POLITICAL ECONOMY
FOR PUBLIC POLICY

POLITICAL ECONOMY
FOR PUBLIC POLICY

Ethan Bueno de Mesquita

PRINCETON UNIVERSITY PRESS
Princeton and Oxford

Library of Congress Cataloging-in-Publication Data

Names: Bueno de Mesquita, Ethan, author.
Title: Political economy for public policy / Ethan Bueno de Mesquita.
Description: Princeton, N.J. : Princeton University Press, 2016. |
    Includes bibliographical references and index.
Identifiers: LCCN 2015047630 | ISBN 9780691168739 (hardcover : alk. paper) |
    ISBN 9780691168746 (pbk.)
Subjects: LCSH: Economics. | Political planning. | Policy sciences.
Classification: LCC HB71 .B785 2016 | DDC 330–dc23 LC record available at
    http://lccn.loc.gov/2015047630

British Library Cataloging-in-Publication Data is available

This book has been composed in ITC Stone Serif and Avenir LT Std

Printed on acid-free paper. ∞

Typeset by Nova Techset Pvt Ltd, Bangalore, India
Printed in the United States of America

1 3 5 7 9 10 8 6 4 2

For my parents, Arlene and Bruce Bueno de Mesquita

Summary of Contents

Contents

Policy Applications

Preface

This is a book about political economy for people interested in public policy. Traditionally, policy analysis and policy education have tended to focus on technocratic concerns—cost-benefit analysis, program evaluation, public administration—and on identifying optimal policies, whether or not those policies could possibly be implemented. A political economy approach takes a different perspective.

The making and implementation of public policy is fundamentally political. The leaders and bureaucrats who write, pass, and enforce our policies operate within political environments that shape and constrain their behavior. A policy that would perfectly address some serious problem, but which could never be passed or enforced because of the politics of the policymaking process, is not optimal. Such a policy, doomed as it is to never be deployed, cannot solve any problems. An optimal policy response to a problem must be optimal given all the constraints, including the political constraints.

The study of political economy for public policy, then, is the study of optimal public policy, taking seriously the constraints imposed by the political process. Understanding these politics is essential for any serious student of public policy and certainly for anyone, in or out of government, interested in leading policy debate or policy change. This is why political economy is, or ought to be, a core element of a public policy education.

For a political scientist, such as myself, the most natural way to think about introducing students to the politics of the policymaking process is to focus on how specific political institutions constrain and shape policy choices. But this is not the approach I take. Before explaining what I do, I want to say a word or two about why I don't go the institutionalist route. I think this will help make clear what I'm up to and why.

Teaching the politics of policymaking through institutions poses some formidable challenges. Let me highlight two.

A first challenge is breadth. The policymaking process involves many political actors—interest groups, elected and appointed officials, grassroots organizations, voters, lobbyists, foreign leaders, the media—working within many institutions—courts, legislatures, bureaucracies, campaigns, international and non-governmental organizations. If you try to teach the details of each actor and institution in a single course you risk covering none well.

A second challenge is the diversity of student backgrounds in many policy schools. Political science majors might find an introductory course in political institutions boring, while students who are new to this material might feel lost if an accelerated pace is adopted. Moreover, with a student body from many different countries, no matter which institutions we focus on, some students will find them familiar while others will be starting from scratch.

In light of these tricky issues, I have eschewed any attempt at exhaustive coverage of political institutions. In my view, such topics are often most successfully covered in more specialized courses. So what do I do instead?

The approach I take is to teach *political economy*. Rather than focusing on details of the policymaking process in any particular country or institutional setting, I develop general principles. These principles are lenses through which we can view the politics of policymaking in any environment. This has the twin virtues of providing a general approach to understanding politics and policy that can be covered in a single course and of offering new material to nearly any student.

There is also a methodological component to my approach that is important to highlight. Almost all policy educations offer a rigorous introduction to policy analysis through micro-economics and statistics. But the approach to teaching politics is more varied. In many places, the view seems to be that experience, rather than analysis or scholarship, is the best guide to politics. I couldn't disagree more. In my view, the rigor that serves us so well in analyzing policy should also be brought to bear in analyzing politics. Thus, I employ the same mathematical and analytical tools to teach about politics that students are accustomed to seeing when they learn economics and statistics. In this way, the political economy approach also helps to unify the standard policy curriculum by offering methodological coherence and drawing clearer connections across fields.

For Whom Is This Book Written?

I wrote this book for my MPP students at the University of Chicago. It is my hope that it will be useful to other policy students. That said, the book has also proven useful to colleagues teaching in other settings. It certainly works as an introduction to modern political economy for advanced undergraduates, as long as they know just a little bit of calculus. Colleagues have also found the book useful for PhD students in political science. The most common such use is for first-year doctoral students, often as a parallel reading in a game theory course, where it provides some context for the formal tools students are learning. In this setting, the book can help students avoid losing the forest for the trees.

A Word on Tone and Technicality

In Parts II and III, I assume that the reader knows some basic game theory (pure strategy Nash equilibrium and subgame perfection) and can use simple calculus to maximize a function. Game theory is a set of mathematical tools that are used to study situations of *strategic interdependence.* An interaction between two or more people features strategic interdependence if the outcome for one person depends not only on her own actions, but also on the actions of others. Since most of life is strategically interdependent, having a theoretical framework with which to study strategic interdependence is useful. Readers who have already had an introductory game theory class should have no problem with the simple models I develop. For readers who have not previously been introduced to game theory, Appendices A and B cover everything that is needed.

This book is full of mathematical models. But it is not super technical. No mathematics beyond the very basics of calculus (maximizing a function of one variable) is required. Nonetheless, the reader should be prepared to sit at a desk, pen and paper in hand, to work through the models.

While my taste in models runs to the formal, my taste in writing does not. You will find that my tone is conversational. For readers accustomed to formal academic writing, this may be a bit jarring at first, so I want to prepare you. My hope is that a conversational tone will perhaps blunt the sharp edge of the mathematics. As one reviewer put it, "At first, I felt that the author's first-person writing style seemed a little casual or chatty for such a text. However, I grew quickly to like that approach. To an extent, the author is the guide, helping students through sometimes difficult material with his good-natured insights and humor." That is precisely what I'm going for. I hope the tone doesn't bother you too much. In any event, I'm not a good enough writer to switch tones at will, so we're both going to have to live with it.

Acknowledgments

I am particularly indebted to Scott Ashworth, with whom I have discussed this material many times over the years. He has provided an enormous amount of feedback and insight. To the extent that this book organizes ideas in a useful way, the credit is as much due to him as it is to me.

I first encountered much of the material in this book when, as an undergraduate at Chicago, I took the course for which the book is named from Duncan Snidal. When I joined the faculty, Duncan graciously allowed me to teach it.

During that time as an undergraduate, I had the great good fortune, privilege, and delight of studying with Amy Kass, a teacher of extraordinary depth and commitment. Mrs. Kass changed my life—inspiring me to take ideas seriously and demanding more than mere cleverness. I believe she would have been pleased that I've written a book whose purpose is to teach.

I am also in the debt of several other colleagues. At Chicago, Chris Berry, Will Howell, Pablo Montagnes, and Anthony Fowler made helpful suggestions on much of the content. More importantly, they make the Harris School, to my mind, the most interesting place in the world to work in political economy.

It is also, I think, important to note that my hot chocolate doesn't hold a candle to Chris's carbonated Manhattan or smoked Brooklyn.

Bruce Bueno de Mesquita read and commented on the first draft and then harangued me until I agreed to stop editing. Andy Eggers and Dimitri Landa provided particularly thoughtful comments on Chapters 1 and 3. Jeff Ely generously allowed me to shamelessly rip off his remarkably clear approach to teaching basic mechanism design in Chapter 9.1–9.2. Several anonymous referees made suggestions that pushed me to rethink structure and style in exceptionally productive ways.

Scarlett Swerdlow and Zhaosong Ruan provided outstanding research assistance.

This manuscript grew out of lecture notes that I developed while teaching an MPP course at Chicago. I am appreciative of the many students who bore with me over the years while I figured out what I think such a course should cover. My apologies to those students who came along early in the process. All I can say is that the contents of this book are what I meant to tell you. Special recognition is due the many students in the 2011–2013 Harris School Political Economy for Public Policy classes who used the earliest drafts of this manuscript. They identified a truly staggering number of typos, mistakes, and places where I could have been clearer, to say the least. Notable among these students for the excellence and sheer number of their suggestions are Boris Angelov, Anthony Austin, Baur Bektemirov, Constance Boozer, Leah Calvo, Matt Chaney, Jennifer Cowhy, Bradley Crawford, Mark Demming, Craig Denuyl, Mary Desmond, Sarah Dickson, Elc Estrera, Kaci Farrell, Jenny Gai, Jonathan Grabinsky, Evan Johnson, Binbin Lin, Laura Martin, Antonio Moreno-Torres Galvez, Sara Beth Hoffman, Gillian Kindel, Emily Modlin, Diane Nimchuk, Song Yoon Park, Corinne Stephenson-Johnson, Elizabeth Stovall, Jacob Rosch, Alice Song, David Spearman, Roberto Gerhard Tuma, Abra Lyons Warren, and Erin Watts. I'm sure at least one of them will find a misplaced comma in this paragraph,

Finally, a word of thanks to my family. I'm privileged to share my life with three outstanding martial artists. I am as deeply appreciative for the love and support of my wife, Rebecca, as I am proud of the extraordinary work she does. My kids, Abe and Hannah, are the best. The best. And who knows, given the family business, maybe one of them will even read this some day.

This book is dedicated to my parents, Arlene and Bruce Bueno de Mesquita. My mother is unrelenting in her dedication to her children. I am where I am today because of her support. My father is the person I know most committed to the idea that the scientific study of politics is genuinely important. His career is an inspiration, even if his productivity is, frankly, offensive. It is a particular pleasure to get to teach some of his most important ideas in Chapter 11. Thanks, Mom and Dad. Sorry about high school.

POLITICAL ECONOMY
FOR PUBLIC POLICY

Introduction

In June of 2013, the Obama administration released its *Climate Action Plan*. The plan starts by making a case for action:[1]

> Climate change is no longer a distant threat—we are already feeling its impacts across the country and the world. Last year was the warmest year ever in the contiguous United States and about one-third of all Americans experienced 10 days or more of 100-degree heat. The 12 hottest years on record have all come in the last 15 years. Asthma rates have doubled in the past 30 years and our children will suffer more asthma attacks as air pollution gets worse. And increasing floods, heat waves, and droughts have put farmers out of business, which is already raising food prices dramatically.
>
> These changes come with far-reaching consequences and real economic costs. Last year alone, there were 11 different weather and climate disaster events with estimated losses exceeding $1 billion each across the United States. Taken together, these 11 events resulted in over $110 billion in estimated damages, which would make it the second-costliest year on record.

The plan proceeds with a list of many proposals for regulations and incentives to reduce carbon emissions and mitigate climate change. These include (among many others) upgrading the electric grid, strengthening regulatory standards for automobile fuel economy and power plant carbon pollution, increasing funding for clean energy, advanced transportation technologies, energy efficient construction, and accelerating clean energy permitting.

There is a fairly simple diagnosis of the source of climate change that is agreed to quite broadly by social scientists. Carbon emissions—from factories, passenger vehicles, or what have you—cause climate change. Each of us who consumes fossil fuels bears only a tiny fraction of the costs associated with our personal emissions. I don't suffer much from the increased probability that you get asthma caused by my car. As a consequence, each of us emits too much carbon relative to what would be socially desirable. Put differently, if we could

---

[1]Executive Office of the President. June 2013. *The President's Climate Action Plan.* https://www.whitehouse.gov/sites/default/files/image/president27sclimateactionplan.pdf

all agree to emit less, we'd all be better off. But each of us, as individuals, has an incentive to keep emitting.

There is also a pretty simple, and widely agreed upon, way to address this kind of problem. Increase the price of carbon so that people's individual costs reflect something closer to the true social costs of emissions. This price-based approach has at least two virtues. First, an increase in prices works directly on individuals' incentives. If the price of carbon is higher, people will use less of it all on their own. They don't need to be monitored or further regulated. Second, a price increase incentivizes people and businesses to reduce carbon consumption in as cost-effective a way as possible. Even among existing technologies, there is uncertainty about whether the most cost-effective way to reduce emissions is through increased fuel economy, greater investment in alternative energy sources, cleaner power plants, or what have you. Moreover, who knows what new approaches to reducing emissions will emerge if people have stronger incentives to innovate? Programs of the sort proposed in the President's Climate Action Plan incentivize particular approaches. A price increase on carbon incentivizes reduced emissions, but is agnostic as to how this should be achieved. This gives people and firms the flexibility to choose the most cost-effective strategies and encourages them to innovate.

As we will discuss throughout this book, there are a variety of political reasons that, despite its merits, a price-based approach might lose out. Policies that work through targeted subsidies and regulations do a worse job at mitigating carbon emissions. But, by creating specific winners from the policy process, they allow political leaders to build a coalition of support. This coalition building is often the critical step in achieving policy change. So perhaps we should not lament this outcome too much.

Suppose, however, that we wanted to think seriously about a price-based approach. Broadly speaking, there are two largely equivalent ways of directly increasing the price of carbon through policy. First, the government could impose a carbon tax. Mankiw (2009) describes studies suggesting the optimal such tax is somewhere between $30 per ton (roughly 8 cents per gallon of gasoline) to $300 per ton (80 cents per gallon). Second, the government could directly cap the level of carbon emissions—issuing permits for emissions and allowing companies to trade those permits. Such a system is typically called *cap-and-trade*.

Textbook policy analysis prefers the carbon tax to cap-and-trade (see Mankiw, 2009, for a clear articulation of this position). Here are two reasons. First, the carbon tax is more flexible. If there is significant fluctuation in the demand for carbon emissions over time, cap-and-trade might impose an inefficiently low level of emissions in a high-demand year. By contrast, a carbon tax allows firms the flexibility to use more carbon, if it is worth it to them, in such years. Second, a carbon tax generates government revenue. Such revenue could be used to offset other, less efficient sources of government revenue. A cap-and-trade system does not generate such revenue unless the permits are auctioned off at the outset. Thus, standard policy analysis suggests that a carbon tax is preferable to cap-and-trade and that if we must do cap-and-trade, we should auction the permits, using the revenues to reduce other distortionary taxes.

These arguments have a lot of merit. But, in my view, they are incomplete. If we are interested in actually reducing carbon emissions and mitigating climate change, we have to take the political incentives just as seriously as the economic incentives.

I would argue that the politics flip the standard policy advice on its head. If you want to achieve an increase in carbon prices and reduction in carbon emissions, you should prefer cap-and-trade without a permit auction (i.e., permits distributed to current emitters) over cap-and-trade with an auction, which you should prefer to a carbon tax. Why do I say that?

First, let's think about adoption. The winners from a carbon tax are the broad public who benefit from mitigating the risks of climate change. But the broad public is a diffuse and unorganized interest. It can exert very little political power. The losers from a carbon tax include oil and gas companies, automobile manufacturers, and emitting industries. These are highly concentrated and organized interests. They can exert significant political power to block a carbon tax. What about cap-and-trade? If cap-and-trade is coupled with an auction for emission permits, the same analysis holds. Powerful, concentrated, and well-organized interests are being asked to pay for emissions that they previously made for free. They have every incentive to block such a policy. But what about if permits are given for free? Now the policy has costs and benefits for emitters. On the one hand, they are being forced to reduce emissions, a cost. On the other hand, they are being given control over a tradable asset of considerable value. Current emitters who believe they can reduce emissions relatively cost-effectively will be able to sell those permits for a profit. This might create the sort of organized and powerful interest needed to move the policy through the political process.

Second, let's think about sustainability. Even if a carbon tax were somehow implemented, the analysis above holds. The supporters of a carbon tax are diffuse, unorganized, and relatively weak. The opponents of such a tax are concentrated, organized, and strong. It would require remarkable vigilance to keep a carbon tax on the books. Cap-and-trade, with or without an auction, is just the opposite. Once permits are issued, they become a valuable financial asset. In addition to the owners of the permits themselves, once a market for such permits emerges, there are brokers, investment bankers, and a variety of financial services providers with a stake in the market. An organized and powerful set of interests will fight to sustain the policy. Again, then, the politics favor cap-and-trade.[2]

I hope you find these arguments provocative. My goal, at this point, is not to convince you about the right way to think about environmental policy. Rather, I want you to see that, while traditional policy analysis is an essential input to thinking carefully about policy, it is not the end of the story. Policy is made in political environments. If you want to understand policy or effect policy change, you must take the politics of the policymaking process seriously. So let's get going.

Three Goals

In service of the broad aim of understanding the politics of public policy, this book pursues three interrelated goals.

The first goal—tackled in Part I—is to spend some time thinking about the normative foundations of policymaking. That is, to ask questions like, "What are the proper goals of public policy?" In so doing, we will discover how difficult it is to come up with a coherent, unified, normative framework to motivate policy decisions. We will arrive at one limited version of such a framework, but we will also see that the ambitious program of formulating a broad conceptualization of the public interest that everyone can endorse might be a fool's errand. Nonetheless, along the way we will discover some useful and provocative ideas that will make our thinking about these issues more structured and nuanced.

The second goal is to think through some fundamental aspects of social life that create opportunities for public policy to make the world a better place. I call these aspects of social life—which are developed in Part II—*social dilemmas*. These social dilemmas are ubiquitous features of human interaction that give rise to predictably regrettable outcomes. We will discuss ways in which policy might improve those outcomes. The objective, in this part of the book, is to develop some habits of mind that let you see the world through a few analytical lenses. I believe you will find that once you get used to viewing the world through the lens of these social dilemmas, you will start to see them everywhere. This may be a bit depressing, but it is also useful in identifying opportunities for policy to do good.

The third goal is to think seriously and conceptually about the politics. As I said in the preface, I'm not going to do this by analyzing the politics of policymaking institution by institution. Instead, in Part III, we look at two classes of explanations for why governments might not always achieve good policy outcomes. The first focuses on *technological constraints*—facts about the

---

[2]This argument is based on the discussion of the success of cap-and-trade in curbing sulphur dioxide emissions in Patashnik (2008, Chapter 8).

policymaking process that limit the government's ability to achieve good policy outcomes even when policymakers are genuinely motivated to do so. The second focuses on *incentive constraints*. Policymakers are people with their own interests and concerns. We analyze how some fundamental facts of politics—most especially leaders' desire to remain in power—interact with political institutions to determine when policymakers have better or worse incentives to pursue good policy. We end this part of the book by looking at a bit of evidence on how the organization of government affects policy outcomes—including an extended discussion of foreign aid policy.

The Role of Models

The main analytic tool we will use in this book is theoretical models—mostly mathematical models. As such, it is important to think a little bit about how to relate to or evaluate a model. What is a model, and what is one good for?

The world—be it physical, biological, or social—is too complicated for us to think through coherently all at once. To make sense of the world, we need to break it up into bite-size pieces that we can think about carefully. The hope is that, in so doing, we will figure out some general principles that help guide our thinking. Models are an attempt at doing this.

Given this, the goal of a model is emphatically not to describe the world in all its richness. A model is an abstraction and a simplification. Its purpose is to isolate some aspect of a problem or phenomenon, so that you can think it through carefully and without distraction. If a model captured all the richness of the world, you would be just as perplexed thinking about your model as you are thinking about the world. That would be a lousy model.

Let me be a little more concrete. A classic example of a model is a map. A map of a city, for instance, is a model of a particular part of the earth. It abstracts away from almost everything that is interesting about that part of the earth—the people who inhabit it, the quality of the restaurants, the crime rate, school districts, in some cases the topography, and so on. To be a successful model, a map must ignore this richness. A map of place and street names isolates precisely those bits of the world that you need to navigate the city. More information would distract from the task at hand—trying to get around. Less information would leave the map insufficiently rich to be useful. It's a delicate balance.

The analogy to a map points to an important fact about models. What a model should and should not include depends critically on what you intend to do with it. Consider two maps—one a street map and the other a topographical map. One cannot say, in the abstract, which of these is the better model of a bit of the earth. If one's goal is to drive, then the street map is the right model. If one's goal is to hike without trails, then your map needs topo-graphical information.

The same holds true with models of social interaction. It is tempting, when presented with a model of human beings, to start listing things that you consider important but that are not included in the model. To react that way, however, is to miss the point of a model—just like criticizing a street map for failing to include restaurant information is to miss the point of a street map. If you evaluate a model by asking whether it captures everything that is interesting about some question or situation, you will be perpetually dissatisfied. The world is an infinitely interesting and wondrous place. Our poor powers to abstract and to generalize are not up to the task of capturing all its richness. So, yes, all our models will leave you wanting, if you expect them to be full representations of the world, or even of some little slice of the world. But this doesn't mean our models are bad. It just means that expecting models to capture everything that is interesting about some aspect of the world is the wrong goal. What, then, is the right goal?

First, for a model to be useful, it cannot be a purely abstract object. We must be able to relate it to some aspect of the world in which we are interested. As the philosopher of science Ronald Giere puts it, models are "artful specifications ... designed so that elements of the model can be identified with (or coordi-nated with) features of the real world" (Giere, 2006, p. 63). Notice the key point here. Some element of the model must correspond with some feature of the world. The model need not capture *everything* that is interesting or important about the bit of reality you are interested in. But it must capture *something* that is interesting or important about it.

Second, the purpose of a model is to help you think through some aspect of the world that is too complicated to think through in its totality. As such, the model should teach you something that you didn't see before you broke the situation up into bite-sized pieces. Otherwise, the model wasn't terribly useful.

In my view, the right way to evaluate a model involves asking something like the following two questions:

1. Is something in the model like something I am interested in out there in the world?
2. Did the analysis of the model teach me something about that aspect of the world that I didn't know before?

If the answer to both questions is yes, then the model has done its job. It has laid out an abstraction that you are able to relate to the world in some way. And the abstraction did in fact help you learn about that aspect of the world. These are the goals of a model.

If this is what a good model does, how should someone interested in public policy think about applying the insights of a model? I like to think of a model as a really smart adviser who understands only one narrow aspect of a policy issue. You, the policymaker, should listen to your model and the ideas it suggests. But you should not do so slavishly. After all, you know a lot more about the world you are dealing with than your model does. A third question, then, that you might want to ask before applying the insights or policy suggestions that come out of your model is something like this:

> 3. Is there something about the world that is missing from my model that I believe would materially change the conclusions of the model were it included?

If the answer is no, then it seems the insights of your model are applicable. If the answer is yes, however, then you should proceed to apply the model's insights only in a cautious and somewhat skeptical way.

With all of this in mind, I should perhaps say a word or two about how I chose and constructed the models that appear in this book. My goal is not to bring you to the technical frontier. Rather, it is to introduce what I take to be some of political economy's most important insights in a rigorous, but accessible, way. As such, two principles guide my modeling choices.

First, I always present the absolutely simplest, least technical version of a model that makes all of the points I want to make. The goal is to make substantive insights clear and rigorous. This requires some technicality. But I emphatically do not want you to get lost in the math.

Second, I only present models whose messages I believe are general. I am not interested in presenting simple models whose main point is fragile. To do so would privilege clever formalization over substance. That's not what I'm about. So, for every simple model I present, I'm asking you to take my word that there is a body of scholarship (too technical for our purposes) that has developed the arguments in sufficient depth to convince me that the main idea is both important and robust. At the end of each chapter, I point the interested reader to some of these further resources.

Why Rationality?

Almost all of our models build on the assumption that people are rational. Rationality, here, means several things. In its most stripped down form, rationality simply means that people have coherent preferences over outcomes and they act to pursue those preferences. I discuss this a bit more formally in Appendix A.1.1.

But we will generally assume something stronger than just coherence of individual preferences. In particular, we will assume that people have coherent preferences over outcomes, that they pursue those preferences, and that those preferences are mostly centered on their own personal welfare. That is, we will assume that people are not primarily motivated by altruism or concern for others, but rather by making themselves better off.

Notice, the assumption of rationality of this kind is already a model. It is a model of human agency. Why should we adopt this particular model? After all, we regularly hear stories of great acts of charity and heroism. Surely a coherent analysis of social life would take into account the fact that human beings are not entirely selfish and avaricious.

I don't disagree. People are, at times, altruistic. (Though the fact that such stories are newsworthy suggests that they may be the exception, rather than the rule.) But, remember, we are building a model. We are trying to simplify the world in a way that is useful for the problems with which we are concerned. And the problems with which we are concerned here are problems of public policy.

Public policy is, at least in one conceptualization, what society does when people, left to their own devices, do not act in one another's interests. Given this, if we are going to think about a model of people to motivate the making of public policy, surely we do not want to assume that people are primarily motivated to look out for one another. If we base our thinking on such an optimistic model of human motivations and proceed to design policies on the basis of that assumption, we may find ourselves disappointed by the actual behavior of our fellow humans. If, instead, we start with the assumption that people are basically selfish, we put ourselves in a position to think about policy interventions that will work even under the worst of circumstances. To be sure, such an assumption may be overly pessimistic, leading us to take precautions against bad behavior in excess of what is necessary. But, in the context of policymaking, this seems like the safer kind of mistake to make, at least as a starting point.

There is another (perhaps more pragmatic) reason for restricting our attention to rational individuals. Doing so massively simplifies many of our analyses. And, remember, the goal of model building is to come up with something that corresponds in some way to the world, but that is simple enough that you can think it through and learn something you didn't see before. For this purpose, the assumption of rationality (in the sense of having coherent preferences, not the assumption of selfishness) is indispensable.

Further Reading

The appendices contain all the game theory you need to understand this book. But if you are looking for an alternative introduction to game theory, there is none better than Martin Osborne's *An Introduction to Game Theory*. If you need a basic calculus refresher, I recommend Daniel Kleppner and Norman Ramsey's *Quick Calculus*.

Many philosophers of science have deep things to say about the role of models. My favorite is Ian Hacking's *Representing and Intervening*. In the chapter, I mentioned Ronald N. Giere's *Scientific Perspectivism*. Perhaps most relevant for the kind of models explored here is Mary S. Morgan's fantastic book *The World in the Model*. The map analogy as a means of explaining the pragmatics of models is certainly not mine. For instance, in her *Essays in the Theory of Economic Growth*, Joan Robinson wrote, "A model which took account of all the variegation of reality would be no more use than a map at the scale of one to one." Paul Krugman's essay "The Fall and Rise of Development Economics," which is the first chapter of his *Development, Geography, and Economic Theory*, has a fantastic discussion of the history of map making, its role in thinking about economic development, and the conceptual importance of simplified models in social science.

PART I

Normative Foundations

In Chapter 1 we look at some models proposed by political philosophers to answer questions like "what are the proper goals of public policy?" but, sadly, fail to arrive at a principled answer. One of the central lessons we draw is that life is full of trade-offs. Pursuing one normatively admirable goal often entails sacrificing another. Reasonable people can disagree about these trade-offs and, consequently, can disagree about the proper goals of public policy.

Undeterred, we push forward with our quest to find a normative foundation on which our notions of good policy or the public interest can rest. In Chapter 2, we consider another path. We want to allow reasonable people to disagree. So we abandon the hope of finding a normative framework that simply identifies good policy. Instead we consider the possibility that, while we disagree on basic normative questions, we might nonetheless agree on a procedure for aggregating our disparate views into a collective view. The idea is that if we can find an aggregation procedure that is itself normatively defensible, then we might all agree to endorse the output of that procedure, even when the output turns out contrary to our own personal views or convictions. Unfortunately, even this more limited approach to determining the goals of public policy yields little in terms of progress toward a coherent notion of the public interest. Though in a limited set of circumstances, majority rule has some appeal.

Finally, we curb our ambitions even further in Chapter 3. We define a notion of the public interest that is arguably uncontroversial—policies that make some people better off and no one worse off. Assuming we can all agree that any such policy is a good policy, we set this as our normative standard, although we will see that there might indeed be principled objections even to this limited notion of the public good. We show that if we are willing to make a few extra assumptions about the kind of preferences people have, then the class of situations where such improvements are possible might not be as limited as it first seems. This discussion motivates our study of social dilemmas in Part II.

1

Normative Frameworks

An important current debate in education policy surrounds the issue of charter schools. Oversimplifying, the basic terms of the debate are the following. In many cities, public schools are struggling to provide good educational outcomes, especially for students from disadvantaged backgrounds. In an attempt to reform the education system, policymakers have embraced "school choice" in the form of charter schools. Charter schools are run by private organizations, but at public expense. Students can opt out of the public schools to attend a charter school. (Although often demand for charter schools outstrips supply, so the charter schools hold admissions lotteries, which turns out to be very helpful for assessing the school's efficacy by creating a natural control group of students who wanted to get in but didn't.)

Evidence on the efficacy of charter schools is mixed. However, there is growing evidence that certain charter schools—so-called "no excuses" schools—are quite effective at improving educational outcomes. The hallmarks of such schools include a longer than typical school day and year, performance-based compensation of teachers, high academic and behavioral expectations coupled with strict behavior norms and discipline, and a focus on traditional college preparatory reading and math skills. The best evidence of which I am aware suggests that no excuses schools improve academic achievement across the board and are particularly successful at improving the performance of the most disadvantaged students (Angrist et al., 2012; Angrist, Pathak, and Walters, 2013).

Given these facts, one might think that almost anyone without a personal interest in preventing the spread of charter schools would favor funding no excuses schools. After all, they seem to improve outcomes for all students and to especially aid those students most in need. So whether one's concern is improving overall social well-being, improving opportunity, reducing inequality of opportunity, or what have you, no excuses schools seem to fit the bill.

Let me muddy the waters just a bit with one more piece of evidence. Although no excuses schools benefit the most disadvantaged students, those students are by far the least likely to seek enrollment in such a school (Walters, 2014). Hence, no excuses schools present the following policy paradox. On the one hand, by helping all students, and particularly the disadvantaged, no excuses schools improve both educational outcomes and educational equality among enrolled students. On the other hand, since disadvantaged students are much less likely to enroll in no excuses schools than are advantaged students, overall, the existence of no excuses charter schools *increases* educational inequality.

Now ask yourself whether promoting no excuses charter schools is good or bad education policy. The answer depends on your framework for normative evaluation. If you think that any policy that improves educational outcomes for some set of students, without hurting anyone else, is good policy, then you are probably a big fan of no excuses charter schools. If you are a person who thinks the top policy challenge for education is to improve equality of educational opportunity, again you might advocate for no excuses charter schools, which provide the opportunity for better educational outcomes across the board. By contrast, if you are primarily concerned with equality of educational outcomes, you might think that no excuses charter schools are bad policy because, while in theory they could decrease inequality, in practice they end up disproportionately benefiting advantaged students. To know what you think about no excuses charter schools, you have to know what you believe the proper goals of public policy are and why. Thinking about normative frameworks is intended to help you wrestle with such questions.

The purpose of this chapter is not to identify *the* normative framework that we can all agree on—such a thing does not exist. Nor is it to convince you that one set of standards is better than another. I have my personal views with regard to these matters, but I'm not so confident in them as to think you should believe them too. Rather, before we dive into theorizing about social dilemmas and their solutions, it seems worth spending a bit of time looking at some normative frameworks that various thinkers have found both compelling and useful in evaluating public policy and social outcomes. Each has its problems, some of which we will discuss. Each also offers useful and thought-provoking insights into thorny questions about the goals of public policy. Reasonable people can disagree about the relative merits of these ideas, but all are, I believe, worth having spent some time with.

Thinking about normative frameworks is not, primarily, the work of social scientists. It is the work of philosophers and, in particular, normative political theorists. I am not an expert in normative political theory, so this discussion will not pretend to be a comprehensive or deeply nuanced take. Indeed, I will purposefully leave out much of the richness and subtlety that exists in the discourse on each of our normative frameworks. My hope is to give you a rough overview of some important ideas and the dialogue amongst those ideas. I do so with three goals in mind.

First, if you are going to use a particular normative standard to set goals for public policy, you should have a clear-minded understanding of the implications of your normative commitments. Similarly, if you are going to advocate for certain positions, it may prove helpful to have a more robust understanding of the kinds of normative arguments that might lead people to disagree with you. Entering into dialogue with your opponents in a way that addresses their actual concerns and values is a more productive means toward reaching understanding (if not agreement) than is simply repeating your own position in an ever louder voice.

Second, in my view, the public discourse on the normative justifications for various public policies is often hopelessly confused. People on different sides of various debates use the same words to mean different things, often without noticing that they are doing so. I hope that a discussion of some core ideas from political philosophy can improve the clarity of your thinking about your own views and values, if nothing else, by disambiguating some important concepts.

The third goal is closely related to the second. One reason that people like to use one word to mean many things is so that they do not have to face the fact that life is full of trade-offs. For instance, there may be real trade-offs between liberty (understood as freedom from coercion) and equality of opportunity. Yet, if we define liberty to mean everyone has the same capacity to pursue his or her goals, rather than everyone is similarly free from coercion, then achieving liberty requires equality of opportunity. This conflation makes the concept of liberty redundant—why not just call it equality of opportunity? This kind of no-trade-offs thinking is insidious. Public officials, for instance, often like to talk as though all good things go together—we can have a cleaner environment and stronger economic growth, lower taxes and more government revenues, and so on. What we will see in the discussion to come is that many of our most cherished values are, at least some of the time, in tension with each other. If we want to hold informed and mature policy positions, we should face up to these trade-offs and take them seriously.

1.1   What Is a Normative Framework?

Defining a normative framework is itself tricky work. So let's try to answer this question, not from first principles, but by thinking about what it is that normative theorists do.

It seems to me that normative theorists focus on three interrelated tasks. First, they identify and clarify various normatively valuable goals. For instance, they might talk about the idea that freedom is normatively valuable and distinguish various notions of freedom from one another. Second, normative theorists often attempt to describe some of the trade-offs that exist between various goals. So a normative theorist might point out that the goal of maximizing freedom from coercion and the goal of equality of wealth are in tension with one another. Third, they offer foundational arguments about which normative goals are actually valuable and how to balance the trade-offs between various normative values. For instance, one theorist might argue that the fundamental standard for all normative decisions is equality and, as a consequence, might advocate for accepting some diminution in freedom from coercion in order to redistribute wealth. Another normative theorist might argue that the fundamental standard for all normative decisions is respect for individual self-ownership and, thus, might advocate for accepting high levels of inequality so as to avoid any compromise on freedom from coercion.

To my mind, it is this third step that is at the heart of normative analysis. A normative framework proposes a system that allows one to think systematically about the trade-offs among competing values. As I've said, it is not my view that any one normative framework is right. Nor do I think that you must commit yourself to one normative framework in order to balance trade-offs in a principled way. Normative policy questions are just not the sort of topic with deeply satisfying foundations like that. (I'm not sure any topic is, but that is another discussion.) What I do believe is that it is a useful exercise to adopt the mind-set of a particular normative framework in order to see what that way of thinking has to teach you about a particular question. Of course, for any given policy question, you may want to repeat that process with several normative frameworks and then think about what you believe the right way to balance all the trade-offs is, informed by your understanding of what different normative frameworks have to say about the issue. Put differently, I want us to treat normative frameworks as different models, each of which may be useful in some circumstances.

1.1.1 Private vs. Public Morality

Normative frameworks provide guidance on two different sorts of questions which are usefully distinguished. The first type of question is about private morality—how ought I to behave? The second type is about public morality—how ought the government to behave? While each of the normative frameworks we will discuss have things to say about both sorts of questions, the questions are not the same. To see why, it is useful to talk about a couple examples.

Imagine a wealthy person who favors a policy of significant redistribution from the rich to the poor, but gives little to charity. Is such a position normatively tenable? If public and private morality are the same, then it seems the answer is no—your normative commitments call for both a policy of redistribution and a personal duty to give your wealth to those less fortunate.

But one can imagine an argument for pulling apart the two moralities. Virtually any individual giving away her personal wealth has essentially no impact on the total level of inequality. Hence, a person might reasonably hold the following position:

> I am happy to give away much of my wealth as part of a societal effort to achieve greater equality. But if the rest of the members of my society are not going to participate, I don't want to make a large personal sacrifice with no appreciable consequences for overall inequality.

This position makes a distinction between private and public morality. Government policy can achieve large-scale redistribution. And so, it says, the government should do so because social equality is important. But individual charity cannot achieve large-scale redistribution. So, it says, an individual is not duty-bound to unilaterally give away her wealth.

One can imagine similar arguments in many settings. Only the government can achieve large-scale reductions in carbon emissions. Hence, one might simultaneously argue that good policy requires reducing emissions and that, absent such a policy, it is okay to drive an SUV. Of course, one might also argue that, in some domains, public and private morality coincide. (Broome (2012) considers both sides of the argument for the case of climate change.)

In other settings, it is straightforward that public and private ethics come apart. Consider a parent's duty to a child. Most (though not all) normative frameworks suggest that parents have a special duty to their children. Indeed, on many views, I have a duty to protect my children, even if that means failing to protect others' children. (To see this, ask yourself whether I would have done the right thing if, in some emergency, I chose to save my own two children, instead of four children of strangers.) But it seems crazy to think that this personal duty implies an analogous public duty. No one (other than me, of course) thinks the government should care more about my children than other people's children.

It is useful, as you think through the various normative frameworks, to keep this public versus private distinction in the back of your mind. Now let's turn to our normative frameworks.

1.2 Utilitarianism

Utilitarianism is the classic example of a *consequentialist* normative framework—that is, a normative framework that assesses the rightness or wrongness of an act based on its consequences. Within the class of consequentialist normative frameworks, it is *welfarist*—the consequence with which it is concerned is human well-being or *utility*. The basic motivating thought of utilitarianism is that good acts, policies, or social arrangements are those that tend to maximize the aggregate utility in society. Each person has his or her own individual preferences over many things. As such, each possible act, policy, or social arrangement has implications for many people's utility—making some better off and others worse off. In a choice between two acts, policies, or social arrangements, the one that results in the larger aggregate utility is taken to be right.

To see how tricky even seemingly simple normative frameworks can be, here's a little thought experiment. One way to define aggregate utility is as the sum of individual utilities. Another perfectly reasonable definition is the average of the individual utilities.

Under both of these definitions, utility is aggregated by adding, treating all individual utilities equally. So, at first blush, these two definitions might seem equivalent. They are not. To take an example, they have very different implications for the desirability of policies that encourage people to have children. On the first definition, it is pretty clearly a good, utilitarian policy to encourage people to have children, at least up until the point of overcrowding. (More people, more total utility in society.) On the second definition, adding a person increases aggregate utility only if that person has higher than average utility. Thus, under this second definition, you'd want a policy that encourages people to have children if their children are expected to have higher utility (be happier) than the average citizen and that discourages people from having children if their children are expected to have lower utility than the average citizen. How you define your utilitarian objective matters.

1.2.1 Why Be a Utilitarian?

There is much to like about utilitarianism. First, it has the important virtue of treating all people equally.

Second, and perhaps most importantly, utilitarianism is a powerful tool for balancing trade-offs. Often, when we think through complicated policy questions, we find multiple competing values. Perhaps in order to save lives, we need to deceive people. Or, in order to improve health or environmental outcomes, we have to reduce economic growth. Under many normative frameworks, it can be hard to see how to make choices among competing, fundamental values. Not for a utilitarian. A utilitarian evaluates such trade-offs simply by figuring out the utility value of each outcome to each individual, adding, and comparing. Utilitarianism transforms philosophical conundrums (how do I compare two fundamental values?) into empirical questions (how much do individuals value these two outcomes?) and, thus, always provides an answer. For this reason, utilitarianism has become the guiding normative framework underlying almost all of modern policy analysis.

A third argument in favor of utilitarianism is less pragmatic and more philosophical. A long-standing tradition in political theory suggests that we think about the legitimacy of a set of societal institutions as deriving from a *social contract*, agreed to in mythical negotiations amongst our ancestors some time in the distant past. This type of contractarian argument is most typically used (for instance, in the Hobbesian tradition) as a way to establish the legitimacy of state authority by allowing the argument that the state rules by the consent of the governed. If we push the contractual analogy a bit, we might also offer a contractarian defense of a more specific social arrangement or set of social goals.

A concern with such a contractarian approach to normative justification is that, during contract negotiations, people will tend to push for a social arrangement that serves their individual interests, not the interests of society. As such, any actual social contract will reflect particularistic interests and power relationships, not the social good.

The economist John Harsanyi proposed a thought experiment (later made famous by the philosopher John Rawls) to develop a theory of normative justification that simultaneously retains some of the appealing features of contractarianism—in particular, the idea that we might all agree to some social arrangement—while also suggesting a way around (at least for the philosopher) the problem of particularistic interests sullying the social contract. Imagine yourself behind a *veil of ignorance*, so that you don't know any of the particularities of yourself—whether you will be smart or dumb, attractive or unattractive, born to rich or poor parents, and so on. Now ask the following: Suppose we were all behind the veil of ignorance and we could sign a contract which would specify the rules for our society. What kind of contract would we sign? Rawls refers to this fictional state of ignorance as "the original position."

Before we get to Harsanyi's answer, let's see what's going on here. The veil of ignorance has two important features. First, we are all identical behind the veil of ignorance. That is, you and I are both equally likely to end up with any particular set of skills, talents, and so on. This makes it easy to agree to a contract, since we all have the same interests. Second, in the absence of any particularistic knowledge about ourselves, we are in the common position of humanity. Hence, from behind the veil of ignorance, whatever decision you come up with about what kind of society you want to live in is not based on particularistic interests. This last fact is the real force of the thought experiment. It lets us get at a notion of the sort of society in which we'd like to live that does not depend on anything about ourselves as individuals, but rather, depends only on our shared humanity.

Harsanyi argues that, behind the veil of ignorance, we are all utilitarians. (Rawls disagrees. We'll talk a bit about this later.) It is worth noting that Harsanyi's position is controversial. Nonetheless, it is an interesting argument worthy of our consideration. Here are its bare bones.

Suppose our society is made up of N individuals. We are choosing a social arrangement from a set, A, of potential social arrangements. A social arrangement is a description of how we will organize our society, what policies we will implement, and so on.

Consider some particular social arrangement, $a \in A$.[1] Under this social arrangement, there will be some person who has the highest utility, some person who has the second highest utility, and so on, all the way down to the person with the Nth highest (i.e., lowest) utility. Call the utility of the best-off person under social arrangement a, $u_1(a)$. This utility is a numerical measure of that person's happiness or well-being. Call the utility of the second-best-off person under social arrangement a, $u_2(a)$, and so on all the way down to $u_N(a)$. We can do likewise for any other social arrangement.

Now, recall, we are behind the veil of ignorance. When evaluating the merits of various social arrangements, you don't know whether you will be the person with the highest utility, the second highest utility, or the person with the lowest utility. You find each equally likely. In particular, since there are N individuals, the probability you are in any given social position is simply $1/N$.

To evaluate the merits of a particular social arrangement from behind the veil of ignorance, we need to know how people deal with uncertainty. It is clear, if offered two certain outcomes, a person prefers the outcome with higher utility. Thus, within a given social arrangement, everyone prefers to be the person with the highest utility to the person with the second highest utility, and so on. But things are less clear if people are offered uncertain outcomes.

To see the issue, imagine a society with two people and two possible social arrangements, a_1 and a_2. Under social arrangement a_1, each person gets a utility of 10. Under social arrangement a_2, the best-off person gets a utility of 100 and the worst-off person gets a utility of 0. From behind the veil of ignorance—that is, not knowing whether you will be the high or low utility person under social arrangement a_2—it is not obvious which social arrangement you should prefer. Social arrangement a_1 offers an okay outcome for sure. Social arrangement a_2 offers a coin toss between a really good and a really bad outcome.

I am a bit more formal about this in Appendix A, but essentially the assumption we will make is that people evaluate such uncertain "lotteries" over various outcomes by calculating the *expected utility*. One calculates an expected utility by multiplying the probability of each outcome times the utility from that outcome and then adding. So, in our example, the expected utility of social arrangement a_1 is just 10, since a person gets a utility of 10 for certain. The expected utility of social arrangement a_2 is $\frac{1}{2} \times 0 + \frac{1}{2} \times 100 = 50$. This calculation comes from the fact that, under social arrangement a_2, a person gets a utility of 0 with probability one-half and gets a utility of 100 with probability one-half. Hence, given these payoffs and probabilities, a person who maximizes expected utility would prefer social arrangement a_2 to social arrangement a_1.

---

[1] If you don't know what the symbol $\in$ means, feel free to ask. There is no sense getting lost in notation. It means "element of." Capital A is a set (or collection) of possible social arrangements. Little a is an element of the set A, which means a is one particular social arrangement from the collection of possible social arrangements, A.

Of course, if the payoffs had been different, preferences over social arrangements might have been different. For instance, suppose there was some third social arrangement, a_3, where one person gets utility 0 and one person gets utility 18. Like under social arrangement a_2, under social arrangement a_3 one outcome is worse than the assured payoff under social arrangement a_1 and one outcome is better. But the expected utility of social arrangement a_3 is $\frac{1}{2} \times 0 + \frac{1}{2} \times 18 = 9$. Thus, from behind the veil of ignorance, a person who maximizes expected utility prefers social arrangement a_1 to social arrangement a_3.

Now, consider your evaluation of some arbitrary social arrangement, a, from behind the veil of ignorance. You think that with probability $1/N$ you will get utility $u_1(a)$, with probability $1/N$ you will get utility $u_2(a)$, and so on. So, your *expected utility* from social arrangement a is

$$EU(a) = \frac{1}{N} \times u_1(a) + \frac{1}{N} \times u_2(a) + \ldots + \frac{1}{N} \times u_N(a).$$

This can be rewritten:[2]

$$EU(a) = \frac{\sum_{i=1}^{N} u_i(a)}{N}.$$

Given this, from behind the veil of ignorance, you strictly prefer social arrangement a to some other social arrangement a' if and only if

$$\frac{\sum_{i=1}^{N} u_i(a)}{N} > \frac{\sum_{i=1}^{N} u_i(a')}{N}.$$

That is, from behind the veil of ignorance, you prefer one social arrangement to another if and only if the average utility is higher under that social arrangement. Thus, Harsanyi concludes that we are all average-social-utility maximizing utilitarians behind the veil of ignorance.[3]

1.2.2 Some Problems for Utilitarianism

Utilitarianism is a powerful normative framework. It provides a clear set of standards, has systematic arguments in its favor, and offers guidance on a wide array of questions. That said, utilitarianism is not without its problems. A utilitarian assessment involves measuring, aggregating, and comparing individuals' utilities. From a conceptual point of view, this is a demanding informational requirement—we must conceive of each individual's well-being as something that can be put on a common scale, so that they can be compared. From a

---

[2]Again, don't let notation get in the way of understanding. The symbol $\sum$ means "sum." So $\sum_{i=1}^{N} u_i(a)$ means the sum of $u_1(a) + u_2(a) + \ldots + u_N(a)$.

[3]Harsanyi's argument, clever as it is, is controversial. A reader interested in a deep, but technically difficult, critique of Harsanyi's argument should consult Roemer (1998, Chapter 4.4).

practical standpoint, this is a demanding measurement requirement—if we want to use utilitarianism to evaluate policies, we need to measure the effects of these policies on a lot of individuals' well-being.

In addition to these conceptual and practical worries about the informational demands of utilitarianism, there are also a variety of concerns about some of the implications of utilitarianism. Before I discuss a few classic examples, let me offer a caveat.

While the coming examples (and the examples I will point to for the other normative frameworks) raise some serious questions about utilitarianism, you should interpret them with some care. Remember, any normative framework is a model, meant to help us think about complicated decisions in a simplified way that clarifies some key issues. No such model could be perfect—for any normative framework, no matter how compelling, we are going to be able to come up with some situations where it seems to lead us astray. It is important to know in what situations it will do so. But it is also important to bear in mind the many situations in which the normative framework provides us with good and useful guidance. As John Rawls puts it in *A Theory of Justice* (p. 52):

> Objections by way of counter-examples are to be made with care, since these may tell us only what we know already, namely that our theory is wrong somewhere. The important thing is to find out how often and how far it is wrong. All theories are presumably mistaken in places. The real question at any given time is which of the views already proposed is the best approximation overall.

PHILISTINES

In Jeremy Bentham's classic formulation of utilitarianism, people's preferences are their own. We have no moral standing to judge that from which another person derives utility. If you derive happiness from great literature and I derive happiness from blowing stuff up in my backyard, we have no way of saying that one activity is more meritorious than the other. (Up to, of course, the point where your enjoyment of some activity causes me to suffer or vice versa.) If being a Philistine makes me as happy as being refined and highbrow makes you, then both are equally moral acts.

An even more extreme version of this same problem is Nozick's idea of a pleasure machine. Suppose we could hook people up to the Matrix (is that reference already dated?) and make them believe they are fantastically happy. Would that be morally preferable to letting people live their actual lives?

Philosophers, at least since John Stuart Mill, have been unhappy with this aspect of utilitarian theories. They've proposed a variety of fixes. But, as a general matter, I think a person committed to a classical utilitarian kind of view has to accept that these problems exist for the theory. I don't find them terribly upsetting. If you derive lots of utility from watching reality TV and drinking bad beer, good for you. I kind of wish I did. It would be cheaper than my taste for avant-garde cuisine and single-malt scotch.

MONSTERS

The problem of monsters is closely related to the problem of Philistines, but perhaps more troubling. Consider a person who derives pleasure from inflicting pain on others. If the utility he derives from inflicting that pain is greater than the utility loss suffered by his victims as a result of the pain, then his actions could be construed as right and proper from a utilitarian perspective.

You may think this is not a serious problem, since no one actually cares about the welfare of such monsters. You are incorrect. I once sat in an academic seminar in which a scholar showed evidence that removing children from abusive homes improved their futures (e.g., less criminal behavior, greater educational attainment) and that the benefits to the kids exceeded the monetary costs of the program. Having presented this evidence, the scholar tried to make a normative claim about the merits of the particular policy intervention he was studying. An audience member quickly jumped in to ask how the presenter could possibly reach such normative conclusions, not having calculated the impact of the policy on all the affected parties' utilities. The presenter seemed confused by the question, since it struck him as obvious that a policy that removed kids from abusive homes and improved future outcomes for those kids in a cost-effective way was normatively desirable. After a bit of back and forth, it became clear that the interlocutor's concern was that the presenter had failed to estimate how much the abusive parents valued keeping (and presumably continuing to abuse) their kids. A fair point from a strictly utilitarian standpoint. But, in my own view, such a thoroughgoing commitment to utilitarianism is fairly alarming.

TRANSPLANTS AND TROLLEYS

Another potential problem for utilitarianism comes from the following two scenarios. (These and many related scenarios have been extensively discussed. Here, I paraphrase thought experiments due to Foot (1967) and Thomson (1985), but also remind you of Rawls's admonition regarding counter-examples.)

1. There are ten people on a trolley that somehow got on an unfinished track. If the trolley continues to the end of the track, it will plunge into an abyss, killing all ten people. A person is standing at the last switch on the track. If the person pulls the switch, the trolley will be diverted onto a siding, saving the people on board. But a worker on the siding will be killed. The people on the trolley will never know how they were saved.

2. There are ten people, each of whom needs a different organ transplant
   through no fault of his or her own. Without the organ transplants
   all ten will die. The head of medicine at the hospital where all ten
   are being treated can call a local thug, who will randomly kill a person
   on the street and bring the body to the hospital for harvesting. All ten
   people will be saved and will never know where the organs came from.

Most people share a common set of moral intuitions about these two cases.
They think the person should pull the switch, but are horrified at the idea of the
doctor allowing the thug to kill a person to harvest organs.

It is difficult to make sense of these intuitions within a utilitarian framework.
In both scenarios one life can be sacrificed to save ten. In both cases the
utilitarian answer is clear—sacrifice the one for the ten. Yet most people find
it hard to wrap their head around the idea that randomly killing people to
harvest their organs is good policy. Perhaps this is a strength of utilitarianism—
the model has taught us something about the situation that we couldn't see
without the model. Or perhaps it is a weakness—killing people to harvest their
organs is insane. (Please don't go around telling people that I taught you that
murder-for-organ-harvesting is good policy.)

In Chapter 1.4 we will revisit these problems and see how another normative
framework may provide a more satisfying approach in such cases.

EQUITY ACROSS GENERATIONS

One of the virtues of utilitarianism is that it treats all individuals equally. But
this also raises some hard questions. Many policy changes affect individual welfares now and in the future. For instance, the costs of an intervention limiting
carbon emissions to slow global warming might well exceed the benefits over
the course of a single generation. After all, it is unlikely that the climate will
change drastically enough over the next twenty years to have a huge impact
on the quality of your or my lives. But suppose that same policy, over the long
run, prevents catastrophic climate change. It might ultimately save the lives of
billions of people. The benefits for future generations could be huge.

And herein lies a deep challenge. The future is essentially endless. And the
population is expanding. This means that if we treat the utilities of members
of each generation equally, a policy that offers even a small benefit to future
generations has a huge positive effect on aggregate welfare, since those future
benefits affect so many people.

This creates two problems. First, if we believe that the members of each
generation should be treated equally in our utilitarian calculations, we ought to
be spending most of our current resources on policies that benefit the future—
even large costs to a few billion people today are a drop in the bucket when
compared to the benefits to hundreds of billions of people over the course of

future generations. I hope you don't like air conditioning, or travel, or meat. Second, since all policies that benefit the future have basically infinite benefits (what with all the people in the future), it is really hard to compare one future-benefiting policy to another. Everything looks either infinitely good or infinitely bad.[4]

Practical utilitarians respond to this problem with an idea called "discounting the future," which derives from the methodology used to analyze how individuals make inter-temporal trade-offs. (The basics of discounting are discussed in Appendix B.7.) Let's see how this works.

For a variety of reasons—impatience, returns on investment, the risk that you won't survive—a dollar today is worth more to you than is the promise of a dollar a year from now. So, suppose that you'd be indifferent between receiving 90 cents today or a dollar a year from now. We say that you discount the value of money a year from now by a factor of 0.9. Now suppose I asked you the same question a year from now. Assuming your time preferences hadn't changed, you'd give the same answer—that is, a dollar in two years is worth 90 cents in one year. Since a dollar in two years is worth 90 cents in a year and 90 cents in a year is worth 81 cents today, a dollar in two years is worth 81 cents today. And, of course, this diminution in the value of a dollar continues as the delivery date moves further and further into the future. A dollar in twenty years is worth about 12 cents today. A dollar in fifty years is worth half a cent today.

When we do a utilitarian cost-benefit analysis for policy, we directly extend this methodology of discounting the future to thinking about the benefits of a policy for future generations. The government justifies this practice along exactly the lines described above. For instance, the United States' Office of Management and Budget says, "Discounting reflects the time value of money. Benefits and costs are worth more if they are experienced sooner."[5] So the further into the future some future generation is, the more we discount its benefits or costs. As you can see, this solves the problem of infinite future benefits. We essentially write off the distant future through discounting and get on with the business of quantifying benefits and costs.

But there is something fishy about this kind of discounting. Discounting for an individual and discounting across generations are different. It makes sense to value a benefit to me today more than an equal benefit to me in thirty years. If you asked me whether I would like the benefit today or in thirty years, I would choose today. After all, I might be dead in thirty years. It is something entirely different, however, to value a benefit to me more than a benefit to my grandchildren, simply because my grandchildren won't be around for another

---

[4]There are theorems along these lines. The basic upshot is that intergenerational equity is incompatible with our standard utilitarian approach. See, for example, Zame (2007).

[5]Office of Management and Budget, "Guidelines and Discount Rates for Benefit-cost Analysis of Federal Programs," Circular A-94, December 1992.

thirty years. If you asked them, "Would you prefer a benefit to granddad BdM when he was 40 or a benefit to yourself when you are 4?" I suspect the ingrates would choose themselves. More fundamentally, if we value everyone's well-being equally, there is just no reason to care less about people in the future than in the present (other than the small chance that the world will cease to exist, so they won't be around to enjoy the benefits). Their happiness or suffering will be no less real for happening a couple generations from now.

It is this kind of logic that led Frank Ramsey (1928)—who in the 1920s laid the intellectual foundations for how we think rigorously about intertemporal considerations in policymaking—to argue that discounting the welfare of future generations "is ethically indefensible and arises merely from the weakness of the imagination." Or, more poetically, as put by the midcentury economist R. F. Harrod (1948), it is "a polite expression for rapacity and the conquest of reason by passion." The great theorist of economic growth, Robert Solow (1974), was perhaps clearest, saying, "We ought to act as if the social rate of time preference were zero."[6]

We discount future generations in policy analysis because, if we don't, we can't quantify costs and benefits in a way that makes for a coherent utilitarian analysis. But once we've accepted discounting, we've given ourselves license to ignore costs or benefits that occur more than a generation or two in the future. If you are discounting at a rate of 0.9 per year and someone asks you for ten million dollars for a policy that is guaranteed to save a billion people in two hundred years, a standard utilitarian cost-benefit analysis would tell you not to do it.[7]

This may sound theoretical, but it has practical implications. For instance, environmental regulators frequently complain that it is difficult to persuade the government to take actions on issues—like global warming—with limited short-run impact, but potentially catastrophic long-run consequences. The reason they cite is that utilitarian-based cost-benefit analysis with discounting just doesn't care much about those long-run consequences because they will be suffered by someone else.

RELATIONSHIPS

Another objection to utilitarianism, and other forms of consequentialism, has to do with the nature of human relationships. In particular, utilitarianism seems to have little room for people to have special duties to certain other people.

---

[6] Arrow (1999) is also interesting on this subject.

[7] If the discount factor is 0.9 and the value of a statistical life is $7 million, the discounted value of a billion lives in 200 years is just under $5 million.

Figure 1.1. Ethan's very cute kids.

To take an extreme example, suppose I could choose to save my own two children from a terrible accident or save four children whom I don't know. I would certainly save my own kids. (See Figure 1.1.) Assuming the parents of the kids I would fail to save love their kids as much as I love mine, my act is not justifiable on utilitarian grounds. But this seems like a failing of utilitarianism to capture an essential aspect of what it means to live a good and moral life—which involves taking seriously the relationships among human beings and their meaning. Indeed, recent research by Bartels and Pizarro (2011) shows that people who choose the utilitarian solution to various moral dilemmas in an experimental setting also have higher scores on measures of "psychopathy, [M]achiavellianism, and life meaninglessness."

Here it is useful to recall the distinction we made earlier between public and private morality. The failure to take relationships seriously is, perhaps, a weakness for utilitarianism as a source of private morality. But it may be a strength for utilitarianism as a source of public morality. Utilitarianism disciplines the policymaker to dispassionately weigh everyone's welfare equally, abstracting away from personal ties.

1.3 Egalitarianism

Utilitarianism is certainly not the only plausible consequentialist framework. Under egalitarianism we judge the rightness or wrongness of an act, policy, or social arrangement by whether it increases or decreases equality, rather than overall well-being.

Defining egalitarianism is itself somewhat tricky. For egalitarians, equality is the key principle of justice. But, as Amartya Sen (1980) puts it, the critical question is "equality of what?" Should society seek to achieve equality of well-being, equality of wealth, equality of opportunity, or what? I'll review several arguments for various kinds of egalitarianism, pointing to some issues along the way.

1.3.1 Equality of Outcomes

There are at least two reasonable definitions of equality of outcomes. To try to get a handle on the issues, think about a society with just two individuals. You might say that the society is more equal under policy a_1 than under policy a_2 if the two individuals have more equal wealth under a_1 than under a_2. Or, you might say that the society is more equal under policy a_1 than under policy a_2 if the two individuals have more equal utility under a_1 than under a_2. The two definitions are not equivalent.

To see this, consider an example. Suppose the two people in our society are named Eeyore and Tigger. Both are happier the more resources they have, but other than that, they are as different as different can be. Eeyore is strongly inclined toward unhappiness, while Tigger is strongly inclined toward happiness. Society has a finite amount of resources to distribute between the two. If we are egalitarians with respect to wealth, then we would split those resources equally. However, if we are egalitarians with respect to well-being, we would give almost all (maybe all) of the resources to Eeyore, since Eeyore, with his negative disposition, has much lower well-being than does Tigger, with his positive outlook.

A similar problem arises when you think about matters of taste. Suppose we have two people with very different tastes. One is made happiest by drinking beer and watching football on broadcast television. The other is made happiest by drinking fancy wine and traveling in the south of France. If we are egalitarians with respect to wealth, these differences in taste don't affect our policy decisions. However, if we are egalitarians with respect to utility, then we believe our friend with expensive taste deserves more resources because he requires those resources to reach the same level of utility as our friend with more down-to-earth preferences.

Given the rather perverse recommendations that come from being an egalitarian with respect to well-being, let's focus on equality of wealth. Although more coherent than equality of well-being, a strict argument for equality of wealth also faces a variety of conceptual challenges. Consider a few.

A first issue is the problem of *prioritization*. Imagine two people, one quite intellectually gifted, the other not the brightest bulb in the chandelier.

Society only has sufficient resources to educate one of them. Left without an education, the smart person will do pretty well on raw talent alone, but the dull person will struggle to make a living. If educated, the smart person will go on to do truly great things—cure cancer, invent a cool iPhone app, or what have you. If educated, the dull person will do nothing special, but will be able to hold down a job and support himself. What is society to do?

From a wealth egalitarian perspective, the dull person should be educated. Society faces a choice between two states of the world. If it educates the bright person, that person is very well off while the dull person fares terribly. If, instead, it educates the dull person, both people do okay. Wealth egalitarianism prefers the latter outcome.

This conclusion stands in stark contrast to that suggested by utilitarianism. From a utilitarian perspective, society should invest its educational resources in the person who will derive the greatest benefit from them and from whom society will benefit the most. If educating the bright person means that we get a cure to cancer, the benefits to society of this contribution far outweigh the costs of the dull person's suffering.

Perhaps the hardest challenge for wealth egalitarianism is the problem of *incentives*. The most direct way to achieve equality of wealth is to collect resources generated by each member of society and redistribute them. Indeed one solution to the prioritization problem discussed above might be to educate the bright person and then give some of her money to the dullard.

A problem with such a system is that it reduces people's incentives to work hard, since they know they will enjoy only a portion of the fruits of their individual labors. Hence, the argument goes, a completely egalitarian society will be a poor one.

A closely related issue is the so-called *leveling down* problem. Imagine a society made up of two people. Under one social arrangement, person 1 has one million dollars and person 2 has half-a-million dollars. Under another social arrangement, each person has half-a-million dollars. Strict wealth egalitarianism prefers the second social arrangement, which seems strange, since all we've done to move from the first arrangement to the second arrangement is make person 1 worse off by destroying some of her resources. That is, we've leveled the wealth in society by dragging one person down, without pulling another person up.

Reasonable people might well prefer the second social arrangement on egalitarian grounds. But what about the following? Under one social arrangement, person 1 has one million dollars and person 2 has half-a-million dollars. Under a second social arrangement, neither person has any resources. Again, from a strictly wealth egalitarian point of view, the second social arrangement is to be preferred. But could any reasonable person actually prefer to level down by destroying everyone's resources rather than allowing some inequality?

These problems notwithstanding, there are more nuanced arguments for various versions of wealth egalitarianism that are more satisfying. Let's consider a few.

UTILITARIAN EGALITARIANISM

Perhaps the most straightforward argument in favor of equality of wealth is a utilitarian argument. We typically believe that people have *diminishing marginal utility in money*. That is, the more wealth you have, the less your well-being increases with each additional dollar. If people have diminishing marginal utility in money, then a dollar is worth more to a poor person than to a rich person. Hence, aggregate well-being increases if wealth is redistributed from the rich to the poor.

The utilitarian argument straightforwardly deals with the problems of incentives, leveling down, and prioritization. In particular, under utilitarianism, wealth equality is not a goal unto itself. It is a goal only insofar as decreasing wealth inequality increases aggregate well-being. Hence, leveling down holds no appeal under a utilitarian analysis. And the problems of prioritization and incentives just become other factors to take into consideration in the utilitarian calculus. For a utilitarian, one simply balances the benefits of redistribution (which come from the diminishing marginal utility of money) with the costs in terms of incentives and efficient targeting of resources (e.g., educating bright people) to identify the optimal amount of wealth equality.

COMMUNITARIANISM

A wholly different kind of argument for egalitarianism comes from thinking not about well-being, but about community. Such an argument goes something like this. In a non-egalitarian society, resources are not shared, but rather competed over. Competing for resources is debasing and dehumanizing. The right way to interact with your fellow humans is in a spirit of cooperation, not competition. But doing so is not possible in the midst of the competition for resources. And so, if we want to live properly human lives, we must share resources equally.

The philosopher G. A. Cohen (2009) provides an analogy to a camping trip, which he views as a metaphor for the ideal society. On a camping trip, he argues, it is unimaginable that someone would say something like, "I cooked the dinner and therefore you can't eat it unless you pay me for my superior culinary skills." Rather, one person cooks dinner, another pitches the tent, another purifies the water, and so on, each in accordance with his or her abilities. All these goods are shared and a spirit of community and dignity uplifts all participants. A camping trip where each person attempted to extract the maximal concessions from the other campers in exchange for the use of his or her talents would quickly end in disaster and unhappiness. Moreover, the experience would be ruined if people were to behave in such a way. So, too, the argument goes, we would all be uplifted and our humanity enhanced by living in a more egalitarian and cooperative society.[8]

It is tempting to reject Cohen's argument for failing to deal with the problem of incentives. But such a dismissal depends on already embracing the view of human nature Cohen is seeking to reject—one in which people are motivated to work by the material returns they get from that work. Cohen, like Marx before him, believes this to be, at best, a partial understanding of human nature.

Neither Cohen nor Marx deny that people, as we observe them today, are in fact motivated to work, at least in part, by the incentives that come from increased personal wealth. However, both deny that this state of affairs is inevitable. In Cohen's view, the social system of competition and incentives in which we are embedded from the earliest age indoctrinates us into behaving in such a way. Were society to be radically transformed along egalitarian lines, Cohen believes, people would behave differently. People embedded in a social framework of sharing and cooperation would find it as natural to produce and share for the collective interest as we, embedded in our competitive and individualistic social framework, find it to produce in service of our individual interests. Hence, the argument goes, it will not do to reject egalitarianism on the grounds that people indoctrinated into behaving competitively would not do well in an egalitarian system. Part of the point of the egalitarian system is to free people from the dehumanizing indoctrination inherent in competition and inequality.

RAWLSIAN EGALITARIANISM

Rawls (1971) makes an argument for a kind of wealth egalitarianism by invoking the veil of ignorance.[9] Rawls believes that, behind the veil of ignorance, rational individuals prefer, say, social arrangement a_1 to social arrangement a_2 if and only if the worst off person under a_1 is better off than the worst off person under a_2. That is, if and only if $u_N(a_1) > u_N(a_2)$. Rawls's analysis is flawed, and I won't discuss it in depth. (You can see the problem by recalling that Harsanyi's argument for utilitarianism proceeds from the same premise

---

[8]Cohen, who admits he isn't actually much of an outdoorsman, seems to camp with a somewhat better class of person than I do. I can certainly remember being in the High Rockies and thinking, "My pack weighs 80 pounds and the pack of the person who divided the gear this morning looks like it weighs more like 65 pounds." Maybe I'm just petty and caught in a competitive mind-set.

[9]While Rawls comes to a somewhat consequentialist, egalitarian conclusion, it is worth noting that his veil of ignorance argument is not consequentialist. Rather, he is making an argument that, in spirit, is a modern version of something like Kant's deontological argument which we discuss in the next section.

and reaches a different conclusion.) Nonetheless, Rawls's argument leads to an interesting and helpful idea, which Rawls called the *difference principle*:

> *Rawls's Difference Principle:* A society should have inequality only to the extent that such inequality tends to increase the welfare of the worst off member of that society.

The difference principle is clearly egalitarian in spirit—giving lexicographic priority to society's worst off. Under the difference principle, one can only change from one policy to another if that policy change makes the worst off person better off. Only once that requirement has been met can one even ask questions about what the policy change does for other people. First and foremost, we worry about the bottom of society.

But the difference principle also differs from what I have called strict wealth egalitarianism in a couple of important ways. First, it avoids the leveling down problem. The difference principle favors the society where one person has a million dollars and the other person has half-a-million dollars over the society where both people have nothing. Second, the difference principle acknowledges incentives. Rawls argues that a just social arrangement must make the worst off person as well off as possible. You might, intuitively, think that this means Rawlsian justice calls for complete equality. But it does not, as the formulation of the difference principle (which suggests some persistent inequality) makes clear. Why not?

As we have already seen, one way to design a society that achieves complete equality is to collect all resources generated by each member of society and redistribute them evenly. But such a system provides only very weak incentives for hard work. Allowing some inequality creates stronger incentives. If people know that some people get to be rich, while others will be poor, and that working hard or taking risks is a necessary condition for becoming rich, then people have some incentive to work hard or take risks. In so doing, people create wealth, knowledge, art, apps, and all sorts of other good stuff. This stuff may well make everyone, even the poor, better off than they would be in a system of complete equality but weak incentives. Thus, Rawls is prepared to tolerate a fair bit of inequality, as long as that inequality has the effect of making even the worst off people better off.

1.3.2 Equality of Opportunity

Equality of opportunity is a considerably less controversial goal than is equality of outcomes. The basic argument goes something like this. People should have the chance to make something of themselves. And so, as a society, we ought to eliminate those disadvantages that are due to discrimination or to the idiosyncrasies of where and to whom an individual was born. Let's start our discussion of equality of opportunity by clarifying exactly what it means and what arguments it has on its behalf.

Cohen (2009) suggests three versions of equality of opportunity. I'll label them as Cohen does, though I don't find the names particularly helpful:

1. *Bourgeois Equality of Opportunity:* Eliminating "status restrictions, both formal and informal, on life chances." The idea is that equality of opportunity requires that a person's access to various opportunities should not be affected by irrelevant facts about that person (e.g., race, gender, parentage, wealth, sexual orientation, and so on). Rather, it should be determined only by that person's fitness for the opportunity.

2. *Left-Liberal Equality of Opportunity:* Eliminating "circumstances of birth and upbringing that constrain not by assigning an inferior status to their victims, but by nevertheless causing them to labour and live under substantial disadvantage." The idea is that irrelevant characteristics of a person should not affect a person's chance of acquiring the relevant fitness for a given opportunity.

3. *Socialist Equality of Opportunity:* Eliminating "inequality that arises out of native differences." The idea is that a person's access to various opportunities also should not be affected by characteristics that are relevant to that person's fitness for a given opportunity (e.g., intelligence, work ethic, physical ability).

The first notion of equality of opportunity—that people ought not be discriminated against based on irrelevant characteristics—is, I suspect, pretty uncontroversial. So too, I would guess, is the second. People should not be denied access to the chance to acquire relevant skills as a result of race, parentage, wealth, or what have you. Indeed, I think this second notion is what most people mean by equality of opportunity. People born to difficult circumstances or to historically mistreated groups should be ensured access to education, networking opportunities, and the like, so that they have the chance to acquire the requisite skills necessary to seize life's opportunities.

The third notion of equality of opportunity strikes many people as going a bit too far for two reasons. First, to be sure, being smart or physically able is, to a large degree, luck. Yet it is hard to think about organizing a society around the idea that those characteristics ought not affect a person's access to opportunity. (Though perhaps Cohen's radically egalitarian society could make this work.) Society might want to compensate or insure people against the risk of various kinds of natural disadvantage. But most people don't think that some highly athletic person and I should have had equal access to the opportunities offered by a college football career. (Though that would have been awesome.)

Second, there is a sense in which the third version of equality of opportunity equivocates too much on who *I* am. It is relatively easy for me to imagine a person who is me, only with a different level of access to education or networking. Thus, I understand what it means to remove the kind of barriers suggested by the second version of equality of opportunity. It is much more difficult for me to imagine a person who is me, only with a different level of intelligence or physical ability. After all, my capacity to think or to run is not separate from me, it is part of me. This leaves me somewhat confused as to what it means that I am disadvantaged by not being terribly bright. A person who was brighter wouldn't be me. He'd be a hedge fund manager.

To try to get a handle on these issues, let's consider two different arguments for equality of opportunity.

LUCK ELIMINATION

Dworkin (1981*b*) posits a classic argument for a certain kind of equality of opportunity. On Dworkin's view, justice requires that a person's fate be determined by things that are within that person's control, not by brute luck. Insofar as differences in well-being are determined by circumstances lying outside of an individual's control, they are unjust. On this argument, inequality of well-being that is driven by differences in individual choices or tastes are acceptable. But we should seek to eliminate inequality of well-being that is driven by factors that are not an individual's responsibility and which prevent an individual from achieving that which he or she values. We do so by ensuring equality of opportunity or equality of access to fundamental resources.

As we saw with Cohen's typology, a challenge is figuring out what factors that affect well-being are within the realm of individual responsibility and what factors are brute luck. We can probably all agree that an individual's racial, ethnic, socio-economic, and genetic background are outside of his or her control. So, on this view, any inequality of well-being due to such factors is unjust and ought to be corrected.

But notice, even this relatively uncontroversial position creates some difficulties. Think about genetic background. Genes affect intellectual capacity, physical ability, creativity, health, appearance, work ethic, and so on. Each of these, in turn, may affect well-being. Do we want to commit ourselves to the position that differences in well-being that are due to, say, differences in intellectual capacity, physical ability, or creativity are unjust and require correction? We might, but it is certainly not obvious.

Consider an even harder case. Are people responsible for their own preferences or values? Preferences—for labor vs. leisure, socially acceptable vs. unacceptable behavior, and so on—affect the choices people make and the actions they take. Those choices and actions affect well-being. Are differences in well-being that are due to differences in preferences a matter of individual responsibility or brute luck? Preferences appear, at least in part, to be determined by a variety of matters of luck—for example, the gene pool, family, and culture into which you happen to have been born. Given this, do we wish to conclude that a person's preferences are beyond his or her control and, thus, that justice mandates that we correct difference in well-being resulting from differences of preference?

Dworkin makes a possibly useful distinction, here, between preferences with which a person does and does not identify. A person identifies with some preference she holds if she is glad she holds it. A person does not identify with some preference she holds if she wishes she didn't hold it. This distinction is useful if you think, for instance, about the case of addiction. An addict might demonstrably hold a strong preference for using drugs that reduce her well-being. But if that addict wishes she didn't hold that preference, even if she has been unable to overcome her addiction, she does not identify with the preference. We might be more comfortable saying that a person is responsible for the consequences of those preferences that she both holds and is glad she holds, but not responsible for the consequences of preferences that drive her behavior, but which she wishes she could overcome.

It is, perhaps, clear at this point that using personal responsibility to draw the line where we stop equalizing opportunity gets us into some thorny issues. The resolution of such issues ultimately turns on the stance we want to take on questions like free will. Once you see that it is reasonable to question whether people are responsible for their own preferences, it is only a hop, skip, and a jump to the question of whether people are responsible for their own actions. At that point we must ask whether we draw the line anywhere or whether everything is just a matter of brute luck? And, if everything is a matter of luck, does that mean that a luck-elimination argument for equality of opportunity ultimately requires complete equality of well-being?

My own view is there is a line to be drawn, but for pragmatic, rather than fundamental, reasons. Deep down, everything (ability, preferences, actions) may well be determined by luck or, put differently, by physics. But that isn't a terribly helpful thought, as it provides little guidance about trade-offs. By contrast, in all sorts of settings, it is useful to think of people using their cognitive capacities to make decisions for which they are responsible, despite perhaps having limited control over their preferences. For instance, such a thought provides a foundation for punishment in criminal justice settings. It also provides a way to acknowledge that education and parenting shape character, while still permitting the possibility that a person is responsible for the consequences of his or her actions. Whether the line is properly drawn at the level of actions, preferences with which a person identifies, or somewhere else, I don't know. But it seems a line must be drawn.

UTILITARIANISM AND EQUALITY OF OPPORTUNITY

All this conceptual confusion suggests that maybe we have the wrong defense of equality of opportunity. Perhaps we shouldn't be defending it on purely egalitarian or luck-elimination grounds. Another defense might be more pragmatic. The world is full of talented, smart, hardworking people born to bad circumstances. It would be a tragedy, not just for them, but for society, to waste those talents. Maybe one such kid could grow up to cure cancer, prevent asteroids from hitting the earth, solve a really cool game theory model, or help the Bears' passing game. Thus, for the good of society, we want to make sure all individuals have access to the opportunity to gain the skills necessary to realize their potential.

This defense of equality of opportunity, while perfectly sensible, is a very different kind of argument than the ones we typically make. In particular, it is a thoroughly utilitarian argument. On this argument, equality of opportunity is no longer an end unto itself. Rather it is a means to an end.

This embrace of utilitarianism as a defense of equality of opportunity is itself interesting. It is another instance of a phenomenon we saw in our earlier discussion of welfare egalitarianism—often values that we cherish can be (at least partially) justified on utilitarian grounds. One advantage of such an instrumental, utilitarian defense is that it also provides a framework for thinking about trade-offs. Just because equality of opportunity tends, all else equal, to increase social utility, doesn't mean that we must slavishly pursue that goal to the exclusion of everything else. Instead, we balance competing goals against one another in proportion to their importance for overall social utility.

But even if we embrace a utilitarian argument for Cohen's left-liberal equality of opportunity, there is a second problem. Suppose we start our society with complete equality of opportunity of this sort. Over the course of a generation, we will not end up with equality of outcomes. People differ in terms of their natural talents, their interests, their willingness to trade off labor and leisure, and so on. As such, even with complete equality of opportunity, some people will end up rich and other people will end up poor.

We didn't set out to achieve equality of outcomes, so this state of affairs might not worry you. And I'd agree, if it weren't for the children. Here is the problem. Most parents want to help their children live happy, productive, successful lives. As it turns out, parents can turn money into opportunities for their children. As such, the first generation's outcomes will be a major input into the second generation's opportunities. A second generation person with successful parents has better opportunities than a second generation person with unsuccessful parents.

This is not good. We created a society with equality of opportunity. But the nature of human relationships intervened and, in just one generation, eradicated equality of opportunity. The only way to get it back, of course, is to impose equality of outcomes on the first (and all subsequent) generations. But as we've already seen, there are lots of problems with equality of outcomes. So it seems that we may be stuck. Although we may very much like equality of opportunity, it might not actually be achievable without sacrificing a lot of other things that we also care about.

1.4 Kantian Deontology

Both utilitarianism and certain kinds of egalitarianism are consequentialist frameworks. A different class of normative frameworks, called *deontological frameworks*, addresses many of the problems of consequentialist normative arguments. Of course, they do so at the expense of introducing new problems. Nonetheless, they are worth spending some time thinking about.

Deontological normative frameworks are those that judge a policy or social arrangement by its conformity to some moral norm or duty, rather than by its consequences. A deontological framework that is familiar in our political discourse concerns rights. Loosely speaking, a person has a right to something if another person can be said to have a duty to allow her to have it. We typically talk about such rights in deontological terms. We think of ourselves as having rights to life, liberty, and the pursuit of happiness, not because the existence of such rights increases the social welfare, but because those are our birthrights as human beings. (We are endowed by our creator with certain inalienable rights and so on.)

It is important that, when we talk about rights, we are asserting something deontological. To see why, notice that there is a tendency in political debate to proliferate claims to rights. Arguments for increasing the scope of government (with respect to health care, education, the economy) are often framed in terms of rights. Arguments for decreasing the scope of government (with respect to gun control, taxation, social programs) are also often framed in terms of rights. But claiming too many rights seems to cheapen the idea.

While it may be a useful rhetorical trick, labeling every policy you like as a right and every policy you dislike as a violation of rights renders the concept of a right more or less useless. It simply comes to mean "good." It is, then, perhaps useful to keep in mind the notion that a right for you entails a duty for others. Asking yourself whether you believe others have a duty to provide you some thing will help to clarify whether you have a right to that thing. For instance, I really can't claim that I have a right to chocolate cake because, much as I might like a piece of chocolate cake, you are under no obligation to provide it to me. (Unless you'd like extra credit.) But I might assert a right to freedom of religion if I believe you have a duty not to prevent me from exercising my religion of choice, and I have the same duty to you.

This idea that the existence of a deontological right or duty is closely tied up in our willingness to extend that right or duty universally comes from Kant, the most important of the deontological philosophers. But for Kant, the source of deontological duties is neither divine revelation nor natural law. Rather, deontological principles are derived from human nature itself.

Humans, on Kant's view, are rational creatures whose fundamental purpose is autonomy, which he understands as full actualization of our rational selves. For Kant, a rational person is autonomous if she is bound only by those moral laws that she would rationally will herself to be bound by. For this to be the case, Kant argues, those laws must be internally generated by the person's own rationality. A person bound by moral laws or duties that derive from outside the individual is said to be heteronomous, the opposite of autonomous.

When Kant insists that moral laws be rationally willed, he means that a rational person would be willing to universalize the law—binding herself, and others, to it everywhere and always. Thus, for Kant, to act autonomously is to behave in a way that is guided by those moral laws and duties that one would be willing to universalize. (It is worth noting that "veil of ignorance" arguments, which we used as a foundational argument for various types of consequentialism, can be viewed as Kantian-style deontological arguments which then yield a certain kind of consequentialism as an implication. Something like this was, in fact, Rawls's view.)

From this basic principle of autonomy, Kant derives his fundamental, deontological, moral precept: the Categorical Imperative. The Categorical Imperative has many formulations, but two are particularly useful, in my view. Here I paraphrase:

1. For an action to be moral, it must be that I would be willing to make the maxim (principle) that motivates the action a universal law (i.e., a principle to be followed everywhere and always by rational agents).
2. We should never treat another person's humanity as merely a means, but rather always as an end unto itself. (Note, this doesn't mean you can never use another person as a means, i.e., as in when you use a professor as a means to learn. But rather, you cannot treat your professor as though he or she were simply a means, rather than having an independent humanity that is an end unto itself.)

Kant's formulations are useful in several ways. First, they provide an example of a deontological framework that is philosophically respectable. Kant does not simply assert some deontological principle of morality. Rather, the Categorical Imperative is derived from axioms (with which you should feel free to disagree). Moreover, the Categorical Imperative is not a specific instruction of some duty you have. Instead, it is a tool by which you can derive a variety of duties. For any action, you can first identify the maxim that underlies it and then question whether you would be willing to universalize that maxim. If yes, then, on Kant's view, you are on firm moral ground. If no, then you are taking an action which is inconsistent with morality and rational autonomy.

Second, a Kantian view raises some interesting questions for thinking about policy, especially if we focus on the latter formulation of the Categorical Imperative above. For instance, consider the relationship of the state to criminals. Kant's analysis admits certain justifications for polices such as incarceration. A rational agent can universalize the maxim that criminals should be punished and security maintained. However, other views of the purpose of incarceration—such as crime deterrence—are inconsistent with a Kantian framework. In particular, to incarcerate a person in order to deter other potential criminals is to use that person as merely a means.

1.4.1 Deontology and the Challenges to Utilitarianism

Deontological frameworks have the advantage of addressing some of the primary objections leveled against utilitarianism. For instance, standard deontological arguments make sense of our shared moral intuitions about the trolley and transplant problems. According to the Categorical Imperative, it is clearly immoral to kill a person to harvest her organs—doing so uses her as merely a means, rather than as an end unto herself. But, according to the Categorical Imperative, it is permissible to pull the switch in the trolley example. The maxim of that action is that you should preserve human life—an easily universalized principle. The key distinction between the transplant and trolley problems is that in the trolley problem, the worker who will be killed is not being used as a means to save the lives of the trolley passengers. Pulling the switch would save those lives whether the worker were on the siding or not. Unlike in the case of transplants, his death is not the means to the end of saving the lives of the trolley passengers. Rather, the worker is just an unfortunate bystander.

Deontological arguments also leave considerably more room than do consequentialist frameworks for taking seriously special human relationships. For instance, in many deontological frameworks, parents have special obligations to their children. One would not want to universalize the maxim that every person should devote enormous time and resources to the care and nurturing of every child. But one can easily universalize the maxim that parents should do so for their children.

1.4.2 Challenges for Deontological Thinking

Although deontological frameworks have some appeal, both philosophically and intuitively, like any normative framework, they also have their challenges. Here I highlight some common critiques of deontological approaches.

A first problem arises when multiple duties come into conflict with one another. (An eventuality that Kant seems to have thought impossible.) Let's look at a classic example.

Standard deontological frameworks give rise to a duty not to lie. To see this in a Kantian framework, think about the maxim underlying a lie—to render communication deceptive. If one were to universalize this maxim, one would will that all communication be deceptive, something a rational agent could not do. Thus, the Categorical Imperative suggests a duty not to lie.

Standard deontological arguments also typically give rise to a duty to respect the lives of fellow human beings. This follows more or less directly from our second formulation of the Categorical Imperative. And so arises a classic question for Kant (and other deontological frameworks). Suppose a murderer asks you the location of his intended victim. Do you have a moral obligation not to lie to the murderer? A similar moral dilemma arises in thinking about problems like the morality of torture in the face of a "ticking time bomb."

While extreme cases, these examples highlight a broader point about deontological theories. There is no reason to believe that duties will not frequently come into conflict with one another. If we cannot adjudicate among duties on the basis of consequences, how are we to know how to act in the presence of competing duties?

A second problem, sometimes called the paradox of deontology, is closely related. You are not permitted to violate a deontological duty, even to prevent others from violating a deontological duty. Thus, on the Kantian argument, it would be wrong for me to deceive you into taking some action, even if that action would prevent ten murderers from killing ten people. Why is this? Because deceiving you into taking an action is using you as a means, rather than an end. And this is forbidden, even if doing so would stop not just a bad outcome (let's not be consequentialists!), but actually prevent many other people from violating deontological duties (e.g., the duty not to murder).

Both of these problems, in some sense, come down to the question of how we weigh different wrongs and make trade-offs in a deontological framework. It is a violation of deontological duty to lie. It is a violation of deontological duty to kill. But those things can't be compared or added. That is, it is not obviously worse to kill than to lie. Nor is it obviously worse to lie twice than to lie once. To say that it is morally permissible to lie in order to prevent two lies is to slip into consequentialism.

A final note on the usefulness of deontology is also merited here. The usefulness of, say, the Categorical Imperative depends on your ability to correctly identify the maxim of your action. For instance, consider whether my slapping my own forehead (perhaps to signal surprise) is moral. If the maxim of that action is "slapping my forehead is moral," then I don't want it universalized, as I do not want to live in a world where anyone feels free to come up and slap me in the head. But if the maxim of that action is "slapping one's own forehead is moral," then fine by me.[10] While silly, this example highlights a real challenge for the applicability of deontological frameworks. Unlike utilitarianism, where the final judgment is an empirical one, for the Categorical Imperative, the final judgment of an act's morality is a conceptual one that depends on what maxim you take to underlie it.

1.5 Libertarianism

Libertarianism can be thought of as a particular type of deontological normative framework. It again provides a stark contrast from either utilitarianism or egalitarianism. Libertarians do not evaluate the merits of policies or social arrangements based on utility (be it the sum or the difference). Instead, they are interested in maximizing human freedom.

Human freedom is an appealing norm for many people. Politicians often frame debates over policy in terms of ensuring our freedom or preventing our freedom from being abridged. Yet, as one can see from those debates, there is considerable disagreement as to what freedom actually is.

Consider, for instance, the debate over same-sex marriage. Both sides of that debate frequently frame the discussion in terms of freedom. Those in favor of legalized same-sex marriage argue that the government should not deny people the freedom to marry the partner of their choice. Those opposed to legalized same-sex marriage argue that the government should not deny people the freedom to live and raise families in communities whose laws reflect their values.

How can it be that both sides of a debate have freedom on their side? The answer, I believe, derives from the fact that freedom means at least two different things in our political discourse. These two meanings are worth pulling apart and thinking about separately, lest we get horribly confused.

What does it mean to be free? One view is that true freedom is about self-actualization. For Kant, to be free means to live in accordance with the dictates of rationality—that is, to achieve autonomy. On Kant's view, if all we do is pursue utility or happiness or wealth, we aren't really free. Rather, we are slaves whose actions are dictated not by our rational wills, but by things external to ourselves.

A second definition of freedom is perhaps more straightforward—freedom is the absence of coercion. That is, a person is free when she is able to do what she wants, subject to the restriction that she not diminish the freedom of others.

---

[10]I thank Scott Ashworth for this example.

These views are, at times, in tension with one another, though they need not always be. Let's first think about why they might be in tension and then come back to how they can, for some thinkers, be reconciled.

If freedom is defined in terms of autonomy, then there can be room for a fairly active government, in service of freedom. A state that seeks to facilitate citizen autonomy can justify all sorts of interventions on the grounds that they advance self-actualization. Some policies that might be justified in this way could strike you as fairly benevolent. For instance, one might argue for universal access to education on the grounds that autonomous individuals must develop critical capabilities. One might also argue for universal access to subsistence on the grounds that the pursuit of autonomy requires physical nourishment.

Autonomy-based freedom arguments can also be used to justify less benevolent-seeming policies. A state that believes people are taking actions that are not in their true interests—say, worshipping a false god, engaging in immoral behavior, pursuing heretical scientific inquiry, or betraying their ethnic group or economic class—might argue that, in order to make people free, it must massively restrict their actions. For some thinkers, true autonomy can only be achieved within a collective—be it one's class (for Marx), one's nation (for Fichte), or what have you. Such notions of autonomy can (though need not) lead to a defense of totalitarian government on the grounds of preserving freedom.

An alternative view is that freedom is maximized when coercion is minimized. Interestingly, as political philosophers at least since Hobbes have noted, the goal of living an uncoerced life requires that one accept no small measure of government coercion. In particular, in order to free oneself from coercion by others, one must accept the rule of law. That is, one must allow the state to use the threat of violence to coerce you and others not to engage in acts of violence against one another. While the rule of law is clearly a constraint on one's actions, it can be defended on the grounds that it increases, rather than decreases, freedom by reducing the risk of other forms of coercion.

This coercion-minimizing view of freedom raises some interesting questions about the proper role of the state. In defense of this sort of freedom, we want the state to use its coercive power to prevent violent coercion by other people. But what of other forms of coercion? A person can be coerced into taking actions she wouldn't otherwise take in a variety of ways. Does it increase or decrease freedom for the state to use the threat of violence to prevent coercion through social sanction? What about coercion through indoctrination? What if the people being indoctrinated are children? These are tricky questions which involve trade-offs of one kind of freedom against another.

Finally, it is worth noting that the two views of freedom need not be in fundamental tension. Kant, for one, believed that true freedom was to be found in autonomy. His vision of autonomy was an individualistic one. As such, in his view, the job of the state is to facilitate autonomy by allowing people to live as uncoerced a life as possible. (Notice, this is another useful distinction between private and public morality.)

For now, we need to make a choice about what we mean by freedom. So, for the remainder of this discussion, I will focus on a view of freedom that is about the absence of coercion, not about self-actualization.

1.5.1 Why Be a Libertarian?

Like utilitarianism and egalitarianism, there are many reasons why one might be a libertarian. Indeed, one might even be a libertarian on utilitarian grounds. (That is, one might think that absence of coercion maximizes incentives, which maximizes societal wealth, which maximizes aggregate utility.) But here I will focus on a freestanding, deontological defense of libertarianism associated with the philosopher Robert Nozick (1974).

Nozick argues that the essential evaluative criterion for a social arrangement is the degree of respect for self-ownership. On Nozick's view, individuals have absolute ownership of their own bodies. This means that if you use your body to create things of value, then you own those things. To take them from you is to deny your self-ownership.

For Nozick, because things of value are created by mixing human labor (and thought) with the natural world, it makes no sense to ask how much stuff each person deserves, as an egalitarian might. Given that people own their own bodies, they are due whatever they create with that body. The things of value in the world are owned by individuals because they were created by individuals. For the social arrangement to take things from one person and give them to another is to deny individuals' ownership of themselves.

To see the force of Nozick's idea, imagine two people born owning equal pieces of the natural world. Suppose one is very professionally ambitious, while the other prefers to spend more time with family. The professionally ambitious person produces a lot from the natural resources he owns and thus becomes wealthy. The family-oriented person produces less material wealth. This is not an unjust or bad outcome for a libertarian. Each person has been respected as a self-owning individual. The fact that they made different life choices, and thus ended up with unequal levels of wealth, is neither here nor there with respect to justice, and certainly cannot be used as a justification for redistributing the professionally ambitious person's (self-owned) wealth to the family-oriented person. (This example also highlights the importance, for consequentialists, of not conflating wealth and utility. It is not clear which of these people has higher utility.)

Nozick's famous parable involves the basketball player Wilt Chamberlain. He imagines a world in which each person starts with equal amounts of wealth. But people are willing to pay to see Wilt Chamberlain play. Each person is made better off by these transactions, since if she is willing to spend some amount of money to see Wilt Chamberlain play, it must be that she enjoys the experience more than the money. Yet, in the end, we end up with lots of inequality. Wilt Chamberlain is very rich. There is nothing unjust, for Nozick, about this outcome. Chamberlain came by his money as a simple extension of his ownership of his own body. And the people who paid to see him play were justified in spending money to enjoy the experience as a simple extension to their self-ownership. The ultimate inequality of wealth is normatively irrelevant.

On Nozick's analysis, both consequentialist and redistributivist views of justice are in contradiction with what is, to him, the fundamental moral fact of human life: self-ownership. Thus, Nozick argues, the right social order is the one that maximizes respect for self-ownership by minimizing coercion, regardless of the consequences.

1.5.2 Some Problems for Libertarianism

Like any normative framework, libertarianism has some places where it runs into problems. Below I discuss a couple important ones.

OWNERSHIP OF PROPERTY

In my description of Nozick's theory of self-ownership, I slipped in what is perhaps the greatest challenge for Nozick's thinking on these issues. Things of value are never created by a human using her body alone. Rather, she mixes her labor and thought with the natural world to create something of value. On Nozick's argument, if I own a part of the natural world and I own my body, then it follows that I own whatever it is that I use my body to make out of the part of the natural world that I own. But, even if you grant this argument, you can still question how I came to own part of the natural world.

Nozick is not unaware of this issue. On his account, at the beginning of time, the natural world is unowned. It comes to be owned by acts of legitimate acquisition, which involve people claiming and improving unowned land. Here he draws on John Locke's thinking about property rights, most clearly articulated in Chapter V of the *Second Treatise of Government*. (It is worth noting that Locke's ideas on the matter were developed, at least in part, to justify colonial expropriation of native lands.)

As a matter of historical record, of course, this is not how things went. Lots of land was owned by one person, in the Nozickian sense, only to have it taken by force by another. Nozick is also aware of this fact. In response, he endorses some kinds of temporary redistribution in order to reset the system of ownership to a justified level once and for all. Following such a rectification, however, Nozick believes that redistribution can never again be justified, since people own the fruits of their labor mixed with their legitimately held property. Nonetheless, one need not think of Nozick as embracing the current status quo, since that status quo may be built on a foundation of unjust property claims. But once such problems are addressed, Nozick believes the state must take a minimal role—basically just protecting property rights—in order to respect people's self-ownership.

TRADE-OFFS

Another potential problem for a libertarianism grounded in an uncompromising commitment to self-ownership (though not a libertarianism that is derived from utilitarianism) is that it does not admit much in the way of trade-offs. One can imagine situations in which small increases in coercion (say, taxation for the purpose of providing education) might yield social benefits well in excess of social costs. Yet the committed libertarian would reject such policies, no matter how large the benefit, because forcible taxation for the purpose of transferring resources to others (as opposed to taxation for, say, the purpose of national defense, which would be permissible) is a violation of the principle of self-ownership. Such is the nature of deontological commitments of this sort.

1.6 Takeaways

- We've looked at several ways people think about how to evaluate or justify the goals of public policy. Each of these various normative frameworks has arguments to recommend it and each also has implications or conceptual limitations that might leave you somewhat uncomfortable. My goal was not to convince you of some particular normative position. Rather, I hope this discussion has, at least to some extent, added a bit of nuance to your normative thinking.
- Various normative frameworks are often in conflict with one another. There are trade-offs in life. For instance, increasing equality through redistribution may require diminishing freedom from coercion. Maximizing overall utility may also sometimes require reducing freedom by engaging in physical coercion (remember the transplants example).
- The same term is often used to mean different things. When this happens, serious deliberation over policy goals becomes difficult. For instance, freedom-as-autonomy and freedom-from-coercion are often both simply called freedom. But they are very different things and if you don't know which your opponent is referring to, you are unlikely to make arguments she finds persuasive.

- Any plausible normative framework has good arguments in its favor and good arguments against it. As such, consensus on the proper normative framework is not a workable goal. Reasonable people can disagree.

- Indeed, I would go further. Arriving at a coherent framework that accounts even just for all of your own personal normative commitments probably isn't a reasonable goal. Sometimes you will be motivated by a concern for freedom. Other times you will be motivated by a concern for overall utility. Deep down, these two normative frameworks may contradict each other. But so what? Physics has unanswered (perhaps unanswerable) questions deep down. Must political philosophy be on firmer footing than physics? That said, in your more self-righteous moments, you might want to remember that lack of deep foundations.

- Normative frameworks are often presented as *the* answer to a set of moral questions. This is nonsense. As we've seen, there are lots of trade-offs and contradictions—not all good things go together all the time. Normative frameworks are better seen as models—conceptual frameworks that help you think through one aspect of a problem. It might be helpful to think of them as all-else-equal claims. All else equal, more freedom is better than less, more utility is better than less, more justice is better than less, and more equality is better than less. But all else is never held equal. So, in coming to a normative judgment on some policy issue, you must weigh the trade-offs. How much do you care about equality versus freedom *in this case*? Your position, then, will not be right everywhere and always, but rather will reflect the particular trade-offs you happen to be willing to make. Reasonable people can and will disagree about those trade-offs.

1.7 Further Reading

Of course, the political philosophy literature is vast. Peter Singer's *Practical Ethics* is a classic, thoughtful introduction to ethics and its application to policy problems. Adam Swift's *Political Philosophy: A Beginners' Guide for Students and Politicians* is a nice, accessible primer on political philosophy. John Broome's *Climate Matters: Ethics in a Warming World* gives a moral philosopher's take on many of the same themes discussed in this chapter in a particular applied policy context.

To my mind, the deepest formal treatment of the sort of issues discussed in this chapter is John E. Roemer's extraordinary *Theories of Distributive Justice*.

Some of the classic works discussed in this chapter are Kant's *Groundwork of the Metaphysics of Morals*, Rawls's *A Theory of Justice*, Nozick's *Anarchy, State, and Utopia*, Cohen's *Why Not Socialism?*, and Dworkin (1981*a,b*). Sen (1980) helpfully asks "equality of what?" The veil-of-ignorance argument for utilitarianism is articulated in Harsanyi (1953) and in his book *Rational Behavior and Bargaining Equilibrium in Games and Social Situations*.

1.8 Exercises

1. Suppose a car company produces a small, light, inexpensive, fuel efficient car. Because the car is inexpensive and fuel efficient, it will be affordable for relatively low-income people, who will use it to get to work, take their children to school, and so on. However, because the car is so small and light, it also turns out not to be as safe as larger cars. Indeed, the manufacturer discovers that the car does not perform well on several crash tests. Addressing these safety issues would require modifications to the car that would significantly increase its cost, making it inaccessible to many low-income potential users.

    Ignoring regulatory issues (i.e., is the manufacturer allowed to sell such a car), use different normative frameworks to make a pro and con argument for each of the following two positions:

    (a) The car company should disclose the safety flaws, but sell the car at the affordable price without alteration.
    (b) The car company should either modify the car and increase the price or not sell the car at all.

2. Consider the proposition that the United States should reduce barriers to immigration, allowing many more people to emigrate from poor countries where they lack opportunity. Take as given that the kind of people who immigrate tend to be low skill, but smart and ambitious.

    (a) Focusing only on the U.S. population and the immigrants themselves, evaluate this proposal from a utilitarian, egalitarian, and libertarian perspective.
    (b) Now expand your analysis to also consider the populations of the immigrants' home countries. Does this alter any of your evaluations?

3. In a recent set of influential articles Sunstein and Thaler argue for a normative position which they call *libertarian paternalism* (Sunstein and Thaler, 2003; Thaler and Sunstein, 2003). Drawing on insights from psychology and behavioral economics, they start with the premise that, left to their own devices, people often make choices that are not in their own interest (e.g., eating more than they would like to eat, saving less for retirement than they would like to save). That is, people are irrational in certain predictable ways. This, in their view, is an argument for a certain

kind of paternalism—because policymakers are aware of these systematic biases in people's behavior, in some circumstances, the policymaker can make decisions that are better for a person than the decisions the person would make him or herself.

However, Sunstein and Thaler are also interested in maintaining certain libertarian principles. In particular, while they want to help people make better choices, they don't want to coerce people. Thus, they suggest "nudging" people towards better choices—for example, making the default choice the "right" one, while always leaving people with the option to act differently.

For instance, they would like companies to have the default be that all employees make the full contribution to a retirement plan (nudging people towards saving), while allowing people the option to opt out of the program. One systematic bias in people's behavior is an overwillingness to stick with the status quo. So, they argue, making the default option the good choice, while leaving people the option to change their decision, has the dual virtues of using people's behavioral biases to push them towards the better choice (paternalism), while not forcing them to make that choice (libertarianism).

(a) To what extent do you think libertarian paternalism in fact fulfills the goals of libertarianism in Nozick's sense of the term?

(b) What would a utilitarian think about libertarian paternalism? Think about this from two perspectives:

  i. Assuming the policymaker really does know what is in the interest of individuals better than they do, what would a utilitarian think about using behavioral methods to nudge people towards better decisions?
  ii. Is the notion that people don't know their own true interests (in the sense that they are unable to act on those interests) conceptually problematic for defining utilitarianism?

4.   In a provocative essay, O'Hare (2015) argues that major art museums should sell off some of their art. Here's the essence of his argument:

Any top-rank museum exhibits no more than a twentieth of its collection, often much less. There is some rotation in and out of storage but, as a rule of thumb, consider the least distinguished object in a gallery, and you can be sure that there are one or two just a teeny bit inferior, and a dozen nearly as good, in a warehouse or the basement. The Met, for example, shows 27 of its 41 Monets, but only three out of its 13 Eugène Boudins....

> Selling just 1 percent of the collection by value—much more than 1 percent by object count—would enable the AIC [Art Institute of Chicago] to endow free admission forever.
>
> ...selling another percent of the museum's collection would pay for 30 percent more exhibition space (either where it is now, or in a big satellite somewhere), to actually show us more art. Let's go crazy and sell another percent—that would endow $17 million a year of operating budget, a fifth of the institute's current "instructional and academic" staff costs, which would enable it to hire something on the order of 200 more full-time researchers, educators, designers, and people studying the audience to understand what really goes on when people get up close to art. All this, and the AIC would still be sitting on 97 percent of the value of its current stockpile, but showing a third more of it, and better.

Adopting two different normative frameworks, make an argument for and against this proposal.

5.   In 1991 Lawrence Summers (a Harvard economist who was then chief economist at the World Bank and later became secretary of the treasury) wrote the following memo:

> Just between you and me, shouldn't the World Bank be encouraging MORE migration of the dirty industries to the LDCs [Less Developed Countries]? I can think of three reasons:
>
> 1) The measurements of the costs of health impairing pollution depends on the foregone earnings from increased morbidity and mortality. From this point of view a given amount of health impairing pollution should be done in the country with the lowest cost, which will be the country with the lowest wages. I think the economic logic behind dumping a load of toxic waste in the lowest wage country is impeccable and we should face up to that.
>
> 2) The costs of pollution are likely to be non-linear as the initial increments of pollution probably have very low cost. I've always thought that under-populated countries in Africa are vastly UNDER-polluted, their air quality is probably vastly inefficiently low [sic] compared to Los Angeles or Mexico City. Only the lamentable facts that so much pollution is generated by non-tradable industries (transport, electrical generation) and that the unit transport costs of solid waste are so high prevent world welfare enhancing trade in air pollution and waste.

3) The demand for a clean environment for aesthetic and health reasons is likely to have very high income elasticity. The concern over an agent that causes a one in a million change in the odds of prostate cancer is obviously going to be much higher in a country where people survive to get prostate cancer than in a country where under 5 mortality is 200 per thousand. Also, much of the concern over industrial atmosphere discharge is about visibility impairing particulates. These discharges may have very little direct health impact. Clearly trade in goods that embody aesthetic pollution concerns could be welfare enhancing. While production is mobile the consumption of pretty air is a non-tradable. The problem with the arguments against all of these proposals for more pollution in LDCs (intrinsic rights to certain goods, moral reasons, social concerns, lack of adequate markets, etc.) could be turned around and used more or less effectively against every Bank proposal for liberalization.

One at a time, briefly evaluate Summers's argument from the perspective of any two of our normative frameworks. Do not dispute Summers's factual assertions (e.g., that the marginal cost of pollution is increasing), but rather offer a normative evaluation, assuming his factual assertions are true.

6. Consider a person of above-average wealth who believes strongly in government redistribution of wealth, but does not give personally to charity. Evaluate the reasonableness of holding these two positions simultaneously from the perspective of utilitarianism and Kant's Categorical Imperative.

2

Collective Goals

We've seen that there are lots of reasonable ways to normatively evaluate policy. This multiplicity of potentially mutually exclusive normative criteria creates something of a problem for our standard discourse about good policy. We often want to say that good policy serves the public interest. But how do we determine what the public interest is if we can't agree on a normative framework?

An alternative approach is to think of these (and other) normative frameworks as reflecting the opinions of individuals within a society. That is, none of them defines the public interest. Rather, they may describe what a particular individual believes the public interest to be. And when we speak of *the* public interest we mean a set of goals or standards that a society—made up of people with their individual opinions—collectively agrees on.

What does it mean for a society of individuals, who disagree on the right set of goals, to nonetheless collectively agree on a notion of the public interest? One possibility is that we might all agree on some procedure for aggregating our individual opinions and then define the public interest for our society as the outcome of that aggregation procedure.

For instance, consider a choice between two policies, which I'll call x and y. The individuals in a society might disagree over which of those two policies is best or right. But they might agree to define the public interest as whichever of x or y a majority prefer. I'm not saying this is a particularly good definition of the public interest. But it is a plausible procedure that takes as inputs contradictory individual opinions and returns as output a vision of the public interest, without asking the individuals to agree with one another as to which of x or y is the better choice.

This notion of the public interest being defined through the aggregation of individual interests is one way of understanding what Rousseau had in mind when he wrote of the "general will" in *The Social Contract*:

> There is often a great deal of difference between the will of all [what all individuals want] and the general will; the general will studies only the common interest while the will of all studies private interest, and is indeed no more than the sum of individual desires. But if we take away from these same wills, the pluses and minuses which cancel each other out, the balance that remains is the general will.

So we have arrived at a potential way forward. We cannot all agree on a normative standard by which to evaluate policies. However, perhaps we can all agree on an aggregation procedure that will take our heterogeneous preferences and turn them into a set of collective goals that we can define as the public interest. This approach, of course, depends on our finding an aggregation procedure that we can all agree on and that will in fact generate meaningful collective goals. In what follows, we explore whether this approach will work. To do so, we first need to develop a little bit of apparatus to formalize the ideas of individual and collective preferences.

2.1 Rational Individuals

Let's start with a model of individual preferences. We assume that each person in our society has preferences over a set of alternatives, A. The elements of this set of alternatives could be a variety of things, but for concreteness, let's think of them as policies.

Consider an individual named i facing a choice between two policies (call them x and y) from the set of alternatives. Person i's preferences indicate whether she likes x at least as much as y (denoted $x \succsim_i y$) or likes y at least as much as x (denoted $y \succsim_i x$). If she likes x at least as much as y but not vice versa, then she strictly prefers x to y (denoted $x \succ_i y$). If she likes x at least as much as y and y at least as much as x, she is indifferent between them (denoted $x \sim_i y$).

We say that a person is *rational* if her preferences satisfy two simple conditions:

1. **Completeness:** For any two policies in the set of alternatives (i.e., $x, y \in A$) person i has a preference (i.e., $x \succ_i y$, $y \succ_i x$, or $x \sim_i y$).
2. **Transitivity:** Consider three policies in the set of alternatives (i.e., $x, y, z \in A$). If $x \succsim_i y$ and $y \succsim_i z$, then $x \succsim_i z$.

Completeness simply says that i always has an opinion. She can say she likes x better than y, y better than x, or is indifferent between them. What she can't say is that she is wholly unable to compare x to y.

Transitivity says that if a person likes x at least as much as y and y at least as much as z, then she likes x at least as much as z. (Transitivity of the weak preference implies transitivity of both the strict preference and indifference.) This is a minimal condition for rationality. A person with intransitive preferences—say, $x \succ_i y \succ_i z \succ_i x$—might constantly cycle in her choices. If she was offered y or z she'd choose y. If offered x or y, she'd choose x. If offered x or z she'd choose z, ending up right where she started. Such a person would potentially be unable to make coherent decisions and, as the following example shows, could be exploited by clever tricksters.

EXAMPLE 2.1.1 (THE MONEY PUMP)

Paul has intransitive preferences over three fruits: apples (*a*), bananas (*b*), and oranges (*o*). In particular, Paul's preferences are such that $a \succ_P b$, $b \succ_P o$, and $o \succ_P a$. Moreover, Paul values each of these preferences at one dollar and ten cents. That is, if you ask Paul how much he'd be willing to pay to trade a banana for an apple, the answer is $1.10. If you ask Paul how much he'd be willing to pay to trade an orange for a banana, the answer is $1.10. Finally, if you ask Paul how much he'd be willing to pay to trade an apple for an orange, the answer is $1.10.

Suppose Paul has an orange and $10. Sally is a fruit seller. One day, Paul enters Sally's store with his orange and his $10. Sally offers to trade Paul one of her bananas in exchange for Paul's orange plus a dollar. Paul would be willing to pay all the way up to $1.10 to trade his orange for a banana, so he eagerly takes the deal. Now Paul has a banana and $9.

Sally, crafty business person that she is, now offers Paul another trade. She will give Paul an apple in exchange for Paul's banana and a dollar. Paul would be willing to pay all the way up to $1.10 to trade his banana for an apple, so he once again eagerly takes the deal. Now Paul has an apple and $8.

Sally offers Paul yet another trade. She will give Paul an orange in exchange for Paul's apple and a dollar. Paul would be willing to pay all the way up to $1.10 to trade his apple for an orange, so he once again eagerly takes the deal. Now Paul has an orange and $7.

Recall that Paul entered Sally's store with an orange and $10! Sally has turned Paul into a money pump. And notice, Sally can keep doing this until Paul runs out of money.

An important point here is that, as we've defined it, rationality has nothing to do with the normative content of preferences. A rational person can think any crazy thing she likes about which policies are better and which policies are worse, as long as those preferences are complete and transitive. This is important because the content of your preferences may well be a function of the normative frameworks to which you are committed. (It may also be a function of other things like your wealth, life experience, or what have you.) And the whole point of our current enterprise is that we lack any principled way to choose among a variety of plausible normative frameworks. Thus, we don't want to label certain kinds of preferences as irrational simply because we happen to disagree with them.

2.2   Aggregation Procedures

For the purposes of our analysis, a society is a collection of rational individuals. That society has to make a decision over some set of alternatives, *A*. Each individual has preferences over those alternatives. Define an *issue* as a set of alternatives and the collection of each individual's preferences over those alternatives.

Remember, our goal is to find an aggregation procedure that, for any issue, takes individual preferences and returns a social preference, so that we can all agree that the outcome of that aggregation procedure yields something we will accept as the public interest on that issue.

What exactly is an aggregation procedure? It is a function that takes as inputs all of the individual preferences and returns as output a social preference. A social preference, just like an individual preference, is simply a rank ordering of all the alternatives in the set A. For concreteness, let's consider one particular aggregation procedure: pairwise majority rule.

Pairwise majority rule aggregates preferences as follows. For any two alternatives, $x, y \in A$, say that society prefers x to y if a majority of individuals in society prefers x to y, society prefers y to x if a majority of individuals prefers y to x, and society is indifferent between x and y if the same number of people prefers x to y as y to x. A simple example will fix ideas.

EXAMPLE 2.2.1 (MAJORITY RULE AGGREGATION)

A society with three members—Beth (B), Charles (C), and Dana (D)—is considering tax policy. There are four possible taxes: None, Low, Medium, and High. That is, the set of alternatives is $A = \{N, L, M, H\}$.

The three members of society have different views about the appropriate tax rate. In particular, their preferences are

$$H \succ_B N \succ_B L \succ_B M$$
$$M \succ_C H \succ_C L \succ_C N$$
$$M \succ_D H \succ_D N \succ_D L.$$

Suppose they agree to define the public interest as the preference ordering determined by pairwise majority rule. What will that social preference be?

Let's denote the social preference under majority rule by $\succ_{maj}$. Comparing High taxes to Medium taxes, we find that a majority (Charles and Dana) prefers Medium taxes. From the perspective of society, under majority rule aggregation, $M \succ_{maj} H$. Comparing High taxes to Low or No taxes, we find that there is unanimous agreement in favor of High taxes. Thus, $H \succ_{maj} L$ and $H \succ_{maj} N$. While there is not unanimity in support of Medium compared to Low or No taxes, a majority (Charles and Dana) does prefer Medium taxes to either of these alternatives. Thus, $M \succ_{maj} L$ and $M \succ_{maj} N$. Finally, comparing

(*Continued on next page*)

Low to No taxes, a majority (Beth and Dana) prefers No taxes to Low taxes. So this analysis gives us the full social preference for this society under pairwise majority rule aggregation:

$$M \succ_{maj} H \succ_{maj} N \succ_{maj} L.$$

Of course, we might have used a different aggregation procedure, such as a scoring rule like the *Borda count*. Under this procedure, if there are k alternatives, each person's first choice gets $k - 1$ points, each person's second choice gets $k - 2$ points, and so on, with each person's last choice getting 0 points. We then sum the total points for each policy and rank order policies by their scores. Let's redo our example under the Borda count.

EXAMPLE 2.2.2 (BORDA COUNT AGGREGATION)

Consider the same society as in Example 2.2.1. Under the Borda count aggregation procedure, point totals are as follows:

- H: $3 + 2 + 2 = 7$
- M: $0 + 3 + 3 = 6$
- L: $1 + 1 + 0 = 2$
- N: $2 + 0 + 1 = 3$

Let's denote the social preference under the Borda count by $\succ_{bor}$. Under this aggregation procedure, we have the following social preferences:

$$H \succ_{bor} M \succ_{bor} N \succ_{bor} L.$$

The examples highlight two key points. First, there are multiple potentially reasonable aggregation procedures for determining social preferences. Second, different aggregation procedures can give rise to different notions of the public interest. For instance, the social preference in our example is different under majority rule than under the Borda count. Given this, we need to look for a principled argument to choose among potential aggregation procedures.

2.3   Evaluative Criteria for Aggregation Procedures

There are a huge number of potential aggregation procedures. So choosing among them is a daunting task. The key approach to narrowing down the set is to start by identifying some intuitively appealing features of social preferences and eliminating aggregation procedures whose outputs (i.e., the social preferences the rule produces) do not have those features.

Before jumping into this task, however, there is an important subtlety to be highlighted. An aggregation procedure is basically just a machine that takes a collection of individual preferences as an input and spits out a social preference as an output. The social preference that an aggregation procedure produces, therefore, depends on the individual preferences that are fed in. Suppose we identify some intuitively appealing feature that we want the social preference produced by an aggregation procedure to have. In trying to figure out whether the social preference produced by an aggregation procedure will or will not have that feature, the answer may well depend on the particular individual preferences with which we started. So what do we do?

Typically, we say that we want an aggregation procedure to satisfy some intuitively appealing criterion *for any* possible collection of rational individual preferences we feed in. This requirement is called *universal domain*.[1] Let me be a little more concrete to fix ideas.

Here's an intuitively appealing criterion. Suppose absolutely everyone in society prefers x to y. Then you might think that any sensible aggregation procedure should say that society prefers x to y. This criterion is called *unanimity*. The universal domain requirement, applied to unanimity, says the following: No matter what issue—that is, set of alternatives and collection of individual preferences—the members of our society happen to face, a sensible aggregation procedure will respect unanimity. *If* everyone agrees about the ranking of two alternatives, the social preference will share that ranking.

We care about universal domain because, when we choose an aggregation procedure, we don't know what issues might arise in the future. We are going to use this same aggregation procedure, no matter the issue. So we want to be sure that the aggregation procedure will behave sensibly in any setting.

Given this, let's start looking at some fairly basic criteria to see which aggregation procedures they rule out.

2.3.1 Transitivity of Social Preferences

The first criterion we will impose is transitivity. Transitivity is a minimal requirement for coherent social preferences, just as it is for individual preferences. If an aggregation procedure returns intransitive social preferences, then it really isn't useful in identifying the public interest. If our social preferences rank x over y, y over z, and z over x, then what exactly do we prefer?

---

[1]The term universal domain refers to the fact that the domain of the aggregation procedure is the set of *all* profiles of individual preferences.

Remember, for any criterion (like transitivity), the principle of universal domain says that an aggregation procedure should satisfy the criterion for any issue with which it is presented. If we can find even one example where a candidate aggregation procedure violates transitivity (or any of the other criteria we will discuss) we will throw it out of contention, since that aggregation procedure is not guaranteed to always yield something that could be sensibly called the public interest.

Strikingly, demanding transitivity of social preferences rules out what, for many people, is the most intuitively appealing aggregation procedure: pairwise majority rule. To see this, consider the following example, known as the Condorcet Paradox.

EXAMPLE 2.3.1 (CONDORCET PARADOX)

There are three alternatives $A = \{x, y, z\}$ and three members of society (person 1, person 2, and person 3). Individual preferences are

$$x \succ_1 y \succ_1 z$$

$$y \succ_2 z \succ_2 x$$

$$z \succ_3 x \succ_3 y.$$

A majority (1 and 3) prefers x to y. A majority (1 and 2) prefers y to z. And a majority (2 and 3) prefers z to x. Hence, under pairwise majority rule, the social preference is intransitive:

$$x \succ_{maj} y \succ_{maj} z \succ_{maj} x.$$

Example 2.3.1 implies that if we want to use an aggregation procedure that is guaranteed to return transitive social preferences, we cannot use pairwise majority rule.

2.3.2 Unanimity

The next criterion we will impose is one mentioned earlier, *unanimity*. Recall that an aggregation procedure satisfies unanimity if, whenever everyone prefers some alternative x to another alternative y, the aggregation procedure says that society prefers x to y as well.

It might seem impossible that any sensible aggregation procedure doesn't respect unanimity. But this is not the case. For instance, consider a procedure inspired by amendment rules in the U.S. Congress.

Suppose there are n alternatives. First randomly label all of the alternatives with letters: $a, b, \ldots, n$. Now begin round 1. Compare a against b by majority rule, the winner against c by majority rule, the winner against d by majority rule, and so on through n. Call the final winner of round 1 the most preferred alternative. Now begin round 2 and do the same procedure on all the remaining alternatives (i.e., on all those other than the alternative that won round 1). Call the winner of round 2 the second most preferred alternative. Continue this process until all alternatives are ranked. Label the social preference under this aggregation procedure $\succ_{amend}$.

To see that the amendment procedure does not respect unanimity, consider the following example. There are three members of society (1, 2, and 3), and five alternatives: ($a, b, c, d,$ and e). Individual preferences are

$$b \succ_1 a \succ_1 d \succ_1 c \succ_1 e$$
$$c \succ_2 b \succ_2 a \succ_2 d \succ_2 e$$
$$e \succ_3 a \succ_3 d \succ_3 c \succ_3 b.$$

Suppose the random procedure places the alternatives in alphabetical order. In the first round, here is what happens:

- b defeats a (it is preferred by 1 and 2)
- c defeats b (it is preferred by 2 and 3)
- d defeats c (it is preferred by 1 and 3)
- d defeats e (it is preferred by 1 and 2)

Thus, d is the most preferred alternative under the social preferences defined by the amendment procedure.

We can stop here. A problem is already evident. The amendment procedure identifies d as society's most preferred alternative. Whatever the rest of the social preferences, we know $d \succ_{amend} a, b, c, e$. But notice, the members of society unanimously prefer a to d! This example implies that if we want our aggregation procedure to always respect unanimity of opinion when forming the social preference, then we cannot use the amendment procedure.

2.3.3 Independence of Irrelevant Alternatives

Our third criterion is called *independence of irrelevant alternatives* (IIA, for short). IIA is slightly more subtle than transitivity or unanimity, but still intuitively appealing. IIA says that the social preference between two alternatives, x and y, should depend only on people's preferences over x and y. That is, whether society likes x better than y or y better than x should depend on what people think about x versus y. But it should not depend on what people think about some irrelevant alternative, z.

The intuitive appeal of such a criterion is perhaps clearest when thinking about what it would mean for an individual to violate IIA. Imagine you are at a restaurant and the waiter tells you that there are two choices: chicken or beef. You choose the chicken. Then the waiter informs you that he's just remembered, there is also fish. Upon hearing this, you change your mind and order the beef.

This is strange behavior. You compared chicken to beef and preferred chicken. Then you heard that there was fish—a fact irrelevant to your evaluation of the relative merits of chicken and beef—and changed your preference from chicken to beef. This is a violation of IIA. Your preference for chicken or beef was affected by the presence of an irrelevant alternative. The IIA requirement says that we don't want social preferences to behave in this strange way.[2]

The IIA criterion rules out another kind of aggregation procedure that we've already seen—scoring rules like the Borda count. To see this, consider the following example. There are 4 members of society and 3 alternatives, $A = \{x, y, z\}$. Preferences are

$$x \succ_1 y \succ_1 z$$

$$x \succ_2 y \succ_2 z$$

$$y \succ_3 z \succ_3 x$$

$$y \succ_4 x \succ_4 z.$$

The Borda count gives first choices 2 points, second choices 1 point, and third choices 0 points. Point totals are

- $x: 2 + 2 + 0 + 1 = 5$
- $y: 1 + 1 + 2 + 2 = 6$
- $z: 0 + 0 + 1 + 0 = 1.$

The social preference under the Borda count is

$$y \succ_{bor} x \succ_{bor} z.$$

Now suppose a fourth alternative, w, is introduced. The new preferences are

$$x \succ_1 w \succ_1 y \succ_1 z$$

$$x \succ_2 w \succ_2 y \succ_2 z$$

$$y \succ_3 z \succ_3 x \succ_3 w$$

$$w \succ_4 y \succ_4 x \succ_4 z.$$

---

[2]There are other justifications for the IIA criterion as well. In particular, IIA is closely related to the procedure not being strategically manipulable, for instance, by people introducing new alternatives that do not win, but alter the outcome.

Notice that no individual's preferences among x, y, and z changed, so w is an irrelevant alternative with respect to x, y, and z.

The Borda count now gives first choices 3 points, second choices 2 points, third choices 1 point, and fourth choices 0 points. Point totals are

- w: $2 + 2 + 0 + 3 = 7$
- x: $3 + 3 + 1 + 1 = 8$
- y: $1 + 1 + 3 + 2 = 7$
- z: $0 + 0 + 2 + 0 = 2.$

In this case, the social preference under the Borda count is

$$x \succ_{bor} w \sim_{bor} y \succ_{bor} z.$$

In the first scenario, y was strictly preferred by society to x. Adding the irrelevant alternative, w, flipped the social preference; x became strictly preferred to y. Thus, if we want our aggregation procedure to always respect the independence of irrelevant alternatives when forming the social preference, we cannot use scoring rules like the Borda count.

2.4   Arrow's Theorem

We could continue adding more criteria and ruling out more aggregation procedures. But, it turns out, at this point we've done enough. We've been listing criteria and using them to rule out possible aggregation procedures. Kenneth Arrow (1950) provides a sweeping result that bypasses this laborious exercise.

Arrow asks whether we can characterize all aggregation procedures that satisfy some appealing set of criteria. It turns out that the answer is yes. And there is even more good news. There is exactly one aggregation procedure that satisfies universal domain, transitivity, unanimity, and IIA. So, assuming you want social preferences determined by a procedure that satisfies these criteria, Arrow's theorem pins down exactly the procedure you should use. There is, however, a little bit of bad news. Here's the theorem.

Theorem 2.4.1 (Arrow's Theorem). Suppose a society has at least 2 people considering at least 3 alternatives. Then there is exactly one kind of aggregation procedure that satisfies universal domain, transitivity, unanimity, and independence of irrelevant alternatives. Those procedures are **dictatorships**—that is, rules that identify one individual and define the social preference as being identical to that individual's preference regardless of what anyone else thinks.

A proof of Arrow's theorem is beyond the scope of this book. I provide references at the end of the chapter.

2.5 Social Decisions Instead of Social Preferences

Arrow's theorem provides a striking impossibility result—there is no non-dictatorial aggregation procedure that is guaranteed to satisfy three minimal requirements (transitivity, unanimity, IIA) for every issue society might confront (universal domain). But it does so for a pretty demanding notion of what it means for an aggregation procedure to tell us the public interest. In particular, the framework on which Arrow's theorem is built involves searching for (and showing we can't find) an aggregation procedure that returns a full social preference over all the possible alternatives.

We don't necessarily need our aggregation procedure to do quite so much to have a notion of the public interest on which we can base public policy decisions. For that purpose, we might make do with knowing what the *best* alternative or alternatives are. We don't really care whether our aggregation procedure yields incoherent social preferences with respect, say, to which alternatives are ranked fifth, sixth, or seventh. We just want it to do a good job telling us which alternative or alternatives are ranked first. This raises a question: does there exist an aggregation procedure that satisfies minimal normative requirements and always identifies an alternative (or set of alternatives) that is the best from a social perspective? If so, we might yet resurrect a procedural notion of the public interest.

Unfortunately, the answer is still no. Under minimal conditions, we can't even find an aggregation procedure that reliably identifies the best alternative(s). The conditions needed to rule out this possibility are somewhat stronger than those needed for Arrow's theorem, but still pretty weak.

The first two requirements are familiar—independence of irrelevant alternatives and unanimity. We can, of course, weaken the transitivity requirement, since we are no longer looking for a social preference over all alternatives, we just want to ensure that the aggregation procedure identifies at least one most preferred alternative. But we will require that an aggregation procedure satisfy a new condition called *positive responsiveness*. Suppose we have some collection of individual preferences such that, under our aggregation procedure, society is indifferent between two alternatives, x and y. Now suppose we hold everyone's preferences fixed except that at least one individual who preferred y to x moves x up relative to y in her preference ranking (i.e., so that now she is at least indifferent between x and y). We say that the aggregation procedure is *positively responsive* if such a change breaks the social indifference, so that society now strictly prefers x to y. One can think of positive responsiveness as a sort of representativeness requirement. It says that, if society is indifferent between two alternatives, if we leave everyone else the same, any individual choosing to move x up relative to y in her rankings should break the indifference.

Let's see how positive responsiveness matters for our ability to identify a most preferred alternative or alternatives. Consider an aggregation procedure that we will call the *unanimity-or-indifference rule*, defined as follows.

- If every individual at least weakly prefers an alternative x to an alternative y and at least one individual's preference is strict, then society strictly prefers x to y.
- If at least one person strictly prefers x to y and at least one person strictly prefers y to x, then society is indifferent between x and y.

This rule satisfies Arrow's unanimity and IIA requirements. Moreover, it is not a dictatorship. It does not always produce a transitive social preference (if it did, it would have been a counter-example to Arrow's theorem). However, it does always identify a most preferred alternative or alternatives. Indeed, it will often produce a huge set of alternatives that are ranked at the top of the social preference, since as long as two people disagree about two alternatives, society is indifferent between them. But the unanimity-or-indifference rule is not positively responsive. To see this, consider a society with three individuals who rank two alternatives as follows:

$$x \succ_1 y$$

$$y \succ_2 x$$

$$y \succ_3 x.$$

Under the unanimity-or-indifference rule, this society is indifferent between x and y. If persons 1 and 2 do not change their preferences, but person 3 changes her mind so that $x \succ_3 y$, positive responsiveness says that the social indifference should be broken in favor of x. But since person 1 and person 2 still strictly disagree, the unanimity-or-indifference rule continues to yield social indifference.

Now that we understand positive responsiveness, we are almost in a position to state a result about identifying most preferred alternatives that is analogous to Arrow's theorem for full social preferences. Before doing so, we need one last concept. An individual is a *weak dictator* if when that individual strictly prefers some alternative x to another alternative y, then it must be that society at least weakly prefers x to y.

With that concept in hand, we can state a result, due to Mas-Colell and Sonnenschein (1972), on the impossibility of finding an aggregation procedure that identifies the socially most preferred alternative(s).

Theorem 2.5.1 (Mas-Colell and Sonnenschein's Theorem). Suppose a society has at least three people considering at least three alternatives. Then any aggregation procedure that always identifies at least one socially most-preferred alternative and satisfies universal domain, unanimity, independence of irrelevant alternatives, and positive responsiveness is a weak dictatorship.

2.6 The Public Interest?

Arrow's and Mas-Colell and Sonnenschein's theorems are quite upsetting, given the project we set for ourselves—defining a coherent procedural notion of the public interest. It appears that looking for such procedures is a fool's errand. None exist, save dictatorship.

So what are we to do? I see a few ways forward.

First, we might abandon this whole notion of the public interest. There are many possible motivations for making public policy. The public interest is only one of them. An option open to us is to dispense with the idea that public policy is about serving some public interest that can be coherently and consistently defined. But in so doing, we lose a powerful motivation for policymaking and are left somewhat adrift in terms of evaluating our policy goals.

Another approach is to weaken our ambitions a bit more. There is a sense in which Arrow's and Mas-Colell and Sonnenschein's theorems are very strong results. They rule out all aggregation procedures, save dictatorship, with appeal to only minimal criteria. There is no need, in generating these impossibility results, to delve into controversial criteria like equality of opportunity, respect for freedom, or other such contested normative standards. But there are also ways in which these theorems are quite weak. Let's explore three ways we might relax the theorems' requirements to make progress.

2.6.1 Only Two Alternatives: May's Theorem

Both impossibility theorems assume that society must choose among at least three alternatives. But there may be policy settings in which the issue boils down to a choice among two options. What can we say about social preference in such settings?

Following our usual approach, we can answer this question by identifying some intuitively appealing normative criteria that we would like our aggregation procedure to satisfy. Here we consider three. The first two criteria are that people and alternatives should be treated equally. People are treated equally if the procedure satisfies *anonymity*—if the preferences of two members of society are switched with one another and nothing else changes, the rank ordering of the alternatives under the aggregation procedure shouldn't change. Alternatives are treated equally if the procedure satisfies *neutrality*—if the preferences of all members of society flipped between the two alternatives, the rank ordering of the alternatives under the aggregation procedure would flip. The final requirement is positive responsiveness, which we've already discussed.

These criteria are related to those from Arrow's theorem. In particular, if an aggregation procedure satisfies anonymity, it clearly is non-dictatorial. If a procedure satisfies neutrality, it respects the independence of irrelevant alternatives. And if a procedure is positively responsive, then it respects unanimity. Hence, one might be worried that no aggregation procedure will satisfy all three criteria. But, because we have restricted attention to a situation in which the choice is between only two alternatives, this is not the case. Instead, we can state our first positive result about the notion of the public interest, due to May (1952).

> **Theorem 2.6.1 (May's Theorem).** Suppose society has at least two people considering exactly two alternatives. The only aggregation procedure that satisfies universal domain, anonymity, neutrality, and positive responsiveness is simple majority rule—if a plurality of individuals strictly prefer one alternative to the other, then so does society and otherwise society is indifferent between the two alternatives.

2.6.2 Ruling Out Some Collections of Preferences: The Median Voter Theorem

May's theorem suggests the desirability of majority rule as a way of defining the public interest, but only when there are exactly two alternatives. If we are willing to relax another of Arrow's criteria, we can construct a different argument for majority rule, even when society is faced with many alternatives. For this argument, the key is to relax universal domain—the idea that an aggregation procedure should satisfy the normative criteria for *all* possible collections of individual preferences.

Let's be clear about what is at stake here. Our impossibility theorems do *not* say that there are no circumstances in which we can aggregate individual preferences into a coherent notion of the social preference. Indeed, there are many such instances. One possible such scenario is an issue on which every member of society agrees. In such a circumstance, majority rule, the Borda count, and many other aggregation procedures will all yield completely sensible social preferences. But we don't actually need universal agreement to get a coherent social preference or decision out of some particular aggregation procedure. For instance, recall Example 2.2.1. That fictional example about tax policy had considerable disagreement among the individuals. Yet majority rule did a perfectly good job of identifying a coherent social preference.

Our theorems say we can't be sure that some aggregation procedure that works for one issue will continue to yield coherent social preferences when the next issue arises. If, on that next issue, we end up with the right (or is it wrong?)

collection of preferences, an aggregation procedure that worked fine in the past might now yield incoherent or bizarre social preferences.

But perhaps we don't need to worry about every possible issue emerging. Perhaps some issues are exceedingly unlikely, so that we can reasonably restrict the domain of collections of preferences our aggregation procedure has to work for.

I will consider one particular such restriction. First, notice that on any given issue, we can line up all the alternatives in any order we like. It will be helpful to describe such an order in terms of an ideological dimension. That is, we can say alternative 1 is to the left of alternative 2 which is to the left of alternative 3, and so on. A little notation is useful here. Consider two alternatives, a_1 and a_2. If alternative a_2 is to the right of (or more conservative than) alternative a_1, we write $a_1 < a_2$.

For any set of alternatives, there are many possible ideological orders. For instance, suppose we have three alternatives, $A = \{a_1, a_2, a_3\}$. One ideological order is $a_1 < a_2 < a_3$. Another ideological order is $a_2 < a_1 < a_3$. Another is $a_3 < a_1 < a_2$. And so on.

Once we have an ideological order of the alternatives, we can try to describe individuals as more liberal or conservative than one another. What do I mean by this? Say that individual i is *more conservative than* individual j under a given ideological order if the following holds: Consider two alternatives, $a_1 < a_2$. If i is more conservative than j, then $a_2 \succsim_j a_1$ implies $a_2 \succsim_i a_1$. That is, i is more conservative than j if whenever j likes the more conservative of two alternatives at least as much as the more liberal alternative, then so does i. We then say that individual i is *strictly more conservative than* individual j if i is more conservative than j and j is not more conservative than i. We can define one person being more liberal than another analogously.

Whether we can describe people ideologically as ranging from liberal to conservative depends on the individual preferences and on the ideological order we choose for the alternatives. To see what I mean let's consider an example.

EXAMPLE 2.6.1

A society with 3 members—Beth (B), Charles (C), and Dana (D)—is considering tax policy. There are three possible tax rates: Low (L), Medium (M), and High (H). The three members of society have different views about the appropriate tax rate. Their preferences are

$$H \succ_B M \succ_B L$$

$$M \succ_C H \succ_C L$$

$$L \succ_D M \succ_D H.$$

(Continued on next page)

There are many possible ideological orders on the alternatives. One natural order is descending tax rates, so that the highest tax rate is identified with the most liberal position and the lowest tax rate is associated with the most conservative position. That is, $H < M < L$.

Under this order, Beth is strictly more liberal than Charles or Dana. To see that Beth is more liberal than Charles, notice that whenever Charles prefers the more liberal option (M over L and H over L), so too does Beth. To see that Beth is strictly more liberal than Charles, notice that there is an instance where Beth prefers the more liberal option while Charles does not (H vs. M). To see that Beth is more liberal than Dana, notice that Dana never prefers the more liberal option, while Beth always does. A similar set of comparisons shows that Dana is strictly more conservative than Beth or Charles. Thus, we can describe these three individuals from liberal to conservative under this ideological order.

If we had chosen a different ideological order, we might not have been able to describe the individuals ideologically. For instance, consider the order $M < H < L$. Here, Charles is strictly more liberal than Beth or Dana. But Beth and Dana are not ranked ideologically. In particular, comparing M to H, Beth prefers the more conservative alternative, while Dana prefers the more liberal. However, comparing M to L, Beth prefers the more liberal alternative, while Dana prefers the more conservative. Thus, Beth and Dana cannot be ranked ideologically under this order.

In Example 2.6.1, we see an issue where if we choose the right ideological order, then the preferences of the individuals can be described ideologically. There are, however, also issues where, no matter what ideological order we choose, individual preferences cannot be described ideologically. To see this, recall Example 2.3.1.

EXAMPLE 2.6.2 (EXAMPLE 2.3.1, REVISITED)

There are three alternatives $A = \{x, y, z\}$ and three members of society (person 1, person 2, and person 3). Individual preferences are

$$x \succ_1 y \succ_1 z$$

$$y \succ_2 z \succ_2 x$$

$$z \succ_3 x \succ_3 y.$$

(Continued on next page)

There are six possible ideological orders. No matter which order we choose, we cannot describe the individuals in ideological terms. Consider all six possible ideological orders:

1. $x > y > z$: Person 3 prefers x (the most conservative alternative) to y, while person 2 prefers y to x. But person 2 prefers y to z (the most liberal alternative), while person 3 prefers z to y. Hence, 2 and 3 cannot be ranked ideologically under this order.

2. $x > z > y$: Person 1 prefers x (the most conservative alternative) to z, while person 3 prefers z to x. But person 3 prefers z to y (the most liberal alternative), while person 1 prefers y to z. Hence, 1 and 3 cannot be ranked ideologically under this order.

3. $y > x > z$: Person 2 prefers y (the most conservative alternative) to x, while person 1 prefers x to y. But person 1 prefers x to z (the most liberal alternative), while person 2 prefers z to x. Hence, 1 and 2 cannot be ranked ideologically under this order.

4. $y > z > x$: Person 1 prefers y (the most conservative alternative) to z, while person 3 prefers z to y. But person 3 prefers z to x (the most liberal alternative), while person 1 prefers x to z. Hence, 1 and 3 cannot be ranked ideologically under this order.

5. $z > x > y$: Person 2 prefers z (the most conservative alternative) to x, while person 1 prefers x to z. But person 1 prefers x to y (the most liberal alternative), while person 2 prefers y to x. Hence, 1 and 2 cannot be ranked ideologically under this order.

6. $z > y > x$: Person 3 prefers z (the most conservative alternative) to y, while person 2 prefers y to z. But person 2 prefers y to x (the most liberal alternative), while person 3 prefers x to y. Hence, 2 and 3 cannot be ranked ideologically under this order.

I will say that an issue is *described by an ideology* if we can find some ideological order on the alternatives such that individuals can be rank ordered from liberal to conservative.[3] The domain restriction I want to consider is to restrict attention only to issues that are described by an ideology.

Example 2.6.2 shows that restricting attention to issues that are described by an ideology does in fact rule out some cases. But it also has a substantive interpretation that explains why it is useful. To get some intuition for what it means for an issue to be described by an ideology, consider redistribution.

---

[3]The term used in the academic literature is that preferences are *single crossing* or satisfy *order restriction*. This condition is distinct from the single peakedness assumption used in Black's (1958) famous median voter theorem. But it yields a more powerful median voter theorem.

Suppose people's preferences for redistribution are driven by their personal wealth—the richer you are, the less you like redistributive policies. Then the issue of the level of redistribution is described by an ideology. Line people up from poorest to richest. Now consider two levels of redistribution, *a lot* and *a little*. Suppose a relatively poor person prefers *a little* redistribution to *a lot* of redistribution. Then any person who is richer than her also prefers *a little* to *a lot*. But a person who is poorer than her may prefer *a lot* to *a little*. Hence, with respect to redistribution, we can order people from more liberal to more conservative by their level of wealth.

What does being able to describe an issue by an ideology buy us? Consider two alternatives, $a_1 > a_2$, such that at least one individual prefers a_1 and at least one individual prefers a_2. If preferences are described by an ideology, then we can identify some individual i such that people who are more conservative than i prefer a_1 and people who are more liberal than i prefer a_2. To see this, suppose person i is just indifferent between a_1 and a_2. Then, by definition, any person who is more conservative than i prefers a_1 at least as much as a_2 and any person who is more liberal than i prefers a_2 at least as much as a_1.

An immediate implication of this fact is that if an issue is described by an ideology, then we can be sure that majority rule will yield coherent preferences. For instance, imagine a society with five individuals considering an issue that is described by an ideology. Suppose the ideology is such that person 5 is more conservative than person 4, person 4 is more conservative than person 3, and so on. Notice that person 3 plus the individuals who are more conservative than her make up a majority of this society. The same is true of person 3 plus the individuals who are more liberal than her. We refer to person 3 as the *median voter*. The median voter is a member of society who (herself included) has a majority to her left and to her right. (Notice, if society has an even number of people, there is not a unique median voter.)

If we compare two alternatives, $x > y$, the majority rule winner will always be whichever is preferred by the median voter. To see this, suppose person 3 prefers x to y. Since person 4 and person 5 are more conservative than person 3, they must also prefer x to y, so x wins a majority vote. Now suppose person 3 prefers y to x. Since person 2 and person 1 are more liberal than person 3, they must also prefer y to x, so y wins a majority vote. Thus, when an issue is described by an ideology, majority rule always yields coherent social preferences—in particular, majority rule induces social preferences that are identical to the median voter's preferences, as stated in the next result, due to Gans and Smart (1996).

Theorem 2.6.2. (Gans and Smart's Median Voter Theorem). Suppose society has an odd number of people and is considering an issue that is described by an ideology. Then social preferences under majority rule are identical to the preferences of the median voter. That is, society prefers an alternative x to an alternative y if and only if the median voter prefers x to y.

Let's notice a couple of things about the median voter theorem. First, the fact that the majority preference is identical to the median voter's preference does not mean that majority rule is a dictatorship. The identity of the median voter is not fixed; it can change from issue to issue. Consider some society with 3 people. On one day it may face an issue on which person 1 is more conservative than person 2 who is more conservative than person 3. On this issue, majority rule induces social preferences that are identical to person 2's preferences. But on the next day society may face an issue on which person 2 is more conservative than person 1 who is more conservative than person 3. On this issue, majority rule induces social preferences that are identical to person 1's preferences. While, on any given issue, the social preference under majority rule corresponds to the median voter's preference, there is no dictator because different issues can have different median voters.

Second, assuming that issues are described by an ideology yields coherent social preferences through majority rule by relaxing the assumption of universal domain. That is, we are no longer allowing for the possibility than any future issue (with any collection of individual preferences) might arise—we are assuming that only issues that can be described by an ideology will arise. Example 2.6.2, which illustrated an issue not described by an ideology, shows why this is important. The preferences in Example 2.6.2 were precisely those that we used in Example 2.3.1 to show that majority rule didn't necessarily yield transitive social preferences. It is exactly these sort of preferences that are ruled out by the restriction to issues that are described by an ideology.

We've now seen two results that give us two conditions under which majority rule will do a good job of identifying social preferences. If there are only two alternatives, May's theorem shows that majority rule is the unique aggregation procedure that satisfies some minimal, normatively desirable conditions. And if there are more than two alternatives, the median voter theorem shows that majority rule will at least yield coherent social preferences if society faces issues that can be described by an ideology.

2.6.3 Intensity of Preferences

So far, in searching for a procedure for aggregating individual preferences into social preferences, we've made another very restrictive assumption, this one on the sort of information that is available about individual preferences. In particular, we have only been using information about individuals' rank orderings of alternatives. We have not spoken about how intensely individuals feel about the relative merits of various alternatives or about how strongly one individual feels relative to another. Without going into details (which are quite technical), it is worth noting that if we allow for the possibility of using more information about relative preferences and intensity of preferences, then we can say more about social preferences.

Roemer (1998) shows the following two results. If we allow for information that informs us about the relative well-being of each individual under given alternatives (i.e., I can say person 1 is better off than person 2, but can't say how much better off), then conditions similar to Arrow's criteria (plus a minimal equity condition) yield a unique rule for aggregating individual preferences into social preferences. The unique aggregation procedure will correspond, loosely, to Rawls's difference principle—one alternative is preferred to another if and only if it is preferred by the person who is worst off. If we allow for even more information—in particular, if we can compare the intensity of individuals' well-being under various alternatives—then conditions similar to Arrow's criteria are consistent only with an aggregation procedure that is identical to utilitarianism.

2.6.4 Agreement

A final approach we might take is to look for situations in which it is likely that any sensible rule will yield the same social choice. The most obvious such situation is one in which we all agree. In such circumstances, it seems uncontroversial to say that there is a public interest. (Though we'll reconsider whether this claim is really uncontroversial in Chapter 3.6.) Of course, for this to be a useful thought, opportunities to enact policies that induce outcomes that we could all agree are improvements over the status quo must arise in the world with some frequency.

In what follows, we develop a conceptual framework for thinking about how and when such circumstances might arise. This will be important because Part II is devoted to showing a variety of common social dilemmas in which this may indeed be the case—good policy might get us to a situation that everyone would agree is an improvement over the status quo.

2.7 Takeaways

- One can approach defining the idea of the public interest procedurally instead of substantively. That is, it is conceivable that people could agree to a procedure that aggregates disparate, individual views into a collective view such that each individual would accept the output of the aggregation procedure as representing the public interest even if it turned out contrary to that individual's particular views.
- Arrow's theorem and Mas-Collel and Sonnenschein's theorem show that if we want the aggregation procedure to be guaranteed to satisfy

some minimal normative standards regardless of what issue a society ends up confronting, then we are stuck with dictatorship.

- Majority rule is a particularly appealing aggregation procedure in at least two settings. First, May's theorem shows that, when there are only two alternatives from which to choose, majority rule is the unique procedure that satisfies minimal normative criteria. Second, regardless of the number of alternatives, the median voter theorem shows that if society only faces issues that can be described by an ideology, then majority rule yields coherent social preferences.

- The key results in this chapter suggest that, in many circumstances, it is not feasible to define a procedural notion of the public interest that everyone will accept and that will always yield a coherent answer.

2.8 Further Reading

My dissertation advisor Ken Shepsle's classic book *Analyzing Politics: Rationality, Behavior, and Institutions* provides another introductory take on much of the material found in this chapter. The definitive source for the technically motivated student is David Austen-Smith and Jeffrey S. Banks's *Positive Political Theory I: Collective Preference*, while Amartya Sen's *Collective Choice and Social Welfare* is the classic overview. Geanakoplos (2005) provides three straightforward proofs of Arrow's theorem.

Myerson (2013) discusses a variety of results from social choice theory and tells us how to think about them. Sen (1970*b*) offers results linking social choice and notions of individual rights.

Black (1958) is the original formulation of the median voter theorem, though the version discussed here is due to Gans and Smart (1996). While not the primary approach I take in the remainder of this book, a long tradition, following on Anthony Downs's *An Economic Theory of Democracy*, makes use of the median voter theorem to study elections, legislatures, committees, and other aspects of democratic politics. Keith Krehbiel's *Pivotal Politics* is a particularly nice application of this approach.

2.9 Exercises

1. Answer true or false as to whether each of the following statements is an implication of Arrow's theorem. In each case, briefly justify your answer.

    (a) Under no circumstances is there a preference ordering which we could sensibly call the public interest.

    (b) Consider the aggregation procedure pairwise majority rule. Now consider some particular society made up of individuals with preferences over some set of alternatives. For that society, majority rule violates at least one of transitivity, unanimity, or IIA.

(c) Consider some arbitrary aggregation procedure that is not dictatorship. There exists a real society in the world (i.e., an actual country, city, or what have you) in which that aggregation procedure violates at least one of transitivity, unanimity, or IIA.

(d) Consider some arbitrary aggregation procedure that is not dictatorship. You can imagine a society (i.e., a collection of individuals with preferences over alternatives), though it may not actually exist in the world, such that the aggregation procedure violates at least one of transitivity, unanimity, or IIA.

2. Consider a society made up of three people—Dan (D), Erin (E), and Fred (F). The society must choose between three immigration policies—Closed Borders (C), Open Borders (O), and Regulated Immigration (R). Suppose preferences are as follows:

$$R \succ_D C \succ_D O$$

$$C \succ_E R \succ_E O$$

$$O \succ_F R \succ_F C.$$

(a) Write down an ideological ordering on the alternative such that this issue is described by that ideology.

(b) What is the preferred policy of the median voter under that ideology?

(c) Use this fact to make an argument for why pursuing that policy might be considered serving the public interest in this setting.

(d) Make an argument for why you might nonetheless reject the idea that this policy is clearly in the public interest or explain why you think there is no such argument.

3. At this point, given our discussion in Chapters 1 and 2, do you find the notion of "the public interest" to be useful for thinking about policy evaluation? Why or why not? (There isn't a right answer here. You should simply try to say something thoughtful.)

4. Consider a society with three workers. Each worker, i, has a wage w_i. Assume $w_1 > w_2 > w_3$. Society is choosing a tax rate, $\tau \in [0, 1]$. If the tax rate is τ, then worker i pays taxes τw_i, so total government revenues are $R(\tau) = \tau w_1 + \tau w_2 + \tau w_3$. The revenues are redistributed back to each worker equally. That is, each worker receives a transfer of $T = \frac{R(\tau)}{3}$. So worker i's

overall income, given a tax rate, τ, is

$$U_i(\tau) = (1 - \tau)w_i + \frac{R(\tau)}{3}.$$

(a) Show that worker 1's income is decreasing in τ.
(b) Show that worker 3's income is increasing in τ.
(c) The median wage is w_2. The mean wage is $\frac{w_1+w_2+w_3}{3}$. Show that worker 2's income is increasing in τ if the mean wage is greater than the median wage. Show that worker 2's income is decreasing in τ if the mean wage is less than the median wage.
(d) Show that, in either case, this issue is described by the ideology where we order taxes from lowest to highest.
(e) If the mean wage is greater than the median wage, what is the majority preferred tax rate? If the mean wage is less than the median wage, what is the majority preferred tax rate?
(f) When the mean wage is much higher than the median, we typically think there is a lot of inequality (the highest paid worker has very high wages). Given this interpretation, provide a substantive explanation of the meaning of your answer to the previous subquestion.

3

Pareto Concepts

Our quest to preserve a notion of the public interest in the face of the negative results from Chapter 2 ended with the thought that a policy intervention might uncontroversially be thought of as in the public interest if everyone agrees it is beneficial. The question, then, is whether such unanimity ever actually exists. That is, are there any policies that make everyone better off, or at least make some people better off without making anyone worse off? And, if so, how do we identify them?

The classic problem for finding such policies is that many interventions that make people better off on average also have significant distributional consequences—making some people better off and other people worse off. Think of free trade. The 1993 North American Free Trade Agreement (NAFTA) created a trilateral trading bloc between Canada, Mexico, and the United States. The goal of NAFTA was to reduce barriers to trade and investment in North America, including the virtual elimination of tariffs, reductions in non-tariff trade barriers, protection of intellectual property, establishment of transportation corridors, and so on.

The idea underlying NAFTA, like any such trade agreement, is that free trade encourages competition and prosperity. Because products can move easily across borders, workers and resources are used in industries for which they have comparative advantage. Increased efficiency and lower input prices yield lower prices for consumers. Overall, the result should be increased wealth and growth.

And, indeed, the evidence suggests that NAFTA did improve overall economic prosperity in North America. Caliendo and Parro (2015) find that, from 1993–2005, trade within the NAFTA bloc increased by 118% for Mexico, 11% for Canada, and 41% for the United States. As a consequence, they report, Mexico experienced a large, net welfare gain, while the United States and Canada experienced a small net welfare gain and loss, respectively.

As Canada's trading loss highlights, even a policy that has large benefits on average may create winners and losers. We can see the same pattern within countries. When trade is liberalized, some industries benefit, but other industries suffer as production and jobs move to other locations. In the case of NAFTA, Americans working in industries in which Mexico had comparative advantage, but that had been protected by trade barriers, were likely to suffer as a result of increased trade openness. Indeed, as McLaren and Hakobyan (2010) point out, so too were people who did not work in such industries but lived in locales dominated by those industries. They give the example of an American worker living in a small town dominated by apparel manufacturing, but working in an industry that does not face pressure from increased trade (e.g., a waiter in a restaurant). Even such a person, McLaren and Hakobyan argue, suffered following NAFTA. Increased trade decreased employment in apparel manufacturing, leading to decreased demand for restaurant food and increased competition for restaurant jobs, leading to a reduction in waiters' wages. And, of course, matters are even worse for a worker in apparel manufacturing, who faces job loss, a shift of industry, and heightened competition. Overall, McLaren and Hakobyan find that, even as the overall economy benefited, people who lived in localities dominated by NAFTA-vulnerable industries experienced slower than average wage growth, particularly for working-class jobs. Further, wages in the most protected industries fell sixteen percentage points relative to unprotected industry wages as a consequence of NAFTA.

And so we see a major challenge for trying to create unambiguously good public policy. Even policies that do a fair bit of overall good, create winners and losers. To get to unambiguously good policy, we have to find a way to move beyond just creating benefits on average.

3.1 Pareto Concepts

A group of related concepts will help us think through these issues. All these concepts are named after the nineteenth-century Italian economist and philosopher Vilfredo Pareto.

We will assume that the value of a policy to a particular individual, call her i, is given by a *utility function* U_i. Although we've already discussed the idea of utility, it will be useful to be a little more formal at this point.

A utility function represents preferences with numbers. We say that person i's utility function represents her preferences if it satisfies the following properties:

1. If person i prefers a policy x to another policy y, then $U_i(x) > U_i(y)$.
2. If person i is indifferent between a policy x and another policy y, then $U_i(x) = U_i(y)$.

Given this, we can now define our Pareto concepts.

Definition 3.1.1. A policy x **Pareto dominates** another policy y if two conditions are satisfied:

1. No one strictly prefers y to x—that is, for all i, $U_i(x) \geq U_i(y)$.
2. At least one person strictly prefers x to y—that is, for at least one person, i, we have $U_i(x) > U_i(y)$.

Pareto dominance formalizes our notion of a choice on which everyone can agree. If some policy y is Pareto dominated by some other policy, then we definitely should not choose y. Moreover, if the status quo policy is y and it is

Pareto dominated by some alternative policy x, then we would all agree that moving from y to x serves the public interest. Of course, there may be policies that some of us prefer even above x, but that is a separate question. All we are saying is that the move from y to x is unambiguously good.

We give this notion of a policy change that is unambiguously in the public interest its own name.

> **Definition 3.1.2.** The move from a policy y to an alternative policy x is a **Pareto improvement** if x Pareto dominates y.

Finally, we can also define the set of policies from which no unambiguously good policy change is possible.

> **Definition 3.1.3.** A policy x is **Pareto efficient** if no other policy Pareto dominates it.

An equivalent definition is that x is Pareto efficient if moving from x to any other policy makes at least one person worse off. I refer to any policy that is not Pareto efficient as *Pareto inefficient*. The notion of Pareto efficiency is important for two reasons. First, the set of Pareto efficient policies is the set of policies from which there are no policy changes that unambiguously serve the public interest, in the sense of making no one worse off. Second, social scientists believe that they know a lot about identifying the set of Pareto efficient policies.

3.2 From Pareto Efficiency to Pareto Improvements

Given that social scientists claim to know a great deal about how to identify Pareto efficient policies, it is unfortunate that our normative benchmark is Pareto improvements rather than Pareto efficiency. The distinction is important because it is entirely possible to move from a Pareto inefficient to a Pareto efficient policy without achieving a Pareto improvement. To see this, consider the following example.

EXAMPLE 3.2.1

A society made up of three people (1, 2, and 3) is choosing between three policies (x, y, and z). The three people have the following utility functions:

$$U_1(x) = 5 \quad U_1(y) = 2 \quad U_1(z) = 4$$
$$U_2(x) = 1 \quad U_2(y) = 3 \quad U_2(z) = 7$$
$$U_3(x) = 4 \quad U_3(y) = 1 \quad U_3(z) = 1.$$

(*Continued on next page*)

> The policy y is Pareto inefficient. In particular, everyone is at least as well off under the policy z as under the policy y and both person 1 and person 2 are strictly better off. The other two policies, x and z, are both Pareto efficient. Any move from either of these policies to some other feasible policy leaves at least one person strictly worse off. So we have two Pareto efficient policies, x and z, and one Pareto inefficient policy y.
>
> A policy change that moves from the Pareto inefficient policy to a Pareto efficient policy need not be unambiguously in the public interest—that is, need not be a Pareto improvement. For instance, consider the move from the policy y to the policy x. This is a move from a Pareto inefficient to a Pareto efficient policy. However, this policy shift leaves person 2 strictly worse off. Hence, it is not a Pareto improvement.

The disconnect between Pareto efficiency and Pareto improvements presents a challenge for us. We have good reason to believe Pareto improvements are good policy. We believe we know some things about how to achieve Pareto efficiency. But, on its own, Pareto efficiency is not obviously normatively compelling.

3.3 A Model of Policies and Preferences

Pareto concepts are only useful in the search to define unambiguously good policy if we think it is in fact plausible to identify opportunities for Pareto improvements. As we saw in Example 3.2.1, simply identifying Pareto efficient policies is not enough. In this section, we develop a framework to help us think about how we might use our knowledge about how to achieve Pareto efficiency to construct Pareto improving policy changes. We do so by building a model of people's preferences over policy that allows us to separate two potential effects of a policy change—the effect on *efficiency* and the effect on *distribution*.

3.3.1 Actions and Transfers

Think of all policies as having two components: an *action* and a monetary *transfer scheme*. The action represents which policy lever is pulled—for example, free trade or protectionism, CAFE standards or a carbon tax, high-stakes testing or an extended school day. The transfer scheme represents redistribution of money from some people to other people.

Suppose our society has n people in it. The set of possible actions is A. For instance, in the case of trade we might have $A = \{$Free Trade, Protectionism$\}$. A transfer scheme consists of a transfer to or from each individual. A transfer scheme is represented by $t = (t_1, t_2, \ldots, t_n)$. The transfer to person i is t_i. If t_i

is negative, then the transfer scheme takes money away from person i. If t_i is positive, then the transfer scheme gives money to person i. If t_i is zero, then the transfer scheme neither takes money away from nor gives money to person i. We will say that a transfer scheme has a *balanced budget* if

$$\sum_{i=1}^{n} t_i = 0.$$

No money is created or lost through a balanced budget transfer scheme. Any transfer to one person must be fully paid for by transfers away from other people. Since money can not be manufactured out of thin air, we will focus on balanced budget transfer schemes. Thus, a *policy* (a, t) is a pair consisting of an action $(a \in A)$ and a budget balanced transfer scheme (t). Consider an example motivated by our opening discussion of NAFTA.

EXAMPLE 3.3.1

A society made up of two people, *Capital* and *Labor*, has to decide between two actions, *Free Trade* and *Protectionism*. A policy for that society would be something like this: (Free Trade, $t_C = -10$ million, $t_L = 10$ million). That is, the society implements free trade and transfers 10 million dollars from *Capital* to *Labor*.

Notice, this framework is flexible. It allows for the possibility that society might pull a policy lever (i.e., choose an action) without making any monetary transfers. Such a policy is represented by an action coupled with a transfer scheme in which everyone receives a transfer of zero.

3.3.2 Quasi-Linearity: A Bridge from Pareto Efficiency to Pareto Improvement

Our model of policy and preferences needs one more piece if we are to construct a bridge between Pareto efficiency and Pareto improvements. The key assumption is that the value of each additional dollar is the same to each person.

To formalize this idea, let the value to player i of an action a (e.g., free trade or protectionism) be given by a function v_i. That is, the value of some action a to person i is $v_i(a)$. Further, let the value of a transfer of dollars, t_i, to person i be exactly t_i. This implies that one dollar is worth exactly one unit of utility to any person. Person i's overall utility (or payoff) from an action a and a transfer t_i is given by the following *quasi-linear utility function*:

$$U_i(a, t) = v_i(a) + t_i.$$

We call these preferences quasi-linear because the utility function is linear in money but need not be linear in the action. (I haven't said anything about how the function v_i behaves.)

Quasi-linearity is a useful starting point for building a bridge between Pareto efficiency and Pareto improvements and clarifying the relationship between these two concepts. (Later we will look at what happens if people do not have quasi-linear utility.) This is because the quasi-linear model of preferences neatly separates efficiency concerns from distributional concerns. Let me illustrate by continuing Example 3.3.1.

EXAMPLE 3.3.2 (EXAMPLE 3.3.1, CONTINUED)

Suppose Capital and Labor both have quasi-linear preferences. Capital's payoffs from the actions are given by $v_C(FT) = 12$ and $v_C(P) = 4$. Labor's payoffs from the actions are given by $v_L(FT) = 2$ and $v_L(P) = 9$. So Capital likes free trade and Labor likes protectionism.

Payoffs from a policy $(FT, (t_C, t_L))$ are

$$U_C(FT, (t_C, t_L)) = v_C(FT) + t_C = 12 + t_C \text{ and } U_L(FT, (t_C, t_L)) = v_L(FT) + t_L = 2 + t_L.$$

Payoffs from a policy $(P, (t_C, t_L))$ are

$$U_C(P, (t_C, t_L)) = v_C(P) + t_C = 4 + t_C \text{ and } U_L(P, (t_C, t_L)) = v_L(P) + t_L = 9 + t_L.$$

Since the budget is balanced, it must be that $t_C + t_L = 0$. Hence, between the two players, the total amount of utility under a policy $(FT, (t_C, t_L))$ is 14, whereas the total amount of utility under a policy $(P, (t_C, t_L))$ is only 13. This implies that if we start at protectionism and move to free trade, we can find a way to make both players better off using transfers.

For instance, suppose we start at the policy $(P, (t_C = 0, t_L = 0))$. Under this policy, Capital's payoff is 4 and Labor's payoff is 9. If we then move to the policy $(FT, (t_C = 0, t_L = 0))$, Capital's payoff is 12 and Labor's payoff is 2. This is not a Pareto improvement because Labor was made worse off. But now suppose we also change the transfers, implementing the policy $(FT, (t_C = -7.5, t_L = 7.5))$. Under this policy, Capital's payoff is 4.5 and Labor's payoff is 9.5. Both players are strictly better off than under $(P, (t_C = 0, t_L = 0))$.

Example 3.3.2 shows how quasi-linearity splits the policy problem into two components. First, we identify the efficient action—i.e., the action that creates the most total utility—in this case, free trade. Then we use transfers to create a Pareto improvement by moving utility among individuals, compensating any losers from free trade with transfers from the winners.

The conceptual value of this division of policy problems into efficiency and distributional concerns is not purely theoretical. It directly influences government thinking about, among other matters, trade policy. For instance, a report of the Congressional Research Service states:[1]

> Congress created Trade Adjustment Assistance (TAA) in the Trade Expansion Act of 1962 to help workers and firms adjust to dislocation that may be caused by increased trade liberalization. It is justified now, as it was then, on grounds that the government has an obligation to help the "losers" of policy-driven trade opening.

Under TAA, American workers who lose their jobs as a consequence of free trade agreements receive relocation assistance, subsidized health insurance, and extended unemployment benefits (or wage insurance for older workers) while they are enrolled in retraining programs.

Extensions of presidential authority to negotiate free trade agreements have typically been coupled in various ways with trade adjustment assistance. TAA was a key condition for ratification of the Tokyo Round of the General Agreement on Tariffs and Trade in the late 1970s. And, while it was scaled back through the 1980s, in the 1990s, President Clinton insisted on TAA expansion as part of the negotiations over NAFTA. In 2002, President Bush sought Congressional approval of Trade Promotion Authority (known as "fast track" or TPA). Under TPA, the president is authorized to negotiate trade agreements with a guarantee of an expedited, up-or-down Congressional vote on ratification. Democrats in Congress opposed fast track authorization and only granted it after reaching a deal on expansion of TAA.

A similar debate recurred in 2015, when President Obama sought Trade Promotion Authority to negotiate the Trans-Pacific Partnership—a free trade deal focused on U.S. relations with the Asia Pacific region. It was commonly understood that TPA was a non-starter without an expansion of TAA. Indeed, at one point, in an attempt to derail trade expansion, Congressional Democrats voted down a bill extending TAA. The eventual compromise again coupled new TAA protections with fast track authority.

Example 3.3.2 also highlights the fact that quasi-linearity creates an equivalence between Pareto efficiency and utilitarianism. Recall that under utilitarianism, we evaluate a policy based on the sum of utilities. When preferences are quasi-linear, the set of Pareto efficient policies is exactly the same as the set of policies that maximize the sum of utilities. Indeed, it is straightforward that, in the example, free trade is the utilitarian optimal action—total utility under free

---

[1] See J. F. Hornbeck. August 5, 2013. "Trade Adjustment Assistance (TAA) and Its Role in U.S. Trade Policy." *Congressional Research Service* R41922. https://www.fas.org/sgp/crs/misc/R41922.pdf.

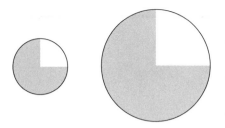

Figure 3.1. Any division of a *Small* pie is Pareto dominated by that same division of a *Large* pie. Here, the left-hand pie is *Small* and divided 3:1 while the right-hand pie is *Large* and divided 3:1. Both people receive a larger amount of pie under the *Large* pie scenario.

trade is 14, while it is 13 under protectionism. Hence, any policy involving the action free trade is Pareto efficient.

To see the equivalence between Pareto efficiency and utilitarianism a little more clearly, consider a society with two members making a policy choice. The society has only two actions available to it, but can choose any budget balanced transfer scheme it likes. People have quasi-linear utility.

One of the two actions is the unique utilitarian optimum (e.g, free trade in our example). That is, it results in more total utility in society. The other action is not the utilitarian optimum (e.g., protectionism in our example). It results in less total utility in society. Let's represent the total amount of utility in society by a pie. If society takes the action that is the utilitarian optimum, it ends up with a *Large* utility pie. If it takes the other action, it ends up with a *Small* utility pie.

I want you to see two things. First, any policy that involves an action that yields a *Small* pie, regardless of the division of that pie (i.e., the transfer scheme), is Pareto dominated by some other policy. To see this, consider the policy that results in a *Small* pie with share p going to person 1 and share $1 - p$ going to person 2. To find a Pareto improvement, simply move to the action that results in a *Large* pie and choose transfers that keep the shares at p and $1 - p$. Both people are now strictly better off. This is illustrated in Figure 3.1.

Of course, one doesn't have to keep the shares fixed to create a Pareto improvement when moving from a *Small* pie to a *Large* pie. All one has to do is make sure that no one's piece of pie shrinks.

The fact that any policy involving a *Small* pie is Pareto dominated by at least one policy involving a *Large* pie implies that a policy can only be Pareto efficient if it involves a *Large* pie—that is, if the action taken is a utilitarian optimum.

The next thing I want you to see is that all policies involving the action that produces a *Large* pie are Pareto efficient. To see this, notice that once the pie is *Large*, all we can do is redistribute shares of the pie between the two people through transfers. Any redistribution of shares, of course, makes one person better off and the other worse off.

The points above are general. They do not depend on there being only two people or only two actions. Whenever people have quasi-linear preferences and transfers are possible, a policy is Pareto efficient if and only if the action

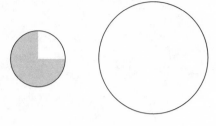

Figure 3.2. The move from a *Small* pie divided 25% to Person 1 and 75% to Person 2 to a *Large* pie divided 100% to Person 1 and 0% to Person 2 is not a Pareto improvement.

involved in that policy is a utilitarian optimum. Moving to a utilitarian optimum increases aggregate utility. And, when transfers are possible and money is worth the same amount to everyone, once you've created extra utility, you can always divvy it up in a way that makes everyone better off. These facts are recorded in the following theorem. (For interested readers, the proof is in the appendix of this chapter.)

Theorem 3.3.1. Assume people have quasi-linear preferences and budget balanced transfers are feasible.

1. If $x \in A$ is a utilitarian optimum, then for any budget balanced transfer scheme, t, the policy (x, t) is Pareto efficient.
2. If the policy (x, t) is Pareto efficient, then x is a utilitarian optimum.

Now it is straightforward that quasi-linearity allows us to build a bridge between Pareto efficiency and Pareto improvements in two steps. First, we choose an action that increases the total amount of utility in society—ideally choosing an action that is a utilitarian optimum. Second, if that action had distributional consequences such that some people are worse off than they previously were, we use transfers to compensate those people. We know that doing so is possible because there is more total utility to share. This is precisely what we did to construct a Pareto improvement in Example 3.3.2.

Let's return to our pies to see this two-step procedure in action. Suppose that our society has two actions available. The two different actions have different implications for the total amount of utility in society (i.e., the size of the pie) as well as for the distribution of that utility (i.e., the division of the pie). In particular, one action results in Person 1 getting 25% and Person 2 getting 75% of a *Small* pie. The other action results in a *Large* pie going exclusively to Person 1. If no transfers are made, the move from the *Small* pie to the *Large* pie is a move from a Pareto inefficient to a Pareto efficient policy, but it is not a Pareto improvement. This is illustrated in Figure 3.2.

The problem is that the change in action that yields Pareto efficiency— that is, the change in action that increases the size of the utility pie—also has distributional consequences that make Person 2 worse off. Importantly,

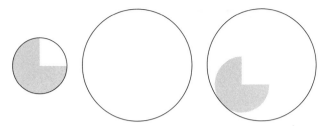

Figure 3.3. The move from a *Small* pie divided 25% to Person 1 and 75% to Person 2 to a *Large* pie divided 100% to Person 1 and 0% to Person 2 is not a Pareto improvement even though the latter alternative creates more overall utility in society. However, by transferring 75% of a *Small* pie back to Person 2, we create a Pareto improvement. That is, the right-hand cell is a Pareto improvement over the left-hand cell.

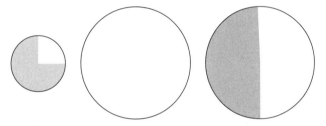

Figure 3.4. The move from a *Small* pie to a *Large* pie, with properly chosen transfers, can make both people strictly better off.

though, there is more overall utility when the pie is *Large*, so we can use transfers to create a Pareto improvement. Imagine that we start at the policy (*Small*, $t_1 = 0, t_2 = 0$). We create a Pareto improvement by switching to the action *Large* and choosing transfers appropriately. In particular, we must use transfers to take pie away from the beneficiary of the action change (Person 1) and give it to the person harmed by the action change (Person 2).

Suppose we choose a policy that yields a *Large* pie and has transfers that give Person 2 exactly the amount of pie she had under the previous policy of (*Small*, $t_1 = 0, t_2 = 0$). Then she is indifferent between the two policies. Moreover, it must be that Person 1 now has strictly more pie than he did under the previous policy (since the total pie is bigger), so he is strictly better off. Hence, we have a Pareto improvement. This idea is illustrated in Figure 3.3.

Of course, this isn't the only way to construct a Pareto improvement after increasing the size of the pie. Indeed, we could choose transfers so that everyone ends up strictly better off, as illustrated in Figure 3.4.

These results offer reasons for optimism. I've told you, and will show you in what follows, that social scientists have some ideas about how to use policy to achieve utilitarian improvements. Normatively, however, we want to achieve Pareto improvements. Not every utilitarian improvement is a Pareto improvement. But the discussion above shows that, when transfers are possible and people have quasi-linear preferences, one can turn a utilitarian improvement into a Pareto improvement by choosing transfers correctly. In particular, when changing actions in a way that simultaneously increases total utility in society and also creates winners and losers, one creates a Pareto improvement by transferring money from the winners to the losers.

3.4   A Bridge Too Far?

Quasi-linearity is a useful model. Treating the efficiency and distributional consequences of a policy change separately is conceptually clarifying. And, as we've discussed, this insight in fact affects the way we think about and build actual policies.

That said, I don't want you to get too optimistic. We've used this model to build a bridge between Pareto efficiency and Pareto improvements. But recall, before we make use of the implications of a model, we should probe their robustness. The bridge we've built between Pareto efficiency and Pareto improvements rests upon two critical assumptions—that preferences are quasi-linear (so that efficiency and distribution can be separated) and that appropriate transfers will in fact be made. If either of these assumptions is false, a focus on actions that yield utilitarian improvements need not result in a Pareto improvement. Let's see why.

3.4.1 Limited Transfers and Distributional Concerns

The bridge between Pareto efficiency and Pareto improvements depends on the necessary transfers actually being made.[2] But there might be lots of reasons to worry that this will not happen. Technological constraints can get in the way of transfers—compensating losers from a policy shift might prove more difficult than the model suggests. Indeed, according to a Congressional Research Service report, one of the reasons that trade adjustment assistance declined in the 1980s was because of a series of studies showing that TAA programs were failing in their mission to help displaced workers transition to new jobs.[3] Informational constraints might make it difficult for the government to identify the people entitled to compensation. Economic constraints might also pose an obstacle to compensatory transfers—collecting and redistributing resources requires significant government infrastructure and may create a variety of other distortions that could make the transfer scheme itself very costly. And, perhaps

---

[2]I don't want to push this transfer point too far. There are ways of compensating for distributional effects that don't involve direct transfers. For instance, a well-known result in trade theory shows that one can achieve Pareto improvements moving from protectionism to free trade without direct transfers by increasing taxes on goods that become cheaper as a result of trade (Dixit and Norman, 1986). Still, the point stands, some policy shift that addresses distributional consequences is necessary to achieve Pareto improvements.

[3]See J. F. Hornbeck. August 5, 2013. "Trade Adjustment Assistance (TAA) and Its Role in U.S. Trade Policy." *Congressional Research Service* R41922. https://www.fas.org/sgp/crs/misc/R41922.pdf

most importantly, political constraints often prevent transfers—for instance, if the losers from some policy change are relatively weak or underrepresented, then political leaders might not have incentives to make the transfers necessary to achieve a Pareto improvement.

If we are to use Pareto efficiency as a normative benchmark, we must take these constraints seriously. Policy actions can have distributional consequences. Without properly chosen transfers, there is no reason to believe that moves toward Pareto efficiency are unambiguously in the public interest, a fact that is often hidden in both political debate and traditional policy analysis—where the fragility of the bridge between Pareto efficiency and Pareto improvements is often left unmentioned.

3.4.2 Non Quasi-Linear Preferences

The other assumption on which the bridge between Pareto efficiency and Pareto improvements rests is quasi-linearity. When people do not have quasi-linear preferences, a dollar to one person may be worth less than a dollar to another person. As such, transfers of money are not equivalent to transfers of utility. Hence, we cannot necessarily neatly separate policy problems into efficiency concerns to be solved with policy levers and distributional concerns to be solved with transfers.

The most obvious substantive objection to quasi-linearity is that it is inconsistent with diminishing marginal utility from money. Under quasi-linear preferences, no matter how much money you have, the next dollar is worth exactly the same to you as the previous dollar—one unit of utility. Typically, however, we think that an extra dollar is worth more to a poor person than to a rich person. Thus, we assume people have diminishing marginal utility in money.

Example 3.4.1 shows that sometimes, when people have diminishing marginal utility from money, one cannot create a Pareto improvement by moving to a utilitarian optimum and choosing transfers carefully. In the example, the losers from the policy change are also the people who value money the least. Thus, to compensate the losers, we must transfer money from people who care a lot about money to people who care very little about money. And that means we have to transfer so much money that we are taking more utility away from the winners (through the negative transfer) than they got from the action change.

EXAMPLE 3.4.1 (THE IMPORTANCE OF QUASI-LINEARITY)
Suppose there are two people: Rich and Poor. Rich has wealth $w_R = \$1,000,000$ and Poor has wealth $w_L = \$1,000$.

(*Continued on next page*)

Each player gets utility from policy and from money. People have diminishing marginal utility from money. In particular, if the action is a and person i receives transfer t_i, then person i's payoff is

$$U_i(a,t) = v_i(a) + \sqrt{w_i + t_i}.$$

(I use the square-root because it is a simple functional form that exhibits diminishing marginal returns.)

There are two possible actions: x and y. Rich prefers action x. Her payoffs from the two actions are

$$v_R(x) = 5 \quad v_R(y) = 0.$$

Poor prefers action y. His payoffs from the two actions are

$$v_P(x) = 0 \quad v_P(y) = 10.$$

Suppose the status quo policy is x with no transfers. So, under the status quo, Rich is making a payoff of

$$v_R(x) + \sqrt{1,000,000}$$

and Poor is making a payoff of

$$v_P(x) + \sqrt{1000}.$$

The action that maximizes the size of the utility pie is y. Suppose we adopt y and the balanced budget transfer scheme that takes t dollars from Poor and gives t dollars to Rich, in order to compensate Rich for the policy change. Can we achieve a Pareto improvement?

In exchange for the action change from x to y, Poor is willing to transfer any amount, t, that satisfies

$$v_P(x) + \sqrt{1000} \leq v_P(y) + \sqrt{1000 - t}.$$

This means the **most** that Poor is willing to transfer is t_P given by

$$0 + \sqrt{1000} = 10 + \sqrt{1000 - t_P}.$$

A little computation shows that Poor is willing to transfer up to approximately $532 in exchange for a shift from x to y.

(*Continued on next page*)

How much would Rich have to be transferred in order for the action change from x to y not to leave her worse off? She would need an amount, t, that satisfies

$$v_R(x) + \sqrt{1{,}000{,}000} \leq v_R(y) + \sqrt{1{,}000{,}000 + t}.$$

Thus, the **least** that Rich must be transferred to leave her no worse off is t_R given by

$$5 + \sqrt{1{,}000{,}000} = 0 + \sqrt{1{,}000{,}000 + t_R}.$$

Again, computation shows that Rich must be transferred at least \$10,025 to compensate her for the change from x to y.

Given that Poor is only willing to pay up to \$532 and Rich must be paid at least \$10,025, there is no way to make the move from x to y a Pareto improvement, even though y maximizes $v_R + v_P$. The problem is that players have diminishing marginal utility in money. On the margin, money is worth less to Rich than it is to Poor. The change from x to y makes Poor better off and Rich worse off. So, although Poor would be willing to transfer enough utility to compensate Rich, Poor isn't willing to transfer enough money to do so.

3.5 Relationship to Cost-Benefit Analysis

At some point in your policy education, you will likely learn about cost-benefit analysis. Loosely speaking, cost-benefit analysis is a process for trying to systematically measure and compare the costs and benefits of some policy or project. It is used both to assess whether a given project is a good idea and to compare the merits of multiple projects. In the United States, cost-benefit analysis is a mandatory component of much of the regulatory process. As Sunstein (2014, p. 170) explains, under Executive Order 13,563, an agency can only proceed with a regulatory action "if the benefits justify the costs and only if the chosen approach maximizes net benefits (unless the law requires otherwise)."

The model underlying cost-benefit analysis is more flexible and robust than a model with quasi-linear preferences, but it is particularly easy to see the relationship between Pareto concepts and cost-benefit analysis when people have quasi-linear preferences.

Here's one model of cost-benefit analysis based on a concept called *willingness to pay*. Consider two possible projects: x and y. Individual i, who has quasi-linear preferences, has payoffs from the two projects given by $v_i(x)$ and $v_i(y)$, respectively. Given quasi-linear preferences, $v_i(x) - v_i(y)$ is person i's *willingness to pay* (in both utility and monetary terms) for a change from y to x. A person with a negative willingness to pay for a project prefers the status quo to that project, while a person with a positive willingness to pay for a project prefers that project to the status quo.

Theoretically, all we need to do to carry out a cost-benefit analysis on some project is to measure each person's willingness to pay and sum these up. If the sum is positive, then the benefits of the project outweigh the costs, relative to the status quo. Thus, it should be clear, with quasi-linear preferences, that there is a close connection between cost-benefit analysis, utilitarianism, and Pareto efficiency. In particular, a project will only satisfy cost-benefit analysis if it is a utilitarian improvement over the status quo. Moreover, the only situations for which there is no new project that survives cost-benefit analysis is one in which the status quo is Pareto efficient.

While I won't go into any detail here, this type of claim extends beyond the environment with quasi-linear preferences. Indeed, quite generally, if a project does not survive cost-benefit analysis, then the project cannot result in a Pareto improvement. Importantly, however, all our earlier caveats about Pareto efficiency still hold. The fact that a project looks good in terms of cost-benefit analysis tells us nothing about whether that project will result in a Pareto improvement. Many projects can perform well with respect to cost-benefit analysis and, yet, make some people much worse off as a result of the distributional consequences. Having larger benefits than costs is a necessary condition for a project generating Pareto improvements. But it is by no means sufficient.

It is also worth noting that there may be times when you wish to pursue a project even though it fails a cost-benefit test. For instance, some project might achieve a distributional goal that you find desirable, albeit in a manner that is not cost effective. Nonetheless, if outside constraints—for instance, politics—prevent you from achieving the distributional goal in a more efficient way, you may be willing to accept the costs of the project to achieve your goals. (We will explore many such issues in Part III.)

The practice of cost-benefit analysis is a field unto itself, with lots of nuance. The simple model based on quasi-linear preferences and willingness to pay that I've just given you certainly does not capture everything that is going on in cost-benefit analysis. However, it does raise what I believe are some important questions about cost-benefit analysis as a normative standard for policy analysis. Whenever a cost-benefit argument is presented, regardless of the methodology used, it is valid and important to ask whether the resulting conclusions are informative relative to the normative standard by which you have chosen to judge policy changes.

3.6 Are Pareto Improvements Unambiguously in the Public Interest?

Having spent this chapter arguing for the virtues of Pareto improvements, let me now briefly take the opposite position. The argument for Pareto improvements goes like this: a policy change that is a Pareto improvement makes some people better off while leaving no one worse off, who could dislike that? The implied answer is "no one." But the actual answer is "lots of people." Let's see why.

When we say that a Pareto improvement is good because it leaves no one worse off and makes some people better off, we are already accepting the proposition that the way one evaluates policies is by their effects on welfare. We've snuck in consequentialism. Perfectly reasonable non-consequentialist normative frameworks might, therefore, reject certain Pareto improving policies because those policies are deemed undesirable on some dimension other than individual welfare.

An example will help to illustrate what I have in mind. Suppose it were the case that banning possession of any gun that holds more than one bullet at a time would eliminate all gun violence in the United States. (I'm not saying it would and I'm not advocating that policy. It's just an example. Please don't send me hate mail.) Since gun violence is so socially costly, it seems likely that, were that the case, the utility surplus generated by massive gun control would be more than sufficient to compensate all the gun owners out there for taking away their weapons, creating a Pareto improvement. However, many people would nonetheless object to such a policy, not on consequentialist grounds, but from a rights-based or liberty-based perspective. That is, they would argue that the right to keep and bear arms is absolute and that any policy that abridges that right is bad, regardless of its welfare consequences.

A similar kind of tension between consequentialist and rights-based normative frameworks can be seen in various historical debates about the protection of civil liberties during times of national crisis (e.g., Lincoln's suspension of habeas corpus, increased surveillance provisions in the Patriot Act, and so on). A reasonable person could make a consequentialist argument on behalf of such policies—curtailing rights during a time of crisis might increase security, making everyone better off. But an equally reasonable person could make a rights-based argument against such policies, even while accepting that such a policy is a Pareto improvement.

Yet another species of this kind of tension comes from the tradition of virtue ethics. Those who subscribe to various notions of virtue ethics also reject pure consequentialist reasoning, instead arguing that there are certain types of behavior and pursuits that are (or are not) consistent with virtue—that is, with proper human living—regardless of the welfare consequences. Perhaps the most interesting place where this type of argument has been influential in modern policy discussions is in the debates over stem cell research.

Most informed people would concede the consequentialist argument—stem cell therapies have the potential to treat huge numbers of diseases and eliminate an immense amount of suffering. In an important consequentialist sense, massive investment in stem cell research would make us all better off. Nonetheless, serious voices in medical ethics have objected to stem cell research on non-consequentialist grounds. Perhaps most prominent among them is Leon Kass, a former University of Chicago professor and chair of President Bush's Council on Bioethics. While acknowledging the consequentialist benefits of stem cell research, Kass categorically opposes such work on the grounds that it is "repugnant" and, thus, inconsistent with human dignity. Here is an example of what he has to say:

> In crucial cases, however, repugnance is the emotional expression of deep wisdom.... Can anyone really give an argument fully adequate to the horror which is father-daughter incest, or having sex with animals, or mutilating a corpse, or eating human flesh.... The repugnance at human cloning belongs in this category. We should declare that human cloning is unethical in itself .... This still leaves the vexed question about laboratory research using early embryonic human clones.... There is no question that such research holds great promise ... that might be used, say, in treating leukemia or in repairing brain or spinal cord injuries.... As a matter of policy and prudence, any opponent of the manufacture of cloned humans must, I think, in the end oppose also the creating of cloned human embryos.[4]

We will proceed for the rest of this book by assuming that Pareto improvements are in fact good policy. And there are strong arguments for doing so. But it is important to see that even this very restrictive normative standard does not really, in the end, get us out of the problems we've encountered throughout this part of the book—reasonable people can, and will, disagree about even the most seemingly uncontroversial normative positions.

3.7 Takeaways

- Pareto improvements are (sort of) unambiguously in the public interest, at least if you are willing to embrace a mild version of consequentialism.
- The quasi-linear model of preferences suggests that we think about achieving Pareto improvements in two steps. First, look for a policy action that increases total utility. Second, address any distributional

---

[4]Leon Kass. "The Wisdom of Repugnance." *The New Republic* 1997.06.02:17–26.

concerns by transferring utility from people who benefited from the policy change to people who were harmed.

- The quasi-linear analysis requires a few caveats. First, since utility is not actually directly transferable, one has to think hard about what kinds of transfers are possible and whether they justify a focus on policy actions that achieve utilitarian improvements. Second, a focus on utilitarian improvements is not justified if transfers are not made—for technological, informational, economic, or political reasons.

- The Paretian normative framework is only useful insofar as plausible situations exist where there are Pareto improvements to be achieved.

- There may well be a variety of reasons to support policies that would not result in Pareto improvements. First, you may be willing to stake out a stronger normative position than simply advocating for Pareto improvements. Second, sometimes the efficient policy may not be politically feasible, but an inefficient policy that achieves similar goals may be. Thus, advocating for policies that are not Pareto improving may be a fine thing to do. But an important lesson is that, when you do so, you should be cognizant of the fact that you are not on unassailable normative ground.

3.8 Further Reading

Edith Stokey and Richard Zeckhauser's *A Primer for Policy Analysis* introduces the classic approach to policy evaluation in an accessible way. Sunstein (2005, 2014) provides a thoughtful argument about the benefits of cost-benefit analysis. For an outsider's deep, and surprisingly sensitive, take on the normative foundations of economic policy analysis, you should read Michel Foucault's *The Birth of Biopolitics*.

3.9 Exercises

1. Consider a society made up of three individuals: Alice, Bob, and Cathy. Currently, this society has a policy $(x, (t_A = 0, t_B = 0, t_C = 0))$ in place, but it is considering the possibility of a new policy. In particular, the society has to choose whether to implement action y, action z, or stick with the status quo action x. The three individuals in the society have quasi-linear preferences, with valuations for the three actions given by the following:

$$v_A(x) = 120 \quad v_A(y) = 30 \quad v_A(z) = 220$$
$$v_B(x) = 75 \quad v_B(y) = 170 \quad v_B(z) = 40$$
$$v_C(x) = 100 \quad v_C(y) = 110 \quad v_C(z) = 90.$$

(a) Suppose that transfers are not possible so that the only policies available are $(y, (t_A = 0, t_B = 0, t_C = 0))$, $(z, (t_A = 0, t_B = 0, t_C = 0))$, or the status quo of $(x, (t_A = 0, t_B = 0, t_C = 0))$. Which policies are Pareto efficient? Which policies involve actions that are utilitarian optima? Are they the same?

(b) Continue to assume transfers are not possible. Suppose we move from action x to the action that is the utilitarian optimum. Is this move a Pareto improvement? Why or why not?

(c) Suppose, now, that it is possible to use any budget balanced transfer scheme. Starting from a status quo policy of $(x, (t_A = 0, t_B = 0, t_C = 0))$, suggest a policy change that is a Pareto improvement.

(d) Is it possible, starting from $(x, (t_A = 0, t_B = 0, t_C = 0))$, to suggest a policy that is a Pareto improvement but is not Pareto efficient? If yes, do so. If no, why not?

2. Imagine a society made up of two kinds of people—the Xs and the Ys. There are an equal number of Xs and Ys. The society is considering three policy actions: a, b, and c. Each individual in the society cares only about his or her personal wealth.

    - Under action a, all members of society have wealth 10.
    - Under action b, the Xs each have wealth 11 and the Ys each have wealth 12.
    - Under action c, the Xs each have wealth 15 and the Ys each have wealth 9.

    (a) Define a policy as an action and a budget balanced transfer scheme. All budget balanced transfer schemes are feasible. People have quasi-linear preferences. Which policies are Pareto efficient?

    (b) Call the transfer scheme where no one gets any transfer t_0. Which of the following is true:
        i. (a, t_0) Pareto dominates (b, t_0).
        ii. (b, t_0) Pareto dominates (a, t_0).
        iii. Neither of these two policies Pareto dominates the other.

    (c) Identify a normative framework that would be in favor of the move from (b, t_0) to (c, t_0) and explain why.

    (d) Identify a normative framework that would be opposed to the move from (b, t_0) to (c, t_0) and explain why.

3. Explain why moving from a Pareto inefficient to a Pareto efficient policy need not be an unambiguously good policy decision. Give a policy example that you think illustrates your point.

4. I argued that allowing for utility transfers and quasi-linear preferences "built a bridge" between Pareto efficiency and Pareto improvements—that is, made

it possible to think about setting Pareto efficiency as a key goal of public policy.

(a) Explain how transferable utility builds this bridge.

(b) Do you find this to be a compelling argument for why Pareto efficiency is an important goal for public policy? Briefly explain your answer.

5.　　For the purposes of this question, a policy is a pair that includes an action (a) and a budget balanced transfer scheme (t). Assume people have quasi-linear preferences and that any budget balanced transfer scheme is possible.

(a) True or False? Consider two actions: a_1 and a_2. Also consider some particular budget balanced transfer scheme (t'). Suppose a_1 is a utilitarian optimum and a_2 is not. Then the policy (a_1, t') definitely Pareto dominates the policy (a_2, t').

(b) True or False? Again assume that a_1 is a utilitarian optimum and a_2 is not. The policy (a_1, t') is Pareto efficient and the policy (a_2, t') is not.

(c) Suppose (a_2, t) is not Pareto efficient. Could there be a policy (a_3, t') that is Pareto dominated by (a_2, t)?

(d) In words (3 sentences or less), what do we mean when we say that Pareto improvements are "unambiguously good policies"? How convincing is that argument?

(e) Suggest an example (4 sentences or less) of a situation in which there might be a policy change that is a Pareto improvement and yet would still be viewed as a bad policy decision by one of our normative frameworks (be specific about what normative framework and why).

3.10　Appendix: Proof of Theorem 3.3.1

Theorem 3.3.1. Assume people have quasi-linear preferences. Suppose the set of policies is any pair including an action drawn from the set A and a budget balanced transfer scheme. If $x \in A$ is a utilitarian optimum, then for any budget balanced t, the policy (x, t) is Pareto efficient. If the policy (x, t) is Pareto efficient, then x is a utilitarian optimum.

Proof. The proof of the first claim is by contradiction. To get a contradiction, assume that some action x is a utilitarian optimum, but that (x, t) is not Pareto efficient. The fact that x is a utilitarian optimum implies that

$$\sum_{i=1}^{n} v_i(x) \geq \sum_{i=1}^{n} v_i(y), \tag{3.1}$$

for all $y \in A$. The fact that (x, t) is not Pareto efficient means that there is some (y, t') that Pareto dominates (x, t). For this to be true, it must be that

$v_i(y) + t_i' \geq v_i(x) + t_i$ for each i and $v_i(y) + t_i' > v_i(x) + t_i$ for at least one i. This implies that

$$\sum_{i=1}^{n} [v_i(y) + t_i'] > \sum_{i=1}^{n} [v_i(x) + t_i].$$

Since t and t' have balanced budgets, this implies

$$\sum_{i=1}^{n} v_i(y) > \sum_{i=1}^{n} v_i(x),$$

which contradicts Condition 3.1. This completes the proof of the first claim.

To prove the second claim we will show that if x is not a utilitarian optimum, then (x, t) is not Pareto efficient. This implies that if (x, t) is Pareto efficient, then x is a utilitarian optimum. If x is not a utilitarian optimum, then there exists a y such that

$$\sum_{i=1}^{n} v_i(y) > \sum_{i=1}^{n} v_i(x). \tag{3.2}$$

Now fix an arbitrary budget balanced transfer scheme t and define a new transfer scheme T such that $T_i = v_i(x) - v_i(y) + t_i$. All people are indifferent between (x, t) and (y, T):

$$\begin{aligned} U_i(y, T) &= v_i(y) + T_i \\ &= v_i(y) + v_i(x) - v_i(y) + t_i \\ &= v_i(x) + t_i \\ &= U_i(x, t). \end{aligned}$$

But T is not budget balanced, on net it makes negative transfers:

$$\begin{aligned} \sum_{i=1}^{n} T_i &= \sum_{i=1}^{n} [v_i(x) - v_i(y) + t_i] \\ &= \sum_{i=1}^{n} v_i(x) - \sum_{i=1}^{n} v_i(y) + \sum_{i=1}^{n} t_i \\ &= \sum_{i=1}^{n} v_i(x) - \sum_{i=1}^{n} v_i(y) < 0, \end{aligned}$$

where the final inequality follows from Condition 3.2. Hence, we can define a new, budget balanced transfer scheme, T', that gives each person $T_i' = T_i + k$ with $k = \frac{\sum_{i=1}^{n} v_i(y) - \sum_{i=1}^{n} v_i(x)}{n} > 0$ (i.e., that gives everyone a little share of the money not distributed by T). Since everyone is indifferent between (y, T) and (x, T), everyone strictly prefers (y, T') to (x, T). Hence, (x, T) was not Pareto efficient.

$\square$

Summing Up Normative Foundations

The next section focuses on trying to identify situations where Pareto improvements can be achieved. Before getting there, let's remember why we are doing this. Our discussion of normative frameworks and various impossibility theorems taught us that we are unlikely, through argument or aggregation, to find a set of criteria that uncontroversially describe a general notion of the public interest. We want to avoid the conclusion that the merits of any policy goal we might set are simply a matter of personal opinion, without any normative foundation. So we've adopted a very limited notion of the public interest on which we can all agree (almost)—achieving Pareto improvements. Then, in order to make this useful, we pointed out that under some extra assumptions (in particular, quasi-linear preferences and feasible transfers), a utilitarian improvement can be turned into a Pareto improvement, if transfers are chosen properly. This allows us to usefully divide the process of finding good policy into two steps. First, identify a policy that increases the size of the utility pie. Then use transfers to compensate anyone whose welfare was harmed by the distributional impact of that change. To paraphrase my colleague Chris Berry: "You wanted to learn how to make the world a better place. We're going to teach you how to make it more efficient."

PART II

Social Dilemmas

The social world is a strategically interdependent place. Virtually every outcome you or I care about depends not only on our own actions, but on the actions of others as well. This is why game theory is so valuable. It provides us with a set of analytic tools to simplify and study some of the most fundamental issues that arise in social interactions.

One of the things that taking strategic interdependence seriously does is highlight some fundamental social dilemmas. A social dilemma, as I will use the term, is a situation in which every individual is acting rationally and yet the outcome is suboptimal. That is, a social dilemma is a situation in which individually rational behavior leads to a Pareto inefficient outcome. In such situations, we could all be better off if we could find a way to behave differently. But, left to our own devices, we can't find a way to behave differently because the way we are behaving is an equilibrium—none of us individually regrets his or her actions, given what everyone else did.

These social dilemmas are ubiquitous—in our economies, schools, governments, communities, bureaucracies, and so on. As such, they constitute a major opportunity for policies that we can all agree are in the public interest—policies that implement Pareto improvements. If you learn to spot these social dilemmas wherever they arise, you will be strongly positioned to find opportunities to make the world a better place through policy. It is my hope that by mastering some simple models, you will begin to view the world through the lens of these social dilemmas—seeing them, and the opportunities they present for good policy, all over the place.

4

Externalities

In 2014, the World Health Organization (WHO) warned of the growing problem of antibiotic resistance. Adaptation and natural selection have given rise to bacteria that are immune to most of the world's antibiotics.[1] The WHO report raises the specter of a future in which diseases that were easily treated in the twentieth century once again become life threatening. One key cause of antibiotic resistance is a combination of doctors prescribing unnecessary antibiotics and patients failing to take the full course of treatment.

Why might physicians overprescribe antibiotics? In interviews with doctors in Britain, Butler et al. (1998) identify several factors. Doctors face pressure from patients, who believe antibiotics will speed their recovery. For instance, Butler et al. (1998, p. 638) report:

> A typical clinician's opinion was, "You can't just say, 'It's viral, you don't need antibiotics, go away,' because they feel they're being fobbed off. They feel that their illness is not being taken seriously."

Patients' desire for antibiotics creates real costs—in terms of time and repeat business—for clinicians who resist overprescribing or attempt to educate their patients. For instance, Butler et al. (1998, p. 639) quote one practitioner saying:

> You spend 15 minutes trying to educate them, when they will go out disillusioned, come back the next day and see someone else, making you feel 5 minutes would be better spent just giving them a prescription and getting rid of them.

Doctors see benefits to prescribing antibiotics and costs to not doing so. Still, one might expect them to resist the temptation to overprescribe. Indeed, admonitions against overprescription are routine in both medical education and official statements of medical best practices.[2] But the diffuse and abstract benefits to society in general that underlie these ethical mandates can seem less than compelling when compared to the immediate and personal benefits to

---

[1] http://www.who.int/mediacentre/news/releases/2014/amr-report/en/
[2] For example, see Cooper et al. (2001); Barnett and Linder (2014).

the doctor and his or her patient. One of Butler et al.'s interviewees articulates precisely this tension:

> In a way it would be better for the community that so many people would not take antibiotics, but I have a feeling that for the individual it is better for him or for her to take antibiotics. So here is a little bit of conflict of interest in a way…now antibiotics are cheap and no harm is done if antibiotics are prescribed once or twice a year for an upper respiratory tract infection or a little bronchitis. Now why should I deprive my patients? (p. 639)

The result of these incentives is massive overprescription. Barnett and Linder (2014) estimate that the rate of antibiotic prescription for sore throats in the United States is six times the appropriate level and has been since the early 2000s despite "decades of effort" to curtail it.

This example illustrates a ubiquitous feature of social interactions—one individual's behavior has spillover effects on the welfare of others. Your actions—be it driving a car, studying hard for an exam, building a factory, vaccinating your children, joining a political protest, prescribing antibiotics, or what have you—impact not just your own well-being, but the well-being of those around you.

Situations in which one person's actions directly affect another person's welfare are called situations with *externalities*. In particular, if person A's action positively affects person B's well-being, we say that person A imposes a *positive externality* on person B. If person A's action negatively affects person B's well-being, we say that person A imposes a *negative externality* on person B. Situations with externalities (negative or positive) constitute our first social dilemma.

Rational individuals, when choosing their actions, ignore the externalities they impose on others—by definition, the externalities an individual imposes on others don't affect her individual payoffs, so they don't affect her best responses. We have a linguistic shorthand for describing the fact that rational people do not take externalities into account when making decisions. We say that people don't *internalize their externalities*. The doctor above who wondered "why should I deprive my patients?" despite acknowledging that doing so "would be better for the community" was failing to internalize his or her externalities.

As the example highlights, externalities can be very important from a social perspective because they affect the overall size of the utility pie. So the fact that externalities are ignored in individual decision making is a serious problem. In particular, it implies that, relative to the social optimum, actions that impose positive externalities are typically done too little and actions that impose negative externalities are typically done too much. Prescribing antibiotics imposes negative externalities. Thus, we have overprescription. By way of contrast, vaccination imposes positive externalities—a vaccinated child is less likely to spread disease to others. Thus, we have under-vaccination.

A policymaker facing a situation of externalities—be they positive or negative—can improve everyone's well-being by getting people to internalize their externalities. Often, policy does so by taxing or fining actions that impose negative externalities and subsidizing actions that impose positive externalities. For instance, a carbon tax is a way of making consumers of fossil fuels internalize their negative environmental externalities. And medical research grants are a way of making scientists internalize the positive externalities created by new medical discoveries.

Of course, such policy interventions sometimes come with problems of their own—for instance, the taxes needed to fund a subsidy might distort other economic decisions—that must be taken into account when formulating a policy response. In this chapter, we look at several models of situations with externalities. Doing so will allow us to get a sense of some of the ways in which externalities matter in the world, as well as to explore the possibilities and challenges of using policy to mitigate the problems they create.

4.1 Collective Action

A thriving society requires teamwork. Holding a government accountable, providing for the common defense, and cleaning up a neighborhood park all depend on costly contributions from a lot of people. As anyone who has ever lived in an apartment with messy roommates or worked in a problem set group with slacker study partners knows, teamwork is not always easily achieved. The problem is each individual's effort may make only a small contribution to achieving the desired outcome, but impose a sizable personal cost. Thus, each individual, acting rationally, may find it optimal to shirk. But an individual's contribution to the collective mission has sizable externalities, since his small contribution benefits all the members of the group. Hence, even if the *individual* costs of effort exceed the *individual* benefits, they may not exceed the *social* benefits. When this is the case, individuals contribute too little.

Think of a protest. A protest aims to achieve some goal. How likely is the protest to succeed? That depends on how many people show up. The more people who show up, the more powerful the protest and the more likely it is to achieve its goal—be that toppling a government, forcing a policy change, expressing solidarity over some issue, generating media attention, or what have you.

Actually, this is a reasonable description of a lot of things. Think of regional theater or the arts. How likely is it that the new dance troupe in your city will survive? That depends how many people show up for the first season of performances. Think of trade sanctions imposed by the United Nations. How likely is it that such sanctions will lead the target to change its behavior? That depends on how many countries choose to enforce the embargo. I invite you to think of examples in your own area of interest.

To get a handle on these issues, let's examine a model of participation in some collective activity in the presence of positive externalities.

Consider a group of $N > 1$ people. They share a goal in common—overthrowing the government, supporting a particular cause, forcing a policy change, etc. The individuals must decide, simultaneously, whether or not to participate in some activity that will increase the likelihood that the goal will be achieved. This could be turning out for a protest, making donations, writing letters to political leaders, and so on. The cost of participating is $c > 0$.

Each individual benefits if the goal is achieved. The value to an individual of having the goal achieved is $B > c$. An individual gets to enjoy the benefit of the goal being achieved whether or not she participated in the activity.

The probability that the goal is achieved is a function of the number of people who mobilize. To keep things simple, assume that if n people participate, the probability that the goal is achieved is $\frac{n}{N}$. That is, the probability of success is equal to the fraction of the population that participates. If everyone participates, they succeed for sure. If no one participates, they fail for sure. If half of the population participates, they succeed with probability one-half.[3]

Suppose a player, i, believes that n other people will participate. Her expected utility from participating is

$$\frac{n+1}{N} \times B - c.$$

The first term represents the probability of the goal being achieved when $n + 1$ people participate (Player i plus the n others she believes will participate) times the benefit to Player i of the goal being achieved. The second term represents Player i's private costs of participating. Player i's expected utility from not participating is

$$\frac{n}{N} \times B,$$

which is simply the probability of the goal being achieved without Player i's participation times the benefit to Player i of the goal being achieved.

Player i's best response is to participate if and only if

$$\frac{n+1}{N} \times B - c \geq \frac{n}{N} \times B,$$

---

[3]This is one of those instances in which I'm choosing the simplest possible model. Nothing about the results I'm going to discuss depends on this particular functional form for probability of success.

which can be rewritten

$$\overbrace{\left[\frac{n+1}{N} - \frac{n}{N}\right]B}^{\text{Incremental Benefit}} \geq \overbrace{c}^{\text{Incremental Cost}}.$$

The term $\left[\frac{n+1}{N} - \frac{n}{N}\right]$ is critical. It is the difference between the probability the goal is achieved with Player i's participation versus without. That is, it constitutes Player i's personal contribution to the collective goal. Call the left-hand side of this inequality Player i's *incremental benefit* of participating—the increase in probability of achieving the goal times the benefit of achieving the goal. The right-hand side is Player i's *incremental cost* of participating. Player i participates if and only if her incremental benefit is greater than her incremental cost.

For most collective goals like this, the presence or absence of any one individual is of essentially no consequence. In the model, if N is reasonably large, an individual has almost no impact on the probability of a good outcome—that is, $\left[\frac{n+1}{N} - \frac{n}{N}\right] = \frac{1}{N}$ is very close to zero. As such, the incremental benefit is miniscule. However, the costs of participation, in terms of time, money, or personal risk can be quite large. Hence, it is typically a best response not to participate. If this is the case, then in equilibrium no one participates.

Let's do an example to see how this works. Suppose our society has ten million people in it—that is, $N = 10,000,000$. Further, suppose the goal is very important. Say achieving it is worth one million dollars to each individual. Will an individual participate to achieve such an important goal?

According to our calculations above, it is a best response to participate if

$$\frac{1}{10,000,000} \times \$1,000,000 \geq c$$

which is the same as

$$\$\frac{1}{10} \geq c.$$

Everyone agrees that the goal is extremely important—the value of achieving it is $1,000,000 per person. Yet, a rational individual is only willing to participate if the cost of doing so is less than ten cents! As you can see from this example, in a model like this, if participation is at all costly, it is virtually certain that no one will participate. And even the cheapest of collective actions—for example, cleaning up the local park, making a donation to NPR—costs something in time or money.

4.1.1 The Social Dilemma

The example illustrates how pathological situations with externalities can be. Continue the example above and imagine the cost of participating is just one dollar. In equilibrium, no one participates. So payoffs are zero for each individual. If, instead, everyone participated, then the goal would be achieved for certain. As a result, every single individual (and there are ten million of them) would gain a benefit worth one million dollars and bear a cost of only one dollar. Thus, the total extra social value created would be

$$10,000,000 \, (\$1,000,000 - \$1) = \$9,999,990,000,000.$$

If everyone would participate, this society would create a social surplus of almost ten trillion dollars! That's a lot of utility pie. Yet, in equilibrium, no one participates. This is what I mean by a social dilemma. With each individual acting rationally, society leaves trillions of dollars in social surplus on the table. A policy intervention that got everyone to participate would be a massive Pareto improvement. Imagine if you could fix even just one such problem in your career.

My numbers may have been chosen to be a bit dramatic. (What can you think of that you value at one million dollars, other than one million dollars?) But the basic point stands. Rational individuals fail to participate even though everyone would be better off if everyone participated. This is a bit of a puzzle, since being rational means doing what is best for you. So what is going on?

In this model, people don't participate because each individual's participation has very little effect on the probability of success, so an individual's expected benefits from participating don't exceed his or her costs from participating. But there are a lot of individuals out there. Individual i's participation benefits each of them a small amount. So if we think about the *social*, rather than individual, benefit of Player i participating, it is quite large. In particular, it is her small contribution to the probability of success times the benefit of success times the large number of people who enjoy the benefit if success is achieved: $\frac{1}{N} \times B \times N = B$. The fact that the individuals don't internalize these positive externalities is the source of the social dilemma. Each individual makes her decision with respect to her personal well-being, ignoring her impact on everyone else's well-being. Hence, participation is lower than is socially optimal.

4.1.2 Interpretations

We've already discussed a variety of interpretations of this model. It is a stylized representation of incentives that exist when we think about many areas of society. As such, I hope it can serve as a kind of template you keep in the back of your mind and compare to real-world situations. Whenever you see a situation in which a large group of people must each individually take a small, but costly, action to achieve a collective goal, you should worry. This might include many everyday situations. For instance, the decision to support local arts, attend a public or community meeting, donate blood, join the governing board of a non-profit organization or neighborhood association, or work hard on a group project might all be subject to collective action problems. On a societal level, collective action problems affect people's incentives to join a volunteer army, register as an organ donor, turn out to vote, or protest policies they dislike.

This is not to say that groups never find ways to overcome these incentives and act collectively. But the incentives to shirk (or "free ride" as we sometimes say)—and thus the likelihood of socially suboptimal outcomes—are there and must be actively overcome. Being cognizant of these incentives may help you identify situations where interventions facilitating collective action would create Pareto improvements.

4.2   Public Goods

Some of what makes life good we must, by necessity, share in common. If the air is clean for me, it is clean for you as well. If the country is safe from foreign threats for me, it is safe for you as well. If NASA develops a technology to detect and deflect asteroids that might end life as we know it for me, it does so for you as well. (That one is a bit of a personal nightmare of mine. Why aren't more people working on this? Did we learn nothing from the dinosaurs?) Scientific discoveries that become available to me, also become available to you.

A *public good* (not to be confused with *the* public good) has two defining characteristics:

1. It is *non-excludable*: My having access to it means you have access to it as well.
2. It is *non-rival*: My using the good does not reduce your access to the good.

Clear air, national defense, not dying in an asteroid-induced mass extinction event, and scientific knowledge are all examples of public goods.

If you understood Section 4.1, on collective action, you might already see where we are going. Situations where people have the opportunity to create public goods are situations with positive externalities. Left to our own devices, we typically underprovide public goods, relative to the social optimum. (This may well be why we are not prepared to avoid mass extinction from space. You heard it here first.) This under-provision of public goods is another example of Pareto inefficiency caused by people not internalizing their externalities.

Here we will consider a model of public goods being provided through the joint efforts of a group of people working as a team. In Chapter 9 we will consider the problem of a government directly trying to provide a public good whose value is uncertain.

Suppose there are $N > 1$ people. Each chooses how hard to work on creating a public good. Call Player i's effort e_i.

The total public good created (G) is simply the sum of all the efforts. That is,

$$G = e_1 + e_2 + \ldots + e_N.$$

This is a simple functional form that captures the idea that the amount of public good which we each get to enjoy depends on each of our individual efforts.

Individuals find effort costly. The cost to Player i of effort e_i is given by e_i^2. A player's payoff is the total public goods provided minus the costs of her individual effort:

$$u_i(e_1, e_2, \ldots, e_N) = e_1 + e_2 + \ldots + e_N - e_i^2.$$

To put some substance to the model, think of a group of people each individually deciding how much of their travel to do by car versus public transportation. You can interpret effort as the amount of personal inconvenience a person chooses to endure to take public transportation. Some people may do a lot, others may do very little. The more effort you put into taking public transportation, the greater your personal costs. This is represented by the cost term e_i^2. But, the more effort you put into taking public transportation, the cleaner is the air in your locality. Clean air is non-rival and non-excludable. Thus, the public good G is increasing in your effort directed at taking public transportation and in everyone else's effort as well.

Let's think about a Nash equilibrium of this game. Suppose Player i believes the efforts by everyone else are given by $\mathbf{e}_{-i} = (e_1, \ldots, e_{i-1}, e_{i+1}, \ldots, e_N)$. Then her best response solves the following maximization problem:

$$\max_{e_i} e_1 + e_2 + \ldots + e_i + \ldots + e_N - e_i^2.$$

To find her best response, we differentiate with respect to e_i and set the first derivative equal to zero:

$$1 - 2e_i^* = 0. \tag{4.1}$$

The first term in the first-order condition in Equation 4.1 represents her marginal benefit from effort—increasing e_i increases the level of public goods she enjoys in a one-for-one manner. The second term represents her marginal cost from effort. At the optimum, marginal benefits equal marginal costs.

Rearranging, we have that Player i's optimal effort is

$$e_i^* = \frac{1}{2}.$$

In this simple model, a player's best response is to choose effort of one-half, regardless of what everyone else is doing. This implies that there is a unique Nash equilibrium—all players choose effort $e_i^* = \frac{1}{2}$.

The total amount of public goods created in this equilibrium is $\frac{N}{2}$. Hence, each player's equilibrium payoff is

$$u_i\left(\frac{1}{2}, \ldots, \frac{1}{2}\right) = \frac{N}{2} - \left(\frac{1}{2}\right)^2 = \frac{2N-1}{4}.$$

4.2.1 Comparison to the First Best or Utilitarian Optimum

You will not be surprised to learn that this equilibrium is not Pareto efficient. This public goods game is a situation with positive externalities, so people contribute too little, relative to the utilitarian optimum. Before showing you how much better players could do if they behaved differently, I want to introduce one more piece of terminology, which will become useful later when we analyze optimal policy interventions.

The term is the *first best*, which is just another name for the utilitarian optimum. I will sometimes refer to the first-best actions, by which I mean the action profile that maximizes the utilitarian welfare. Having defined this terminology, let's solve for the first best to see how much better off players could be in our public goods game.

Suppose that the society produces a total amount of public goods, G, with each player contributing an equal share: $e_i = \frac{G}{N}$. (This is precisely what is happening in equilibrium, with $G = \frac{N}{2}$.) How much would be socially optimal to produce?[4]

In such a situation, each individual's payoff is $G - \left(\frac{G}{N}\right)^2$. So the total utilitarian payoff for the society is

$$N\left(G - \left(\frac{G}{N}\right)^2\right).$$

To find the *first best* we maximize this utilitarian payoff:

$$\max_G N\left(G - \left(\frac{G}{N}\right)^2\right).$$

---

[4]It is, in fact, socially optimal for each individual to take equal effort.

Differentiating and setting the first derivative equal to zero, we find that the first-best level of public goods provision (denoted G^{FB}) satisfies

$$N\left(1 - \frac{2G^{FB}}{N^2}\right) = 0 \Rightarrow G^{FB} = \frac{N^2}{2}.$$

The first best involves each individual contributing $\frac{N}{2}$, which, in a large group, is a lot more than the equilibrium contribution of $\frac{1}{2}$.

Why does the utilitarian optimum require people to contribute so much more than they do in equilibrium? As we've already seen, in equilibrium, a person contributes until her personal marginal benefit equals her personal marginal cost. She ignores the benefit of her effort for $N - 1$ other people—that is, she doesn't internalize her externalities. At the utilitarian optimum, each person internalizes her positive externalities. She keeps contributing until the marginal benefit of her effort *to the whole society* equals her effort's marginal cost. This means she internalizes the fact that N people benefit from each increment of effort, not just one person. And, consequently, to achieve the first-best level of public goods, each individual works N times harder.

If individuals are working harder at the utilitarian optimum, why are they better off? The key is that each individual benefits from the fact that everyone else is also working harder. If everyone contributes $\frac{N}{2}$ to providing the public good, each individual's payoff is

$$N \times \frac{N}{2} - \left(\frac{N}{2}\right)^2 = \frac{N^2}{4},$$

which is greater than the payoff to an individual under the Nash equilibrium ($\frac{2N-1}{4}$). Players are better off if everyone does the socially optimal level of effort, rather than the equilibrium level of effort. Moreover, the more people there are, the larger the gap between the two payoffs. These facts are illustrated in Figure 4.1.

4.2.2 Interpretation

A few examples will hopefully highlight the ubiquity of the incentives that lead to the under-provision of public goods. Governments expending effort to fight a transnational threat such as terrorist groups, drug traffickers, global warming, or the spread of a disease may fail to internalize their positive externalities on other countries. Similarly for individuals and corporations taking costly actions to reduce pollution. Scientific research leading to knowledge with broad benefits for humanity is likely to be under-provided because the individual researchers do not fully internalize the benefits of their research for others. Some individuals are inclined to turn down access to vaccination, deworming, or other health improving actions. Those individuals typically justify

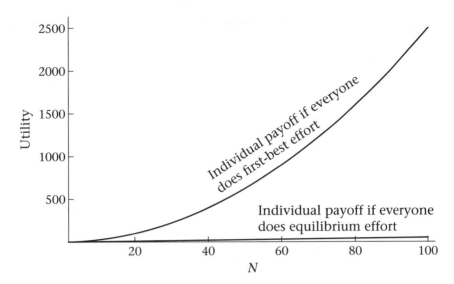

Figure 4.1. Each individual's payoff is higher if everyone does the first-best level of effort rather than the equilibrium level of effort. This becomes increasingly true as society gets large so that externalities loom large.

their choice in terms of their individual rights, but are failing to internalize the externalities generated by vaccines and the like—when an individual is treated, it benefits others by reducing their exposure to disease. Members of corporate boards are supposed to monitor the behavior of executives. While board members have some incentives to do so, those incentives are unlikely to be strong enough to fully internalize the positive externalities generated for shareholders when executive behavior is closely monitored.

4.2.3 Concentrated vs. Diffuse Interests

The collective action and public goods problems are particularly important for understanding how the politics of special interests impact policy outcomes. Because of failure to internalize externalities, it is difficult to organize support for a policy that benefits a large, diffuse group of people. In a setting with *diffuse interests*, each individual has trouble imagining that his or her contribution matters. By contrast, it is relatively easy to organize support for a policy that strongly benefits a small group of people. In a setting with *concentrated interests*, there are fewer externalities and each individual's participation is more important. Hence, the logic of externalities suggests that concentrated interests will be overrepresented, relative to diffuse interests, in the policymaking process.

There are many examples of this phenomenon. Public sector unions are better organized and more influential in debates over pension reform than are citizens' groups. The financial industry was more influential in banking reform than were consumers. It is difficult to curtail pork-barrel spending in Congress because each individual congressperson is willing to work hard on behalf of his or her individual district, but not against pork barreling in general. And so on.

The relationship between urban planning and the construction of the interstate highway system in the United States provides a particularly striking example of the advantages concentrated interests have relative to diffuse interests.[5] In 1956, President Eisenhower approved construction of a national, interstate highway system. This was an exceptionally ambitious public works project that ultimately resulted in the construction of over 42,000 miles of road, crisscrossing the country. Interstate highways set the course for patterns of economic development, internal migration, housing, urban policy, manufacturing and shipping, and much else that characterized the second half of the twentieth century in the United States.

A major issue for highway planners was the relationship between the interstates and urban centers. The population and retail decline of industrial cities had taken hold by the 1950s. One problem the highway system had to address was how to meet the ever-increasing demand to move workers efficiently from the suburbs into the city and back. The solution was the familiar hub-and-spoke pattern of inner- and outer-belt highways that connected suburbs with the urban core.

But this issue was intimately tied up with the racially fueled politics of "urban revitalization." In the three decades that followed World War II, millions of southern African Americans migrated to northern and midwestern city centers. The combination of middle-class suburbanization, racial housing segregation, and massive migration created urban ghettos and slums which were of great concern to urban political leaders, as well as business and real estate developers.

Highway advocates seized on this "urban blight" problem as a key argument for the construction of the interstates. They claimed that strategic placement of expressways would facilitate urban redevelopment by forcing the destruction of low-income housing and tenements. In particular, they proposed running highways through the middle of poor, residential districts in the inner city, using the government's land acquisition rights to force out poor residents and make room for high-rise and retail development.

Of course, such a policy had both winners and losers. Urban politicians, real estate owners and developers, and various industries benefited from the construction of the interstates. These are classic examples of concentrated interests. Urban real estate owners and developers were represented by the Urban Land Institute (ULI). According to Rose and Mohl (2012), p. 101, "The ULI's Central Business District Council focused on freeways as 'the salvation of the central district, the core of every city.'" Road builders, the concrete industry,

---

[5]This discussion is based on Rose and Mohl (2012).

and automobile manufacturers also all participated in lobbying. For instance, Rose and Mohl, p. 101–102 report:

> As early as 1949, in a letter to President Truman, the ARBA [American Road Builders' Association] defended the use of highway construction in slum clearance. Urban express highways, the ARBA contended, were necessary to alleviate traffic congestion, but through proper right-of-way planning they also could "contribute in a substantial manner to the elimination of slum and deteriorated areas.". . .
>
> [T]he American Concrete Institute, which had an obvious interest in highway construction, championed the use of urban expressways in "the elimination of slums and blighted areas." Build highways through the city slums, urged the ARBA and the ACI, and solve the problems of urban American. . . .
>
> [T]he Automotive Safety Foundation assured readers that freeways were desirable, beneficial, and beautiful; they stimulated rising land values and prevented "the spread of blight and. . .slums."

On the losing side were poor, African American, city residents—a classic example of a diffuse interest. These communities did not successfully organize in opposition to the interstate highways in the 1940s and 1950s, when the system was planned. As a consequence, Rose and Mohl, p. 96, report that "[b]y the 1960s, federal highway construction was demolishing 27,000 urban housing units each year." It was not until the massive costs of these highways became clear that organized opposition emerged, primarily under the auspices of the civil rights movement. But by then it was too late to change much.

Nashville's Interstate 40 is a case in point. As Rose and Mohl, p. 105, describe:

> [H]ighway planners went out of their way to put a "kink" in the urban link of Interstate-40 as it passed through the city. The expressway route gouged a concrete swath through the North Nashville black community, destroying hundreds of homes and businesses and dividing what was left of the neighborhood. The decision for the I-40 route had been made quietly in 1957 at a nonpublic meeting of white business leaders and state highway officials. By 1967, after years of denying that the expressway would adversely affect the community, the state highway department began acquiring right of way, displacing residents, and bulldozing the route.

Residents eventually organized in opposition to the highway, gaining a temporary restraining order, but ultimately losing in federal court. The highway was constructed as planned. Similar stories played out in cities throughout the country. And while some highway construction was halted and some highways were rerouted, the overwhelming majority of the stories end with the interstates following precisely the plans established by the concentrated interests starting in the 1940s.

Let's look at a model to see that externalities can lead to the differential power of concentrated versus diffuse interests.

Imagine a setting in which, say, a factory owner is making profits by polluting the water supply of a town. A regulator must decide whether to regulate the factory. Both the factory owner and the citizens of the town can invest in lobbying the regulator. Each hour of lobbying costs $100. The regulator can be influenced through lobbying. If the citizens do C hours of lobbying and the factory owner does F hours of lobbying, the probability that the regulator sides with the citizens and factory owner are

$$\frac{C}{C+F} \quad \text{and} \quad \frac{F}{C+F},$$

respectively. If the two sides spend equally, they win with equal probability. But the more one side spends relative to the other, the more likely it is to win.

There are N citizens in the town. If the factory stops polluting, each citizen experiences a benefit of $b > 0$. Polluting allows the factory owner (who lives elsewhere) to make an extra profit of π. Assume that $b < \pi < Nb$, so that the factory owner values polluting more than any individual citizen, but the utilitarian outcome is for the regulator to prevent pollution.

The citizens and factory owner each choose an amount to contribute towards lobbying. The factory owner (being only one person) is a concentrated interest, while the citizens are a diffuse interest. As we will see, even though the utilitarian outcome is for the factory to be regulated, in equilibrium the factory owner will yield more influence than the citizens and, as a result, almost certainly will not be regulated.

Consider a citizen, i, who believes that each of her fellow citizens will contribute enough to purchase c hours of lobbying and that the factory owner will buy F hours of lobbying. Citizen i believes that if she contributes enough money to purchase c_i hours of lobbying, then the total amount of lobbying in support of regulation will be $C = c_i + (N-1)c$. Hence, she believes the probability of regulation will be $\frac{c_i+(N-1)c}{c_i+(N-1)c+F}$. Given this, citizen i makes a contribution, c_i, that solves

$$\max_{c_i} \left(\frac{c_i + (N-1)c}{c_i + (N-1)c + F} \right) b - 100 c_i.$$

Taking the first-order condition and rearranging, citizen i's best response is

$$\text{BR}_i(c, F) = \frac{\sqrt{bF}}{10} - F - (N-1)c.$$

Since the citizens are identical, focus on the case in which each makes the same contribution (given F). Call this contribution $BR_i(F)$. Since all citizens make the same contribution, it must satisfy

$$BR_i(F) = \frac{\sqrt{bF}}{10} - F - (N-1)BR_i(F).$$

Rearranging, each citizen's contribution purchases the following number of hours of lobbying:

$$BR_i(F) = \frac{\sqrt{bF} - 10F}{10N}. \tag{4.2}$$

If the factory owner believes that the citizens will purchase a total of C hours of lobbying, he solves

$$\max_F \left(\frac{F}{C+F}\right)\pi - 100F. \tag{4.3}$$

Maximizing this function, the factory owner's best response is

$$BR_f(C) = \frac{\sqrt{C\pi} - 10C}{10}.$$

Equations 4.2 and 4.3 give us the two best responses. If we substitute the right-hand side of Equation 4.3 for F in Equation 4.2, we find the Nash equilibrium:

$$c^* = \frac{b^2\pi}{100(b+\pi)^2 N} \quad \text{and} \quad F^* = \frac{b\pi^2}{100(b+\pi)^2}.$$

What does this imply about which side's lobbying efforts are likely to prevail? Total lobbying by the citizens is

$$C^* = Nc^* = \frac{b^2\pi}{100(b+\pi)^2},$$

while total lobbying by the factory owner is

$$F^* = \frac{b\pi^2}{100(b+\pi)^2}.$$

Since $\pi > b$, it is straightforward that the factory owner's investment in lobbying is larger than the sum total of the citizens' investments. Thus, the factory owner is more likely to prevail. In particular, the probability that the citizens win and pollution is stopped is

$$\frac{C^*}{C^* + F^*} = \frac{\frac{b^2\pi}{100(b+\pi)^2}}{\frac{b^2\pi}{100(b+\pi)^2} + \frac{b\pi^2}{100(b+\pi)^2}} = \frac{b}{b + \pi} < 1/2.$$

This outcome is inefficient. As a group, the citizens value stopping the pollution more than the factory owner values polluting. For instance, suppose $b = 1000$, $N = 100,000$, and $\pi = 1,000,000$. The citizens' total value of stopping pollution is \$100,000,000. The factory owner's value of polluting is only \$1,000,000. Yet the probability that the regulator stops the pollution is tiny:

$$\frac{1000}{1000 + 1,000,000} = \frac{1}{1001}.$$

Because the citizens are a diffuse interest, their efforts to organize are hampered by an externalities problem. Each individual benefits only a small amount from her individual contribution. But that contribution also benefits all the other citizens. Hence, each citizen under-contributes. They all would be better off if they could find a way to all contribute more to the cause.

4.3 The Tragedy of the Commons

In February of 2009, an American commercial communications satellite (Iridium 33) and a defunct Russian military communications satellite (Kosmos 2251) collided in low earth orbit traveling over 42,000 km/hour. Both satellites were destroyed on impact. According to the European Space Agency, the collision and destruction of the satellites generated 2200 trackable fragments of space debris.[6] In 2012 one such fragment passed close enough to the international space station that astronauts were forced to take refuge in "life boats" as a precaution against a collision. All told, the international space station has had to reposition itself to avoid space debris at least fifteen times.[7]

Though dramatic, this story is in some sense not surprising. Low earth orbit (approximately 200 to 2000 kilometers above the earth) is the least costly part of space to access. Moreover, because of its close proximity to earth, communications can be achieved with relatively low power. However, because objects in low earth orbit circle the globe quite quickly (relative to the rotation of the planet), they do not stay over a fixed position on earth. A constellation of interconnected satellites is, thus, required to provide uninterrupted coverage. As a consequence of these facts, an enormous number of objects—scientific

---

[6]http://www.esa.int/Our_Activities/Operations/Space_Debris/About_space_debris
[7]http://www.esa.int/Our_Activities/Operations/Space_Debris/FAQ_Frequently_asked_questions

equipment, satellites used for communications, spying, global positioning, weather and environmental monitoring, and so on—have been sent into low earth orbit.

While several international treaties regulate space, the underlying legal framework leaves the peaceful use of space as a right of sovereign nations. As the example of space debris highlights, this creates externalities problems.

Space in low earth orbit is a finite resource. When one country or firm launches a satellite into orbit, it reduces available space for others. This is a situation of negative externalities—countries and firms suffer only a small portion of the costs associated with crowding space with debris. Thus, we should expect there to be too much space debris, relative to the social optimum. And, indeed, the European Space Agency estimates that there are over 600,000 pieces of debris of at least 1 cm in size orbiting the earth. This debris is the result of thousands of satellites, rockets, and instruments launched into orbit since the space age began. In fact, prior to the collision, the defunct Kosmos 2251 was itself space debris.

A related issue arises for satellites in geostationary orbit at much higher altitude (almost 36,000 kilometers above the earth). Objects in geostationary orbit circle the globe directly above the equator, at the same speed as the earth rotates on its access. As a consequence, they stay above a fixed position on earth at all times. This stationarity is particularly valuable for communications, since a single satellite can guarantee continuous coverage of a particular part of the globe. The problem for geostationary orbit is not primarily debris. It is limited space. Because the radio frequencies used by such satellites can interfere with one another, they must be spaced appropriately. As a result, there are a very limited number of spots, especially above desirable parts of the globe. Moreover, satellites must stay in a very narrow altitude band to remain geostationary (if they fall out of that band, they cease to remain over a fixed location). Hence, satellites must reposition relatively frequently, a process which can again interfere with signals sent by nearby satellites.

While there is an international registry to coordinate positioning of satellites in geostationary orbit, the right to launch and to reposition satellites again rests with sovereign nations. As with space debris in low earth orbit, then, there are significant externalities problems. Individual countries and firms fail to internalize the full costs of putting a satellite in orbit or of repositioning that satellite. As a consequence, we expect inefficient overuse.

In the previous section we explored externalities in the context of public goods—goods that are neither excludable nor rival. The problem of overcrowding in space illustrates an externalities problem that is very closely related, but arises with another type of good—the commons. The commons (sometimes also called a common-pool resource) is a good that is non-excludable, just like a public good, but is rival, unlike a public good. As you'll recall, a non-excludable good is one that has the property that if anyone has access to it, everyone has access to it. A rival good is a good where my use of it diminishes the supply of the good left for you—that is, the resource in question can be depleted. Other classic examples of the commons include fish stocks within a fishery, grazing land, space on the road, internet bandwidth, water, and so on.

Because of its rivalrous nature, the commons presents a situation with negative externalities. If I use a lot of bandwidth to stream movies to my TV in the evening, I slow down everyone else's internet connection. But I don't take those negative externalities into account when using the commons. As such, typically people use too much of the commons, relative to the social optimum. Hence, the tragedy of the commons. Think about that next time you are downloading movies from BitTorrent. The real crime isn't stealing intellectual property. It's the negative externalities you are imposing on my internet speed as I try to stream Netflix legally.

To be a little more precise, let's consider a simple model of a commons that is a little more down to earth than geostationary orbit, a fishery. The fishery is small enough that, no matter how much fishing is done, it does not affect the price of fish on the market. The price per fish is \$2. There are two firms running boats in the fishery: firm 1 and firm 2. The firms simultaneously choose how many fishing boats to run: b_1 and b_2. It costs \$20 to run a boat. We will assume that, if they want to, firms can run partial boats, so that b_1 and b_2 are real numbers rather than integers. (This is just for technical convenience.)

Fish are a depletable resource. So the more boats out fishing, the lower the density of fish in the fishery and the fewer fish caught per boat. In particular, if the total number of boats in the water is $B = b_1 + b_2$, then the number of fish caught per boat is $100 - B$.

The firms care about profits. If a firm runs b_i boats, then its profits are

$$\$2(100 - B)b_i - \$20b_i.$$

The first term represents revenues: two dollars per fish times $(100 - B)$ fish per boat times b_i boats. The second term represents costs: \$20 per boat.

How many boats will each firm run? Suppose firm i believes the other firm will run b_{-i} boats. Then it chooses a number of boats to maximize profits:

$$\max_{b_i} 2(100 - b_i - b_{-i})b_i - 20b_i.$$

The optimal number of boats for firm i is given by $\mathrm{BR}_i(b_{-i})$, which (if it is positive) satisfies the following first-order condition:

$$200 - 4\mathrm{BR}_i(b_{-i}) - 2b_{-i} - 20 = 0.$$

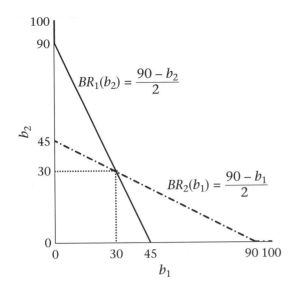

Figure 4.2. Best response correspondences in the Tragedy of the Commons game.

Rearranging we have

$$\mathrm{BR}_i(b_{-i}) = \begin{cases} \frac{90-b_{-i}}{2} & \text{if } b_{-i} \leq 90 \\ 0 & \text{otherwise.} \end{cases} \tag{4.4}$$

We can use these best response correspondences to find a Nash equilibrium. A profile (b_1^*, b_2^*) is a Nash equilibrium if and only if the following conditions hold:

$$b_1^* = \mathrm{BR}_1(b_2^*) \quad \text{and} \quad b_2^* = \mathrm{BR}_2(b_1^*). \tag{4.5}$$

Figure 4.2 draws both best response correspondences. The solid line is firm 1's best response correspondence. For any number of boats run by firm 2 (on the y-axis), you find the best response for firm 1 by moving horizontally to this line and then dropping down to the horizontal axis. The dash-dot line is firm 2's best response correspondence. For any level of boats by firm 1 (on the x-axis), you find firm 2's best response by moving vertically to this line and then moving leftward to the vertical axis. The best response correspondences intersect at an equilibrium—each firm runs 30 boats.

One can also see this algebraically. Substituting the best responses from Equation 4.4 into Equation 4.5, if the firms run fewer than 90 boats, then at an equilibrium we have

$$b_1^* = \frac{90 - b_2^*}{2} \quad \text{and} \quad b_2^* = \frac{90 - b_1^*}{2}.$$

Substituting the second equation into the first we get

$$b_1^* = \frac{90 - \frac{90 - b_1^*}{2}}{2}.$$

Rearranging yields

$$b_1^* = 30 \quad \text{and} \quad b_2^* = \frac{90 - 30}{2} = 30.$$

Given that each firm runs 30 boats, each firm's equilibrium profits are

$$\$2(100 - 30 - 30)30 - \$20 \times 30 = \$2400 - \$600 = \$1800.$$

4.3.1 A Pareto Improvement

You won't be surprised to learn, given the negative externalities, that the equilibrium involves overfishing. To see this, imagine that each firm ran 20 boats instead of 30. Under this scenario, profits are

$$\$2(100 - 20 - 20)20 - \$20 \times 20 = \$2400 - \$400 = \$2000 > \$1800.$$

By running 20 rather than 30 boats each, the firms actually keep revenues exactly the same (\$2400) but save the costs of running an extra 10 boats each. This works because, by not running so many boats, the firms are able to catch more fish per boat.

4.3.2 The First Best

It turns out that running 20 boats each is not the utilitarian optimum for these firms. It was simply a convenient example to show that the firms could do better by both fishing less. Let's now figure out how many boats are socially optimal.

Suppose that the total number of boats run is B and each firm runs an equal number. Then the sum of the two profits is

$$\$2\left(100 - \frac{B}{2} - \frac{B}{2}\right)\left(\frac{B}{2} + \frac{B}{2}\right) - \$20\left(\frac{B}{2} + \frac{B}{2}\right).$$

We can find the B that maximizes this sum of profits (which we will call B^{FB} for the "first best") by differentiating and setting the first derivative equal to zero:

$$\$2\left(100 - 2B^{FB}\right) - \$20 = 0.$$

Rearranging, the first-best number of boats is

$$B^{FB} = 45.$$

4.3.3 Interpretation

We opened with an example of a tragedy of the commons in space. As the model highlights, another famous setting typically viewed as a commons is fisheries or grazing land. Perhaps the most famous such example is the collapse of Canada's Grand Banks cod fishery in the 1990s. Hutchings (1996) reports that the Grand Banks fishery was once the world's largest cod fishery. However, beginning in the 1960s, technological innovations (e.g., larger trawlers, electronic navigation, sonar) increased the rate at which cod were caught. For a while, this led to record catches. Eventually, however, the density of cod in the fishery began to decline, leading to ever smaller catches. The annual catch fell from over 800,000 tons in 1968 to under 200,000 tons by the late 1970s. According to Hutchings, between 1962 and 1992, there was a 94% decrease in the abundance of cod old enough to be commercially fished. In 1993, amid concerns of permanent collapse, the fishery was closed down.

There are many other such examples in environmental policy. For instance, deforestation due to overlogging is a classic example of a tragedy of the commons which has played out in tropical forests throughout south Asia, Africa, and South America.

Another particularly striking example is the Pacific trash vortex (also known as the Great Pacific garbage patch). This enormous gyre of marine debris in the Pacific Ocean is estimated by the U.S. Environmental Protection Agency (EPA) to stretch from Hawaii to Japan and contain approximately 100 million tons of garbage.[8] The garbage patch is a source of significant environmental problems. For instance, the EPA reports that concentrated marine debris results in degraded habitat, harm to coral reefs, accumulation and transport of high levels of contaminants (including PCBs and pesticides), and direct damage to animal life through ingestion and entanglement.

The vortex is the consequence of marine pollution that gets trapped and consolidated by oceanic currents. The EPA reports that

> [t]he primary source of marine debris is the improper waste disposal or management of trash and manufacturing products, including plastics (e.g., littering, illegal dumping).... Debris is generated on land at marinas, ports, rivers, harbors, docks, and storm drains. Debris is generated at sea from fishing vessels, stationary platforms and cargo ships.

Such an outcome is not surprising. Clean and well-functioning oceans are a common pool resource. The logic of the tragedy of the commons, then, implies that, absent intervention, we should expect overpollution. And in this case,

---

[8]U.S. Environmental Protection Agency Pacific Southwest/Region 9, "Marine Debris in the North Pacific A Summary of Existing Information and Identification of Data Gaps." http://www.epa.gov/region9/marine-debris/pdf/MarineDebris-NPacFinalAprvd.pdf

where there are so many possible ways for debris to flow into the sea, it may be particularly difficult to solve the problem.

There are also applications outside the context of environmental policy. As already mentioned, various forms of traffic—vehicular, internet, cell phone, radio, satellite, and so on—share the strategic structure of a tragedy of the commons. Anyone can get on the highway or the internet. But the more people who use the highway or the internet, the slower the traffic moves. Hence, your presence on the highway imposes a negative externality on me by depleting a resource that we share—open road, as it were.

The metaphor can extend even further. For instance, Berry (2009) argues that the structure of local government in the United States creates a tragedy of the commons with respect to taxation. In many localities in the United States, citizens are represented by a large number of overlapping, local governments— a city, a county, a school district, a parks district, a water reclamation district, a library district, a mosquito abatement district, and so on. Many of these districts have independent taxation authority. Hence, they are all drawing government revenues from a common pool of the citizens' depletable, taxable resources. The consequence is overtaxation by local government in those areas where there are many overlapping districts.

And, indeed, Berry finds precisely this effect in the data by studying how taxation and service provision change in a county when the number of overlapping jurisdictions in that county changes. In the United States, increasing jurisdictional overlap in a county from the 25th to the 75th percentile (this is a move from 2 to 5 overlapping jurisdictions) leads to an 11% increase in government revenue, about $130 per capita. Moreover, this increase in revenue comes with no appreciable increase in government services, suggesting that it really is the result of common pool incentives, rather than expanding service provision.

4.4 Policy Interventions

All of our models point to a common policy prescription. If a policymaker could get people to internalize their externalities, outcomes could be vastly improved, making everyone better off. But how?

4.4.1 The Failure of Persuasion

A common intuition is that we could achieve a better outcome by simply explaining to people how much better off they would be if everyone internalized their externalities. It is important to see that this will not work. Let's think about the public goods model from Section 4.2.

The incentive for an individual to undercontribute to public goods persists even if players believe everyone else will do the socially optimal thing.

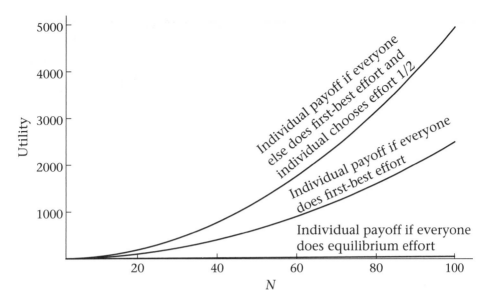

Figure 4.3. An individual's payoff is higher if everyone else does the first-best level of effort and she does her individual best response.

In particular, if I believe that all other players will choose effort $\frac{N}{2}$, I still want to choose effort $\frac{1}{2}$. Yes, I am better off with everyone (including me) choosing the first-best level of effort ($\frac{N}{2}$) than with everyone choosing the equilibrium level of effort ($\frac{1}{2}$). *But I am even better off if everyone but me chooses the first-best level of effort and I get to free ride on them.* In particular, my payoff if everyone but me chooses $\frac{N}{2}$ and I choose $\frac{1}{2}$ is

$$(N-1)\frac{N}{2} + \frac{1}{2} - \frac{1}{2}^2 = \frac{2N^2 - 2N + 1}{4},$$

which is even larger than the payoff under the first-best: $\frac{N^2}{4}$. (Check if you want to practice your algebra.) This point is illustrated in Figure 4.3.

The same is true in the tragedy of the commons. An agreement to each run fewer than 30 boats is not self-enforcing. Indeed, if firm 1 knew that firm 2 would run, say, 20 boats, firm 1 would exploit the greater fish density by running even more boats than in equilibrium. You can see that fact through the following calculation:

$$\mathrm{BR}_1(20) = \frac{90 - 20}{2} = 35.$$

Even though both firms are better off under a deal where they each run fewer than 30 boats, neither firm has an incentive to honor such a deal.

The point that players do not internalize their externalities, regardless of what others do, is important for two reasons.

First, as I've already indicated, a common reaction to this type of model is to say, "This argument doesn't make any sense. If everyone thought like this, nothing would get done. So let's just explain that to people and they'll act differently." But that response doesn't hold water. Suppose it was the case that everyone didn't "think like this." Indeed, suppose you knew that everyone else in your society would contribute a lot to producing a public good (or attending a protest). Then it is still a best response for you to shirk.

Second, this logic highlights the challenge for policy interventions. It is not enough for a leader to explain that everyone would be better off if everyone would pitch in. True as that might be, if everyone else is pitching in, I still don't want to. And if everyone faces that same calculation, then we are right back where we started—underproviding public goods, over-consuming the commons, and so on. Some more active kind of policy intervention is called for in these circumstances. Indeed, this is why we typically think of providing public goods—national defense, environmental protection, scientific research, roads, air traffic control, safety from enormous rocks falling from space, and so on—as one of the essential roles of government.

4.4.2 Pigovian Subsidies and Taxes

Taxes and subsidies are the most direct way to induce people to internalize their externalities. When an activity imposes negative externalities, a tax incentivizes people to do less of it. When an activity imposes positive externalities, a subsidy incentivizes people to do more of it. These kinds of subsidies or taxes are often referred to as Pigovian, after the economist Arthur Cecil Pigou. Examples of such policies include carbon taxes—designed to curb the use of fossil fuels, which impose negative externalities—or subsidies for scientific research—designed to expand the creation of scientific knowledge, which imposes positive externalities.

Let's look at how a Pigovian subsidy works in a bit more detail in our public goods model. (In the exercises you can explore a Pigovian tax in our Tragedy of the Commons model.)

Suppose a subsidy, σ, is paid to each player in our public goods game for each unit of effort she contributes. We must collect revenue through taxation to fund the subsidy. Unfortunately, taxation itself results in some inefficiencies. This might be due to reduced incentives for work, distortions in behavior to focus on less productive tasks that are taxed at a lower rate, the need to build a bureaucracy to collect the taxes, or what have you. We will model this inefficiency in as simple a way as possible. It costs taxpayers $\$\tau > \$1$ for each dollar of revenue the government requires. That is, to disburse $\$T$ in subsidies, the government must collect $\$T \times \tau$ in revenues.

Assume that each member of society pays an equal share of the tax burden to fund subsidies for everyone other than herself. For instance, suppose Player i

earns a subsidy of $e_i \times \sigma$. Then each of the $N - 1$ other taxpayers must pay taxes of $\frac{e_i \times \sigma \times \tau}{N-1}$ to fund Player i's subsidy. This implies that, if tax revenues of T are needed to fund the subsidies for all citizens other than Player i, then Player i pays a total tax equal to $\frac{T \times \tau}{N-1}$.

Suppose Player i believes everyone else will use the strategies given by $\mathbf{e}_{-i}$. If the subsidy is σ, Player i's best response solves

$$\max_{e_i} \overbrace{e_1 + e_2 + \ldots + e_i + \ldots + e_N}^{\text{Public Goods}} + \overbrace{e_i \sigma}^{i\text{'s subsidy}} - \overbrace{e_i^2}^{i\text{'s costs}}$$

$$- \frac{\overbrace{(e_1 + e_2 + \ldots + e_{i-1} + e_{i+1} + \ldots + e_N)\sigma\tau}^{i\text{'s tax burden}}}{N-1}.$$

Taking the first-order condition, and labeling i's best response given the subsidy, $\text{BR}_i(\mathbf{e}_{-i}, \sigma)$, we have

$$1 + \sigma - 2\text{BR}_i(\mathbf{e}_{-i}, \sigma) = 0.$$

This first-order condition looks much like the first-order condition without a subsidy. (See Equation 4.1.) The key difference is that the marginal benefit of contributing to the public good is now larger, reflecting the presence of the subsidy.

Rearranging, an individual's best response is now to contribute

$$\text{BR}_i(\mathbf{e}_{-i}, \sigma) = \frac{1+\sigma}{2}. \tag{4.6}$$

If we set the subsidy at $\sigma = 0$, then people will each choose the level of effort they did in our original model, $1/2$. If we set the subsidy at $\bar{\sigma} = N - 1$, then people will choose the first-best level of effort:

$$\text{BR}_i(\mathbf{e}_{-i}, \bar{\sigma}) = \frac{1+N-1}{2} = \frac{N}{2}.$$

The intuition is simple. The subsidy that induces players to choose the first-best level of effort is the one that makes them fully internalize the positive externalities of effort. The externalities from effort are the benefit given to the $N - 1$ other people in society. Thus, the subsidy that fully internalizes the externalities must provide Player i with the benefit that all the $N - 1$ other people enjoy.

Importantly, $\bar{\sigma}$ is not the socially optimal subsidy. Because raising revenues to pay for the subsidies is itself costly, the social welfare maximizing subsidy balances the benefits of increased public goods that higher subsidies induce and the costs of increased distortionary taxation that higher subsidies require.

The socially optimal subsidy, therefore, lies somewhere between zero and $\overline{\sigma}$. We explore this in detail in Section 4.5.

4.4.3 Regulation

An alternative to a Pigovian subsidy or tax is to directly regulate the externality generating activity. If the government can mandate how much carbon people can emit, how many fish a firm can catch, how much medical research scientists must do, and so on, then it is straightforward to implement the utilitarian optimum. Of course, problems may arise.

One problem with direct regulation is that the government must monitor the relevant activities. It might be, for instance, much easier to impose a tax on carbon at one or two points in the production process than to monitor all the end uses of carbon.

A second problem is that the government may not know precisely what the optimal level of activity is. Hence, it may not be certain exactly how to regulate. This, of course, is also a problem for the Pigovian approach. If the government doesn't know the optimal level of activity, it is uncertain what the right regulation or the right Pigovian subsidy or tax is. We will return to the issue of what the government does when it lacks relevant information in Chapter 9.

A third important downside to direct regulation, relative to the Pigovian approach and related to the information problem, is flexibility. Suppose the government wants to limit carbon emissions because of negative externalities. At the time it decides to pursue this policy goal, perhaps the most efficient way to do so is to shift to some mix of natural gas and renewable energy. But, over time, there may be technological innovations that suggest even better alternatives. One wants a policy that allows firms to switch to those better solutions and, as importantly, gives firms incentives to look for such innovations. If the government promulgates a regulation that simply says that x percent of an industry's energy needs must be met with natural gas and y percent must be met with renewables, carbon emissions will be reduced. But firms will not be able to flexibly shift to new alternatives as they become available and, so, will not have incentives to look for such alternatives. By contrast, if the government imposes a Pigovian tax on carbon, firms have incentives to avoid carbon as inexpensively as possible and, so, have incentives to innovate.

4.5 The Theory of the Second Best

No policy intervention is perfect. Any policy lever that the government pulls to address some issue is likely to cause at least some new problems in some other domain. Hence, the art of designing good policy involves balancing benefits and costs. It is this insight that leads to one of the most important ideas in policy analysis—the theory of the *second best* (Lipsey and Lancaster, 1956).

As we've already discussed, we use the term first best to describe the efficient outcome. The second best, by contrast, is the best outcome that can be achieved, given all the constraints faced by the government. One of the most important lessons that comes from the theory of the second best is the following. When faced with a situation in which there are constraints that imply that matters will not be efficient in one domain, it is not always the best policy to try to achieve efficiency in some other domain.

To be a little less abstract, let me give you a famous example of the theory of the second best. It is a well-known fact from basic microeconomics that monopolies create inefficiency. A monopolistic firm has incentives to hold production down, thereby raising prices and profits. This is inefficient because it creates a situation in which there are consumers who would be happy to buy the monopolist's product for more than the monopolist's marginal cost of production, but who are left unserved. Forcing higher production—through regulation or increased competition—increases utilitarian social welfare. Hence, standard policy advice is to break up monopolies.

But now suppose there is a monopolist in an industry, say mining, that imposes negative externalities through pollution. Moreover, suppose that this particular type of mining is inherently polluting—there is simply no way to do it without producing the pollution. Is it still a good idea to break up the monopoly?

Here, there are two domains of concern for social welfare—the inefficiency associated with monopolistic underproduction and the inefficiency associated with externalities from pollution—and so there are competing effects of breaking up the monopoly. On the one hand, production goes up, prices go down, and more consumers are served. This tends to increase social welfare. On the other hand, production goes up, so the negative externalities from pollution go up. This tends to decrease social welfare.

The optimal policy regarding how competitive the mining industry should be must balance these costs and benefits of increased production. The *second-best policy* optimally balances this trade-off. The key is that, because of the constraint that says that matters will not be efficient in the pollution domain, the second-best policy involves less competition (and, so, less production) in the mining industry than would the first best (a completely competitive market).

The theory of the second best is critical for thinking about the optimal use of Pigovian taxes and subsidies. Pigovian taxes and subsidies offer a powerful lever that policymakers can use to get decision makers to internalize their externalities. However, like any policy intervention, they are not perfect. As we've already discussed, the use of taxes to collect government revenue creates costs.

We captured such costs in Chapter 4.4.2 by assuming that it costs taxpayers $\$\tau > \$1$ for each dollar of revenue the government requires. Let's see this more specifically in our public goods model.

4.5.1 The Second-Best Pigovian Subsidy

Given that taxes are distortionary, the theory of the second best implies that the subsidize-and-tax plan that implements the first best, $\overline{\sigma}$, is not the socially optimal subsidize-and-tax plan. Inefficiencies on one dimension (distortionary taxes) imply that the optimal policy does not achieve complete efficiency on another dimension (the first-best level of public goods). This is a subtle and very important point, so I want to spend a bit of time on it.

We call the level of public goods provided under the socially optimal subsidize-and-tax plan the *second best*. Here, the first best is the socially optimal level of public goods unconstrained by concerns about how you achieve it. The second best is the level of public goods that is socially optimal, taking into account the unfortunate inefficiencies created by the very policy interventions meant to get us closer to the first best. The second best, then, is the best outcome that society can actually hope to achieve.[9] An important, and sometimes confusing point given the terminology, is that the second-best policy yields *higher* social welfare than the policy that induces the first-best action.

> **Definition 4.5.1.** The *second-best policy* is the policy that maximizes the utilitarian social welfare, taking into consideration all the various effects of the policy. The *second-best action* is the action players are induced to take when the second-best policy is implemented.

Let's solve for the second best in our public goods game. To do so, we are going to engage in an analysis that is somewhat different than what we have done previously. In Equation 4.6 we solved for the level of effort each individual will take, in equilibrium, for any given subsidy σ. Our task now is the following:

1. We take that equilibrium effort as a function of the subsidy, σ, as given.
2. Given the equilibrium effort induced by a given subsidy, σ, we calculate the utilitarian social welfare as a function of σ.
3. We find the σ that maximizes that social welfare. The σ that does so is the second-best subsidy and the effort it induces is the second-best effort.

---

[9] As we will emphasize in Part III, even achieving the second best is not a realistic goal, since policymakers have their own incentives to pursue policies other than the social optimum.

Recall, from Equation 4.6, that for any level of subsidy, σ, each individual will choose effort $\frac{1+\sigma}{2}$. Let's label that level of effort

$$e^{*,\sigma} = \frac{1+\sigma}{2}.$$

To fund such a subsidy for the $N-1$ other people, an individual must pay a tax equal to

$$\frac{(N-1) \times e^{*,\sigma} \times \sigma \times \tau}{N-1} = e^{*,\sigma} \times \sigma \times \tau.$$

Hence, for a given subsidy, σ, an individual i's payoff is

$$\overbrace{N \times e^{*,\sigma}}^{\text{Public Goods}} + \overbrace{e^{*,\sigma} \times \sigma}^{i\text{'s subsidy}} - \overbrace{(e^{*,\sigma})^2}^{i\text{'s cost}} - \overbrace{e^{*,\sigma} \times \sigma \times \tau}^{i\text{'s tax burden}}.$$

The first term is the payoff from the public goods created, the second term is individual i's personal subsidy, the third term is individual i's cost of effort, and the fourth term is individual i's tax burden. Substituting for $e^{*,\sigma} = \frac{1+\sigma}{2}$, this can be rewritten:

$$N\left(\frac{1+\sigma}{2}\right) + \left(\frac{1+\sigma}{2}\right)\sigma - \left(\frac{1+\sigma}{2}\right)^2 - \left(\frac{1+\sigma}{2}\right)\sigma\tau.$$

A total of N people make this same payoff. So, given the equilibrium effort and taxes induced by a subsidy σ, the utilitarian social welfare as a function of σ is

$$U(\sigma) = N\left[N\left(\frac{1+\sigma}{2}\right) + \left(\frac{1+\sigma}{2}\right)\sigma - \left(\frac{1+\sigma}{2}\right)^2 - \left(\frac{1+\sigma}{2}\right)\sigma\tau\right].$$

To find the second-best subsidy, we maximize U by differentiating with respect to σ and setting the derivative equal to zero (labeling the resulting subsidy σ^{SB}, for second best). Doing so, and rearranging, shows that for any $\tau < N$, the second-best subsidy is[10]

$$\sigma^{SB} = \frac{N-\tau}{2\tau-1}.$$

This implies that the second-best level of effort is

$$e^{*,\sigma^{SB}} = \frac{1+\frac{N-\tau}{2\tau-1}}{2} = \frac{N-1+\tau}{2(2\tau-1)}.$$

There are three points worth noting.

First, the more inefficient is taxation (higher τ), the lower are the second-best subsidy and effort.

---

[10]If $\tau \geq N$, then the inefficiency of taxes is so large that it swamps the benefits of internalizing externalities, so it is optimal to offer no subsidy.

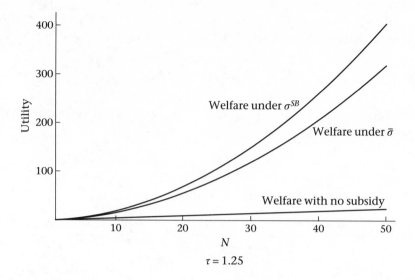

$\tau = 1.25$

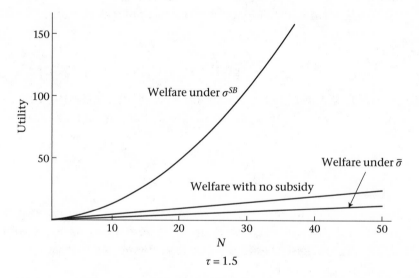

$\tau = 1.5$

Figure 4.4. For two different levels of tax inefficiency ($\tau = 1.25$ and $\tau = 1.5$), the figures show individual welfare (as a function of the size of society) under the second-best subsidy, the subsidy that implements the first-best effort, and no subsidy.

Second, for any τ that is greater than 1 and less than N, social welfare is higher under the second-best subsidy than with no subsidy or with the subsidy that implements the first-best effort. This fact is illustrated in Figure 4.4, which shows individual payoffs under each of these policies for two different values of τ. A point worth noting from the figure is that, as society gets large, such that externalities matter a lot, it becomes particularly important to implement a good subsidy policy.

Third, for any $\tau > 1$, the second-best subsidy is less than the subsidy that gets people to choose the first-best effort:

$$\sigma^{SB} = \frac{N - \tau}{2\tau - 1} < N - 1 = \overline{\sigma}.$$

This straightforwardly implies that the second-best level of effort, and therefore the second-best level of public goods provided, is in between the no-intervention equilibrium level of public goods and the first-best level of public goods.

This is perhaps easier to see graphically. In the first panel of Figure 4.5, the dotted line shows the subsidy that implements the first-best level of effort for the case where society has 1000 people in it. As we have already seen, this subsidy is $\overline{\sigma} = N - 1 = 999$. The solid curve shows the second-best (i.e., optimal) subsidy as a function of how inefficient taxation is. When $\tau = 1$, taxation is not at all inefficient. That is, each dollar of taxes collected turns into a dollar of subsidy. As you can see, in this case there is no trade-off, so the second-best subsidy is the one that implements the first-best level of effort. But as taxation becomes more inefficient (i.e., τ gets larger), the second-best subsidy gets smaller and smaller.

This logic carries through to the second panel of Figure 4.5. The dotted line shows the first-best level of effort. As we've already seen, this is $\frac{N}{2} = 500$. The solid curve shows the effort that will be chosen if the government imposes the second-best subsidy. Again, as we saw above, this is $e^{*,\sigma^{SB}} = \frac{N-1+\tau}{2(2\tau-1)}$. Finally, the dashed line is the effort chosen in equilibrium if there is no subsidy, $e^* = \frac{1}{2}$. The figure shows that if taxation is not very inefficient, then the second-best effort gets very close to the first-best effort. (Indeed, if $\tau = 1$, so that taxation is not at all inefficient, then second-best effort is equal to first-best effort.) However, as taxation becomes more inefficient (i.e., τ gets big), this is no longer the case. As we saw in the first panel, the subsidy gets smaller and smaller. And, consequently, as we see in this panel, effort gets smaller and smaller. Indeed, as τ gets very large, the second-best subsidy goes to zero and the second-best effort approaches the equilibrium effort with no subsidy.

4.6 Alternative Responses

While regulation and Pigovian taxes or subsides are the most straightforward policy solutions to externalities problems, they are not the only approach. Below we consider various less direct ways of addressing externalities. Some of these require intervention by the policymaker much earlier in the process. Others suggest the possibility that society might, sometimes, be able to solve these problems without a policy intervention, or at least with a less prescriptive intervention.

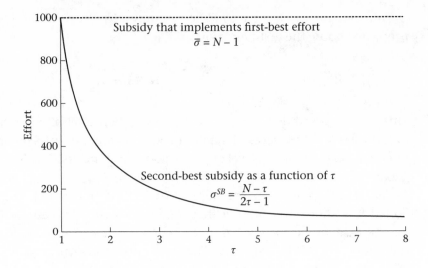

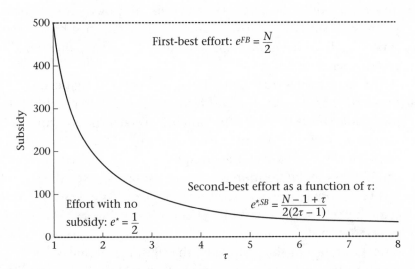

Figure 4.5. The upper panel shows the subsidy that implements the first-best effort and the second-best subsidy as a function of τ, for the case of $N = 1000$. The lower panel shows the first-best effort, the second-best effort, and the equilibrium effort with no subsidy.

4.6.1 Altruism

We've seen that simple persuasion is unlikely to solve externalities problems. But that is not to say that things wouldn't be better if people had a greater sense of obligation to one another. In the models we've looked at, people's preferences are entirely focused on their own individual well-being.

If people had direct concern for one another's well-being, they would (at least partially) internalize their externalities. So, if society can find ways to teach or persuade people to feel more altruistically toward one another the situation might improve.

Let's see this in our model of collective action. Suppose that an individual in that model values benefits to other people, as well as benefits to herself. Let $\alpha \in (0, 1)$ be the amount she values benefits to another person relative to benefits to herself. This change in preferences could have a big effect on her behavior.

Consider an example with N people, each of whom values the outcome at \$100 and finds the cost of participating to be \$10. A person, i, who believes n other people will participate has an expected payoff from participating given by

$$\frac{n+1}{N}\left(\$100 + (N-1) \times \alpha \times \$100\right) - \$10.$$

The first term reflects the probability of success times the \$100 benefit of success directly enjoyed by person i plus the α-share of \$100 per person (for all $N-1$ people other than person i) that person i internalizes in terms of her concern for the benefits to others.

Person i's payoff from not participating is

$$\frac{n}{N}\left(\$100 + (N-1) \times \alpha \times \$100\right).$$

Comparing, she participates if

$$\alpha \geq \frac{1}{10}\left(\frac{N-10}{N-1}\right).$$

The right-hand side is bounded above by $\frac{1}{10}$. Hence, in this example, even with just 10% altruism, it is an equilibrium for everyone to participate. People have less of an incentive to free ride when concern for others leads them to internalize at least some of the positive externalities they impose on others.

Of course, it remains an open question whether you can actually educate or persuade people to have this kind of altruistic view. You might not want to count on it.

4.6.2 A Market in Externalities

Another way to move toward efficiency in the face of externalities is to clearly define property rights and facilitate private exchange. That is, assign someone the right to impose an externality and then make it easy for that person to sell that right to the person (or people) who will bear the externality. Let's see how this works in the context of another famous example of negative externalities.

Suppose that train tracks run through a neighborhood with one resident. The railroad company gets a net benefit, $B > 0$, from running the trains. The resident of the neighborhood suffers a cost, $C > 0$, from the trains running, due to pollution (or what have you). Assume both the railroad and the resident have quasi-linear preferences.

In this model, running trains imposes a negative externality on the resident of the neighborhood. (Alternatively, we could say that the resident of the neighborhood living in peace and quiet imposes a negative externality on the railroad.) When the railroad decides whether to run trains, it ignores the resident's costs. Hence, the railroad might make a socially suboptimal decision. Indeed, the railroad always wants to run trains, since $B > 0$. But it is only socially optimal to run trains if $B > C$.

Let's do a little thought experiment. Imagine two property rights arrangements:

1. The railroad owns the right to decide whether or not trains run.
2. The neighborhood resident owns the right to decide whether or not trains run.

If the railroad and resident can negotiate costlessly, then the first best will be achieved regardless of who owns the property right. To see this, we'll break our example up into two cases: (*i*) when it is socially optimal to run trains ($B > C$) and (*ii*) when it is socially optimal not to run trains ($B < C$).

Start by assuming $B > C$, so running trains is socially optimal. Now, imagine the railroad owns the property right. What will happen? The railroad makes a profit of B from running the trains. The resident is willing to pay up to C not to have the trains run. But $B > C$, so the resident is not willing to pay the railroad enough to convince it not to run trains. Hence, trains run.

Now suppose the resident owns the property right. What will happen? Again, the railroad makes a profit of B from running trains and the resident bears a cost of C. Since $B > C$, the railroad is willing to pay the resident more than C to be allowed to run trains. The resident finds this deal worthwhile and sells the railroad the right to run trains. Hence, just like when the railroad owns the property right, trains run.

The same logic applies if running trains is inefficient (i.e., if $B < C$). If the railroad owns the property right, the resident is prepared to pay the railroad more than B not to run trains. Hence, the railroad won't run trains. If the resident owns the property right, the railroad is not willing to pay enough to convince the resident to let it run trains, so trains won't run. Either way, trains don't run.

What have we seen? If transactions between the railroad and the resident can be made without cost, then trains run if it is socially optimal and don't if it is not, regardless of who owns the property right. Of course, the final individual welfares depend on who owns the property right, since the property right is valuable. So the point is not that the assignment of property rights is irrelevant for individual welfare. It simply doesn't affect whether or not trains run because the socially optimal action maximizes the size of the pie. And with costless transfers, the two sides always want the largest amount of total utility to split between themselves.

The logic illustrated above is an example of an idea known as the *Coase theorem*, after the economist Ronald Coase. If the right to impose an externality can be bought and sold without transaction costs, and if the property right to the externality is clearly defined and enforced, then bargaining between the concerned parties leads to efficient outcomes.

It is worth noting that the example we just analyzed exhibited two interesting features:

1. The outcome is Pareto efficient.
2. The outcome (trains run or not) is invariant to the initial assignment of property rights.

As I discussed in the introduction to this book, it is important, when thinking about a model, to ask which features of it are robust and which might not stand up to a small change in assumptions. It turns out that the first feature of this model—that bargaining between parties without transaction costs yields a Pareto efficient outcome—is pretty robust.[11] However, the second feature of the model—that the actual outcome is invariant to the assignment of property rights—depends on some special assumptions we made. In particular, this result need not hold if players don't have quasi-linear preferences.

To see this, suppose the resident has payoffs from money given by the square root of her final wealth and that she starts with wealth $w > C^2$. Let's see when she'd now be willing to buy the property right if the railroad owns it and when she'd be willing to sell the property right if she owns it.

If the railroad owns the property right, the resident would be willing to buy it from the railroad for an amount t if

$$\sqrt{w - t} > -C + \sqrt{w},$$

---

[11]Though there is an important caveat. Myerson and Satterthwaite (1983) show that if people don't know each other's preferences (i.e., the railroad is uncertain of C and the resident is uncertain of B), then bargaining is not certain to yield an efficient outcome, even when transaction costs are zero.

which is true if

$$t < 2C\sqrt{w} - C^2.$$

Assuming the railroad still has quasi-linear preferences, it is willing to sell for $t \geq B$. Hence, if the railroad starts with the property right, the outcome will be:

- The railroad runs trains if $B > 2C\sqrt{w} - C^2$.
- The resident pays the railroad to not run trains if $B < 2C\sqrt{w} - C^2$.

Now suppose the resident owns the property right. She is willing to sell it to the railroad for an amount t if

$$-C + \sqrt{w + t} > \sqrt{w},$$

which is true if

$$t > 2C\sqrt{w} + C^2.$$

The railroad is willing to pay any amount $t < B$. So, if the resident starts with the property right, the outcome will be:

- The railroad pays the resident to allow trains to run if $B > 2C\sqrt{w} + C^2$.
- The resident prevents trains from running if $B < 2C\sqrt{w} + C^2$.

In all cases, the outcome is Pareto efficient—there does not exist another outcome that makes at least one person better off and no one worse off. But whether or not trains run is not invariant to the initial assignment of property rights. If the railroad owns the property right, trains run if $B > 2C\sqrt{w} - C^2$. If the resident owns the property right, trains run if $B > 2C\sqrt{w} + C^2$, which is a more demanding requirement.

Leaving aside outcome invariance, the Coase theorem raises a provocative question: given that allowing for buying and selling externalities gets us Pareto efficiency, why are we worried about externalities at all? There are several answers.

First, in many circumstances it may be infeasible or undesirable to define property rights. What would it mean to give one person or another a property right to clean air, the oceans, or the internet? How would we decide who owns that right? Surely there are things which, because of our shared humanity, we must actually share in common.

Second, even if we are prepared to dole out property rights to the air and seas, how would one think about enforcing those property rights? If I own one patch of sea and you own another, but fish can swim between them, who owns the right to catch the fish? If a river runs through multiple countries, and each depends on it for drinking and agriculture, does it make sense to say one country or another owns a property right to the water? (For a real example of conflict over such a question, consider the Jordan River.) Similar problems exist for oil reserves, clean air, and so on. Thus, technological feasibility is often a constraint on establishing and enforcing property rights. If property rights can't be enforced or defined, how can they be traded?

Third, a key assumption of these efficiency results is that the railroad and resident can reach agreements and transfer utility for free. In actuality, such transactions require attorneys, loans, bankers, meetings, and so on. As a result, it could well be that $B > C$ and yet, if the resident owns the property right and there are transaction costs (T) that are large ($T > B - C$), it is not worth it to the resident and the railroad to reach a deal whereby trains are run. Hence, the presence of transaction costs can prevent us from achieving efficiency.

A final issue involves the presence of multiple parties. The example we looked at involved two parties reaching an agreement. Things become more complicated when there are multiple parties, some winners and some losers from a transaction. Imagine that instead of a railroad and a resident, there was a railroad and a collection of many residents. Those residents might like to negotiate with the railroad to reach a Coasean agreement, but they may face an internal collective action problem. That is, as in our discussion of diffuse interests in Chapter 4.2.3, they may fail to organize to negotiate, leaving opportunities for Pareto improvements between the residents and the railroad unfulfilled.

For all of these reasons, while it is always important to think about these sort of decentralized policy solutions, we cannot use the Coase theorem to justify ignoring the problem of externalities and hope that clear assignment of property rights will always solve the problems associated with them.

4.6.3 Ongoing Relationships and Self-Organization

In her classic book *Governing the Commons*, Elinor Ostrom tells the story of water irrigation in the Spanish cities of Murcia and Orihuela. The Segura River runs through these cities on its way to the Mediterranean. Water is scarce in the region and so the river plays a critical role in local agriculture. This creates an externalities problem akin to the tragedy of the commons. Individual farmers can extract water from the river to irrigate their fields. But there is not enough water for everyone. The social optimum involves sharing the water. But upstream farmers have incentives to extract as much water as they need, leaving too little for those downstream.

During the Middle Ages, no government authority regulated water use in these cities. And, so, based on our analysis thus far, one might have expected that terribly inefficient outcomes prevailed. But Ostrom reports otherwise.

Player 2

	Cooperate	Defect
Cooperate	2, 2	–1, 3
Defect	3, –1	0, 0

Player 1

Figure 4.6. Prisoner's Dilemma.

The farmers of Murcia and Orihuela self-organized, creating norms of water sharing whereby farmers had the right to irrigate their fields on a rotating basis. The norms made it possible for everyone to have access to at least some water.

There is a significant puzzle here. Our analysis suggests that upstream farmers should not have been willing to follow the sharing norms. While such norms create social efficiency, it is individually rational to defect from such an agreement and, instead, extract all the water you need. But according to Ostrom, the water-sharing norms worked successfully for hundreds of years.

As Ostrom explains, the farmers did more than simply reach an agreement. They created informal institutions to enforce the agreement. Farmers were empowered to monitor one another's water use. Farmers found to be taking water to which they were not entitled could be reported to the larger community and punished (with fines, social sanctions, and so on). While there was no formal governmental authority to enforce the agreement, the farmers were able to self-enforce.

The key difference between this story and the models of externalities we have studied thus far is the ongoing nature of the relationship among the farmers. In our models, people interact once and then the game ends. In reality, people often interact with one another repeatedly. In settings where this ongoing relationship is valuable, groups may be able to self-organize into cooperative agreements. In such an arrangement, each individual has an incentive to engage in good behavior to maintain relations with the community. Something like this seems to be at the root of the success of the farmers of Murcia and Orihuela. They were a small and sufficiently tight-knit community that they could monitor one another and coordinate on punishing people who misbehaved. And, in this way, they were able to avoid the tragedy of the commons.

Let's look at a model that incorporates this idea of ongoing relationships to see how self-organization might emerge. To do so, I'll focus on a particularly simple model of externalities called the prisoner's dilemma (represented in Figure 4.6). Two people interact. Each can either deal honestly with the other (cooperate) or cheat the other (defect). There is a payoff to cheating the other player. And there is a cost to being cheated—if they both cooperate, they engage in a productive interaction.[12]

The dilemma is this. It is a best response to play Defect regardless of what the other player will do. Hence, the game has a unique Nash equilibrium, (Defect, Defect), even though that outcome is Pareto dominated by (Cooperate, Cooperate). The prisoner's dilemma has negative externalities—if you play Defect, you make me worse off. Thus, you can think of this inefficiency coming from a failure to internalize externalities.

To get a handle on the logic of ongoing relationships, we will study a model of people playing the prisoner's dilemma over and over again, indefinitely. In Appendix B.7, I explain how we model players thinking about the value of payoffs in the future. Here I assume you know that material. Players discount future payoffs according to the discount factor $\delta \in (0, 1)$.

Suppose players use strategies that call on them to behave differently depending on how they have interacted in the past. One such strategy is called the *Grim Trigger*:

- Begin the game playing Cooperate.
- If we have both always played Cooperate in the past, play Cooperate today.
- If either of us has ever played Defect in the past, play Defect today.

The Grim Trigger creates a benefit to cooperating. If I cooperate today, then I anticipate that we will both cooperate in the future. But if I defect today, then I anticipate both defecting forever after. Thus, defecting today means forgoing the benefits of cooperating in the future. The hope is that this concern about future payoffs is sufficient to get us both to play cooperatively today. Let's see.

First, notice that if both players play the Grim Trigger, then they will in fact cooperate with each other forever. How do I know this? The strategy calls on players to start the game cooperating. It then calls on them to keep cooperating as long as they have both always cooperated in the past. If they in fact both play the Grim Trigger strategy, they will have always cooperated in the past, so they will never actually have to switch to defecting. So if both players playing the Grim Trigger is a Nash equilibrium, then the players are able to overcome the social dilemma through repeated interaction. We determine whether both players playing the Grim Trigger is a Nash equilibrium as we always do in a

---

[12]The prisoner's dilemma got its name from the story that originally motivated it. Two people jointly commit a crime. The police put the two criminals in separate rooms and offer each the following deal: If you confess and your partner does not, I'll let you go and I'll throw the book at him. If neither of you confess, I'll still prosecute, but you'll be convicted of a somewhat lesser crime. If neither confesses, you'll likely both get off with a minor charge.

game—by asking whether either player has a unilateral incentive to change her behavior.

Suppose the two players are in some period in which both players have always cooperated in the past. Let's focus on Player 1 (Player 2 is exactly symmetric). To see if Player 1 has a unilateral incentive to change her behavior, we assume Player 2 is using the Grim Trigger strategy and then ask whether Player 1 can make a higher payoff by using some strategy other than the Grim Trigger.

If Player 1 sticks with the Grim Trigger, then the two players will continue to cooperate forever. So Player 1 anticipates that, if she sticks with the Grim Trigger, she will get a payoff of 2 in every period. That is, she will make a payoff of

$$2 + \delta \times 2 + \delta^2 \times 2 + \delta^3 \times 2 + \ldots = 2(1 + \delta + \delta^2 + \delta^3 + \ldots) = \frac{2}{1-\delta}.$$

What if, instead, she changes behavior by defecting? Then she will make a payoff of 3 today, which is a short-term benefit. But in the future, Player 2 (who is assumed to play the Grim Trigger) will always defect. Thus, in all future periods, Player 1 will make payoffs of at most 0 (if she also defects). Hence, Player 1 thinks the payoff of her best unilateral change of behavior (which is to defect forever) is

$$3 + 0 \times \delta + 0 \times \delta^2 + 0 \times \delta^3 + \ldots = 3.$$

Player 1 faces a trade-off. On the one hand, if she unilaterally defects, she gets a short-term benefit: making 3 today instead of 2. On the other hand, she pays a long-term cost: making 0 in future periods rather than 2. Is this short-term benefit worth the long-term cost? That depends on how much Player 1 cares about future payoffs. In particular, there is not a profitable unilateral change of behavior if

$$\frac{2}{1-\delta} \geq 3 \Rightarrow \delta \geq \frac{1}{3}.$$

Since Player 2's incentives are exactly the same as Player 1's, if we did this calculation for Player 2 we'd find the same constraint.

If the players care enough about the future, then it is a Nash equilibrium of the infinitely repeated prisoner's dilemma for both players to play the Grim Trigger. In this equilibrium, the players cooperate with each other, achieving efficiency despite the social dilemma that exists in the one-shot game.

Here we have an equilibrium that appears roughly like the kind of self-organized cooperation that Ostrom describes emerging among the farmers of Murcia and Orihuela. Players use the leverage generated by their ongoing relationship to establish a kind of cautious trust, whereby they internalize their externalities because of the threat of future punishment if they fail to do so.

This is a very exciting result. Perhaps the social dilemma isn't so bad after all. In many important spheres, people interact repeatedly. The analysis and example above suggest that, as long as people care enough about the long run, they can self-organize to achieve efficient outcomes even without a policy intervention. (Good news if you are a person. Bad news, perhaps, if you are getting a public policy degree.) Before you despair of a career in public policy, let's think about how far we want to push this argument for non-governmental solutions to social dilemmas.

OTHER EQUILIBRIA

Our analysis of the infinitely repeated prisoner's dilemma shows that if people care enough about the future, then the game has an equilibrium in which players cooperate with one another. That said, it also always has equilibria in which there is no cooperation.

To see this, consider the strategy profile in which both players always choose Defect. This strategy profile is also an equilibrium of the repeated prisoner's dilemma. In any given period, regardless of what you do, the other player will always defect in the future. Thus, you face a choice, period after period, of either defecting (and making 0) or cooperating (and making −1). Clearly, if the other player will always choose Defect regardless of what you do, your best response is to always choose Defect. Hence, we have a Nash equilibrium in which players never cooperate.

Let's be clear about what this means. It is not the case, no matter how patient players are, that the only possible outcome of the repeated prisoner's dilemma is cooperative. It is always an equilibrium for players to defect against each other. So, while a self-organized solution to the externalities problem is sometimes feasible, there is no guarantee that it will happen.

This fact points to a potentially important role for leadership. Earlier we argued that neither communication nor moral suasion were likely to be effective in situations characterized by externalities. But that need not be the case when there is a possibility to use repeated interaction to achieve self-organized cooperation. In such circumstances, good outcomes depend on society reaching the right equilibrium. It might be that effective leadership and communication can help push society in that direction by helping to organize self-enforcing norms of good behavior and sanctions for bad behavior. And, since the good outcome is in fact an equilibrium, if a leader can get people to settle on that pattern of behavior, it will be stable. We will return to this theme in Chapter 5.2.

LARGE SOCIETIES

There is a cooperative equilibrium in the repeated prisoner's dilemma when the short-run benefits of defecting are outweighed by the long-run costs in terms of forgone cooperation. Our analysis thus far indicates that this will be true when players are sufficiently patient. But there are other factors, besides patience, that might affect the long-run costs of defection and, thus, the feasibility of self-organized solutions.

Suppose you live in a large society. Each day you interact with someone by playing the prisoner's dilemma. But you may not interact with the same person day after day. The relative anonymity offered by a large society significantly lowers the costs of defecting. In a large society, if I defect against someone today, odds are I won't have to interact with that person again for quite some time. Consequently, it probably won't be until some point in the far future that I suffer any punishment for my misdeeds. This suggests that, in large societies, it may be harder for people to solve social dilemmas without policy interventions.

To make this a bit clearer, let's think about a model. There are N people (with N even for simplicity). In each period, each person is randomly paired with another person to play the prisoner's dilemma. Players only observe what happens in their own personal interactions, not what happens in interactions in which they are not involved. The probability Player i meets Player j in a given period is $p_{i,j}$.

Consider a strategy profile in which everyone plays the following strategy, which is analogous to the Grim Trigger:

- Play Cooperate with anyone you have never met before.
- If interacting with a player you have met before, Cooperate today if you have both always played Cooperate against each other in the past.
- If interacting with a player you have met before, Defect today if either of you has ever played Defect against the other in the past.

Under what conditions is this modified Grim Trigger strategy profile a Nash equilibrium in our game with a large society?

Suppose that two players, i and j, are paired in some period and that they have always cooperated with one another in the past. Let's focus on Player i. If Player i sticks with the Grim Trigger (i.e., cooperates), she will get a payoff of 2 in every period in which she and Player j interact. Moreover, this interaction will have no effect on her payoff when interacting with any other player. Call her expected payoff from an interaction in some period in which she doesn't interact with Player j $v_{i,-j}$. In any given period, she interacts with Player j with probability $p_{i,j}$ and with other players with probability $1 - p_{i,j}$. So, if Player i cooperates with

Player j, she will make an expected payoff of

$$2 + \delta \left(p_{i,j}2 + (1 - p_{i,j})v_{i,-j} \right) + \delta^2 \left(p_{i,j}2 + (1 - p_{i,j})v_{i,-j} \right)$$
$$+ \delta^3 \left(p_{i,j}2 + (1 - p_{i,j})v_{i,-j} \right) + \ldots .$$

This can be rewritten as

$$2 + \delta \left(p_{i,j}2 + (1 - p_{i,j})v_{i,-j} \right) \left(1 + \delta + \delta^2 + \delta^3 + \ldots \right),$$

which can be rewritten

$$2 + \frac{\delta}{1 - \delta} \left(p_{i,j}2 + (1 - p_{i,j})v_{i,-j} \right).$$

What if, instead, Player i defects against Player j? She will make a payoff of 3 today, which is a short-term benefit. But in the future, Player j will always Defect when they meet. Thus, in all future interactions with Player j, Player i will make a payoff of 0. Player i's defection has no effect on her interactions with players other than j. So her expected payoff from interacting with a player other than j in the future remains $v_{i,-j}$. Hence, Player i's expected payoff from her best unilateral change of behavior (which is to defect against j forever) is

$$3 + \delta \left(p_{i,j}0 + (1 - p_{i,j})v_{i,-j} \right) + \delta^2 \left(p_{i,j}0 + (1 - p_{i,j})v_{i,-j} \right)$$
$$+ \delta^3 \left(p_{i,j}0 + (1 - p_{i,j})v_{i,-j} \right) + \ldots .$$

This can be rewritten as

$$3 + \delta(1 - p_{i,j})v_{i,-j} \left(1 + \delta + \delta^2 + \delta^3 + \ldots \right),$$

which is equal to

$$3 + \frac{\delta}{1 - \delta}(1 - p_{i,j})v_{i,-j}.$$

Player i faces a trade-off similar to the trade-off in the two-person repeated prisoner's dilemma. On the one hand, if she unilaterally switches to defecting, she gets a short-term benefit: making 3 today instead of 2. On the other hand, she pays a long-term cost: making 0 in future interactions with Player j rather than 2. But the long-term cost is lower than it was in the repeated prisoner's dilemma with only two players. This is because Player i does not interact with Player j every period. We can compare the two expected payoffs in the N-player game to find that there is not a profitable unilateral change in behavior if

$$2 + \frac{\delta}{1 - \delta} \left(p_{i,j}2 + (1 - p_{i,j})v_{i,-j} \right) \geq 3 + \frac{\delta}{1 - \delta}(1 - p_{i,j})v_{i,-j}.$$

Rearranging, this implies that Players i and j can cooperate if

$$\delta \geq \frac{1}{1 + 2p_{i,j}}. \tag{4.7}$$

There are a couple of things to note here. First, if $p_{i,j} = 1$ (so that Players i and j meet every period), this condition reduces to $\delta \geq \frac{1}{3}$, precisely the condition we got in the two-player repeated prisoner's dilemma. This is as it should be.

Second, and more importantly, the smaller $p_{i,j}$ is (i.e., the less likely it is that the two players meet in any given interaction), the higher δ must be for it to be a best response for Player i to cooperate with Player j. This is intuitive. When $p_{i,j}$ is very small, the cost of defecting is very low, since Player i will seldom interact with Player j and, so, will only rarely be punished for defecting. Hence, temptation is great and cooperation is hard to sustain—a fact that is reflected in needing ever more patient players.

What might make $p_{i,j}$ small? Several factors come to mind. Two players may be unlikely to interact if they are in different ethnic groups, live in different areas, work in different industries, or are simply part of a larger society. In all of these cases, cooperative behavior is harder to sustain among players who expect not to see and interact with one another frequently. Self-organized solutions are most likely to emerge in smaller or more tightly knit groups.

More generally, the model suggests that as the pool of people one interacts with increases, it becomes harder and harder to sustain cooperation without a policy intervention. To see this, suppose that all players are equally likely to be paired. Then, for any pair (i, j), $p_{i,j} = \frac{1}{N-1}$. Given this, as society gets larger, the probability of any two particular people interacting in any given period gets smaller. Condition 4.7 tells us how patient players must be, as a function of the size of society, for cooperation to be sustainable in equilibrium:

$$\delta \geq \frac{1}{1 + \frac{2}{N-1}}.$$

This condition is illustrated in Figure 4.7. As the figure shows, for even moderately sized groups of potential partners, cooperation becomes difficult to sustain.

This implies two key facts. First, small, tight-knit groups are more likely than larger groups to successfully self-organize to solve externalities problems without intervention. In large groups, players are too anonymous, resulting in low costs to defection. Thus, while small groups are not guaranteed to find cooperative equilibria (remember, non-cooperative equilibria always also exist), it is more likely that doing so will be feasible for such groups.

Second, one key problem of using repeat play to achieve cooperation in large groups is a lack of information. If players could observe how people other

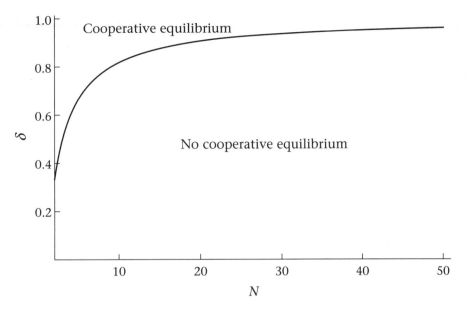

Figure 4.7. How high δ must be to sustain cooperation in equilibrium, as a function of the size of the population.

than those they directly interacted with behaved, then they could punish bad behavior that was directed against others. Hence, institutions or actors that facilitate information sharing might be a fairly non-intrusive way to facilitate efficiency by allowing broader-based punishment strategies. As an example, think of rating services on Amazon, eBay, or Uber, which allow cooperative behavior to emerge among large groups of people who do not know one another at all. These ratings allow broad-based punishment for bad behavior. If a seller were to cheat a buyer, the buyer would report that seller's bad behavior, allowing *other buyers* to stop interacting with that seller. And if a buyer were to cheat a seller, the seller would report that buyer's bad behavior, allowing *other sellers* to stop interacting with that buyer.

IMPERFECT MONITORING

Another problem that might limit the ability of people to achieve efficiency without government intervention is imperfect monitoring. The use of punishment strategies requires that I know whether you defected against me or not. But suppose there is some chance that I mistakenly believe you acted well when you acted poorly or vice versa. In such a circumstance, whether or not you are punished is tied less directly to your behavior, diminishing the costs of defection and the benefits of cooperation. The effects of this are not unlike the effects of a large society. If I think I will only be punished some of the time if I defect (and will only be rewarded some of the time if I cooperate), then I am more inclined to defect. Hence, in an environment where the behavior of individuals is difficult to observe or monitor, it is less likely that people can successfully self-organize to solve externalities problems.

4.7 Takeaways

- A situation in which one person's actions affect another person's payoffs is called a situation with *externalities*.
- Because people don't take the externalities they impose on others into consideration when making decisions, externalities create socially inefficient outcomes.
- Collective action and public goods provision are both examples of situations with positive externalities. The commons is an example of a situation with negative externalities.
- Pigovian subsidies for actions with positive externalities induce people to internalize their externalities and move society in the direction of Pareto improvements. Pigovian taxation of actions with negative externalities does likewise.
- Typically, policy interventions that help people internalize their externalities impose their own, new, inefficiencies. Hence, the socially optimal policy intervention is typically not the one that actually gets people all the way to the first best. Rather, it trades the benefits of increased internalization of externalities off against the costs of the intervention itself. The socially optimal intervention and the associated actions are referred to as the *second best*.
- In settings with repeated interaction, it is sometimes feasible for groups to self-organize a solution to externalities problems. Such self-organized solutions are most likely in close-knit and small groups. But even in such groups, they are not certain to emerge.

4.8 Further Reading

Any intermediate microeconomics textbook will include an extensive discussion of externalities. There are lots of good ones.

Mancur Olson's *The Logic of Collective Action* is the classic statement of the collective action problem, while Hardin (1968) articulates the tragedy of the commons. Mankiw (2009) is a nice, accessible introduction to Pigovian taxation.

Coase (1960) provides the intellectual foundations for the Coase theorem. It is worth noting that Coase clearly believed that transaction costs were typically high and, thus, that a purely market-based approach was not a feasible way of addressing externalities problems.

There is also much worth reading on the topic of decentralized solutions. Elinor Ostrom's celebrated *Governing the Commons* is an essential source on the success and failure of self-organization. Milgrom, North, and Weingast (1990) is a classic game theoretic and historical analysis of the role of repeat interactions in self-organization. Fearon and Laitin (1996) discuss these issues in the context of interethnic conflict and cooperation.

4.9   Exercises

1.   Reanswer Problem 6 from Chapter 1 in light of the lessons of this chapter.

2.   Consider an example of the collective action model from Section 4.1 in which there are one thousand people. Each individual values the outcome at $100 and finds the cost of participation to be $10.

   (a) Is it a best response for a player to participate or not participate?

   Suppose, now, that you offer everyone a subsidy if they participate. The subsidy is funded through inefficient taxation. Raising $1 of revenue costs the taxpayers τ. As in the chapter, an individual's subsidy is funded by everyone other than her paying an equal share of the necessary tax (so my taxes go to fund everyone's subsidy other than my own).

   (b) What is the lowest subsidy that would make it a best response for a player to participate?
   (c) Suppose the government were to offer that subsidy, so that everyone were to participate. What would be an individual's tax burden?
   (d) Given this, what would be the social payoff with the subsidy?
   (e) Given this, for what values of τ is it better for utilitarian social welfare to offer this subsidy rather than offer no subsidy?

3.   As we saw in Section 4.3, the first-best number of boats in the tragedy of commons game is 45. But, if taxes are distortionary, then the socially optimal (i.e., second-best) number of boats is not equal to the first best.

   Let's assume we tax each boat at a rate of t dollars and then redistribute the revenues—giving the revenues collected from firm 1 to firm 2 and the revenues collected from firm 2 to firm 1. As in Section 4.4, there is some inefficiency associated with taxation—for each dollar distributed, the government must collect $\tau > 1$ dollars. That is, if the two firms run b_1 and b_2 boats, total taxes collected are $t(b_1 + b_2)$, but firm 1 gets back only $\frac{tb_2}{\tau}$ and firm 2 gets back only $\frac{tb_1}{\tau}$. We can explore the second-best number of boats in this setting.

(a) Given the tax policy, t, what are firm i's expected payoffs, if it believes the other firm will run b_{-i} boats?

(b) Calculate firm i's best response to the tax rate t and b_{-i} boats by the other firm ($\mathrm{BR}_i(b_{-i}, t)$).

(c) By substituting one firm's best response into the other's, what is the equilibrium number of boats each firm will run, given a tax rate t?

(d) Given equilibrium behavior, for any tax rate t, what is each firm's total payoff?

(e) Use your answer to the previous question to write down the utilitarian social welfare as a function of the tax rate t.

(f) Use your answer to the previous question to compute the second-best tax rate and the implied second best number of boats run by each firm.

(g) Show that the second best number of boats is larger than the first-best number of boats run by each firm.

4. Consider the model of cleaning an apartment in Appendix A.2.3. Suppose the government offers a subsidy, σ, for each unit of effort by each person. So if person i chooses effort s_i, she receives a subsidy of $\sigma \times s_i$.

The subsidy is funded through taxation. Each player pays the tax for the other person's subsidy. Moreover, taxation is inefficient. Each dollar of subsidy paid costs the tax payer $\tau > 1$ dollars. So if person 1 receives a subsidy of $\sigma \times s_1$, then player 2's tax burden is $\sigma \times s_1 \times \tau$.

(a) Write down each player's utility given a strategy profile (s_1, s_2) and a subsidy rate σ.

(b) Solve for each player's best response as a function of the other player's strategy and the subsidy.

(c) Identify the Nash equilibrium level of effort by the players, given a subsidy σ.

(d) Write down each player's payoff in equilibrium as a function of the subsidy.

(e) Use your answer to part (d) to write down the utilitarian social welfare as a function of σ.

(f) Use your answer to part (e) to solve for the second-best subsidy and effort.

(g) The first-best effort in this model is 2. Show, given the inefficiency of taxes, that the second-best subsidy leads to higher payoffs than either no subsidy or a subsidy that leads players to choose the first-best effort.

5. An influential argument makes the following claim: A well-functioning democracy requires that voters actually know what policies would be in

their interests so that they can vote for politicians who implement such policies. However, the argument continues, in a democratic system there is a "public goods problem" with respect to information leading to systematically bad vote decisions and, thus, policy choices in democracies.

(a) Explain what externality this argument is pointing to in claiming there is a public goods problem.

(b) Consider the following model. There are three voters a, b, and c and two candidates advocating two different policies 1 and 2. None of the voters know which policy would be better for her. Moreover, the voters believe it is equally likely that they each prefer either policy.

Each voter, individually, can either invest in becoming an informed voter (at cost C) or not (at cost 0). If a voter invests, she learns the policy she prefers, but she does not have the opportunity to communicate it to the other voters. Moreover, let's assume (for simplicity) that, were they all informed, all the voters would prefer the same policy (i.e., there is a correct policy). The payoff of having the correct policy chosen is $B > C$. The payoff of having the wrong policy chosen is 0.

Assume all voters vote and that if a voter is uninformed she flips a coin to choose between 1 and 2.

   i. Suppose a voter expects the other two voters not to become informed. What has to be true about the relationship between B and C for her to become informed?
   ii. Suppose a voter expects one of the other voters to become informed and one of the other voters not to become informed. Under what conditions on B and C will she become informed?
   iii. Suppose a voter expects both other voters to become informed. Under what conditions on B and C will she become informed?
   iv. Given the answers above, there are two things that can happen in equilibrium. What happens in equilibrium if $C < B/4$? What happens in equilibrium if $C > B/4$?

(c) Compare this to a model with one voter who simply chooses the policy. Under what conditions does this single voter become informed?

(d) How does the comparison of the results from parts (b) and (c) illustrate the public goods problem in democracy?

(e) Suggest a policy one could implement to increase the number of voters who become informed.

(f) What do you think would happen as we increased the number of voters in part (b)? Why?

6.   Consider a public good created through costly effort by individuals. Since there are positive externalities, the outcome is Pareto inefficient. As such, the government decides to implement subsidies. But the tax used to fund the subsidies also creates inefficiencies.

     (a) Which is higher: the first-best or second-best level of public goods? Why?

     (b) Is the utilitarian payoff higher if the government chooses the subsidy that induces the first-best or second-best level of public goods? Why?

7.   Describe a substantive policy issue (that I didn't talk about in the chapter) where you think that people are imposing (positive or negative) externalities.

     (a) Is the result of the externalities, in your example, too much or too little of a particular kind of behavior relative to the social optimum?

     (b) What sort of policy intervention do you think might be effective at mitigating the problem?

     (c) Give at least one reason why the socially optimal policy intervention is *not* the intervention that would give rise to the first-best original behavior, but instead, some lesser amount of policy intervention that gives rise to second-best behavior.

8.   A medical researcher is trying to cure a disease. For each unit of effort she puts into her work, she generates a utility benefit of 10 for each member of society. There are 1,000 people in society besides the medical researcher.

     The medical researcher doesn't care about other people. She is in it for the glory. For each unit of effort she puts into her work, she gets a utility benefit of 1000 (which is inclusive of the 10 that she gets for being a member of society, plus a payoff of 990 in glory). If she exerts effort e, she also suffers cost e^2.

     (a) The medical researcher's payoff from exerting effort e is $1000e - e^2$. What level of effort, e^*, will she exert?

     (b) Suppose a policymaker who was a committed utilitarian (including caring about the medical researcher's glory, since the medical researcher cares about it) was to choose the level of effort the medical researcher exerts. That policymaker would add up the total utility in society (including the medical researcher's utility) from any given level of effort and choose the level of effort that maximizes that aggregate utility.

       i. What (social) utility function would the policymaker maximize?

       ii. Would the policymaker like the medical researcher to exert more or less effort than your answer to part (a)? Why? (Use words, not math, to answer this.)

      iii. What level of effort, e^{FB}, would the policymaker demand of the medical researcher?

      iv. Suppose that the policymaker wanted to implement this first-best policy (e^{FB}) by paying the medical researcher a subsidy σ for each unit of effort. What level of subsidy, σ^{FB}, must the policymaker offer to get the medical research to choose the first-best level of effort?

(c) Suppose, now, that our policymaker can only pay for the subsidy through inefficient taxation. In particular, assume that if a total subsidy of $e\sigma$ must be paid to the researcher, then a total amount of revenues $2e\sigma$ must be collected. The tax burden will be shared equally by everyone except the medical researcher (who pays no taxes). Assume taxes come linearly out of the payoffs of each member of society. Suppose the policymaker chooses the subsidy that maximizes the utilitarian payoff, taking account of these taxes and the level of medical research.

      i. What (social) utility function would the policymaker maximize?

      ii. Will the subsidy she chooses, σ^{SB}, be higher or lower than the subsidy, σ^{FB}, that implemented the first-best effort? Why?

      iii. Calculate the second-best subsidy that the policymaker will implement.

9.   Two people, A and B, are deciding whether to put effort into producing a public good or not. Each person, i, can either choose no effort ($s_i = 0$) or yes effort ($s_i = 1$). The total public good produced is $G = s_A + s_B$. The cost of doing no effort is 0. The cost of doing yes effort is 1.5. The payoff to a player is the total public goods provided (G) minus her personal costs.

(a) Given a choice by player B, s_B, write down player A's utility from choosing no effort.

(b) Given a choice by player B, s_B, write down player A's utility from choosing yes effort.

(c) Comparing these two utilities, calculate player A's best response correspondence and write it down.

(d) Noticing that player B's problem is identical to player A's, what is the unique Nash equilibrium of this game?

(e) What is the utilitarian optimum in this game?

(f) In four sentences or less, explain why the Nash equilibrium represents a social dilemma and how this relates to the idea of positive externalities.

(g) Suppose that you can offer a subsidy of 1 for choosing yes effort, but that for each person you pay that subsidy you must collect tax revenue equal to $\tau > 1$. Assume that you will split the tax burden equally among the two players, regardless of who participates. For what values of τ is it Pareto improving to offer the subsidy-and-tax plan?

5

Coordination Problems

In 1933, the United States Congress passed the Tennessee Valley Authority Act, putting in motion one of the largest economic development projects in American history. The act created the Tennessee Valley Authority (TVA), a federally owned corporation with a mandate to rapidly modernize the economy of the Tennessee Valley—a swath of land covering much of Tennessee, Alabama, Kentucky, and Mississippi—which was among the poorest and least-developed parts of the United States.

Over the course of the 1940s and 1950s, the TVA built dozens of hydroelectric dams and hundreds of miles of navigation canals. It also invested in significant new road networks, schools, and flood control. Kline and Moretti (2014) report that during these two decades the TVA spent over $14 billion (measured in 2000 dollars). During the height of its spending in the 1950s, subsidies through the TVA amounted to 10% of average household income per family in the Tennessee Valley.

What was the effect of the TVA? In 1930, the Tennessee Valley had an overwhelmingly agricultural economy. By the mid-1940s, it was the largest supplier of electricity in the country. Moreover, Kline and Moretti find that during the period of peak investment by the TVA (i.e., the 1940s and 1950s) the ten-year growth rate in both agricultural and manufacturing employment was 10–12 percentage points higher than it would have been absent the TVA.

But most interesting are the different trajectories of the Tennessee Valley's agricultural and manufacturing sectors. Once federal subsidies began to decline (starting in the 1960s), not only did growth in the agricultural sector cease, but the gains that had been made during the 1940s and 1950s disappeared. After 1960, counties in the TVA saw a 13–16 percentage point decrease in the ten-year agricultural employment growth rate relative to non-TVA counties. This decline was sufficiently large that, by the end of the twentieth century, Kline and Moretti estimate the agricultural sector had declined on net.

Manufacturing is an entirely different story. Once federal subsidies stopped, the extraordinary growth rates in manufacturing declined. But they did not reverse. Indeed, Kline and Moretti show that manufacturing employment continued to grow at a rate approximately 3 percentage points higher in TVA counties relative to non-TVA counties.

Kline and Moretti argue that the TVA affected agriculture and manufacturing so differently because of what are known as *economies of agglomeration*. There are spatial returns to scale in certain industries. These returns to scale can come from many sources. For instance, if many firms are producing similar products in a particular city or region, then there are likely to be many qualified workers available locally. This decreases the costs of production. Similarly, when multiple firms in the same region work in the same industry, it becomes cost-effective to invest in industry-specific infrastructure, attracts industry innovators, and so on.

Such agglomeration economies give firms within an industry incentives to coordinate on locating in specific regions. As the number of firms in some industry increases in a region, locating in that region becomes more attractive to other firms within the same industry. It is typically thought that manufacturing has increasing returns to scale as a result of economies of agglomeration (Greenstone, Hornbeck, and Moretti, 2010), but that agriculture does not (Hornbeck and Naidu, 2014).

Given this, it is not surprising that the effects of the TVA were long lasting in manufacturing, but not in agriculture. The early investments from the TVA spurred manufacturing growth which put in motion a virtuous cycle of increasing returns. The TVA disappeared, but the agglomeration economy did not, so a positive effect on manufacturing persisted. No such agglomeration economy exists for agriculture. Thus, the early investments spurred agricultural employment through straightforward subsidization, but did not create increasing returns. Hence, once the subsidies disappeared, the positive effects disappeared as well.

This example highlights many of the most important features of our second type of social dilemma, coordination problems. In many situations, good outcomes require actors to coordinate their behavior in the right way. But two things can go wrong. First, actors may fail to coordinate entirely. For instance, different companies within an industry may locate in different regions, never realizing the benefits of agglomeration.

Second, actors may coordinate on a bad outcome, rather than a good outcome. Think about the much-discussed problem of *poverty traps* in economic development. The fundamental idea behind a poverty trap is a failure of coordination. A poor country lacks infrastructure and human capital (this is similar to the problems of a region lacking agglomeration economies). If that poor country could attract outside investors, it could raise revenues to build infrastructure and human capital. If an outside investor believes that other outside investors are going to invest, she believes the poor country will raise the necessary revenue and, thus, will want to invest herself. But if that outside investor believes other outside investors are not going to invest, she doesn't believe the poor country will raise the necessary revenue and, thus, does not invest herself. Each investor wants to do what the other investors are going to do, creating the possibility of a self-confirming poverty trap, whereby poor countries stay poor because everyone believes they will stay poor.

Collier (2007) explicitly links poverty traps in Africa and parts of Asia to agglomeration economies. He argues that in the 1980s and 1990s manufacturers moved production from the developed world to relatively stable, low-wage countries in Asia. This set off the virtuous cycle of agglomeration, as those economies grew, created infrastructure, and invested in human capital. Other countries missed this initial wave of offshoring. And now, because they lack both political stability and agglomeration economies, they are not attractive to manufacturers. Thus, these countries are trapped in poverty, at least until the wage differential between these truly poor countries and the middle-income manufacturing countries of Asia grows large enough that manufacturers are willing to relocate despite the absence of agglomeration economies.

There are many situations with the basic structure of a coordination problem. For instance, the adoption of a new technology often involves coordination. Whether you should purchase a Blu-ray or HD DVD player depends on which will become the dominant technology. And that depends on whether more people buy Blu-ray or HD DVD players. Thus, you want to buy a Blu-ray player if everyone else is going to buy a Blu-ray player and an HD DVD player if everyone else is going to buy an HD DVD player, regardless of which is actually the better technology. If you buy the wrong one, you will end up like all those people with eight-tracks and Betamaxes in their basements. You can tell a similar story about the adoption of business software (e.g., Excel vs. Lotus) and many other technologies.

You might think similarly about whether to buy an electric or hybrid car. Electric cars might be attractive, if the government and industry make an investment in the necessary infrastructure (e.g., lots of charging stations or exchangeable batteries). But the government and industry will only make such an investment if lots of people buy electric cars. So, again, you want to do what everyone else is doing.

An example closely related to the poverty traps story arises in thinking about public schools in urban environments. A common concern is that educated parents send their children to private schools, draining the public schools of a valuable resource. If educated parents believe other educated parents will send their children to the public schools, they might also be inclined to send their children to the public schools. The key, for any given parent, is to coordinate— sending their kids to the same kind of school as all the other educated parents.

Coordination games model these type of situations, characterized by what we call *strategic complementarities*—the benefit to one person of taking some action is larger the more that action is being taken by other people. Broadly speaking, coordination games come in three varieties.

First, there are pure coordination games, in which the only thing players care about is that they successfully coordinate. They are indifferent as to what action they coordinate on. This might, for example, describe the decision of which side of the road to drive on.

Second, there are coordination games with distributional consequences. Consider national governments trying to harmonize financial standards. All governments might agree that sharing a set of financial standards is good, as it encourages trade and foreign investment. However, if different countries have different economies, natural resources, financial institutions, and so on, then they may disagree on the optimal financial standards.

Third, there are coordination games with a Pareto dominated equilibrium. That is, games where everyone wants to coordinate, but in which we can all agree that coordinating on one outcome is better than coordinating on another. Think about bank runs. Suppose that if everyone withdraws their money but you don't, then you lose all your money because the bank folds. But if nobody withdraws their money, and you also don't, you make a reasonable interest rate. There are incentives to coordinate in such a scenario—if everyone else is going to withdraw their money, you want to withdraw yours, but if everyone leaves his or her money on deposit, you want to leave yours too. We can all agree that not having a bank run is preferable to having one. So, although we have coordination incentives, we prefer coordinating on one outcome rather than another. The public versus private school example discussed above might describe another such situation. Parents might prefer to coordinate on public schools, thereby saving tuition expenses. Poverty traps are another such example.

All three of these types of coordination games share some features. Importantly, we want to avoid coordination failure in all of them. But the last class of games—those with a Pareto dominated equilibrium—also suggest another set of issues. In particular, these games present the possibility of coordinating, but on the wrong outcome.

In this chapter, we consider both kind of problems. In Section 5.1 we focus on coordination failure due to strategic uncertainty—a dilemma that can arise in any of these situations. In Section 5.2 we turn our attention to coordination traps—the problem of coordinating on the wrong outcome in games with a Pareto dominated equilibrium.

5.1 Coordination Failure

For a company to list its shares on a stock exchange, that company must comply with national securities regulations. One particularly important such regulatory hurdle is producing books in compliance with relevant accounting rules.

| | Government | |
	Pump	Outlet

		Pump	Outlet
Car company	Hybrid	2, 2	0, 0
	Electric	0, 0	2, 2

Figure 5.1. A coordination game.

There are many stock exchanges in the world, including major exchanges in Frankfurt, London, New York, Hong Kong, and so on. In order to facilitate access to global capital markets, companies would often like to list on multiple exchanges. But historically there has been a problem. Each national securities regulator imposes a different set of accounting standards. This lack of harmonization forces companies that wish to list on multiple exchanges to bear the significant costs of producing multiple sets of books. It also reduces transparency for investors, since different accounting standards can produce wildly different pictures of a company's performance. For instance, Simmons (2001) relates the story of the German company Daimler Benz deciding in 1993 to list on the New York Stock Exchange in addition to the Frankfurt Stock Exchange. Under German accounting rules, Daimler reported a profit of 615 million deutsche marks for 1993. Under U.S. Generally Accepted Accounting Principles, it reported a loss of 1.8 billion deutsche marks for that same year.

The failure of coordination on a set of internationally recognized accounting standards imposes unnecessary costs on stock exchanges, investors, and corporations. Yet it has persisted for decades.

Let's study coordination failure in the simplest possible environment—a two-player, two-action, pure coordination game. For instance, consider the following model of a game between a car company and the government. The car company must decide whether to invest in hybrid or electric technology. The government must decide whether to encourage infrastructure investment in fuel pumps or electrical outlets. The two players are equally happy with hybrids or electrics becoming the new standard—but they want to coordinate. The game is represented in Figure 5.1.

I will talk about this particular game, but it should be clear that the game between the government and car company is just a metaphor for coordination problems in general. Change the names of the players and actions and you could think of this as a model of many different kinds of coordination— companies deciding what type of technology to invest in, governments choosing accounting standards, etc. Moreover, nothing that I am going to tell you depends on this being a situation of pure coordination. The same issues arise in all situations in which people have an incentive to coordinate—whether or not there are, for example, also distributional concerns.

Government

	Pump	Outlet
Hybrid	$2 + \theta_C, 2 + \theta_G$	0, 0
Electric	0, 0	2, 2

Car company

Figure 5.2. A coordination game with strategic uncertainty.

Start by noticing that this game has two (pure strategy) Nash equilibria: (Hybrid, Pump) and (Electric, Outlet). Given this, you might think that we are in the clear. Our prediction is that there will be no coordination failure.[1]

But suppose players face some *strategic uncertainty*. That is, the car company is uncertain how the government will behave and vice versa. This could be the case for a variety of reasons. Perhaps the car company thinks there is some chance that the government will be unduly influenced by special interests or that voter opinion could change and lead the government to reverse course. Perhaps the government thinks there is some chance the car company will make an important technological breakthrough, leading it to prefer one or the other type of car unexpectedly. There could be lots of reasons for players to feel uncertain about the strategy the other player will use.

We will model this strategic uncertainty in a particularly simple way—players are uncertain of each other's payoffs. Let's assume that there are two random variables, θ_C and θ_G, that represent this uncertainty. We refer to these as the players' *types*. Each player's type can take a value of 1 or −1. The two values are equally likely. The random variables are independent—so the value that θ_C takes provides no information about the value θ_G will take and vice versa. We will assume that the car company's payoff from the outcome (Hybrid, Pump) is $2 + \theta_C$ and, similarly, the government's payoff from (Hybrid, Pump) is $2 + \theta_G$. This modified game is represented in Figure 5.2.

Each player knows her own type, but not the other player's. Consequently, the players are uncertain which outcome the other player prefers. From the car company's (respectively, the government's) perspective, with probability 1/2 the government (respectively, the car company) gets a payoff of 3 from (Hybrid, Pump) and so prefers it to (Electric, Outlet). And from the car company's (respectively, the government's) perspective with probability 1/2 the government (respectively, the car company) gets a payoff of 1 from (Hybrid, Pump) and so prefers (Electric, Outlet). What do the Nash equilibria look like in this modified game with strategic uncertainty?

---

[1] As I do throughout, I'm not going to study mixed strategy Nash equilibria. Instead, below, I model strategic uncertainty explicitly.

A strategy profile specifies how each type of each player will behave. Hence, we can think of each player having four possible strategies. The car company's strategies are as follows:

- Always play Hybrid
- Play Hybrid if $\theta_C = 1$ and Electric if $\theta_C = -1$
- Play Hybrid if $\theta_C = -1$ and Electric if $\theta_C = 1$
- Always play Electric

The government's strategies are as follows:

- Always play Pump
- Play Pump if $\theta_G = 1$ and Outlet if $\theta_G = -1$
- Play Pump if $\theta_G = -1$ and Outlet if $\theta_G = 1$
- Always play Outlet

Call a strategy in which a player takes the same action regardless of her type *non-responsive* and a strategy in which a player's action depends on her type *responsive*. Notice, if Player *i* is using a responsive strategy, then from the perspective of the other player, Player *i* is randomizing between her two possible actions, playing each with probability 1/2.

The two equilibria we have identified in this game prior to introducing strategic uncertainty persist. If the government always plays Pump, the car company's best response is to always play Hybrid and vice versa. If the government always plays Outlet, then the car company's best response is to always play Electric and vice versa. Hence, (Always play Hybrid, Always play Pump) and (Always play Electric, Always play Outlet) are Nash equilibria of this game.

The presence of strategic uncertainty now also creates the possibility of another equilibrium, one in which players play responsive strategies. As we've already noted, if the government plays either of its responsive strategies, then from the perspective of the car company, the government is playing the action Pump with probability 1/2 and the action Outlet with probability 1/2. What is the car company's best response?

If the car company believes the government is using a responsive strategy, then the car company's expected payoff from the action Hybrid is

$$\frac{1}{2} \times (2 + \theta_C) + \frac{1}{2} \times 0.$$

Its expected payoff from the action Electric is

$$\frac{1}{2} \times 0 + \frac{1}{2} \times 2.$$

Comparing these expected payoffs, the car company strictly prefers the action Hybrid if $\theta_C = 1$ and strictly prefers the action Electric if $\theta_C = -1$. Hence, the car company's best response to either responsive strategy by the government is to play Hybrid if $\theta_C = 1$ and Electric if $\theta_C = -1$.

If the government believes the car company is playing a responsive strategy, it's calculations are very similar. The government's expected payoff from the action Pump is

$$\frac{1}{2} \times (2 + \theta_G) + \frac{1}{2} \times 0.$$

Its expected payoff from the action Outlet is

$$\frac{1}{2} \times 0 + \frac{1}{2} \times 2.$$

Comparing these expected payoffs, the government strictly prefers the action Pump if $\theta_G = 1$ and strictly prefers the action Outlet if $\theta_G = -1$. Hence, the government's best response to either responsive strategy by the car company is to play Pump if $\theta_G = 1$ and Outlet if $\theta_G = -1$.

This analysis implies that the game with strategic uncertainty has three Nash equilibria—the two equilibria in non-responsive strategies already described, and an equilibrium in responsive strategies in which the car company plays Hybrid if $\theta_C = 1$ and Electric if $\theta_C = -1$ and the government plays Pump if $\theta_G = 1$ and Outlet if $\theta_G = -1$.

This last Nash equilibrium formalizes the idea that strategic uncertainty can lead to coordination failure. In both of the Nash equilibria where players use non-responsive strategies, there is no chance of coordination failure. But in the Nash equilibrium where players use responsive strategies, each possible outcome—(Hybrid, Pump), (Hybrid, Outlet), (Electric, Pump), and (Electric, Outlet)—is equally likely. This means that, because no player can be sure what the other player will do, the players fail to coordinate half the time.

Coordination failure due to strategic uncertainty is inefficient. Both players are better off coordinating than not coordinating (since all coordinated outcomes provide positive payoffs, while all non-coordinated outcomes provide zero payoffs). Hence, coordination failure is a social dilemma. Players would all be better off if they could guarantee coordination.

To see this even more clearly, let's compare expected payoffs across the equilibria. In the equilibrium in which the car company always plays Hybrid and the government always plays Pump, each player makes a payoff of 3 with probability 1/2 and a payoff of 1 with probability 1/2. Hence, each player's expected payoff is 2. In the equilibrium in which the car company always plays Electric and the government always plays Outlet, each player makes a payoff of 2 for certain. Finally, in the responsive-strategy equilibrium, four things can happen, each with equal probability:

1. If $\theta_C = 1$ and $\theta_G = 1$, the players coordinate on (Hybrid, Pump) and each makes a payoff of 3.
2. If $\theta_C = 1$ and $\theta_G = -1$, the players fail to coordinate—the outcome is (Hybrid, Outlet)—and each makes a payoff of 0.
3. If $\theta_C = -1$ and $\theta_G = 1$, the players fail to coordinate—the outcome is (Electric, Pump)—and each makes a payoff of 0.
4. If $\theta_C = -1$ and $\theta_G = -1$, the players coordinate on (Electric, Outlet) and each makes a payoff of 2.

A player's expected payoff in this equilibrium is

$$\frac{1}{4} \times 3 + \frac{1}{4} \times 2 = \frac{5}{4} < 2.$$

The equilibria in which coordination is achieved for certain Pareto dominate the responsive-strategy equilibrium in which strategic uncertainty creates the possibility of coordination failure.

5.1.1 Interpretation

We opened this chapter with the case of the long-standing failure of coordination on international accounting standards. And, indeed, there are many such examples of coordination failure in regulation.

Consider the case of automobile safety standards. Within the United States, the process of regulatory harmonization began in 1926, when the federal Uniform Vehicle Code (UVC) emerged as a potential replacement for a variety of state and local regulations on automobile safety. By 1946 only 30 states had adopted the UVC in full. Regulatory harmonization increased with the construction of the Interstate Highway System in the 1950s. Many laws were passed and regulations promulgated throughout the 1960s. Most significant was the National Traffic and Motor Vehicle Safety Act of 1966, which imposed federal standards on state highway safety programs and empowered the secretary of commerce (later the secretary of transportation) to issue federal safety standards for motor vehicles. During floor debate, the need to solve coordination failure was specifically raised. For instance, Connecticut Senator Abraham Ribicoff argued, "The Federal Government must have a role. It is obvious the 50 states cannot individually set standards for the automobiles that come into those 50 States from a mass production industry" (*Congressional Record*, vol. 112, Part I (June 24, 1966)).

In Europe, safety regulations developed separately for each country into the 1950s. In 1952, as part of the process of European economic integration, the United Nations Economic Commission for Europe established a working group with the objective of "worldwide harmonization or development of technical regulations for vehicles." A 1958 UN agreement that came out of this working group established harmonized standards inside much of Europe. However, because doing so would require recognition of regulatory standards established by non-American authorities, the United States did not join the UN agreement. Thus, U.S. and European automobile standards remain unharmonized.[2]

This lack of harmonization in safety regulations comes at real cost for manufacturers and consumers. Most importantly, like with unharmonized accounting standards, variation in safety regulations makes it difficult for automobile manufacturers to sell models across markets. Consider just a few differences between the United States and Europe. U.S. rules require that cars demonstrate certain safety protections for passengers not wearing a seat belt, while Europe has no analogous regulation. U.S. bumper tests focus on damage to the automobile, while European bumper tests focus on protection of pedestrians. Standards for crash tests are different—for example, U.S. and European regulations mandate barriers with different physical properties, different crash dummy positioning, and so on. There are further differences concerning lighting color, door locks, head restraints, side lights, electronic stability control, and many other features.[3] All of these regulatory coordination failures increase costs, with little if any benefits for safety.

There are also many examples of coordination failure outside the sphere of government regulation. Often competition among competing technologies leads to coordination failure. Cell phone manufacturers each use a differently shaped power supply. Computer manufacturers have not coordinated on a standardized set of ports for connecting peripherals. And so on.

5.2 Coordination Traps

Terrible social conventions—from honor killings, to genital mutilation, to caste systems—persist for long periods of time throughout the world. In many cases, all parties might be better off if the social convention were altered. But the risk of social sanction for non-conformity keeps the undesirable practice in place.

Mackie (1996) tells the story of foot binding, a form of female mutilation involving tight wrapping to contort a young girl's feet that persisted in China for a thousand years. The practice, according to Mackie, "was extremely painful in the first 6 to 10 years" and led to many complications including "ulceration, paralysis, gangrene, and mortification of the limbs." Studies suggest that 10% of girls did not survive having their feet bound.

---

[2]The previous two paragraphs draw on Congressional Research Service Report "U.S. and EU Motor Vehicle Standards: Issues for Transatlantic Trade Negotiations." https://www.hsdl.org/?view&did=751039

[3]http://www.nbcnews.com/id/26444467/ns/business-autos/t/perfectly-safe-car-just-not-us/

Foot binding first emerged during the Sung dynasty (around the turn of the millennium). Over the course of several centuries, it spread from a practice of the royalty, to the nobility, to the upper classes, and finally to the middle and lower classes. Mackie reports that "[f]ootbinding was the normal practice by the Ming Dynasty (1368–1644). As measured in 1835, it prevailed in the whole empire among the Chinese, affecting 50 to 80 percent of women." Although foot binding was understood to be both economically costly (it prevented women from participating in the agricultural economy) and physically cruel, it was enforced through strong social norms. Perhaps most importantly, foot binding was associated with suitability for marriage. Despite its deleterious effects, the practice was so strongly entrenched that it even survived being formally banned by the Manchu conquerors in the seventeenth century.

In the late nineteenth and early twentieth century, public opinion began to shift with the emergence of a "natural foot" movement. According to Mackie, the natural foot movement "propagandized the disadvantages of footbinding in Chinese cultural terms, promoted pledge associations, and subtly conveyed international disapproval of the custom." Interestingly, consistent with the idea that foot binding was a practice sustained only through mutually reinforcing social pressure, once it started to decline, it disappeared extraordinarily rapidly. For instance, Mackie cites a study showing that "the population of Tinghsien, a conservative rural area 125 miles south of Peking, went from 99 percent bound in 1889 to 94 percent bound in 1899 to zero bound in 1919."

Foot binding illustrates a different type of coordination problem. Here, we don't see a bad outcome occurring because people fail to coordinate. Rather, we see people successfully coordinating, but on an equilibrium that is itself Pareto dominated by another equilibrium. We refer to such a situation as a *coordination trap*—people are trapped in a self-reinforcing pattern of behavior that they regret.

Coordination traps are important for understanding a variety of policy relevant outcomes. These include cultural phenomena like foot binding or honor killings; economic phenomena like bank runs, financial crises, and persistent underdevelopment; political phenomena like failures of accountability, the longevity of dictatorial governments, and revolutions; and social phenomena like educated parents sending their children to private schools.

To make clear what these environments have in common, it will be useful to study a couple of models.

5.2.1 A Basic Model of Coordination Traps: Investment in Developing Countries

Let's start with a simple model with two players and two actions, inspired by our earlier discussion of poverty traps. Suppose there are two firms, each deciding whether to invest in a developing country. The country lacks infrastructure.

	Firm 2	
	Invest	Don't invest
Invest	4, 4	–1, 0
Don't invest	0, –1	0, 0

Figure 5.3. Coordination with a Pareto dominated equilibrium.

As a result, neither firm wants to invest on its own—doing so would result in a loss. However, the firms believe that if they both invest, the economy will grow, the government will be able to build infrastructure, and the investments will be profitable. If neither firm invests, they make no profits, but suffer no costs.

The model is illustrated in Figure 5.3. There is no uncertainty. The game has two pure strategy Nash equilibria—(Invest, Invest) and (Don't Invest, Don't Invest).

The players agree that one equilibrium is better than the other—both prefer the (Invest, Invest) outcome to the (Don't Invest, Don't Invest) outcome. Nonetheless, if a firm believes that the other firm will not invest, then it is a best response not to invest. So (Don't Invest, Don't Invest) is also an equilibrium.

The equilibrium in which neither firm invests illustrates a simple coordination trap. It is stable for the players to coordinate on not investing, even though it is inefficient. The players are trapped—Firm 1 doesn't invest because it believes Firm 2 won't invest and vice versa.

As we discussed at the outset of this chapter, coordination traps like this lie at the heart of the way much of the policy community thinks about economic development and foreign aid. Investing in countries that lack infrastructure, human capital, and the other features of an agglomeration economy is not profitable. But to build infrastructure and human capital, countries must attract investment. Hence, poor countries can get caught in poverty traps. The idea behind short-run economic aid is to give the government an infusion of money (sometimes called a "big push") so that investors don't need to coordinate—if the government can unilaterally build infrastructure, each individual company will find investment worthwhile even if others don't invest. Indeed, this was the idea behind the Tennessee Valley Authority, a point we will come back to shortly.

You may be tempted to dismiss coordination traps as unrealistic. Surely, you might think, players could find their way out of such situations by talking. If these two firms could sit down and agree to invest, they'd both be better off.

But finding a way out of a coordination trap may sometimes be difficult. There may be many players, making communication difficult or costly. Further, in some situations, players may find it risky to communicate a desire to shift equilibria. For instance, this same model might describe how societies get caught in unpleasant cultural practices like foot binding or honor killings. People want to coordinate on following social norms. Failing to act as others do leads to social sanctions. Although almost everyone would presumably prefer to coordinate on not engaging in honor killings or the like, once a society is in that equilibrium, expressing a preference for change is often risky or dangerous. Hence, escaping a coordination trap may be more difficult than it seems at first blush.

5.2.2 A Model of Bank Runs

To flesh the story out a bit more, and to see another set of applications, let's turn to a coordination model with many people. Suppose there are N people, each with \$1000 deposited in a bank. Each person decides whether to *Withdraw* or *Leave* his or her money in the bank. The bank has sufficient cash reserves to pay $T < N$ people. So if fewer than T people withdraw their money, they all get it back and everyone else gets paid interest of r. If some number of people n greater than T withdraw their money, then the bank becomes insolvent. A person who tried to withdraw her money has a $\frac{T}{n}$ chance of getting it back. Anyone who didn't withdraw loses his money for certain.

People care only about how much money they have. No one has short-term need for the money (maybe they all have credit), so there is no direct benefit from withdrawing the money early.

Let's look for equilibria of this game. If everyone leaves his or her money in the bank, everyone makes a payoff of \$1000(1 + r). A person who withdraws her money would only make a payoff of \$1000. So everyone is happy leaving the money in the bank and we have an equilibrium in which the bank is solvent.

If some positive number of people, $n \leq T$, withdraw their money, they each make a payoff of \$1000. But if one such person instead left her money in the bank, she would make a payoff of \$1000(1 + r). Hence, this is not an equilibrium.

If some positive number of people, $n \in (T, N)$, withdraw their money, the bank fails. A person who didn't withdraw her money makes a payoff of 0. If instead she withdrew her money, she'd make an expected payoff of $\frac{T}{n+1} \times$ \$1000. So she should have withdrawn. Hence, this is also not an equilibrium.

This argument points toward the logic of bank runs. If I believe that more than T people will withdraw their money, I should withdraw my money. That is, like other coordination games, this is a game where players' actions are strategic complements—the more other people withdraw their money, the larger the benefit to me of withdrawing my money.

If everyone withdraws their money, each person makes an expected payoff of $\frac{T}{N} \times$ \$1000. If instead some individual had left her money in the bank, she would make 0. So this is an equilibrium in which everyone attempts to withdraw and the bank fails.

This situation is very similar to the two-person model we discussed above. Again there are two pure strategy equilibria. In one equilibrium, all deposits are left in the bank. In the other, everyone attempts to withdraw his or her money. The equilibrium in which everyone attempts to withdraw is Pareto dominated by the equilibrium in which everyone leaves his or her money deposited. Nonetheless, if a person is convinced that everyone else will withdraw their money, it is indeed a best response for her to withdraw her money. So bank runs can occur in equilibrium as part of a coordination trap.

As described at the beginning of this chapter, a variety of phenomena can be usefully thought about with models like this one. The key feature of such models is that players get trapped in an undesirable pattern of behavior because each individual believes all the other individuals will behave in that way and no one wants to be the only person to behave differently.

5.2.3 A Model of Revolutions

Thinking about coordination in this way also gives us some insight into the logic of revolutions. Again consider a group of N people. Each person can choose to *Participate* or *Not Participate* in a protest. The number of people who participate affects the probability that the revolution succeeds.

Just as in our model of collective action from Chapter 4.1, if n people participate, the probability that the regime falls is $\frac{n}{N}$ and the benefit to an individual of regime change is B. But now we will change one crucial assumption. Assume that the costs of participating are decreasing in the number of other participants. In particular, if n other people participate, the cost to me of participating is $\frac{c}{n+1}$.

The assumption that individual costs are decreasing as participation increases seems pretty natural. For instance, one is more likely to be arrested or hurt as one of only a few protestors, than as a relatively anonymous participant in a group of tens-of-thousands. Importantly, when costs are decreasing in participation, the revolution game becomes a situation of strategic complementarities. The more other people participate, the smaller are the costs of participating and, so, the more tempting it is to participate.

Think about best responses. Suppose a player believes that n other players will participate. The payoff to participating is

$$\frac{n+1}{N} \times B - \frac{c}{n+1}.$$

The payoff to not participating is

$$\frac{n}{N} \times B.$$

Comparing these payoffs, if a player believes n other players will participate, it is a best response for her to participate if

$$\frac{B}{N} \geq \frac{c}{n+1}. \qquad (5.1)$$

Let's ask whether there is an equilibrium in which everyone participates. From Equation 5.1, if a player believes everyone else will participate (so $n = N - 1$), then it is a best response for her to participate if

$$\frac{B}{N} \geq \frac{c}{N},$$

which is true since we assumed $B > c$ in Chapter 4.1. If I believe everyone else will participate, then the costs of participating are quite low. As such, I want to participate too. This means there is an equilibrium with full participation.

Next consider a strategy profile in which no one participates. Again, from Equation 5.1, if a player believes no one else will participate, then it is a best response for her *not* to participate if

$$\frac{B}{N} \leq c.$$

This looks just like our collective action model. If a player believes no one else will participate, then unless the benefits of regime change are implausibly large, she too will not participate because the costs of participating are high. Hence, as long as $c \geq \frac{B}{N}$ there is an equilibrium in which no one participates.

The existence of these two equilibria creates the possibility of a coordination trap that drives bad governance. Imagine a ruler who will lead in ways that benefit the people if and only if she believes that, if she follows bad policies, the people will revolt. If the society that she leads is coordinated on an equilibrium in which the people revolt when the leader does a bad job, then the leader has an incentive to pursue good policies that benefit the public. But if the society is coordinated on an equilibrium in which the people don't revolt even when the leader does a bad job, then the leader has no incentives to pursue good policies. Hence, a country can get trapped into having a non-responsive government if the citizens coordinate on the bad equilibrium so that the leader knows that no matter what, she won't be held to account.

A model like this might also help us understand "spontaneous revolutions" like those witnessed in the Arab Spring. Sometimes small events might be capable of changing people's beliefs about how their fellow citizens think. For instance, perhaps Egypt was stuck in a bad equilibrium where its leaders knew the people would never revolt. The revolution in Tunisia may have changed these beliefs, making Egyptians think of themselves as part of a society whose people stood up for their rights, mobilizing for revolution when circumstances called for it. The model we've just studied shows that this change of beliefs, on its own, could be enough to move people to a new equilibrium in which everyone turns out to protest the government.

5.2.4 Interpretation

As already mentioned, there are many situations in which coordination traps are possible. As you begin to think about the world in terms of coordination problems, you will see them all over the place. Reiterating a few canonical examples might help to highlight the idea. As we've discussed, bank runs and other financial panics, participation in mass protests or revolutions, and investment in economically developing countries might all be characterized by coordination problems. Agglomeration creates the possibility of coordination problems. A related set of issues arises in urban renewal. If a school district or neighborhood is considered failing, then people will be disinclined to live there, making it difficult for the school district or neighborhood to turn around. However, if people came to believe that the school district or neighborhood was going to turn around, they might be inclined to participate, creating a self-fulfilling prophecy. Social norms, from silly fashion trends to terrible social institutions like foot binding, rest on a set of mutually self-reinforcing beliefs about others. And the adoption of new technologies often rests on coordination—among competing technologies, the winner will not necessarily be the better technology, but the one everyone comes to believe everyone else will adopt.

5.3   Policy Responses

Addressing coordination problems is quite different from addressing externalities problems. In the case of coordination problems, a successful policy intervention involves finding a way to shift players from a bad equilibrium to a good one. This is not the case for externalities problems, where a policy intervention has to fundamentally shift players' best responses. Thus, when thinking about policy interventions aimed at resolving coordination problems, we focus on fairly different approaches.

5.3.1 Communication

Communication can be a powerful corrective tool for both coordination failures and coordination traps. People want to coordinate on good outcomes. They fail to coordinate because they haven't found a way to get themselves to the right equilibrium—whether that means avoiding the risk of coordination failure due to strategic uncertainty or the unnecessary costs associated with being stuck in a coordination trap. So if you can find a way to "put them in a room" they might be able to simply talk their way into a better outcome.

This is a fundamental difference between coordination problems and externalities. As we discussed in Chapter 4.4, a deep challenge in addressing externalities problems is that, even if you are convinced that everyone else will take a socially optimal action, you still want to free ride. Hence, in an externalities setting, if people agreed to choose a socially optimal action, they would have strong reasons not to trust one another, since everyone would be claiming they would take an action that is not a best response. This is not the case in coordination games. Put differently, what makes an agreement to take a socially optimal action credible is that the agreement be self-enforcing—that is, a Nash equilibrium. In an externalities setting, such a self-enforcing agreement does not exist. In a coordination setting, one does.

That said, there is one important link between externalities problems and coordination problems. In Chapter 4.6.3, we discussed the idea that ongoing relationships might allow groups to self-organize solutions to externalities problems. But we also saw that, even when such a cooperative equilibrium exists, it is not the only equilibrium—inefficient equilibria always exist in situations with externalities. In this sense, the idea of self-organization through repeated interaction transforms an externalities problem into a coordination problem. The issue shifts from whether policy can get people to internalize their externalities to whether policy can get people to play the equilibrium in which they compel one another to internalize their externalities. Hence, like in other situations where there is a risk of coordination failure or coordination traps, leadership and communication can play a role in creating self-organized solutions to externalities problems.

It is also important to note that there are situations where simple communication might not solve coordination problems.

When there are many players, communication may be extremely difficult (or dangerous, in the case of revolutions). Once the panic associated with the bank run equilibrium sets in, it may be difficult to talk people back into the Pareto improving equilibrium of leaving their money deposited.

Further, when deeply held social norms—like foot binding, honor killings, or racial bias—are involved, it may be profoundly difficult to change people's beliefs about how one another will act or think.

Finally, distributional considerations can also mitigate the efficacy of communication. For instance, consider the problem of regulatory harmonization—for example, accounting standards or automobile safety. As we've discussed, there are significant benefits from governments coordinating on mutually accepted standards. But individual governments may also strongly prefer their particular regulations for a variety of economic and political reasons. Overcoming these distributional concerns may be difficult. Entrenched interests—for example, regulators, accountants, engineers, domestic producers—push for coordination on that country's preferred outcome. This suggests that, sometimes, a more direct type of intervention might be needed to solve coordination problems.

5.3.2 Short-Run Intervention

Direct government intervention is, of course, another possible strategy to address coordination problems. Importantly, in the case of coordination problems, often a short-run intervention that pushes players into a better equilibrium is all that is required. Once coordination is achieved, if the government intervention stops, there is no reason for players to fall back into a bad pattern of behavior, since the good pattern of behavior is self-reinforcing.

This, again, is a difference between coordination failure and externalities. A regulation, tax, or subsidy meant to address an externalities problem must be ongoing. If the government ever stops its intervention, the players have an incentive to revert to inefficient behavior. But if the government stops its intervention in a coordination game, then assuming players have learned that they are all now playing the new equilibrium, efficient behavior will persist.

The long-run effects of the Tennessee Valley Authority illustrate the point. As we discussed at the outset of this chapter, manufacturing benefits from economies of agglomeration, while agriculture does not. As a result, the TVA worked quite differently for these two industries. In the case of manufacturing, TVA subsides helped to overcome a coordination trap by building up the infrastructure necessary to create the virtuous cycle associated with economies of agglomeration. Hence, when the TVA subsidies disappeared starting in the 1960s, the growth in manufacturing persisted. As predicted in the case of a coordination trap, the short-run TVA intervention pushed the Tennessee Valley into a new equilibrium—one with higher returns to manufacturing—that did not disappear when the policy disappeared. In the case of agriculture, there was no coordination trap to solve. In the agricultural sector, the TVA subsidies were simply a transfer to agriculture, the effects of which disappeared as soon as the money dried up.

5.3.3 Insurance and the Second Best

Another intervention that is common in settings like that described by the bank run model is government insurance. For instance, if the government can guarantee players that they will not face a bad outcome, even if everyone runs on the bank, then the players have no incentive to withdraw their money. Interestingly, by insuring everyone against the risk of a bad coordination outcome, the government can sometimes actually eliminate the risk of such an outcome occurring. Policies like this, that insure people against negative coordination events, can be very powerful. By promising to spend money if needed, the government can achieve a Pareto improvement without ever actually having to spend a dime.

In the United States, as asset values plummeted during the Great Depression, bank runs were a recurring problem. Banks began to fail and depositors became increasingly concerned about the security of their assets. This led to a rush of withdrawals, causing further insolvencies and further bank runs. The Banking Acts of 1933 and 1935 created the Federal Deposit Insurance Corporation (FDIC) for precisely the reasons outlined above. The FDIC was charged with providing deposit insurance, reassuring depositors of the security of their assets, and thereby stemming the tide of destructive bank runs.

Importantly, the idea that government insurance might alleviate the problem of coordination traps also points back toward the idea of the second best. Government insurance against bank failure reduces incentives for depositors to run on the bank. But it also reduces incentives for depositors to favor banks that invest prudently. As a result, competition for depositors becomes a less effective tool for disciplining banks to behave responsibly. So, once deposits are insured, banks may have an incentive to make investments that are too risky.

This is the well-known *moral hazard* problem that was much discussed during the financial crisis of 2007–2008. During that crisis there was considerable concern that if the government bailed out major financial institutions, then those institutions would behave even more irresponsibly in the future. The fact that government insurance prevents runs but creates moral hazard leads governments to further regulate the behavior of insured banks. For instance, the United States government requires that banks keep a certain amount of liquid capital (in proportion to their liabilities) on deposit at the Federal Reserve. These capital requirements are intended to reduce the risk that the banks behave in a way that leads to the government actually having to make good on deposit insurance. Of course, leaving capital on deposit with the Federal Reserve may not be the optimal use of that capital. Hence, a new source of inefficiency is created by the capital requirements that the government imposes to address the moral hazard problem that is caused by the deposit insurance that is needed to avoid coordination traps in the form of bank runs. And, so, we see a return of the theory of the second best. A policy intervention like deposit insurance has benefits and costs. The optimal (second-best) policy balances these costs and benefits.

5.4 Takeaways

- Coordination games describe situations in which players all benefit if they take coordinated actions.
- Strategic uncertainty can lead to inefficient coordination failure.
- Some coordination games have equilibria that are Pareto dominated by other equilibria. In such situations, it is possible for players to be caught in a coordination trap—playing a Pareto dominated equilibrium

despite the fact that all would agree that some other equilibrium is more desirable.

- Sometimes coordination failure or coordination traps are solvable by communication. However, in situations where there are many actors or in which stating a counter-normative opinion might carry risks of social sanction, communication alone may be insufficient to solve coordination problems.
- Often short-run interventions that move people to a coordinated or Pareto improving equilibrium can address coordination problems. Since coordination problems are solved by moving people to a new pattern of behavior that is also an equilibrium, it may not be necessary to engage in long-run interventions.

5.5 Further Reading

The classic treatment of coordination problems is in Schelling's stunning *The Strategy of Conflict*. For a modern, technical take on models of coordination, see Morris and Shin (2003).

For fairly academic treatments of agglomeration economies, you should read Edward Glaeser's *Agglomeration Economics* and Paul Krugman's *Geography and Trade*. For a non-technical introduction in the context of urban economics, have a look at Glaeser's *Triumph of the City*.

Weingast (1997) and Fearon (2011) relate failures of democratic accountability to coordination traps. Azariadis (1996) overviews the relationship between coordination and poverty traps, while Kraay and McKenzie (2014) ask the empirical question, "Do poverty traps exist?"

Kwame Appiah's *The Honor Code* is a thoughtful historical and philosophical take on how honor codes are sustained and overcome.

Friedman and Schwartz's great book, *A Monetary History of the United States, 1867–1960*, discusses the role of bank runs in American economic history in detail. The classic model of bank runs and deposit insurance is Diamond and Dybvig (1983). Cooper and Ross (2002) extend the analysis to include moral hazard and capital requirements.

5.6 Exercises

1. Consider a model of revolutions. Society is made up of $N > 1$ people. Simultaneously, each person chooses whether or not to participate. If n people participate, the probability the revolution succeeds is $\frac{n}{N}$. If the revolution succeeds, each member of society receives the benefits of a public good worth B. In addition, each person who participated in the revolution

receives a benefit R if the revolution succeeds. (This extra benefit, called a *club good*, might represent special access to government jobs for people who helped unseat the government once the new government is formed, or it might just represent an expressive benefit of having participated in a victorious revolution.) The cost of participating is $c > 0$. Assume that $R > c$ and that $B + R < N \times c$.

(a) Suppose a player believes n other people will participate. What is her expected utility from participating?
(b) Suppose a player believes n other people will participate. What is her expected utility from not participating?
(c) Write down a player's best response correspondence.
(d) Identify all of the pure strategy Nash equilibria of this game.
(e) Calculate the utilitarian payoff associated with each equilibrium.
(f) Does this game have the potential for a coordination trap? Explain why or why not.
(g) What feature of this game makes it a situation that exhibits strategic complementarities?

2.   Consider a society of 2 people trying to achieve a collective goal. Each individual, i, must choose an effort $e_i \geq 0$ at cost e_i^2. We will study two different scenarios:

Scenario 1 The society produces a public good $G = e_1 + e_2$. Each individual's payoff is

$$u_i(e_1, e_2) = G - e_i^2.$$

Scenario 2 The society produces a public good

$$G = \begin{cases} e_1 + e_2 & \text{if } e_1 + e_2 \geq 2 \\ 0 & \text{if } e_1 + e_2 < 2. \end{cases}$$

Each individual's payoff is again

$$u_i(e_1, e_2) = G - e_i^2.$$

Notice, players bear the costs of their individual efforts even if society ends up producing $G = 0$.

(a) The first-best level of effort is the same in both scenarios. What is it?
(b) What is the Nash equilibrium in scenario 1?
(c) Is that same strategy profile a Nash equilibrium in scenario 2?

(d) Is it a Nash equilibrium in scenario 2 for no one to exert any effort?

(e) Is it a Nash equilibrium in scenario 2 for each player to exert the first-best effort?

(f) Suppose, in scenario 1, that a policymaker were able to convince player i that the other player will choose the first-best level of effort. Will player i choose the first-best level of effort?

(g) Suppose, in scenario 2, that a policymaker were able to convince player i that the other player will choose the first-best level of effort. Will player i choose the first-best level of effort?

(h) What do your answers to the previous two questions show about how different kinds of policy interventions work for different kinds of social dilemmas?

(i) Suppose the policymaker could subsidize effort in scenario 1, but doing so required funding through inefficient taxation. Without doing any calculations, if she implemented the second-best subsidy, how would the induced second-best efforts compare to the equilibrium efforts and the first-best efforts? Why?

3. Suppose there are five firms in an industry. Each must individually decide in which of two cities to locate its manufacturing plant. If firm i locates in city j, its profits are $\pi \times n_j$, where $\pi > 0$ and n_j is the number of firms from this industry that locate in city j (including itself).

(a) Give a substantive explanation for why profits might look like this.

(b) Identify all of the Nash equilibria of this game.

Now suppose that one of the cities (city 1) is better for this industry than the other (city 2). A firm that locates in city 1 makes profits $\pi_1 \times n_1$ and a firm that locates in city 2 makes profits $\pi_2 \times n_2$. Assume $\pi_2 < \pi_1 < 5\pi_2$.

(c) Have the Nash equilibria of the game changed?

(d) Explain how your answer suggests that agglomeration economies can create coordination traps.

(e) Often local governments offer incentives to induce a few large firms in some industry to relocate to their city. Evaluate the likely efficacy of such a policy in light of this model.

4. Explain why short-run policy interventions can help to solve Pareto inefficiencies caused by coordination traps, but are unlikely to solve Pareto inefficiencies due to externalities.

5. Let's revisit Exercise 4 from Chapter 1. In O'Hare's (2015) discussion of why it is so difficult to convince major museums to consider selling some of their

art to fund other activities (e.g., free admissions, expanded space, educational staff) he writes:

> If you open this discussion with museum people, as I have done, you find out very quickly that you have walked into a hornet's nest called the "deaccessioning debate." Deaccessioning is fancy art language for selling, and the first thing the director you have provoked will tell you about is the museum directors' code of ethics, which forbids him to ever sell art except to buy more art. If he did, he could never lend anything to other museums or borrow any art from them. He probably couldn't have coffee with his pals at the next convention either: outer darkness, and how appropriate for unethical behavior.

For the sake of argument, assume major museum directors generally agree with O'Hare that museums should sell off a small amount of their art to fund other activities. Explain how the above passage implies they are caught in a coordination trap and suggest an intervention that might move them to a better outcome.

6

Commitment Problems

In 2012, the government of Argentina nationalized its largest energy company, YPF, a majority stake of which had been owned by the Spanish energy company Repsol. The temptation to nationalize was clear—in 2011, Argentina became a net oil importer for the first time in decades. Moreover, the nationalization followed quickly on the heals of the discovery, by Repsol, of vast reserves of shale oil in Argentina's Neuquén province. Argentina's government saw an opportunity to simultaneously take control of a valuable economic resource and claim credit for turning around the oil industry.

There was, however, a problem with this plan. Extracting shale oil requires both expertise and capital—tens, perhaps hundreds, of billions of dollars—that Argentina lacks. The only way for Argentina to exploit its shale oil reserves is through partnership with foreign oil companies. But, fearful that their assets might ultimately suffer the same fate as Repsol's, such companies are understandably reluctant to invest in Argentina. As a consequence of the government's limited ability to credibly commit to respecting the property rights of foreign firms, to date, Argentina has made little progress in developing its shale resources.

This story is an example of a general phenomenon called a *commitment problem*. Party A could take some action—investing in a new technology, setting a good policy, resolving a conflict through negotiated settlement, etc.—that would benefit both himself and Party B. However, Party A anticipates that, in the future, Party B will have the power to exploit him, taking the benefits for herself and leaving Party A worse off than if he hadn't taken the initial action. As a consequence, Party A doesn't ever take that initial action. But if Party B could credibly commit not to exploit her future power, Party A would take the action and they'd both be better off. Party B's inability to credibly commit yields a Pareto inefficient outcome.

The unwillingness of foreign firms to invest in countries where the risk of government expropriation is high is a classic example of the inefficiency caused by commitment problems. If the government could commit not to nationalize valuable resources, foreign firms would invest, making both the firm and the government better off. But if a government has a reputation for not respecting property rights, foreign investors fear that the government will seize any profits, leaving them worse off than if they hadn't invested. Consequently, investment is inefficiently low.

In this chapter we will explore two models of commitment problems to see the variety of ways in which this social dilemma creates opportunities for public policy to yield Pareto improvements. First, we will look at a model of how commitment problems give rise to costly conflicts—wars, lawsuits, strikes, and so on. Second, we will consider how the structure of certain markets creates a commitment problem inside the supply chain that can cause inefficiently low levels of investment. Finally, we will discuss policy interventions that might help mitigate commitment problems.

6.1 A Model of Conflict

From the Easter Rising of 1916 through the signing of the Good Friday Agreement in 1998, the armed conflict over independence, known as the Troubles, defined much of twentieth-century Irish history. The Troubles were a tragedy for both sides. Thousands of lives and billions of dollars were lost in seemingly intractable conflict.

Throughout this history, both sides made intermittent attempts to negotiate a settlement. A reasonable observer might wonder why such negotiations did not succeed. Since conflict is costly, there should be a deal that avoids conflict and makes both parties better off. That is, in any setting of costly conflict (war, lawsuits, labor strikes), there should be a negotiated settlement that is a Pareto improvement over fighting.

To see the logic of this puzzle, imagine the British and Irish are in a dispute over a prize of value R. They believe that if they fight, the Irish will win with probability p and the British will win with probability $1 - p$. Conflict imposes a cost of c on each of them—these costs reflect loss of life, destruction of infrastructure, and time and resources spent fighting. So the expected utility to the British of a conflict is

$$U_B(\text{conflict}) = (1 - p) \times R - c,$$

while the expected utility to the Irish of a conflict is

$$U_I(\text{conflict}) = p \times R - c.$$

Clearly, both sides would be better off with a negotiated settlement that splits the prize, giving the Irish a p-share and the British a $(1 - p)$-share. So why don't they reach such a settlement?

There are several possibilities. First, the prize might be indivisible and utility might not be transferable. For instance, a major problem in finding a negotiated settlement between Israelis and Palestinians is that it is difficult to divide Jerusalem between them while preserving its value to either. Hence, while the sides might be better off reaching a deal that divides the prize, such a deal might not be technologically feasible.

Second, the players may disagree about how likely each of them is to win a dispute. If they are both overly optimistic, then there may be no deal they are both willing to take. For instance, if they are both certain they would win the conflict, neither would settle for less than $B - c$ in the agreement.[1]

Third, there may be commitment problems. While a mutually beneficial deal exists, the players may have concerns that the deal will not be honored. Such lack of trust was an important part of the story in the case of the Irish Troubles. One can see this most clearly in disputes over weapons decommissioning, which proved a stumbling block in many negotiations between the British and Irish Republicans. The British demanded that the Irish Republican Army (IRA) decommission its weapons, first as a precondition to negotiations and later as a precondition for concessions. The IRA feared the British would renege on promises were it to disarm before concessions were made. As a spokesman for the IRA stated in 1996:

There will be no decommissioning either through the front or the back doors. This is an unrealistic and unrealizable demand which simply won't be met. The IRA will under no circumstances leave nationalist areas defenseless this side of a final settlement.[2]

The story is straightforward. The IRA had the power to extract concessions from the British because they were armed. The British promised such concessions in exchange for decommissioning. But the IRA believed that, if it were to decommission, its power would be diminished and the British would no longer have an incentive to honor the promised concessions. Hence, the inability of the British to credibly commit to concessions led to a conflict that was in neither side's interest.

We are going to look at a simple model of this commitment problem logic. It was originally proposed by Fearon (1998) as an account of the spread of ethnic civil wars. I will present it in terms of negotiations between the British and IRA.

We will build up the model in steps. There are two groups, the British and IRA, in dispute over resources of value R. The British make a take-it-or-leave-it offer of a division of the resources between themselves and the IRA.

---

[1]The mutual optimism story is actually quite a subtle one and there is some dispute in the literature as to whether or not it is a coherent account of conflict. In particular, the question is, can rational players really persist in being mutually optimistic throughout the run-up to conflict? See Fey and Ramsay (2007) for a discussion of these issues.

[2]Quoted in English (2003, p. 326).

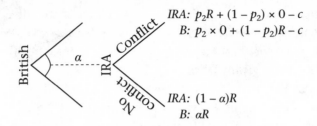

Figure 6.1. A model of negotiations and conflict.

In particular, the British propose to keep a share $\alpha \in [0, 1]$ for themselves, offering the balance, $1 - \alpha$, to the IRA. The IRA decides whether to accept the offer, making a payoff of $(1 - \alpha)R$, or start a conflict. The IRA wins the conflict with probability p_2. The winner gets the full resource, but conflict imposes a cost of c on each player.

This game is represented in Figure 6.1, where the fact that the British face a continuous choice (any α between 0 and 1) is represented by the curve and dashed line coming from the British decision node.

We can solve this game for its subgame perfect Nash equilibria via backward induction. At the final stage of the game, the IRA strictly prefers to accept an offer of $1 - \alpha$ if

$$p_2 R - c < (1 - \alpha)R \Rightarrow \alpha < 1 - p_2 + \frac{c}{R}.$$

Similarly, it strictly prefers to reject an offer if $\alpha > 1 - p_2 + \frac{c}{R}$. So the IRA has a unique best response to every possible offer, α, with one exception. If $\alpha = 1 - p_2 + \frac{c}{R}$, the IRA is indifferent between starting a conflict and accepting the British offer.

Suppose the IRA accepts any $\alpha \leq 1 - p_2 + \frac{c}{R}$ and rejects any $\alpha > 1 - p_2 + \frac{c}{R}$. What offer will the British make? If the British make an offer that is rejected (i.e., $\alpha > 1 - p_2 + \frac{c}{R}$), then there is conflict and their payoff is $(1 - p_2)R - c$. If the British make an offer that is accepted (i.e., $\alpha \leq 1 - p_2 + \frac{c}{R}$), then there is no conflict and their payoff is αR. Given this, the British want to make an offer that is accepted if they can do so with some α satisfying

$$\alpha R > (1 - p_2)R - c \Rightarrow \alpha > 1 - p_2 - \frac{c}{R}.$$

What have we seen? Any α that is less than or equal to $1 - p_2 + \frac{c}{R}$ will be accepted. Any α that is greater than $1 - p_2 - \frac{c}{R}$ is better for the British than conflict. Since $1 - p_2 - \frac{c}{R} < 1 - p_2 + \frac{c}{R}$, the British can make an offer that they prefer to conflict and that the IRA will accept. The largest such offer is $\alpha = 1 - p_2 + \frac{c}{R}$. Thus, there is a subgame perfect Nash equilibrium of this game

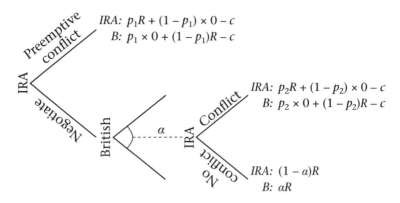

IRA: $p_1 R + (1 - p_1) \times 0 - c$
B: $p_1 \times 0 + (1 - p_1)R - c$

IRA: $p_2 R + (1 - p_2) \times 0 - c$
B: $p_2 \times 0 + (1 - p_2)R - c$

IRA: $(1 - \alpha)R$
B: αR

Figure 6.2. A model of conflict due to commitment problems.

involving the following strategy profile:

- The British offer $\alpha = 1 - p_2 + \frac{c}{R}$.
- The IRA accept any $\alpha \le 1 - p_2 + \frac{c}{R}$ and reject any $\alpha > 1 - p_2 + \frac{c}{R}$.

No conflict occurs in equilibrium.[3]

One critical fact to notice about this game is that because the British get to make a take-it-or-leave-it offer, in equilibrium the IRA ends up indifferent between conflict and no conflict—in either case the IRA's payoff is $p_2 R - c$. (You can see this algebraically by plugging $\alpha = 1 - p_2 + \frac{c}{R}$ into $(1 - \alpha)R$.) Substantively, this is because the British keep as much of the prize for themselves as possible, subject to the constraint that the IRA take the deal. The British, thus, make concessions just sufficient to leave the IRA exactly indifferent between accepting the offer and fighting.

Now that we've understood that interaction, let's add an earlier stage to the game. Suppose that the IRA can start a preemptive conflict before the British make their offer. Moreover, assume that the IRA wins this preemptive conflict with probability $p_1 > p_2$. There might be several reasons this would be the case. First, if the British demand decommissioning of weapons as precondition for talks, then the IRA might be stronger prior to the negotiations. Second, the process of negotiating may undermine some of the operational and personnel secrecy that give the IRA power as a clandestine organization. Third, the process of negotiating may allow the British to consolidate control or public support, weakening the IRA. The game is illustrated in Figure 6.2.

---

[3]This equilibrium is unique. If we consider the case where the IRA breaks indifference in favor of conflict, we find that the British want to offer the largest α that is *strictly* less than $1 - p_2 + \frac{c}{R}$. Since there is no largest α that is strictly less than $1 - p_2 + \frac{c}{R}$, there is no such equilibrium. This issue is discussed in more depth in Appendix B.6.4.

Our previous analysis tells us what happens in most of this extended game. The only question left is what the IRA will do at the beginning of the game.

If the IRA negotiates, it will end up accepting an offer that results in a payoff of $p_2R - c$. If the IRA starts a preemptive conflict, its payoff is $p_1R - c$. Since $p_1R - c > p_2R - c$, the IRA starts a preemptive conflict rather than entering negotiations.

6.1.1 Inefficient Conflict

The IRA starts a preemptive conflict because it understands that, if it enters negotiations, it will be in a weaker position and will end up with a negotiated settlement whose terms are worse than the expected payoff of fighting at the outset. Although preemptive conflict is rational, the equilibrium outcome is also clearly inefficient, since conflict is costly. At root, the source of the inefficiency is the British inability to commit to giving the IRA a sufficient share of the resources once negotiations get going.

To see the inefficiency, notice that in equilibrium the IRA makes an expected payoff of $p_1R - c$ and the British make an expected payoff of $(1 - p_1)R - c$. Suppose the British could credibly commit to proposing $\alpha = 1 - p_1$. The IRA would accept such a proposal rather than fight at the second stage. Moreover, such a commitment would convince the IRA not to start a preemptive conflict, since $p_1R > p_1R - c$. Finally, such a commitment would also make the British better off (relative to the equilibrium with preemptive conflict), since $(1 - p_1)R > (1 - p_1)R - c$. Thus, if the British could make this commitment, inefficient conflict would be avoided and both sides would be better off—a Pareto improvement.

The problem, as we've already seen, is that once negotiations start, the British have gained strength relative to the IRA and so have no incentive to honor such a commitment. Indeed, at the time the British make a proposal, they know that the IRA will take a much worse offer. As such, the British will choose a higher α—that is, will keep more resources for themselves. Anticipating this fact, the IRA distrusts any promise the British make. This distrust leads the IRA to start a preemptive conflict rather than negotiate. Hence, the commitment problem leads to inefficiency.

6.1.2 Interpretation

I've couched this model in terms of a commitment problem that arises when a government demands, say, that a rebel group disarm prior to negotiations. Fearon originally proposed it as a way to understand the spread of ethnic civil wars after the fall of the Soviet Union. There the mechanism was the same, but the anticipated power shift that drives the commitment problem derived from a different source.

During the Cold War, the Soviets served as a third-party guarantor of the peace within the Eastern Bloc. There were many ethnic groups that did not trust one another, but the Soviets, through military strength, prevented the abuse of ethnic minorities. With the fall of the Soviet Union, there was no longer a third-party guarantor. Ethnic minorities suddenly felt threatened by ethnic majorities. The ethnic minorities believed that once the majorities consolidated power, establishing control of the government and the military, they would use their increased strength to exploit minority groups. There was nothing the majorities could do to credibly promise not to do so. And so, the argument goes, the ethnic minorities started preemptive wars, fighting for autonomy before the majorities consolidated power.

This logic played out in a fairly interesting way in Croatia in the early 1990s. In 1991, Serb nationalists began to consolidate control over Yugoslavia. Ethnic Croats saw themselves as a vulnerable minority. Following the logic of the model, in June of 1991, Croatia preemptively declared independence, sparking a war between Croats and Serbs that lasted until 1995.

What happened once the Croatians established independence is even more interesting. Within Croatia, the Croats were a majority and the Serbs, who had been part of the majority prior to the separation of Croatia from Yugoslavia, were a minority. These ethnic Serbs, who were primarily located in the Croatian region of Krajina, now viewed themselves as a potentially exploitable minority within the newly independent Croatia. As a result, they started another preemptive conflict to separate from Croatia—an attempt that was ultimately unsuccessful.

Thus, in Croatia, we see the logic of the model play out twice in a series of cascading civil wars. First a Croatian minority starts a preemptive war in response to the Serbian majority's inability to commit not to exploit its Croatian minority. Then a Serb minority within the newly independent Croatia starts another preemptive war in response to the Croatian majority's inability to commit not to exploit its Serb minority.

While Fearon presented this as a model of ethnic conflict, its basic mechanism—conflict due to commitment problems borne of shifting power—can be thought of much more broadly. As we will see in Chapter 8.3, many types of government policy may be distorted because of commitment problems. For instance, a political party might resist immigration reform if it is concerned that immigrants will vote for another party. But there are also examples within many other kinds of organizations. Let me give a few possible examples.

Imagine a company or organization controlled by a group of elites (e.g., senior executives, tenured faculty). Those elites have to decide whether to allow or block the adoption of a new technology. This new technology will lead to increased growth. But it also makes it more likely that the elites will lose power because younger members of the organization have greater facility with the new technology. The board and shareholders cannot credibly commit not to transfer authority to these younger employees as the current elites' knowledge becomes obsolete. Hence, the elites block the new technology for as long as they can. This is inefficiency due to a commitment problem. If the board or shareholders could commit to not challenge the elites' authority, then the elites would allow the technology, making the company more profitable. But because they can't commit, the company is kept stagnant. A related argument, sometimes made in academic circles, is that one of the benefits of tenure is that it frees faculty to hire new assistant professors whom they believe to be smarter or better trained than themselves.

Consider a union negotiating with management. Management wants the union members to take a small pay cut. However, the union believes that if they take a small pay cut now, then fewer shops will join the union in the future, weakening the union relative to management. Consequently, the union worries that management will exploit the effects of a small pay cut today to demand even larger pay cuts in the future. As a result, the union strikes rather than taking a small pay cut, an inefficient outcome. If management could credibly commit not to demand more concessions in the future, then costly conflict could be avoided. But such a promise is not credible.

6.2   The Hold-Up Problem

In many industries, local dealerships have the exclusive right to sell certain products. For instance, in the United States, a variety of state laws protect local automobile dealerships from both competition and sanction by automobile manufacturers. All states require that dealerships be licensed, restricting new dealerships from entering the market. Many states limit the circumstances under which a manufacturer can terminate a dealership franchise and require manufacturers to repurchase unsold cars from terminated dealers. The vast majority of states also directly protect dealerships from local competition with restrictions on "encroachment."

For example, Massachusetts General Law Part I, Title XV, Chapter 93B, Section 6, includes the following provisions:

> It shall be a violation ... for a manufacturer, distributor or franchisor representative without good cause, in bad faith or in an arbitrary or unconscionable manner to ... grant or enter into a franchise agreement with a person who would be permitted under or required by the franchise agreement to conduct its dealership operations from a site any boundary of which is situated within the relevant market area of an existing motor vehicle dealer representing the same line make.

States are likely willing to provide these protections because they generate significant tax revenue from dealerships. But such restrictions also create inefficiencies. They allow dealerships to demand a larger share of profits from manufacturers by restricting the ability of manufacturers to sell to consumers through other outlets. As a result, the dealership structure and its various policy protections likely raise prices for consumers and reduce investment and innovation by manufacturers, who don't expect to enjoy a large percentage of the fruits of such investments.[4]

This is another instance of inefficiency caused by commitment problems. This particular type of commitment problem is called the *hold-up problem*. Let's look at a model.

Imagine a simple supply chain. There is an *upstream* producer who produces $e \geq 0$. The cost to the upstream producer of producing e is $c \times e^2$, with $c > 0$.

There is a *downstream* user who values the product at $\alpha \times e$. The next best use for the product is for the upstream producer to sell it to some other user for $\beta \times e$ with $\beta < \alpha$. This lower value reflects the fact that the product is in some way particularly well suited to the downstream user. Perhaps it is designed specifically for the downstream user, the upstream producer has to pay a penalty for selling to a different user because of regulatory protections, or the downstream user is especially good at marketing the upstream producer's product.

The game is played as follows. First, the upstream producer chooses a production level. Then the downstream user offers the upstream producer a price p per unit of the product. The upstream producer can take it or reject it.

The upstream producer's payoffs are $pe - ce^2$ if he accepts the offer. His payoffs are $\beta e - ce^2$ if he rejects the offer. The downstream buyer's payoffs if the offer is accepted are $\alpha e - pe$ and if the offer is rejected are 0. This game is represented in Figure 6.3.

At the final stage of the game, the upstream producer strictly prefers to take the downstream user's offer if $p > \beta$ and strictly prefers to reject it if $p < \beta$. The upstream producer is indifferent if $p = \beta$. As in our conflict model, there is only an equilibrium if the upstream producer accepts an offer of $p = \beta$. So the upstream producer accepts any offer of $p \geq \beta$ and rejects any offer of $p < \beta$.

Anticipating this, what will the downstream user offer? If the downstream user offers $p < \beta$, she makes a payoff of 0. If she offers $p \geq \beta$ she makes $(\alpha - p)e$. Clearly, if the downstream user is going to make an offer that will be accepted, she wants to offer as little as possible. Hence, she offers $p = \beta$.

What level of investment will the upstream producer make? The upstream producer anticipates that he will get a price of $p = \beta$ from the downstream user. So he chooses his investment level to solve

$$\max_{e} \beta e - ce^2.$$

---

[4]See Lafontaine and Morton (2010) for details.

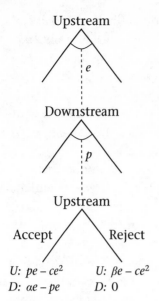

U: $pe - ce^2$ U: $\beta e - ce^2$
D: $\alpha e - pe$ D: 0 Figure 6.3. Hold-up problem.

Maximizing, the equilibrium production level, e^*, is given by the following first-order condition:

$$\beta - 2ce^* = 0 \Rightarrow e^* = \frac{\beta}{2c}.$$

This equilibrium is inefficient. Since the product will end up with the downstream user, its final value is αe and its cost is ce^2. Hence, the efficient level of production solves

$$\max_{e} \alpha e - ce^2.$$

The first-best investment is

$$\alpha - 2ce^{FB} = 0 \Rightarrow e^{FB} = \frac{\alpha}{2c}.$$

Comparing the first-best investment to the equilibrium investment, it is clear that the equilibrium has inefficient underproduction:

$$e^{FB} = \frac{\alpha}{2c} > \frac{\beta}{2c} = e^*.$$

The problem is that while the social value of the product is α, the upstream producer knows he will not be paid a price of α. He will only be paid a price of β. If the downstream user could commit to pay α, the upstream producer would invest efficiently. But the downstream user cannot credibly commit to do so. Once production decisions are made, the downstream user has an incentive to "hold up" the upstream producer—paying only enough to match the upstream producer's next best option.

6.2.1 Interpretation

The hold-up problem suggests that a lack of credible commitment leads to inefficiently low levels of investment. This sort of problem might emerge in a variety of settings.

In many industries, an upstream supplier must bear up-front costs (e.g., new technology, a specialized workforce) to build products to a downstream user's specifications. By making downstream user-specific products, the upstream supplier diminishes the outside marketability of the upstream product. This means the upstream supplier is particularly subject to hold-up. Hence, the upstream supplier will be disinclined to bear the up-front costs, leading to inefficiency.

Firms invest in research to develop a new product (e.g., medicine, technology). If the buyers of those products have significant market power, then the research firm can be held up, leading to underinvestment in research and development. For instance, a concern about adverse effects on investment in new treatments is sometimes raised when large medical insurers or government agencies use their market power to negotiate lower prices for prescription medication.

When consumers purchase software, they anticipate that it may require future modification or updating that they cannot do on their own—for example, tax or accounting software. Once a consumer has purchased the software, the company that has the capacity to modify the software can hold up the consumer (who doesn't want to switch platforms) by charging a high price for future updates. This potential for hold-up will lead to underpurchasing of such software.

Inside a partnership—for example, a law firm or medical practice—some partners invest in technical expertise and other partners invest in client relationships. The partner with client relationships can later threaten to leave with the clients, holding up the partner with technical expertise for a greater share of profits. Hence, partners might have incentives to overinvest in client relations and underinvest in technical know-how.

6.3 Policy Responses

In the case of both costly conflict and the hold-up problem, some future action cannot be credibly committed to even though, from an ex ante perspective, both actors would be better off if a credible commitment could be made. Thus, one can think of a lack of enforceable contracts as the fundamental issue. This lack of enforceability might be because the relevant information (e.g., how hard someone worked) is unobservable by a court and therefore can't be contracted. It might also be because of a lack of institutional capacity for enforcing contracts, as in the case of the absence of a third-party guarantor for agreements during civil war. The basic insight of both models is that non-contractibility leads to inefficiency of various sorts—conflict, underinvestment, and so on. And so the policy challenge is to find ways—legal, institutional, or informal—to facilitate credible commitment.

In the context of conflict, one approach is for the international community to serve as a third-party guarantor. The most direct approach is sending peacekeepers to enforce agreements. But international institutions, such as the International Criminal Court, which have the ability to hold actors to account for illegal acts, also play such a role.

In the context of the hold-up problem, economists have thought a fair bit about how firms and other economic actors might try to solve commitment problems on their own. One provocative idea is that firms themselves are a response to problems like hold-up. The argument is that a vertically integrated firm might solve the hold-up problem by unifying upstream and downstream actors within one overarching economic agent. If both actors can be placed in a setting in which they only care about firm profits, then the hold-up problem disappears. While this is a powerful idea, there are at least some reasons to be skeptical about vertical integration as a solution to the hold-up problem. In particular, it is often the case that units within a firm view themselves as in competition. If this is the case, it might well be that the hold-up problem is re-created within the firm.

In the context of other commitment problems, social scientists argue that various kinds of institutions might aid with commitment. For instance, a government that faces a potential rebellion might like to promise all sorts of policy concessions to avoid revolution. However, such a commitment may not be credible if the revolutionary threat itself diminishes over time. If the government democratizes (i.e., changes institution), then it actually places at least partial control of government decisions in the hands of the people considering rebelling, perhaps credibly committing to follow compromise policies and avoiding a costly rebellion (Acemoglu and Robinson, 2001, 2006). Of course, this idea raises deep questions about why democracy itself constitutes a credible commitment, but we will leave those questions for another day.

Actors can also find less dramatic ways to limit future discretion in order to solve commitment problems. We discussed the idea that strikes might be caused by management's inability to commit not to exploit increased power that comes from union wage concessions in future contract negotiations. In such a setting, management might willingly give up some of its future negotiating power, for instance by subjecting future contract disputes to binding arbitration, in order to avoid a strike.

6.4 Takeaways

- Commitment problems arise in dynamic settings due to the absence of enforceable contracts and shifting power (political, military, social, market, or legal). These commitment problems give rise to inefficient behavior "up the tree." This inefficient behavior can take many forms: underinvestment, conflict, and so on.
- One way to solve commitment problems is to create institutions (formal or informal) that allow players to credibly commit (e.g., democracy as a commitment device for policy change).
- Another solution to commitment problems is to find ways for players to write binding and enforceable contracts.

6.5 Further Reading

Fearon (1995) provides the classic discussion of the puzzle of costly conflict. Fearon (1998) is the clearest articulation of the basic workings of the relationship between commitment problems, shifting power, and inefficient conflict. The most general characterization of this relationship is Powell (2004).

For classic work on the relationship between the hold-up problem and the theory of the firm, see Williamson (1975, 1985), Klein, Crawford, and Alchian (1978), and Hart (1988).

6.6 Exercises

1. Consider the following model of a budget process. At the beginning of the game, a Leader chooses a punishment to impose on all players if the Congress fails to pass a budget. Call this punishment p. The Leader can choose $p = 0$ (i.e., no punishment) or $p = 1.5$. The Congress then either compromises or it does not compromise. If the Congress compromises, a reduced budget is passed. If the Congress fails to compromise, then the status quo budget is passed and the penalty is implemented.

    Payoffs are as follows. The payoff to the Leader of the status quo is 0 and the compromise is 1. The payoff to the Congress of the status quo is 1 and the compromise is 0. Thus, the game is represented in Figure 6.4 (where the first payoff is always the Leader's):

    (a) Write down all of the Leader's strategies. Write down all of the Congress's strategies.

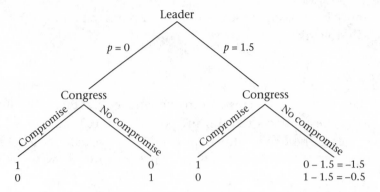

Figure 6.4. Budget game.

(b) Write down the unique subgame perfect Nash equilibrium of this game. Describe what happens in this equilibrium.

Now suppose that, should Congress fail to compromise, the Leader gets to choose whether or not to impose the punishment. That is, the game is now the one represented in Figure 6.5:

(c) In this revised game, write down all of the Leader's strategies and write down all of the Congress's strategies.
(d) In this revised game, write down any one subgame perfect Nash equilibrium. What happens in this equilibrium?
(e) Explain how comparing the equilibrium outcomes in these two models illustrates how an inability to commit can make a player worse off.

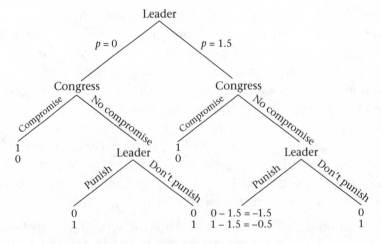

Figure 6.5. Budget game without commitment.

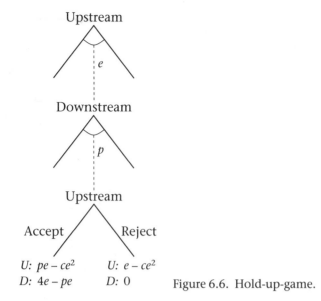

U: $pe - ce^2$ U: $e - ce^2$
D: $4e - pe$ D: 0   Figure 6.6. Hold-up-game.

2. Consider the model of hold-up in Figure 6.6. At the beginning of the game, player U chooses a level of effort, e. Then player D offers a price, p. Finally, player U chooses to accept or reject the offered price.

   If U accepts, it gets pe in revenues. If it rejects, it can use what it produced at value 1, so gets revenues e. The cost to U of effort is ce^2 (where $c > 0$ is a parameter that affects U's marginal cost of effort, which, differentiating, is $2ce$).

   D values e at $4e$. So if U accepts, D's payoff is $4e - pe$. If U rejects, D's payoff is 0.

   (a) Solve for the unique subgame perfect Nash equilibrium.
   (b) Assuming that the outcome involves the price being accepted, what is the utilitarian payoff in this game? (Your answer will be a function of c.)
   (c) What is the utilitarian optimum level of investment? (Your answer will be a function of c.)
   (d) Explain why the equilibrium and utilitarian levels of investment are different.
   (e) Now, suppose that D could actually commit, up-front, to a price. That is, suppose the payoffs stay the same, but the order of play changes so that the game is as in Figure 6.7. What is the unique subgame perfect Nash equilibrium of this game?
   (f) Is the equilibrium identified in (e) a Pareto improvement relative to that identified in (a)?
   (g) Does your answer to (f) suggest that D did or did not suffer from a commitment problem in the original game?

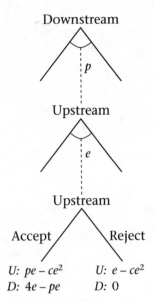

$$U: pe - ce^2 \quad\quad U: e - ce^2$$
$$D: 4e - pe \quad\quad D: 0$$

Figure 6.7. Hold-up game with commitment.

3. In Stanley Kubrik's classic satirical film, *Doctor Strangelove*, a nuclear-armed, American bomber is on its way to bomb the Soviet Union and cannot be recalled. Upon learning this, the Russian ambassador is forced to reveal to the Americans that the Soviets have built a doomsday machine—a machine that will automatically detonate enough nuclear weapons to destroy the earth if Russia is attacked or if anyone tries to disarm the doomsday device. Such doomsday devices were indeed discussed by policymakers during the height of the Cold War. Explain why such devices might have some appeal in terms of commitment problems.

4. Figure 6.8 is a model in which the "people" can credibly threaten revolution if a leader does not democratize.

    The best outcome for the people is to get democracy without revolting. The second-best outcome is to get democracy after threatening a revolution. The third-best outcome is to get no democracy and not revolt. The worst outcome is to get no democracy and have to revolt.

    The best outcome for the leader is to neither democratize nor have a revolution. The second-best outcome is to democratize without being threatened. The third-best outcome is to democratize under threat of revolution. The worst outcome is to not democratize and then actually face a revolution.

    (a) Write down all of the strategies for each player.
    (b) Identify all the SPNE of this game.

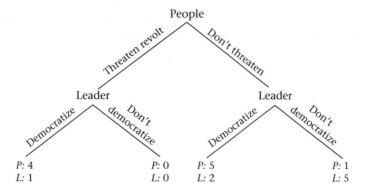

Figure 6.8. First revolution game.

Now consider the alternate game in Figure 6.9, in which the leader moves first and the people only consider revolting if there is no democratization.

(c) Write down all of the strategies for each player.
(d) Identify all the SPNE of this game.
(e) Suppose we define democratization as "good policy" here. (That is, we are not focused on Pareto improvements or utilitarianism, we just want democracy.) Use a comparison of (b) and (d) to explain how a commitment problem can give rise to a bad policy outcome.

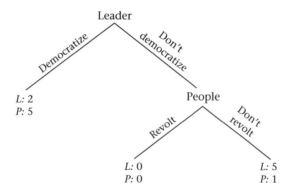

Figure 6.9. Second revolution game.

5.   (This problem was inspired by a problem from Ben Polak.) A company is considering building a new factory. The factory will cost c to build. To operate, the factory requires 100 workers. Once operating, it will generate profits of π. If the company builds the factory and hires the workers at wage w, it makes a payoff of

$$\pi - 100w - c.$$

If the company builds the factory but fails to hire workers, it makes a payoff of $-c$. If it doesn't build the factory, it makes 0.

The workers currently have jobs that pay a wage of v. The workers' payoff is equal to their wages (either at the new factory or in their current jobs).

(a) Suppose the workers can be hired at their current wage—that is, $w = v$. For what values of c will the firm build the factory?

(b) Suppose that, after the factory is built, the workers' union can make a take-it-or-leave-it wage demand to the firm. The firm's only choice is to pay that wage or have the factory not operate (thereby losing its up-front investment of c). What demand will the union make? Anticipating this, for what values of c will the firm build the factory?

(c) Explain how the difference between your answers to parts (a) and (b) are the result of a hold-up problem.

Summing Up Social Dilemmas

In Part II we learned about three kinds of social dilemmas—externalities, coordination problems, and commitment problems. Each of these models describes a broad array of social phenomena. Moreover, when any one of them occurs, the right policy intervention could achieve a Pareto improvement. The hope is that having a conceptual understanding of these dilemmas clarifies where there are opportunities for policy to do good.

Importantly, different dilemmas require different types of policy responses. Table 6.1 offers a summary, showing the policy technologies best matched to each social dilemma.

We also discussed the idea that for certain types of social dilemmas, ongoing relationships may make it possible for people to self-organize a solution. This is particularly likely in tight-knit and relatively small groups. Importantly, even when self-organization is possible, it requires coordination. Hence, another role for policymakers is to use the tools appropriate for addressing coordination traps to help groups self-organize solutions to externalities and commitment problems.

TABLE 6.1. Social Dilemmas and Policy Interventions.

Social Dilemma	Types of Intervention	Length of Intervention
Externality	Pigovian tax or subsidy Regulation	Long Run
Coordination Problem	Leadership and Communication Insurance	Short Run Long Run
Commitment Problem	Enforceable contracts Limit discretion Vertical integration	Long Run

PART III

Constraints on Good Governance

The ubiquity of social dilemmas creates many opportunities for good policy to yield Pareto improvements. Yet much of the policy implemented by governments does not look like the textbook policy solutions we've described. To be sure, there are examples of Pigovian taxes in response to externalities, publicly provided insurance that eliminates coordination traps, and so on. But there are also many actions taken by policymakers that are hard to make sense of in terms of social dilemmas or Pareto improvements.

Indeed, a widely held view among political economists is that much policy is motivated not by opportunities to do good, but by *rent seeking*—that is, using policy to benefit particular individuals or groups. Stigler (1972, p. 100) provides some classic examples:

> Particular industries and occupations obtain from the state a variety of economic privileges which are injurious to the vast majority of the population. Farm subsidies, oil import quotas, tariffs, and occupational licensing are examples.

Let me offer a few specifics.

The price of sugar in the United States is more than twice its price in much of the rest of the world. The reason is a series of U.S. policies—import restrictions, price guarantees, etc.—designed to protect the domestic sugar industry. These policies benefit certain agricultural interests, including both sugar producers and corn growers (demand for corn syrup is driven by high sugar prices). But they impose costs on many other domestic constituencies. Most directly, they harm U.S. food producers and consumers. They also impose costs on taxpayers, who foot the bill for a program in which the government buys surplus sugar when prices drop. Finally, a study by the U.S. Commerce Department estimates that, for every job in the sugar industry saved by U.S. sugar subsidies, three jobs are lost in industries that use sugar as an input.[1] Beghin et al. (2003) estimate that, on net, the U.S. sugar program generates half a billion dollars (in 1999 dollars) in annual deadweight loss. Sugar subsidies are, of course, just one among many such policies involving price supports and import restrictions in the United States and around the globe.

Concern about the anti-competitive effects of professional licensing date to at least Adam Smith, who, in Chapter 10 of the first volume of *The Wealth of Nations*, argues that such restrictions harm welfare "by restraining the competition in some employments to a smaller number than would otherwise be disposed to enter into them." As Kleiner (2006, p. 189) summarizes, Smith worries about "the ability of the crafts to lengthen apprenticeship programs and limit the number of apprentices per master, thus, ensuring higher earnings for persons in these occupations." Kleiner notes that by 2000, over 20% of U.S. workers required some sort of licensing. To be sure, in some settings, licensing may play an important role monitoring quality, enforcing ethics, and informing consumers. But, as Smith and many observers since have noted, licensing also has costs. By restricting entry into the market place, licensing requirements decrease supply, benefiting a small group of incumbents at the expense of new entrants and consumers. These issues arise in a wide array of venues. In some areas—like the efforts of physicians' groups to use licensing requirements to restrict the type of care that can be provided by nurse practitioners or the attempts by lawyers' groups to restrict the services that can be provided by paralegals—there may be serious questions about how to weigh the trade-offs between ensuring high quality service, on the one hand, and fostering competition, on the other. In other areas—like the attempts by taxi drivers to use licensing requirements to avoid competition from ride-sharing companies like Uber or the mandate that bartenders, barbers, and cosmetologists be licensed in many states—it is hard to imagine a compelling public interest argument for the practice of professional licensing.

The reason we observe such inefficient policies, of course, is because public policy is not made by a Pareto improving machine. Public policy is made by governments, which is to say by politicians and bureaucrats. Political decision making is a (perhaps *the*) critical determinant of what kinds of policies get made and enforced. Policymakers are people, with their own beliefs and incentives, working within strategically complicated environments to achieve their goals. Indeed, all of the dilemmas we studied in Part II as a

---

[1] U.S. Department of Commerce International Trade Administration. 2006. "Employment Changes in U.S. Food Manufacturing: The Impact of Sugar Prices." http://trade.gov/media/Publications/pdf/sugar06.pdf

motivation for policymaking—externalities, coordination problems, commit-ment problems—and many others, also exist within the governmental orga-nizations in which policy gets made. Moreover, the people and organizations that are governed by policy are also strategic actors who work hard to influence the policy process to suit their own interests. Hence, if you want to understand policy, you must understand the politics of the policymaking process. And if you want to be a leader of policy debates, you must be able to work within these political constraints.

In what follows, we will examine some reasons why governments might fail to achieve Pareto improvements in the face of social dilemmas. Broadly speak-ing, we will consider two classes of explanations—*technological* and *incentive* constraints.

By a technological constraint I mean some factor in the world that limits even a well-intentioned policymaker's ability to achieve good outcomes. The tech-nological constraints we will consider include people's ability to adjust their be-havior to avoid a policy's intended effects, policymakers' limited commitment power, and lack of information needed to make optimal policy decisions.

By an incentive constraint I mean features of the politics of the policymaking process that affect policymakers' interests. We will consider various ways in which the governed attempt to influence policymakers, including through interest group politics and lobbying, political donations, and electoral politics. We will also look at how the institutional rules that govern how a leader maintains power shape policymakers' incentives.

It is worth reiterating a point made in the introduction to this book. I do not provide a fine-grained analysis of the legislative, judicial, or bureaucratic politics of the policymaking process. Understanding those politics is also essen-tial for understanding policy. But the details of those subjects are, in my view, best covered in more specialized courses and books. My goal, here, is to offer general principles that lend insight into government decision making across many institutions. Just as with the treatment of social dilemmas, in so doing, I hope to provide models that clarify how one thinks about the challenges of moving from a good policy idea to successful policy reform. Along the way, I will also present some evidence that these kinds of governance challenges and constraints really do matter for policy and welfare.

Finally, let me highlight one other important point. In what follows, I will provide a variety of examples and models in which governments fail to implement optimal policy solutions. This should not be taken as an argument against or critique of government or public policy. That is emphatically not the point I am trying to make. Rather, I want you to see something more nuanced. Traditional policy analysis stops at the point of identifying policy solutions that would be effective if faithfully implemented. Such an analysis has a hidden, and unrealistic, assumption about how governments act. A more thoroughgoing policy analysis takes these political constraints seriously as first-order concerns for policy design and implementation. The various analyses that follow are meant to move us in the direction of this more satisfying notion of what constitutes good policy, all things considered.

7

Strategic Adjustment

Corporate Average Fuel Economy (CAFE) standards, which regulate the fuel efficiency of fleets of cars produced by a given manufacturer, were first implemented in the 1970s. The goal was to improve the fuel economy and reduce the environmental impact of automobiles. And, indeed, fuel economy improved dramatically in the United States starting in the 1980s.

But CAFE standards also had another effect. Because light trucks are used in agriculture, they were not treated as cars for the purpose of CAFE standards. They were subject to laxer fuel economy regulation. In effect, CAFE standards reduced automobile manufacturers' costs of selling light trucks relative to cars. In response, the auto industry all but eliminated the station wagon (which was classified as a car), substituting minivans and SUVs (both of which were classified as light trucks) into their personal vehicle fleets. They could sell these large vehicles cheaply (relative to cars) because of the regulatory advantage. A combination of well-intentioned regulation, government failure to anticipate strategic adjustments by automobile manufacturers, and good old-fashioned American love of big stuff are, at least in part, to thank for the rise of the SUV as a passenger vehicle.

The Clinton-era "welfare to work" reform seems to have had a similar unintended consequence.[1] Welfare to work was meant to move people toward self-sufficiency by making public assistance conditional on finding work. And a first glance at the data suggests it was a major success. The number of welfare recipients dropped from about 5 million families in 1995 to about 2 million families in 2010. But it is worth digging a little deeper.

Since much of the financial burden of public assistance fell to state governments, welfare to work gave states strong incentives to move people into the work force. Of course, one way to do so was to actually help people find jobs. But state governments also found other ways to do so—for instance, by turning unemployed workers into disabled workers. People who qualify as disabled are not counted as unemployed. Moreover, since they qualify for federal disability payments, disabled workers don't cost the states anything. So, following the adoption of welfare to work, the states started working hard to help people

---

[1] See Chana Joffe-Walt. *Unfit for Work: The startling rise of disability in America.* National Public Radio. http://apps.npr.org/unfit-for-work/

who might otherwise end up on public assistance instead apply for disability. Many states hired private companies to search lists of welfare recipients for people who could make disability claims and to assist those people through the application process. And, indeed, just as the welfare rolls started their dramatic decline, the federal disability rolls started a significant increase, from about 4 million former workers in 1995 to about 8 million in 2010.

One last example comes from my own industry, higher education. A variety of federal government policies in the United States seek to make higher education more affordable. Most notably, the government offers education tax credits and subsidized student loans. It might seem obvious that such policies lower the price of college for students, but let's think about it a little more.

Offering a college tax credit or subsidized loan is equivalent to lowering the price of college for students. If tuition stays fixed, this will in fact help with affordability. The problem is that colleges are free to increase tuition to whatever level the market will bear. Even at current prices, admission to a research university is very competitive. If the price of tuition drops as a result of new federal subsidies, demand will increase. Two things can happen in a market when there is excess demand. Supply can increase or prices can go up.

The thing about education at a research university, unlike many other businesses (e.g., gas stations, grocery stores), is that it is very hard for supply to increase in the short- to medium-run. Research universities depend on enormous, very expensive infrastructures (physics labs, libraries, dorms, faculties, and so on). They also depend on reputation. So an entrepreneur cannot easily increase supply by creating a new research university where there wasn't one before. Another way that supply might increase is for research universities to admit more students. Universities are willing to do so to some extent in response to excess demand. But that extent is limited because universities care about selectivity, student to faculty ratios, and the like.

If the supply of research universities can't expand to meet the excess demand created by a new federal subsidy, only one other thing can happen. Prices go up. That is, universities increase tuition or decrease internal financial aid to suck up those new federal benefits. In this scenario, the federal subsidy doesn't make college more affordable. The real cost to students stays the same. The policy is simply a transfer from taxpayers to research universities.

Recent evidence demonstrates that research universities do in fact strategically adapt to policy changes in this way. The best study concerns the Pell Grant Program, which in 2011 provided over nine million low-income college students with subsidies of $35 billion (Turner, 2014). Research universities appear to reduce institutional financial aid by about 66 cents for every dollar a student receives in federal grants. So the federal subsidies help students a bit, but most of the money flows to the colleges. Interestingly, the same is not true at community colleges and technical schools, where it is easier for supply to expand to meet excess demand. As a result, such schools are not able to adapt in a way that captures all of the benefits of government subsidies. And, indeed, subsidies do appear to increase affordability for students at these schools.

Each of these examples illustrates a key insight that comes from thinking game theoretically. Actions taken "up the tree" affect behavior "down the tree." This idea is particularly important when thinking about public policy. Often in policy debates, people estimate the expected effects of some policy change assuming that behavior won't change in a meaningful way when the policy shifts. As we've just seen, this is a mistake that can lead to bad policy choices. In the remainder of this chapter we consider two models that illustrate particularly important forms of strategic adaptation and how they create challenges for policymakers.

7.1 Strategic Adversaries

In many policy settings—policing, counterterrorism, regulatory oversight—the government has limited resources which it must use to prevent bad behavior by non-governmental actors. For instance, police must deploy a finite number of patrols across neighborhoods, counterterrorists only have the resources to harden a limited number of potential targets, and nuclear regulators must decide which plants to monitor. In deciding how to deploy its resources, it is critical that the government think about how other actors' behavior will shift in response. Let's consider a simple model in the context of counterterrorism.

There are two potential terrorist targets: A and B. A government allocates counterterrorism resources between the targets. Let $\alpha \in [0, 1]$ be the resources devoted to protecting A and $1 - \alpha$ be the resources devoted to defending B. The terrorists then choose to attack one or the other target.

The probability that an attack against a given target succeeds depends on the counterterrorism resources devoted to protecting that target. For simplicity, assume that if the counterterrorism resources devoted to protecting a particular target are x, then the probability of an attack on that target succeeding is $1 - x$. For now, let's assume the terrorists value the two targets equally.

We can solve this game via backward induction. What will the terrorists do, given the government's counterterrorism strategy, α? There are three cases to consider:

1. If the government chose $\alpha > \frac{1}{2}$, an attack against target A succeeds with lower probability than an attack against target B. So the terrorists' unique best response is to attack target B.
2. If the government chose $\alpha < \frac{1}{2}$, an attack against target A succeeds with higher probability than an attack against target B. So the terrorists' unique best response is to attack target A.

3. If the government chose $\alpha = \frac{1}{2}$, the terrorists are indifferent between attacking A or B. (It turns out that, to sustain an equilibrium, the terrorists randomize between the two targets, but don't worry about that for now.)

What does this imply about how the government should allocate its counterterrorism resources? If the government expends more resources protecting one target than another, those resources are wasted because the terrorists will adapt, attacking the other target. All the government can do is to spread its resources thin, defending both targets equally. Several points are interesting here.

First, the optimal counterterrorism policy is not responsive to how much the government cares about the two targets. Even if the government cares massively more about defending target A than target B, it still isn't the right decision to devote more resources to target A. The reason is the strategic adaptation of the terrorists. If the government devotes lots of resources to the target it cares most about, the terrorists will simply attack the other target, and so the government would have been better off devoting more resources to protecting that target.

Second, the optimal counterterrorism policy is responsive to how much the terrorists care about the two targets. Suppose the value to the terrorists of an attack against A is v_A and against B is v_B. The terrorists strictly prefer to attack A if

$$(1 - \alpha)v_A > \alpha v_B,$$

which can be rewritten

$$\alpha < \frac{v_A}{v_A + v_B}.$$

Thus, the terrorists' best response correspondence is now

$$\text{BR}(\alpha) = \begin{cases} \text{Attack } A & \text{if } \alpha < \dfrac{v_A}{v_A + v_B} \\ \text{Attack either} & \text{if } \alpha = \dfrac{v_A}{v_A + v_B} \\ \text{Attack } B & \text{if } \alpha > \dfrac{v_A}{v_A + v_B}. \end{cases}$$

So the government again spreads its resources thin in the optimal counterterrorism scheme, but weighted by how much the terrorists care about each target, so as to equalize the terrorists' expected value of attacking any given target.

Third, this logic holds even more starkly if there are lots of potential targets, rather than just two. In particular, the optimal counterterrorism policy looks like this. Start by spending on the target considered most valuable by the terrorists. Keep spending until the terrorists' expected value from attacking it is equal to their expected value from attacking the second most valuable target. Then spend on both of those until the expected value of attacking either of them is equal to the expected value of attacking the third most valuable target. Then spend on all three of those until the expected value of attacking any of them is equal to the expected value of attacking the fourth most valuable target. Continue this process until you are out of money. Thus, if there are lots of targets, the government must spread its resources very thin because of the terrorists' capacity to strategically adapt.[2]

7.1.1 Do Terrorists Really Strategically Adjust?

You might think that we are leaning a little too heavily on the rationality of terrorists in this story. The only reason the government's optimal policy calls on it to spread its resources so thin is because our hyperrational terrorists strategically adapt whenever the government fails to do so. Let me offer you a little bit of evidence to suggest this isn't so crazy.

Starting in the mid-1960s, hijacking became a serious problem in American civil aviation. Over 80 airplanes were taken by hijackers in 1969 alone. The hijackers included Americans, Croatians, Cubans, Japanese, North Koreans, Palestinians, and many others. Their motivations ranged from simple ransom to nationalist, leftist, and other global political causes.

In the early 1970s, in response to this growing assault on air safety, the United States and European countries increased airport security. Most importantly, metal detectors were installed in every major American airport by early 1973. We'd taken our first step on the road toward only using toiletries that come in three-ounce packages and not being able to wear socks with holes to the airport.

Did this heightened security work to increase public safety? In one sense, the answer is clearly yes. The upper cell of Figure 7.1 (which is a simplified replication of the analysis from Enders and Sandler (1993)) shows hijackings decreased fairly dramatically right after metal detectors were installed in 1973. But that is not the whole story. After metal detectors were installed, other kinds of terrorist hostage takings became more frequent, as shown in the lower cell of Figure 7.1. Indeed, Enders and Sandler show that during the course of the 1970s there is almost a one-for-one relationship between the decline in hijackings and the increase in other types of hostage-taking terrorist attacks.

There are a couple of points to see here. First, there is a general point for thinking about counterterrorism, policing, and so on. Trying to protect individual sites—airports, nuclear reactors, tourist destinations, skyscrapers, government buildings, and so on—requires us to spread our resources thin. Thus, such a policy is unlikely to be terribly effective in the presence of a large

---

[2]See Bueno de Mesquita (2007) and Powell (2007) for discussions of these and related issues.

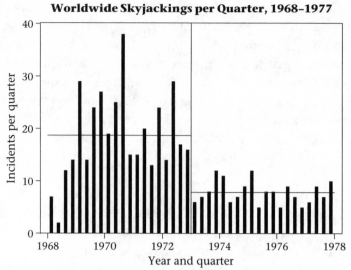

Worldwide Skyjackings per Quarter, 1968–1977

Horizontal line is average incidents per quarter before and after 1973:Q1.

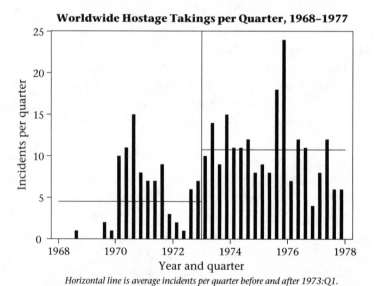

Worldwide Hostage Takings per Quarter, 1968–1977

Horizontal line is average incidents per quarter before and after 1973:Q1.

Figure 7.1. Change in hijackings and non-hijacking hostage takings following installation of metal detectors. The data are from Mickolus (1982). The analysis is a simplified version of that in Enders and Sandler (1993).

number of potential targets. Much better are policies that are broad-based in the sense of protecting everything at once. Such policies might include restricting terrorist financing or access to weapons, intelligence gathering to detect attacks, border security, and the like.

Second, these adjustments suggest that a major portion of the U.S. government's response to the 9/11 attacks may have been suboptimal. In policing and counterterrorism, there is often a tendency to fight yesterday's war. If the terrorists attack airplanes, we protect airports. If there is a rash of crime in a particular neighborhood, we send police to that neighborhood. But such policies may fail due to strategic adaptation.

7.1.2 The War on Drugs

The problem of disrupting the drug trade is not unlike the problem of preventing terrorist attacks. If the government tightens airport security, terrorists take hostages in some other location. If the government makes it more difficult to move drugs into the United States through some entry point, the drug smugglers find a different one, often with toxic effects along the new route.

The Mexican drug war resulted from precisely this kind of adaptation. In the 1970s and early 1980s, very few drugs reached the United States through Mexico. The transshipment route of choice was from Colombia through the Caribbean and into Florida. In 1980, the Drug Enforcement Administration launched Operation Swordfish—a major offensive against the Colombian drug cartels. The government deployed thousands of agents and considerable naval and air power to shut down the Caribbean transshipment route.

Not unlike the case of metal detectors, there is a sense in which Operation Swordfish and other U.S. government efforts in the Caribbean and southern Florida were a stunning success. By the mid-1980s, the Colombian drug cartels were actively pulling out of the Caribbean and the flow of drugs into Florida diminished considerably. In 1985, 75% of all cocaine seized by authorities was captured in the Caribbean. By the early 1990s that number had fallen to around 10%.[3]

But to call these outcomes a victory is to ignore the fact that drug smugglers adapt. The reduction in drugs flowing through the Caribbean and into Florida in the 1980s does not reflect a reduction in drugs flowing to the United States during that period. Indeed, drugs continued to enter the United States at increasing rates, as evidenced by the fourfold decrease in cocaine prices during the course of the 1980s—from a wholesale price of around $200 per pure gram in 1980 to under $50 in 1989—despite soaring demand.[4]

So what did happen? The Colombian cartels abandoned the Caribbean in favor of Mexico. In 1989, one-third of all cocaine in the United States entered through Mexico. Just three years later, that number had increased to one-half. Today, 90% of cocaine sold in the United States is smuggled up from Mexico.

---

[3]See United Nations Office on Drugs and Crime. 2010. "The Globalization of Crime: A Transnational Organized Crime Threat Assessment." Chapter 4. http://www.unodc.org/documents/data-and-analysis/tocta/TOCTA_Report_2010_low_res.pdf

[4]See Office of National Drug Control Policy. October 2001. "The Price of Illicit Drugs: 1981 through the Second Quarter of 2000." https://www.whitehouse.gov/sites/default/files/ondcp/policy-and-research/bullet_5.pdf

This adaptation by the drug traffickers has had devastating effects on Mexico. Throughout the 1990s, the Mexican drug trafficking organizations became larger and more powerful. They shifted from being middlemen for the Colombians to having their own suppliers and distribution networks. In the course of this expansion, Mexican drug trafficking organizations became more violent. In 2010, the Mexican drug war claimed over 1,000 lives per month. The Mexican government struggled to exert basic control over parts of the country.

Suppose the Mexican government were to succeed in preventing drugs from flowing across the Mexican border into the United States. What would happen? We can't know for sure. But both our model of adaptation and past history suggest that, since American demand for drugs doesn't seem to be going anywhere, the drug trafficking organizations would find a new transshipment route. The most depressing scenario I can think of is that they would go right back to the Caribbean, where American interdiction efforts are no longer focused. If this were to happen, the expenditure of several decades of government efforts, billions of dollars, and an untold number of lives would have been undone by the basic logic of strategic adaptation. We'd be right back where we were in 1975. On the up side, maybe they'd bring back Don Johnson and *Miami Vice*.

Well, that was quite depressing. Let me leave this subject on a somewhat more optimistic note. As we've seen, the fact that people strategically adapt makes a lot of trouble for drug policy. But, if you are really clever, sometimes you can also make adaptation work for you. Kleiman (2011) offers the cleverest such suggestion that I've seen. Here's what he has in mind.

Kleiman's proposal starts with the Mexican government crafting and making public a measure of how violent each drug trafficking organization is. Armed with this information, the United States and Mexican governments could then focus their drug enforcement resources on the most violent organization. The Mexican police would attack the organization directly in Mexico. The United States government would direct its investigative and enforcement efforts against drug distribution networks that imported drugs sourced from the most violent Mexican drug trafficking organization.

What would be the result of such a policy? In Mexico, the most violent drug trafficking organization would find itself at a significant disadvantage relative to the other drug traffickers. Presumably the remaining organizations would pick up the slack, so total drugs exported to the United States would be unlikely to change. But life and business would be bad for the most violent organization.

In the United States, drug distributors that sourced from the most violent drug trafficking organization would also find themselves at a disadvantage. They would face greater risk, more police infiltration, and so on. Again, other drug distributors might pick up the slack domestically, but life and business would be bad for those American distributors who sourced their drugs from the most violent Mexican organization.

If other organizations pick up the slack, so that drug exports and drug dealing aren't actually disrupted by targeting the most violent organization, what good is this policy? Here is where you have to think about strategic adaptation. The most violent Mexican drug trafficking organization faces two bad situations. First, the Mexican government is going to focus its anti-drug resources on this organization. Second, because of U.S. policy, its customers in the United States are going to look to source their drugs from one of the other Mexican drug suppliers.

There is a straightforward way for the most violent Mexican drug organization to avoid this fate—adapt, by reducing its use of violence so that some other organization becomes the most violent one. Once that happens, the next most violent organization becomes the focus of the two governments' attention and faces the same incentives to adapt. Once it does so, the third most violent organization becomes the focus and has incentives to reduce violence. When all is said and done, then, this policy induces a *race to the bottom*. Each organization wants to avoid being the most violent. The only way to avoid being leapfrogged into the position of most violent is to keep becoming less violent until there is basically no violence in the Mexican drug business.

I must confess I love this idea. Its brilliance is that it exploits strategic adaptation by drug traffickers—the historic bane of drug enforcement policy—to induce a race to the bottom in violence. On the down side, it does nothing to reduce the amount of drugs entering the United States. But we are already failing to stop drugs from entering. At least under this policy tens of thousands of people's lives won't have to be sacrificed in the service of getting those drugs to market.

7.2 Incentivizing Multiple Tasks

My sister is a public school teacher. She is pretty intrinsically motivated. She didn't get into teaching for the money. She got into it to help kids learn. Like any public school teacher in the United States in the twenty-first century, she spends a lot of her time worrying about standardized tests. Her fate, the fate of her students, and the fate of her school depend on test scores. And so she describes what is a very familiar story to anyone who follows contemporary education debates. Given the pressure to help her students perform well on tests, she focuses a fair bit of effort on teaching test-relevant skills, sometimes at the expense of other skills that may be more important for the student in question but are less useful for the test.

Her story illustrates a classic problem—how do we create incentives for achieving an outcome that requires multiple inputs, when some of the inputs are better measured than others? The output we care about in primary education is how well the children are educated in some encompassing sense. But this is very hard to observe. Some of the inputs might include teacher effort devoted to math, teacher effort devoted to literacy, and teacher effort devoted to socio-emotional skills. Each of these is also difficult for an outsider to observe directly. Instead we observe coarse performance measures, like test scores. These scores are probably informative about both the outcome we care about (overall education) and each of the inputs. But they are certainly not equivalent to any of them. Moreover, a performance measure like test scores is likely more informative about some of the inputs (like math skills) than others (like socio-emotional skills). So, when you give teachers incentives based on test scores, you push them to emphasize the skills that translate into test scores at the expense of the skills that don't.

Similar incentives are at work in medicine. The outcome we care about is something like the amount of patient health provided per dollar spent. Patient health depends on many inputs from the doctor. But the final outcome may not be observable. Instead, programs like Medicare compensate physicians for particular procedures. Thus, physicians are incentivized to provide observable and well-compensated procedures, at the expense of other inputs that may be more effective, if those alternative inputs are not as easily observed or as well compensated.

Settings like this—and, of course, there are many besides education or health care—are another key arena in which strategic adaptation limits the power of policy to improve outcomes. The key problem is that we have two goals:

1. We want to give some agent (e.g., a teacher) incentives to work hard.
2. We want the agent to allocate his effort appropriately across various tasks.

As we will see, sometimes there is a trade-off between these two goals. The more we give the agent incentives to work hard, the more effort he will devote to tasks that are influential for observable performance, whether or not such tasks are the most important input to the actual outcome. Surprisingly, this implies that sometimes, as our ability to measure one task relative to another improves (e.g., we start testing kids in a way that is more informative about math skills than socio-emotional skills), we should actually reduce the extent to which we use such information to provide incentives. Let's see this in a model.

There is some output, π, that is produced through two inputs, a_1 and a_2. The production function is simple:

$$\pi = \alpha a_1 + (1 - \alpha)a_2,$$

with $0 < \alpha < 1$. The parameter α measures how important task 1 is relative to task 2 in producing the output. We can think of π as representing the overall quality of a child's education, while a_1 and a_2 are the teacher's investment in teaching test preparation and socio-emotional skills, respectively. The bigger α is the more important the test preparation skills are, relative to socio-emotional skills, for overall education.

Neither the inputs nor the output are observable. We can only observe some performance measure that is also increasing in the inputs, but is not identical to the output. The performance measure is

$$p = \beta a_1 + (1 - \beta)a_2,$$

with $\beta \neq \alpha$. We can think of p as test scores. Then β represents how responsive test scores are to task 1 relative to task 2. Put differently, β represents how well measured task 1 is relative to task 2. I will focus on the case where

$$\beta \geq 1/2,$$

so that task 1 is assumed to be the better measured input. Notice, inside this model, we can use β to think about policy changes. If we introduce a new standardized test, β increases, because a teacher's investment in teaching skills relevant to the test (a_1) becomes better measured relative to that teacher's investment in socio-emotional skills.

There is a single agent, let's call him the teacher, who must choose how much effort to devote to the two tasks. The teacher is paid both a salary, s, and a pay-for-performance wage, $w \in (0, 1)$. If measured performance is p, the teacher's total compensation is $s + wp$.

The teacher is also intrinsically motivated to work on each task (i.e., he gets a direct benefit). We measure his intrinsic motivation by $I > 1$. That is, in addition to his pay, the teacher gets an additional benefit $I \times (a_1 + a_2)$ because he finds his work inherently meaningful.

Finally, the teacher has costs for effort, given by

$$c(a_1, a_2) = \frac{a_1^2 + a_2^2 + a_1 a_2}{2}.$$

These costs are like others we've already seen, in that they are quadratic in effort devoted to each task. The additional term $a_1 a_2$ means that if effort is higher on task 1, then the marginal cost of effort on task 2 is higher (and vice versa). This captures the idea that increasing effort on one task may crowd out effort on the other task.

Let's start by solving for how much effort the teacher will devote to each task. He solves the following problem:

$$\max_{a_1,a_2} s + wp + I(a_1 + a_2) - \frac{a_1^2 + a_2^2 + a_1 a_2}{2}.$$

Substituting for p, this is the same as

$$\max_{a_1,a_2} s + w\left(\beta a_1 + (1 - \beta)a_2\right) + I\left(a_1 + a_2\right) - \frac{a_1^2 + a_2^2 + a_1 a_2}{2}.$$

We maximize this function by taking the two first-order conditions (with respect to a_1 and a_2), which yield

$$w\beta + I = a_1^* + \frac{a_2^*}{2}$$

and

$$w(1 - \beta) + I = a_2^* + \frac{a_1^*}{2}.$$

Solving these two equations in two unknowns, we have

$$a_1^* = \frac{2}{3}\left(I + w\left(3\beta - 1\right)\right) \quad \text{and} \quad a_2^* = \frac{2}{3}\left(I + w\left(2 - 3\beta\right)\right).$$

There are several things to see here.

First, consider the total effort that the teacher exerts as a function of the amount of performance pay he receives:

$$\text{Total Effort}(w) = a_1^* + a_2^* = \frac{2}{3}(2I + w).$$

Total effort is increasing in w—increasing pay-for-performance leads to an increase in teacher effort.

Now consider how an increase in pay-for-performance affects the teacher's effort on each task separately:

$$\frac{da_1^*}{dw} = \frac{2(3\beta - 1)}{3} \quad \text{and} \quad \frac{da_2^*}{dw} = \frac{2(2 - 3\beta)}{3}.$$

Since $\beta > 1/2$, a_1^* is clearly increasing in w (i.e., $\frac{da_1^*}{dw} > 0$)—increasing pay-for-performance increases effort on task one. However, a_2^* may be increasing or decreasing in w. If $\beta < 2/3$, then a_2^* is increasing in w. If $\beta > 2/3$, then a_2^* is decreasing in w. This implies that if one of the tasks is reflected much more strongly than the other task in measured performance (p), then an increase in pay-for-performance leads to an increase in total effort, but a decrease in effort allocated to the less well-measured task. The intuition is that as pay-for-performance increases, the teacher has an incentive to adjust her behavior toward the task that has the larger impact on measured performance. Doing so tends to crowd out effort toward the other task.

In light of this, we might wonder when pay-for-performance is good policy. On the one hand, it increases total teacher effort. On the other hand, it can distort the allocation of that effort. To assess the policy, consider the effect of pay-for-performance on the output we actually care about, $\pi = \alpha a_1^* + (1 - \alpha)a_2^*$. Plugging in the teacher's equilibrium effort choices as a function of w, we have

$$\pi(w) = \alpha \left(\frac{2}{3}(I + w(3\beta - 1)) \right) + (1 - \alpha) \left(\frac{2}{3}(I + w(2 - 3\beta)) \right).$$

How does a change in pay-for-performance affect this overall outcome?

$$\frac{d\pi}{dw} = \frac{2}{3}\left(\alpha(3\beta - 1) + (1 - \alpha)(2 - 3\beta) \right)$$

The overall outcome is improved by an increase in pay-for-performance if this derivative is positive, which is true if

$$\frac{\alpha}{1 - \alpha} > \frac{3\beta - 2}{3\beta - 1}.$$

It is clearly possible for this condition not to hold—increased pay-for-performance can be counterproductive. In particular, the outcome we care about (π) is decreasing in pay-for-performance (w) if β is relatively large and α is relative small. This fact is illustrated in Figure 7.2. In each of the two upper cells, the horizontal axis represents the amount of pay-for-performance and the line traces out the actual outcome we care about, π, as a function of w. I fix α low (1/8), so the first task is relatively unimportant for the outcome we care about. In the left-hand cell β is large (3/4), so the first task is very important for the performance measure. As a result, the quality of the outcome is decreasing in pay-for-performance. In the right-hand cell β is smaller (1/2), reducing mismatch between the outcome and the performance measure. As a consequence, the quality of the outcome is increasing in pay-for-performance. In the lower cell, α is on the horizontal access and β is on the vertical access. The shaded region identifies situations in which the mismatch is sufficiently large that pay-for-performance is counterproductive.

Why is the outcome sometimes decreasing in w when total effort is increasing? The answer has to do with the allocation of efforts across the tasks. As we've seen, if $\beta > 2/3$, then when pay-for-performance goes up, a_1^* increases and a_2^* decreases because task 1 is reflected better in the performance measure

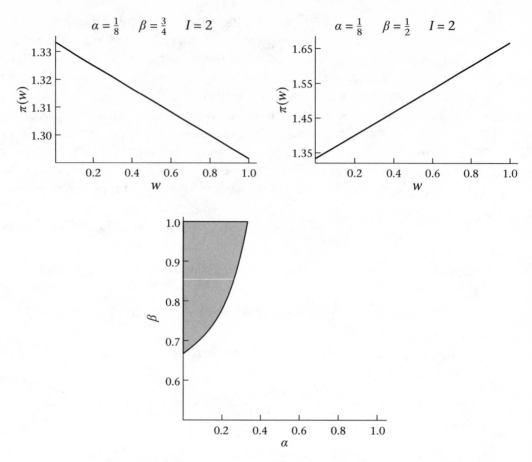

Figure 7.2. Depending on the extent of mismatch between the outcome of interest and the performance metric, increasing pay-for-performance can make outcomes better or worse. In the upper left-hand cell there is considerable mismatch and the quality of the outcome is decreasing as pay-for-performance increases. In the upper right-hand cell there is less mismatch and the quality of the outcome is increasing in pay-for-performance. The shaded area of the lower cell indicates the set of parameter values where mismatch is sufficiently severe that pay-for-performance is counterproductive.

than is task 2. The problem is, when α is relatively small, task 2 is more important for the actual outcome we care about than is task 1. As a result, in this case, an increase in w increases the mismatch between the allocation of the teacher's effort (which is primarily devoted to task 1) and the allocation of effort that is optimal for generating the outcome we care about (which puts greater emphasis on task 2). If this mismatch is sufficiently large (which is true when β and α are far apart), this increased misallocation can have a large enough negative effect to more than offset the benefits of greater total effort. Hence, as a result of strategic adaptation toward the more measurable task by the teacher, sometimes giving stronger incentives actually leads to worse outcomes. This is particularly likely to be the case when there is a mismatch between the import and measurability of various inputs.

It is important to recall that I've emphasized an interpretation of the model in an educational setting. But the basic problem of multitask incentives is quite general.

7.2.1 High-Stakes Testing

In recent years, and especially with the adoption of the No Child Left Behind Act, high-stakes testing has become an increasingly important part of American education policy. Under high-stakes testing, students only advance grades or graduate if their scores on various standardized tests meet some minimum threshold. Our model suggests that teachers will strategically adapt, focusing on those activities most relevant for getting students over the test thresholds and on those students most likely to move from one side of the threshold to the other.

Let's start by seeing evidence that teachers are in fact responsive to incentives to meet these standardized test thresholds. Jacob (2005) studies the effect of the first move to high-stakes testing in mathematics and reading by the Chicago Public Schools. In 1996, Chicago began tying student promotion to performance on the Iowa Test of Basic Skills (ITBS)—a standardized test that students had already been taking. Following the move from low- to high-stakes testing, there was a clear increase in test performance in Chicago relative to other large midwestern cities.

But Jacob also finds several pieces of evidence that this improvement in test scores was, at least in part, the result of strategic adaptation by teachers.

First, test scores in math and reading improved at two to four times the rate of test scores in science and social studies—subjects whose exams were not subject to high-stakes testing. This suggests that teachers and schools may have shifted resources away from social studies and science and towards math and reading. We do not know whether or not this reallocation of resources was optimal for student education.

Second, because the test scores of special education students are not counted towards the overall performance of a school, the move to high-stakes testing gave teachers and schools an incentive to shift low-performing students into special education. And, indeed, Jacob finds that the advent of high-stakes testing is associated with a roughly 8% (one percentage point) increase in the number of students classified as special education. Moreover, this reclassification happened overwhelmingly in schools in the bottom quartile of performance, precisely the schools that were at risk of sanction for poor test performance. For similar reasons, high-stakes testing led to roughly a 64% (two percentage point) increase in the number of students held back a grade, especially among low-performing schools.

Another, and perhaps more disturbing, form of strategic adaptation high-stakes testing might cause involves distorting how teachers allocate their efforts across students. Only a small segment of students actually benefit from teaching to the test. The strongest students will pass standardized tests no matter what. The weakest students are likely to fail the standardized tests no matter what. If high-stakes testing motivates teachers to get as many of their students to pass the exam as possible, then not only will they teach to the test, they will devote a disproportionate amount of their efforts and attention to those students just on the cusp of passing.

Neal and Schanzenbach (2010) provide evidence that high-stakes testing can have precisely this effect of pushing teachers to focus on the students near the margin. Neal and Schanzenbach begin their study with a quotation from a middle school teacher, taken from the *Washington Post*. The teacher, speaking of high-stakes testing, lays out exactly the kind of adaptation we've been talking about:

> We were told to cross off the kids who would never pass. We were told to cross off the kids who, if we handed them the test tomorrow, they would pass. And then the kids who were left over, those were the kids we were supposed to focus on.

To show that these distortionary incentives are real, Neal and Schanzenbach study the second implementation of high-stakes testing in the Chicago public schools. For years, the state of Illinois has administered the Illinois State Aptitude Test (ISAT) to third, fifth, and eighth graders. For most of this time, the test was relatively low stakes—not tied to promotion to the next grade, school resources, and so on. The stakes changed in 2002, when the ISAT became the test that the Chicago Public Schools used to comply with the federal No Child Left Behind Act.

Neal and Schanzenbach compare students who were fifth graders in 2001 to students who were fifth graders in 2002. The ISAT was low stakes when both of these cohorts took it in third grade. For the 2001 cohort, it was still low stakes when they took it as fifth graders. But, for the 2002 cohort, the ISAT had become high stakes when they took it as fifth graders. Focus, for a moment, on students who were in fifth grade in 2001. One can calculate how much improvement different types of students showed from third grade to fifth grade. For instance, you can group the students into 10 groups based on their scores in third grade. Then you can calculate how much students who were in the bottom decile in third grade improved by fifth grade, how much students who were in the 2nd decile in third grade improved by fifth grade, and so on for each decile. Doing so tells you, under low-stakes testing, how much each type of student is expected to improve from third grade to fifth grade.

Now, do this same thing for the students who were in fifth grade in 2002 when testing became high stakes. If teachers don't change their behavior in response to high-stakes testing, then you should expect to see the same pattern for these kids as you do for the 2001 kids. But if, once the test becomes high stakes, teachers focus their efforts on students who are on the cusp of passing the test, then you'd expect to see a different pattern between the 2001 and 2002 groups. In particular, you'd expect less improvement by 2002 kids who were at the very bottom and very top of their third grade classes, since starting in 2002 the teachers are incentivized to focus on them less. You'd also expect more improvement by 2002 kids who were in the middle of their third grade class, since in 2002 teachers have more incentive to focus on these kids.

This is precisely what Neal and Schanzenbach find, as reflected in Figure 7.3. Fifth graders in 2002 who were in the middle of their third grade class show a bigger improvement in their test scores than did 2001 fifth graders who were in the middle of their third grade class. But the same is not true of 2002 fifth graders who were at the bottom or top of their third grade class.

7.3 Takeaways

- People adapt in response to policy changes.
- In order to anticipate the effect of a policy change, one must take into account how behavior will change.
- In order to minimize strategic adjustment, implement policies that target the broadest category of behavior your policy is aimed at. For instance, if your goal is to reduce greenhouse gas emissions, a tax on carbon is more effective than an increase in CAFE standards because it is more difficult to adjust behavior to dodge the use of carbon. If your goal is to improve security from terrorism, increased intelligence is more effective than increased airport security because intelligence degrades terrorist capacity for all types of attacks, whereas airport security only degrades terrorist capacity to attack airplanes, which allows for strategic adaptation.
- To minimize the negative effects of strategic adaptation towards observable tasks, sometimes, as you measure certain inputs better, it is optimal to provide weaker, rather than stronger, performance-based incentives.

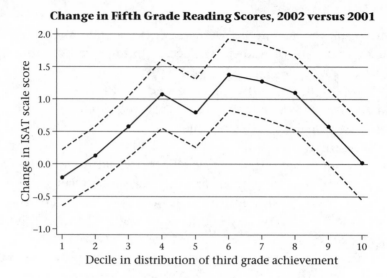

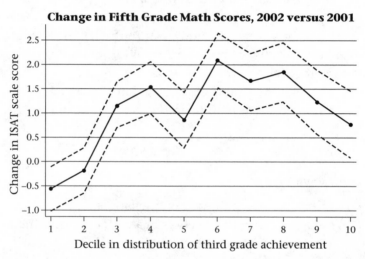

Figure 7.3. Students close to the passing threshold improve more than other students only after tests become high stakes. The figure replicates Neal and Schanzenbach's (2010) Figure 1 using estimates reported in their Table 1.

7.4 Further Reading

Holmström and Milgrom (1991) is the original statement of the multitask problem, though the formulation I use in Section 7.2 is closer in spirit to the models of Feltham and Xie (1994), Baker (2002), and Gibbons (2010). It isn't reading, but you should also watch the video of John Roberts explaining the weak incentives idea at the London School of Economics available at https://www.youtube.com/watch?v=K-2vJVppBgk.

7.5 Exercises

1. A city experiences a spate of crime and decides to try to arrest more criminals. To do so, it increases the size of the police force. After pursuing the policy for four months, the city receives the following data on arrest rates in the four months prior to and following the policy intervention.

Month	−4	−3	−2	−1	1	2	3	4
Number of Arrests	150	220	175	190	80	85	82	91

    The press reports that the policy is a failure, as the increase in police presence did not result in "more criminals being taken off the streets." Explain why the fall in the number of arrests might constitute good news for the efficacy of this policy. (A really great answer to this question would propose, informally, a simple model that would yield these results in equilibrium.)

2. Suppose there are two states—*A* and *B*—that border one another. State *A* has 1 poor person living in it. State *B* has 10 poor people living in it. Any poor person can move states at any time for a cost of $100.

    The government of State *A* would like to give some money to the poor. Suppose that State *A*'s government's payoff from giving an amount of money, t, to the poor is equal to $1000t - t^2$. This implies that the government of State *A* would be willing to give up to $1000 to the poor and would most like to give $500. However, it also implies that the government of State *A* would prefer to give nothing to the poor than give more than $1000. The government of State *B* is uninterested in helping the poor.

    (a) The government of State *A* notices it has only 1 poor person and sets up a program whereby any poor person living in State *A* is entitled to $500. Has the government of State *A* implemented a policy that is consistent with its goal (as defined by its utility function) of supporting the poor while giving away no more than $500? If so, why? If not, what is the problem?

    (b) Suppose the government of State *A* is not allowed to discriminate among its poor residents. It can only choose policies of the form "we give X dollars to each poor person living in State *A*." Given its goals (as defined by its utility function), what is the best such policy that the government of State *A* can implement?

    (c) What happens to this policy if the number of poor people living in State *B* increases? Why?

3.   The Transportation Security Administration runs a program in which Behavior Detection Officers attempt to use behavioral cues to identify terrorists at the airport. Critics of this program point out that, in its decade-long history, this program has never successfully identified and arrested a terrorist. (The most common arrest associated with the program is undocumented immigrants.)

   (a) If you were a defender of the TSA, how might you use the arguments from our models of strategic adjustment to defend the program against such critics?
   (b) If you were a critic of the TSA, how might you use the arguments from our models of strategic adjustment to critique the program?

4.   Two potential patients come to a doctor, who has time to see only one of them. One patient is sicker than the other, which the doctor can observe. In particular, untreated, patient one will have an overall health outcome of θ_1 while patient two will have an overall health outcome of $\theta_2 > \theta_1$, so patient one is sicker than patient two.

   The doctor first chooses which patient to treat. She then chooses to expend effort e on treating the patient. Her effort makes more of a difference for the sicker patient. In particular, if she exerts effort e treating patient 1, the patient's health outcome is $h_1(e) = \theta_1 + 2e$. If she exerts effort e treating patient 2, the patient's health outcome is $h_2(e) = \theta_2 + e$. The doctor bears costs e^2 for effort.

   The doctor has two motivations. First, she is intrinsically motivated. In particular, she cares directly about each patient's health (regardless of which patient she takes). Second, she is paid a fee for good health outcomes for whichever patient she takes. The policymaker who pays for the good health outcomes cannot observe how sick the patients were coming in, nor can he observe the effort the doctor expended. He just observes a measure of the patient's overall health outcome. So if the health outcome for the doctor's patient is h, the policymaker pays the doctor a fee $h \times w$.

   Putting this all together, if the doctor takes patient 1 and exerts effort e, her payoff is

$$(\theta_1 + 2e)(1 + w) + \theta_2 - e^2.$$

   If the doctor takes patient 2 and exerts effort e, her payoff is

$$\theta_1 + (\theta_2 + e)(1 + w) - e^2.$$

(a) How much effort does the doctor exert if she takes patient 1? What is her total payoff?

(b) How much effort does the doctor exert if she takes patient 2? What is her total payoff?

(c) If the policymaker cares about the sum of health outcomes, which patient would he prefer the doctor take?

(d) If $w = 0$, which patient does the doctor take?

Now, to keep things simple, suppose $\theta_1 = 1$ and $\theta_2 = 10$ (so person 1 is much sicker than person 2).

(e) If $w = 1$, which patient does the doctor take?

(f) If $w = 0$, given the patient choice and equilibrium effort, what is the sum of health outcomes?

(g) If $w = 1$, given the patient choice and equilibrium effort, what is the sum of health outcomes?

(h) Comparing these two answers, explain what it has to say, substantively, about how high-powered incentives can create perverse outcomes in multitask environments.

(i) Substantively, in this case, what is the strategic adaptation that is giving rise to the perverse outcome?

8

Dynamic Inconsistency

The launch of the HealthCare.gov website in October 2013 constituted a significant policy setback for the federal government. The website was intended to provide online marketplaces to facilitate the purchasing of mandatory health insurance under the 2010 Patient Protection and Affordable Care Act. However, it did not work as intended—users had trouble accessing the site, experienced long delays, and were unable to enroll in health insurance.

Many factors contributed to the problems at HealthCare.gov. The United States Government Accountability Office (GAO) reports that one important factor was a failure of oversight inside the Centers for Medicare & Medicaid Services (CMS).[1] According to the GAO report, in early 2013, CMS identified significant problems in the work done by one of its major contractors, CGI Federal. Although CMS had the authority to hold CGI Federal accountable, the GAO reports that CMS "delayed key governance reviews" and "chose to forgo actions, such as withholding the payment of fee, in order to focus on meeting the website launch date."[2] Indeed, in August of 2013, CMS sent a letter stating it "would take aggressive action, such as withholding fee ... if CGI Federal did not improve or if additional concerns arose," but quickly withdrew the letter in order to "better collaborate with CGI Federal in completing the work in order to meet the October 1, 2013, launch."[3] It was only after the actual website launch failure that CMS took any significant actions to hold CGI Federal to account, transitioning responsibility from CGI Federal to Accenture Federal Services in January 2014.[4]

This episode illustrates a general problem in governance—dynamic inconsistency. To try to create incentives for good performance, CMS asserted that the contractor would be held accountable for actions taken throughout the process. But once a given task was completed, CMS was primarily concerned with achieving good outcomes going forward. As such, it was willing to renegotiate

---

[1] See GAO-14-694, "HEALTHCARE.GOV: Ineffective Planning and Oversight Practices Underscore the Need for Improved Contract Management," July 2014. http://www.gao.gov/assets/670/665179.pdf

[2] GAO-14-694, page 1.

[3] GAO-14-694, page 34.

[4] GAO-14-694, page 37.

along the way in order to optimize incentives going forward. This commitment problem meant the standards announced early in the process were not credible.

Governments face a variety of such problems of dynamic inconsistency. In this chapter we consider three—commitment problems that undermine the credibility of policy promises of the sort just described, the desire to pass costs for current projects onto future generations, and incentives to take inefficient actions that preserve the current power structure.

8.1   Time Inconsistency

Sometimes even benevolent governments face commitment problems that lead to inefficiency. The *time inconsistency* problem is a classic example. A benevolent government announces a policy that it plans to implement in the future. That policy is Pareto improving. However, anticipating the policy, people make decisions today that influence the optimal policy tomorrow. As a result, when tomorrow comes, the still-benevolent government wants to implement a different policy than previously announced. Hence, the people were wrong to believe the initial promise, although at the time the government meant it. The people, of course, can anticipate this, so the government is in fact unable to make promises that will be believed. Before we look at a model, let me give you a couple of heuristic examples that stick a bit closer to the model than the real-world example from HealthCare.gov already discussed.

Suppose at some mythical university, a professor cares only about how much her students learn. Moreover, she believes each student learns more if all of the students study hard. That is, there are positive externalities from studying. So, even though students are also motivated to learn, they study too little relative to the social optimum.

At the beginning of the quarter, the professor announces that the course will have a final exam. She does so not because she cares to evaluate the students, but to incentivize the students to study harder and therefore help others learn. Students want to make good grades, so anticipating the exam, the students study harder, getting closer to the social optimum.

On the day of the exam, students have already chosen whether or not to study. The professor, who cares only about learning, should now cancel the exam and instead lecture, since the exam can no longer affect the amount of learning. But this means the students were wrong to study harder in anticipation of the exam in the first place. The professor's announced exam policy was *time inconsistent*. Hence, in equilibrium, the professor cannot use the threat of an exam to achieve a Pareto improvement.

The classic time inconsistency problem comes from thinking about monetary policy. An important empirical pattern—known as the Phillips curve—suggests that in the short run central banks face a trade-off between high inflation and low unemployment. The standard economic analysis says that this relationship depends on expectations about inflation. A central bank can use inflation to lower unemployment only if inflation exceeds expected inflation. (This explains why this is only a short-run relationship. In the long run, expectations are correct.) Hence, the central bank would like the market to expect low inflation, so that it can lower unemployment without increasing inflation too much.

Imagine that a benevolent central bank announced a policy of low inflation. If the market believed the central bank and expected low inflation—setting wages, household budgets, prices, and so on, accordingly—these low inflation expectations would leave the central bank with a favorable inflation-unemployment trade-off. By increasing inflation a bit, the central bank could reduce unemployment. The benevolent central bank would be tempted to do so, making the market's expectations incorrect. That is, a low inflation policy is not time consistent for a central bank that also cares about unemployment. It is precisely this sort of time inconsistency analysis that is sometimes used to argue that central banks should have limited discretion, so that, for instance, pledges of low inflation policies are made credible.

Now that we have a sense of what the time inconsistency problem is, let's look at a model to be a little more precise.

Our game has two kinds of players. There is a government and there are consumers. Each consumer has one unit of money. We will assume that there is a very large number of consumers. In particular, there are so many consumers that each consumer's wealth is negligible relative to the size of the economy.[5] This assumption simplifies the analysis because, as we will see, when a consumer makes a savings decision, she will not worry about how that decision affects the total amount of taxes collected by the government, since she is so small relative to the tax base.

The game is played as follows:

1. The government announces a planned future tax rate on capital (i.e., savings), t_0. This tax rate is not binding.
2. Each consumer divides her money between consumption (c) and savings ($1 - c$). Savings earn a return $r > 1$.
3. The government sets a capital tax rate, t.
4. The government spends the revenues it collects on providing a public good. The total public good provided, given revenues R, is $G = \gamma R$.

---

[5] Formally, there is a continuum of consumers of mass 1.

Assume that the monetary return to private savings is larger than the monetary return to public goods investment, but not too much larger. In particular, $r - 1 < \gamma < r$.

A consumer's utility is given by

$$c + (1 - t)r(1 - c) + 2\sqrt{G}.$$

The first term is consumption in the first period. The second term is after-tax consumption in the second period. The third term is the payoff from public goods, which we assume has diminishing marginal utility (thus the square root, which is a simple increasing function with diminishing marginal returns).

8.1.1 The First Best

Money invested instead of consumed generates positive returns. Hence, the first best involves $c = 0$, since saving everything maximizes the total resources available. Given this, the first-best tax rate solves

$$\max_t 0 + (1 - t) \times r \times 1 + 2\sqrt{G}.$$

Since $G = \gamma tr(1 - c)$, this can be rewritten

$$\max_t 0 + (1 - t)r + 2\sqrt{\gamma tr}.$$

To find the first-order condition, we will use the fact that $\frac{d2\sqrt{\gamma tr}}{dt} = \frac{\gamma r}{\sqrt{\gamma tr}}$. Now, the first-best tax rate, t^{FB}, satisfies the following first-order condition:

$$-r + \frac{\gamma r}{\sqrt{\gamma t^{FB} r}} = 0 \Rightarrow t^{FB} = \frac{\gamma}{r}.$$

8.1.2 What Will the Government Do?

Now let's see what happens in equilibrium. We solve by backward induction.

Suppose that the government has made some promise, t_0, and the consumers have all made some choice c. What tax policy will the government actually implement?

Being benevolent, the government will choose a tax rate that maximizes social welfare (given the choice of c). Notice, this means that the government will ignore its promised policy (t_0). The government identifies the socially optimal tax rate by balancing the costs of taxation, in terms of forgone consumption, against the benefits of taxation, in terms of increased public goods. For any c, the government chooses a tax rate to solve

$$\max_t c + (1 - t)r(1 - c) + 2\sqrt{\gamma tr(1 - c)}.$$

Using the fact that $\frac{d2\sqrt{\gamma tr(1-c)}}{dt} = \frac{\gamma r(1-c)}{\sqrt{\gamma tr(1-c)}}$, the first-order condition for this problem is

$$-r(1-c) + \frac{\gamma r(1-c)}{\sqrt{\gamma t^* r(1-c)}} = 0 \Rightarrow t^* = \frac{\gamma}{r(1-c)}.$$

Since t^* is part of a strategy, it tells us what tax rate will be chosen for any c. So we should really write the tax rate the government chooses for any given c as a function, $t^*(c)$. Importantly, since $t^*(c)$ is a tax rate, it must be less than or equal to 1. This means that the first-order condition only gives the government's choice if $\frac{\gamma}{r(1-c)} \le 1$, which is equivalent to $c \le 1 - \frac{\gamma}{r}$. If $c \in (1 - \frac{\gamma}{r}, 1)$, the best response is a corner solution, $t^*(c) = 1.^6$ If $c = 1$ anything is a best response because there is no revenue to be collected. Thus, given an investment level c, the government's choice of a tax rate is

$$t^*(c) = \begin{cases} \dfrac{\gamma}{r(1-c)} & \text{if } c \le 1 - \dfrac{\gamma}{r} \\ 1 & \text{if } c \in \left(1 - \dfrac{\gamma}{r}, 1\right). \\ \text{anything} & \text{if } c = 1. \end{cases} \tag{8.1}$$

Notice, the government really is benevolent. If the consumers choose to save all of their resources (i.e., $c = 0$), then the government chooses the first-best tax rate:

$$t^*(0) = \frac{\gamma}{r} = t^{FB}.$$

8.1.3 How Much Will a Consumer Consume?

Recall, each consumer in this model is infinitesimally small relative to the size of the whole economy. As such, each consumer's individual consumption choice has essentially zero impact on overall consumption. Suppose a consumer believes that overall consumption by the other consumer will be C. Then, she believes that, regardless of her own choice, the tax rate will be $t^*(C)$ and the total level of public goods will be $G = \gamma t^*(C)r(1 - C)$. Given this, a consumer solves the following problem:

$$\max_c c + (1 - t^*(C))r(1 - c) + 2\sqrt{\gamma t^*(C)r(1 - C)}.$$

Rearranging, we can rewrite this as

$$\max_c \left(1 - \left(1 - t^*(C)\right)r\right)c + (1 - t^*(C))r + 2\sqrt{\gamma t^*(C)r(1 - C)}.$$

It is straightforward that a consumer's payoff is strictly increasing in her personal consumption if $1 - (1 - t^*(C))r > 0$. This is equivalent to $t^*(C) > 1 - \frac{1}{r}$.

---

^{6}A corner solution means the government would like to choose $t > 1$ but isn't allowed to because t can't be bigger than 1. So it is stuck at the "corner," 1.

Similarly, a consumer's payoff is strictly decreasing in her personal consumption if $1 - (1 - t^*(C))r < 0$, which is equivalent to $t^*(C) < 1 - \frac{1}{r}$. This implies that, if the consumer believes the tax rate will be $t^*(C)$, her best response is

$$\text{BR}(t^*(C)) = \begin{cases} c = 0 & \text{if } t^*(C) < 1 - \frac{1}{r} \\ \text{anything} & \text{if } t^*(C) = 1 - \frac{1}{r} \\ c = 1 & \text{if } t^*(C) > 1 - \frac{1}{r}. \end{cases} \tag{8.2}$$

8.1.4 Is the Government Time Consistent?

Now let's ask whether the government's promise of a tax rate, t_0, is credible. Doing so will also let us find the equilibrium of this game.

First, suppose the government promises a tax rate of $t_0 < 1 - \frac{1}{r}$. If the consumers believe that promise, then Equation 8.2 shows that each consumer's best response is to consume nothing in the first period (i.e., $c = 0$). If the consumers behave in this way, what tax rate will the government actually choose? Clearly, $0 < 1 - \frac{\gamma}{r}$. So, from Equation 8.1, if all consumers choose $c = 0$, the government's best response is to choose a tax rate of

$$t^*(0) = \frac{\gamma}{r}.$$

But notice that $\frac{\gamma}{r} > 1 - \frac{1}{r}$. (We know this because we assumed at the beginning of the model that $r - 1 < \gamma$.) So the government is not keeping its promise to choose a tax rate $t_0 < 1 - \frac{1}{r}$. The government's promise was not time consistent.

What is the cause of this time inconsistency? The consumers save because of the low promised tax rate. But the high savings rate then makes taxation particularly appealing to the benevolent government because, with high savings, the government can collect a lot of revenue and provide a lot of public goods. Hence, there is an inconsistency between the high savings that a promise of low taxes induces and actually implementing these low taxes, even for a benevolent government.

Next, suppose the government promises a tax rate of $t_0 > 1 - \frac{1}{r}$. If the consumers believe the promise, then each consumer will best respond by consuming everything and save nothing—that is, $c = 1$. Of course, if the consumers actually save nothing, any tax rate is a best response by the government, since there is no actual revenue to be collected. So a promise of high taxes which results in low savings is time consistent.

In equilibrium, then, there are low savings and high taxation. This is surprising. The government is benevolent and the social optimum calls for high savings and intermediate taxes. But if savings are actually high, the government will implement high taxes so as to provide lots of public goods. At that point, doing so is socially optimal. But, anticipating this, consumers don't save.

Hence, a commitment problem on the part of the benevolent government prevents society from achieving the socially optimal savings rate.

8.1.5 Time Inconsistency and Externalities

What is really going on here is that consumer saving imposes positive externalities on other consumers because the tax revenues from individual savings go to providing public goods for everyone. The benevolent government, in choosing the tax rate, takes those externalities into consideration. But the individual consumers, when making their individual consumption decisions, do not. Hence, when there is a lot of saving, the benevolent government wants to tax a lot (to provide lots of public goods). However, if there is going to be high taxation, individual consumers don't save, because they want to free ride on the savings of other consumers. In this sense, this time inconsistency problem hinges on there being a wedge between the preferences of the benevolent government and the individual investors. This wedge means that the consumers (who do not internalize their externalities) strategically adjust their behavior, up the tree, in anticipation of the government's socially optimal behavior down the tree.[7]

8.1.6 Rules vs. Discretion

We've just seen a model in which a benevolent government that has full discretion to choose any tax policy fails to achieve a Pareto efficient outcome. Part of the problem is that the government has too much discretion. Saving is efficient. But the consumers anticipate that, if they save, their money will be taxed. As a result, they attempt to free ride on one another by saving too little (from the utilitarian point of view).

This raises an intriguing possibility. Perhaps the government, despite being benevolent, could achieve better outcomes by reducing its discretion. In particular, suppose the government could commit to a tax rule up-front. The downside of such a commitment is that it eliminates the government's ability to implement the socially optimal tax, given the consumers' savings decisions. The upside of such a commitment is that it allows the government to commit to a lower tax, thereby encouraging savings.

Let's see, in our model, whether eliminating government discretion, by committing to such a rule, in fact improves welfare. Recall that, when the government can't commit (i.e., when the government has discretion), the equilibrium involves no savings and no public goods provision. Hence, equilibrium social welfare is 1.

---

[7]One way to convince yourself that this is indeed what is going on is to ask what would happen in this model with exactly one consumer, so there are no externalities. A good challenge is to re-solve the model under this assumption and see that the outcome is efficient.

Now suppose the government's announcement, t_0, is in fact a binding commitment. For any choice of t_0, the consumers will each save according to the best responses in Equation 8.2. So, for instance, if the government chooses $t_0 = 1 - \frac{1}{r}$, it is a best response for the consumers to save everything. And since $1 - \frac{1}{r} \le t^{FB}$, this is the best outcome that can be achieved. In this scenario, social welfare is $1 + \sqrt{\gamma(r-1)} > 1$. Taking away the government's discretion allows the government to commit to a tax rate that makes everyone better off by increasing savings and public goods.

8.1.7 Applications

The global financial crisis sparked by the 2007 banking crisis in the United States exposed an important time inconsistency problem at the core of the governance structure of the European monetary union.[8] The member countries of the eurozone share a common currency. However, each country is nonetheless empowered to issue its own sovereign debt. This arrangement creates externalities problems—if one country borrows irresponsibly, it may devalue the currency for all the other eurozone members.

The Stability and Growth Pact—one of the treaties governing the eurozone—includes provisions meant to mitigate the risk. First, it sets a limit on borrowing—a country's annual budget deficit and its total debt are not to exceed 3% and 60% of its GDP, respectively. Second, it articulates a "no bailouts" principle—countries are responsible for meeting their individual debt obligations, they cannot expect aid from other eurozone countries. However, given the externalities problem, this latter position is of questionable credibility. Should either a lender or leader believe that other eurozone countries will refuse to aid a country at risk of defaulting on its debt, if such a default would have devastating spillovers on the regional economy?

As it turns out, the no bailouts commitment was not credible. Starting with the collapse of the U.S. investment bank Lehman Brothers in September of 2008, the banking crisis became a global financial crisis. The effect on global lending and construction had a massive negative impact on many eurozone economies, most notably in Greece, Ireland, and Portugal. As a result, by late 2009, it became clear that several eurozone member states were no longer in compliance with the debt-to-GDP rules.

Greece was the most dramatic case. Following an October 2009 election, a new Greek government released a revised budget projecting a deficit of almost 13% of GDP, more than four times the allowed limit and more than twice previous forecasts. As a consequence, the market lost faith in the Greek government's ability to meet its debt obligations. Greek bond yields (i.e., the price of debt) skyrocketed. By May of 2010, Greece was shut out of the

---

[8]This discussion is based on the overview provided by Lane (2012).

bond market. A looming Greek debt default threatened the integrity of the eurozone. Perhaps more importantly, because so much of Greece's debt was held by French and German banks, a Greek default posed a significant risk for the French and German economies. And so, contrary to stated policy, the European Union (EU) and International Monetary Fund (IMF) stepped in to bail out the Greek government, covering its debt obligations in exchange for commitments of fiscal austerity and structural reform. Over the course of the next two years, the EU and IMF were forced to provide bailouts for Ireland and Portugal, as well as a second bailout for Greece. The non-credible commitment not to bailout eurozone countries had neither prevented the governments of those countries from excessive borrowing, nor bound the eurozone governments not to intercede when they found it in their interests to do so, the classic time inconsistency problem.

The French and German governments did learn certain lessons from the Greek crisis. Greek debt was restructured during the course of the second bailout in 2012. As a consequence, Greece's debt was now owed to official creditors (i.e., the French and German governments), rather than private banks. This had two important effects. First, it reduced the risk of massive negative economic spillovers from a Greek default, since the French and German governments stand on firmer financial footing than even the most solvent private banks. Second, it changed the political equation, making French and German voters less sympathetic to Greece. The combination of these two effects made it easier for the French and German governments to take a harder line on future bailouts. And, indeed, in 2015 they forced Greece to miss debt payments in order to push Greece to accept very unfavorable terms for a third bailout.

Another, and very different, example of time inconsistency involves the policy of not negotiating with terrorists held by many governments (Lapan and Sandler, 1988). In the United States this policy was first articulated by President Nixon in response to an attack in which the group Black September took American (and many other) diplomats hostage in Sudan. The idea of the policy is straightforward. If you refuse to negotiate with terrorists, you reduce incentives for such hostage takings. But the commitment problem is also straightforward. When the United States refused to negotiate, the terrorists killed the American diplomats. A government that anticipates this outcome may have a hard time sticking to its guns, undermining the very incentives the policy was meant to create.

And, indeed, the United States has negotiated with terrorists many times. During the Iran hostage crisis, the Reagan administration facilitated the sale of arms to Iran, despite an arms embargo, to attempt to secure release of the American hostages. In 2002, the Bush administration arranged to pay a ransom to the terrorist group Abu Sayyaf in an attempt to win the release of American missionaries who were held hostage in the Philippines. In 2010 the Obama administration exchanged the terrorist leader Qais al-Khazali for a British hostage held in Iraq. In 2014, the Obama administration released five prisoners held in Guantanamo Bay to gain the release of an American soldier.[9] And in 2015, the Obama administration changed policies, permitting kidnap victims' families to negotiate for their release. When the stakes are high enough, the commitment not to negotiate is not credible.

8.2   Fiscal Manipulation

State and local governments across the United States face serious financial problems due to underfunding of pension funds for public sector workers. No state looks worse than Illinois, where I live. According to a report of the Illinois Commission on Government Forecasting and Accountability, in fiscal year 2014, the state had unfunded pension liabilities of approximately $105 billion. The cumulative funded ratio of the state's retirement plans was only about 43%.[10]

My hometown of Chicago can give the state a run for its money. As of 2015, Chicago's pension plans had over $20 billion in unfunded liabilities. In 2013, the city paid under $500 million of the over $1.7 billion it was was supposed to contribute to its pension plans. The unpaid $1.2 billion is equivalent to over 40% of the city's annual budget.[11]

Let me tell you one other story about fiscal management in Chicago. In 2008, the mayor of Chicago reached a deal to privatize the city's parking meters. While the deal is complicated, the rough outline is this—the city received a one-time payment of $1.15 billion in exchange for a lease that gives a private company the rights to the parking meter revenues for 75 years. A report by the Office of the Inspector General of the City of Chicago found that the city sold the parking meter concession for less than half of its value.[12] And, perhaps more importantly, although the lease is for 75 years of revenue, roughly 90% of the $1.15 billion payment was spent in just five years.[13]

---

[9] Most of these examples are reported by Joshua Keating. May 7, 2015. "We Do Negotiate with Terrorists." *Slate*. http://www.slate.com/articles/news_and_politics/politics/2015/05/negotiating_with_terrorists_s_stop_pretending_we_don_t_and_craft_better.html

[10] Commission on Government Forecasting and Accountability. February 2015. "Illinois State Retirement Systems: Financial Condition as of June 30, 2014." http://cgfa.ilga.gov/Upload/ FinConditionILStateRetirementSysFeb2015.pdf

[11] Nuveen Asset Management. April 2015. "Chicago Fiscal Stress: New Term, Same Problems." http://www.nuveen.com/Home/Documents/Default.aspx?fileId=65715

[12] Office of the Inspector General, City of Chicago. June 2, 2009. "An Analysis of the Lease of the City's Parking Meters." http://chicagoinspectorgeneral.org/wp-content/uploads/2011/03/Parking-Meter-Report.pdf

[13] The Civic Federation. November 10, 2010. "Expiring Parking Meter and Skyway Funds." http://www.civicfed.org/civic-federation/blog/expiring-parking-meter-and-skyway-funds

When policy analysts think about how to address the looming fiscal crises in state and local governments, they tend to focus on technical concerns—accounting rules, pension-smoothing schedules, revenue generation. But each of these examples points to an incentive issue that will persist, no matter the technical response. Elected officials have a strong interest in spending money they don't have. This may be true both because doing so pleases voters and because the politicians have policy agendas they care about. Since they are uncertain whether future politicians will agree with them, they'd rather set priorities now, while they have the power.

A straightforward way to determine the policy priorities on which future resources are spent is to borrow money from the future and spend it today. The federal government does so by running a deficit. But almost every state government is compelled by law to balance its budget each year. So state and local leaders have to be more creative—spending their grandchildren's money by delaying pension payments, selling the rights to parking meters or toll roads, promising raises to public sector employees that don't take effect for five or ten years, and a host of other forms of fiscal manipulation. (I hope it hasn't escaped your notice that the fact that state and local leaders find ways to avoid the constraints placed on them by balanced budget policies is itself a lovely example of the kind of strategic adaptation discussed in Chapter 7.)

Let's consider a simple model of the timing of public policy expenditures to see how this might work. In this model, we will capture the idea that politicians prefer to spend money today by assuming politicians have policy priorities that may not be the same as those of future voters or politicians.

There are three players: a voter, a left-wing politician, and a right-wing politician. There are two periods, 1 and 2. Prior to each period, the voter elects one of the two politicians. During each period, there is a budget of size 1 to be spent on public policy. In addition, in period 1, the politician in office has the option to borrow an amount $b \in (0, 1)$. If the politician borrows in period 1, the money must be paid back in period 2. Thus, if the politician borrows, the period 1 budget is $1 + b$ and the period 2 budget is $1 - b$.

There are two possible ways to spend the budget in each period. It can be spent in a way consistent with the right-wing agenda (R) or the left-wing agenda (L). In each period, one of these two agendas is in fact more effective than the other. The value to a citizen of money spent on the more effective agenda is $\lambda \in \left(\frac{1}{2}, 1\right)$, while the value to a citizen of money spent on the less effective agenda is $1 - \lambda$. The idea is that circumstance affects the efficacy of different approaches to public policy. For instance, perhaps voters prefer different fiscal policies during times of economic recession versus times of economic expansion.

In addition, in each period, the stakes of public policy can change. In particular, in period t, the stakes are α_t. I assume that, in each period, α_t is equally likely to be any real number between 0 and 1. This implies that the expected value of each α_t is one-half. The stakes of public policy are independent across the two periods.[14] This difference in the stakes of public policy will imply that sometimes it is optimal to borrow money in period 1 because the stakes of public policy are particularly high. Substantively, we might think that α is particularly high during times of war, recession, natural disaster, or other crises.

Unlike regular citizens, politicians are biased towards one of the two agendas. The right-wing politician values money spent on the right-wing agenda at λ regardless of which agenda is more effective. Similarly, the left-wing politician values money spent on the left-wing agenda at λ regardless of which agenda is more effective.

Politicians and voters both observe which agenda is more effective before choosing which politician to have in office. Thus, in each period, the voter will elect the politician whose partisan bias is consistent with the more effective agenda. The value of α_t is observed after the election, but before policy is set.

8.2.1 The First Best

Let's start the analysis by thinking about the first-best borrowing decision— that is, the borrowing policy that maximizes the voter's welfare.

Suppose, in period 1, the stakes of policy are α_1. The politician in office will spend whatever resources she has on her agenda, which is of value λ to the voter. If the politician in office in period 1 borrows, the voter's payoff in the first period is $\alpha_1\lambda(1+b)$. The voter will then choose whatever party is aligned with her interests for the second period and her payoff in the second period will be $\alpha_2\lambda(1-b)$. Of course, at the time of the borrowing decision, α_2 is unknown. Its expected value is one-half. Hence, the voter's expected second period payoff, if the first period politician borrows, is $\frac{1}{2}\lambda(1-b)$. This gives us the voter's overall expected welfare if the politician borrows in the first period:

$$U_V(\text{borrow}|\alpha_1) = \overbrace{\alpha_1\lambda(1+b)}^{\text{Voter's 1st Period Welfare}} + \overbrace{\frac{1}{2}\lambda(1-b)}^{\text{Voter's Expected 2nd Period Welfare}}.$$

Following a similar logic, if the politician in office in period 1 does not borrow, the voter's expected payoff is

$$U_V(\text{don't borrow}|\alpha_1) = \alpha_1\lambda + \frac{1}{2}\lambda.$$

---

[14]A little more precisely, each α_t is an independent, uniform random variable on $[0, 1]$.

Comparing these, the first-best policy involves borrowing if

$$\alpha_1 > \frac{1}{2}.$$

This makes sense. In this simple model, there are no direct costs to borrowing (e.g., there is no interest). Borrowing simply moves resources from the second period to the first period. As such, it is optimal to borrow if the stakes of policy in the first period are higher than average. This is the canonical argument for the value of government borrowing—in some circumstances, it is efficient to be able to spend resources now that you won't actually have until later. We want our government to be able to borrow during times of crisis.

8.2.2 Electoral Risk

Now that we know the efficient policy, let's think about what will happen in equilibrium. Suppose, again, that the stakes of policy in the first period are α_1. Further, suppose that the politician in office in the first period believes that the probability that the voter will again find her agenda more effective in period 2 is $p \in (0, 1)$. When will the first period politician borrow?

If the first period politician borrows, her payoff in the first period is $\alpha_1 \lambda (1 + b)$. Her payoff in the second period will depend both on the stakes of policy in the second period and on which party is in power. With probability p her party will remain in power and her payoff will be $\alpha_2 \lambda (1 - b)$. With probability $(1 - p)$ the other party will come to power and her payoff will be $\alpha_2 (1 - \lambda)(1 - b)$. Since the expected value of α_2 is one-half, the overall expected payoff of the politician in power in period 1, if she borrows, is

$$U_1(\text{borrow}|\alpha_1) = \alpha_1 \lambda (1 + b) + \frac{1}{2}\Big(p\lambda(1 - b) + (1 - p)(1 - \lambda)(1 - b)\Big).$$

Following a similar logic, if the politician in office in period 1 does not borrow, her expected payoff is

$$U_1(\text{don't borrow}|\alpha_1) = \alpha_1 \lambda + \frac{1}{2}\Big(p\lambda + (1 - p)(1 - \lambda)\Big).$$

Comparing these, the first period incumbent borrows if

$$\alpha_1 > \frac{p\lambda + (1 - p)(1 - \lambda)}{2\lambda}.$$

It is straightforward to see that the right-hand side of this inequality is less than one-half, the first best. Thus, in equilibrium, the politician borrows more often than is welfare maximizing for the voter.

Why is this? The incumbent politician is concerned that she may be out of power tomorrow. When she is out of power, public funds are spent on her less preferred policy agenda. By borrowing, she increases the share of public funds spent on her preferred agenda. This is because borrowing shifts funds from the future, when she might not be in power, to the present. Thus, she is sometimes willing to borrow funds even when the stakes of policy are relatively low.

Here we see a source of inefficiency clearly related to the examples with which we started. A politician, with her own policy priorities, who faces the prospect of not being in power in the future, has incentives to borrow money from the future, even if doing so is inefficient.

8.2.3 Discounting the Future

Intergenerational considerations suggest yet another possible source of inefficiency. Suppose we think of the two periods as two separate generations and assume that politicians care about payoffs for their own generation more than they care about future generations. To model this, let the period 1 politician discount period 2 payoffs by $\delta \in (0, 1)$. Now, even if the politician has no concern that her party will lose power, she will borrow too much because doing so allows her to spend her children's money on herself.

To see this, suppose the politician is certain her agenda will still be the preferred one in the next period. (This is equivalent to $p = 1$.) If she borrows, her expected payoff is

$$U_1(\text{borrow}|\alpha_1) = \alpha_1 \lambda (1 + b) + \delta \frac{1}{2} \lambda (1 - b).$$

If she doesn't borrow, her expected payoff is

$$U_1(\text{don't borrow}|\alpha_1) = \alpha_1 \lambda + \delta \frac{1}{2} \lambda.$$

Comparing, she will borrow if

$$\alpha_1 > \frac{\delta}{2}.$$

Again, the politician borrows more often than is efficient. Here she does so not because of political concerns, but because she values payoffs to future generations less than payoffs to her own generation.

This story is a political version of our earlier discussion, in Chapter 1, about the philosophical problems with discounting the future for policy evaluation. A politician who discounts the future is too willing to sacrifice future generations' interests in service of her own generation's interests. This suggests that we might expect it to be difficult to incentivize politicians to take costly actions on issues, such as global climate change, that require up-front costs for long-term benefits. Not taking costly actions today to mitigate a future threat is just like borrowing money today that will have to be repaid in the future. For a politician who discounts future interests, doing so is tempting. And so, dynamic political considerations help to explain why even politicians who might be ideologically inclined to take action on issues such as climate change find it politically difficult to do so. Moreover, as we discussed in Chapter 1, governmental rules that require discounting the future in cost-benefit analyses exacerbate such incentives.

8.3   When Policy Affects Future Power

Acemoglu and Robinson (2001) observe that in many policy domains, governments seem to pursue a particular goal with inefficient, rather than efficient, policy tools.

Consider the case of agricultural subsidies. Suppose the world economy has changed in a way that makes farming in, say, the United States, a less viable activity today than it was thirty years ago. It is very difficult for a fifty-year-old farmer to retrain and change industries. Hence, the government might well want to use policy to help that farmer. As Acemoglu and Robinson point out, if the United States government wants to support current farmers, it would be efficient to provide direct transfers, rather than pursuing the current policy of propping up prices, restricting imports, and subsidizing agricultural inputs. Such policies distort prices and lead to an inefficiently high level of investment in agriculture rather than other, more productive, industries. Agricultural subsidies are, thus, an inefficient way to compensate farmers for changing economic conditions.

One can, of course, make related arguments about a variety of policies. For instance, price supports and other forms of protectionism for manufacturing jobs are a distortionary response to outsourcing. Similarly, Acemoglu and Robinson argue, labor market regulations—for example, restrictions on firing, closed shops, minimum wages—are an inefficient way to redistribute wealth to workers. Such rules distort economic decision making, reduce the sorting of workers into the jobs for which they are well-suited, increase unemployment, and so on. If the government is concerned with improving the welfare of workers it would, again, be more efficient to directly transfer resources to those workers, rather than regulate employers. And, as we've already discussed, professional licensing requirements are a way of insulating a group of producers from competition from new entrants to the market in a way that drives up prices and reduces innovation.

It is unsurprising that organized interests seek rents. But the inefficient form that such rents often take is a puzzle in its own right. Even if policymakers want to give particularistic benefits to certain groups, why do they do so in ways that shrink the overall size of the utility pie? Acemoglu and Robinson's answer has to do with the dynamics of political power.

Policy changes can affect society in ways that alter future political power. For instance, a policy that subsidizes some activity with positive externalities—say food production, building weapons for national defense, or pharmaceutical research—may also strengthen certain industries relative to others in ways that allow those industries to exercise power over future policy. Hence, it is not always right to think of the political system as a fixed constraint on policymaking. Sometimes policy is made because of the changes it will induce in the political system itself. This kind of dynamic feedback has two important implications for the relationship between political power and policy. First, policymakers may sometimes pursue inefficient policies precisely because those policies will preserve the current power structure. Second, sometimes policies that appear to be socially beneficial (say eliminating an externality) may actually be socially harmful when one considers not just the direct economic consequences of the policy, but also the political consequences.

The first of these points suggests a way in which the dynamics of power may distort government incentives away from pursuing efficient policies. The second point is a cautionary tale for anyone trying to identify good policies. While much of the time good policy involves addressing social dilemmas of the sort we studied in Part II, one must always think about the possible unintended consequences (political and otherwise) of any policy change. As we will discuss, this latter point can be seen as a political application of the theory of the second best.

In Acemoglu and Robinson's model, young workers are disinclined to enter a declining industry. The declining industry is currently large and powerful enough to extract some rents from the government. If the government simply transfers money to people currently working in that declining industry, the policy will have no effect on the decision of future generations about whether to enter that industry. As the number of people working in the industry shrinks, the industry loses political power. Consequently, the current members of the industry fear that it will be more difficult to extract rents in the future. So, instead, the industry wants the government to make policy concessions that not only generate rents, but preserve the industry's power by giving the new generation incentives to enter the industry. Inefficient policies, like price supports and input subsidies, achieve this political goal in a way that efficient policies, like direct transfers, do not. Hence, a powerful group's desire to preserve its power leads to inefficient policymaking. Let's see how this works in a simple model inspired by Acemoglu and Robinson (2001).

Consider a society with N members, divided into two generations. The share of the population in the new generation is $\delta \in (0, 1)$ and the share of the population in the old generation is $1 - \delta$.

Each member of the old generation works in one of two industries: farming or manufacturing. A share, λ, of the old generation are farmers and a share $1 - \lambda$ are manufacturers. The members of the new generation have not yet chosen an industry. We assume that, while the old generation's farmers are a majority of the old generation ($\lambda > 1/2$), they are not a majority of the whole population ($(1 - \delta)\lambda < 1/2$).

The industries differ in two ways. First, farming is less productive than manufacturing. Each farmer produces F, while each manufacturer produces $M > F$. Second, for simplicity, we will assume that it is possible to tax the income from manufacturing, but not from farming, perhaps because farmers can directly consume their products. (This latter assumption is not substantively important, but it simplifies the model.)

The game is played as follows.

1. At the beginning of the game, the old generation chooses one of three policies by majority vote:

   a. Tax manufacturers at rate t and redistribute to the existing farmers through a lump sum transfer. (This benefits only existing farmers.)
   b. Tax manufacturers at rate t to fund price supports for agriculture. (This benefits existing farmers and anyone who becomes a farmer from the new generation.)
   c. Don't tax manufacturers.

2. The new generation observes the policy and then chooses which industry to enter. First-period production then occurs.
3. A new tax policy is set by a majority vote of both generations.
4. Second-period production occurs and the game ends.

Each player has utility equal to the sum of her individual production and her individual transfers.

Before we solve for the equilibrium of this game, note that, in this model, taxes are not inherently distortionary. Hence, the utilitarian payoff (and, so, Pareto efficiency) is determined entirely by the total amount produced. Since manufacturing is more productive than farming, any utilitarian optimum involves the new generation becoming manufacturers. Any policy choice that leads the new generation to instead become farmers is inefficient.

Now let's turn to analyzing the subgame perfect Nash equilibrium of this game to see how concern over future political power can lead to inefficient policy choices. We will focus on an equilibrium in which all of the members of the new generation join the same industry.

Consider the end of the game. If the members of the new generation become farmers, then there are $((1 - \delta)\lambda + \delta)N$ farmers and $(1 - \delta)(1 - \lambda)N$ manufacturers. The farmers, who hold the majority, will impose a tax of t on the manufacturers, redistributing the proceeds to farmers either through a lump sum transfer or through price supports. (In the second period, the two forms of redistribution are equivalent.) Each farmer's transfer is

$$T_F = \frac{t(1 - \delta)(1 - \lambda)M}{(1 - \delta)\lambda + \delta}.$$

Hence, if the new generation become farmers, in the final period, each farmer makes a payoff of

$$F + T_F$$

and each manufacturer makes a payoff of

$$(1 - t)M.$$

If, instead, the members of the new generation become manufacturers, then there are $((1 - \delta)(1 - \lambda) + \delta) N$ manufacturers and $(1 - \delta)\lambda N$ farmers. The manufacturers, who hold the majority, will impose no taxes. Hence, if the new generation become manufacturers, each farmer makes a payoff of F and each manufacturer makes a payoff of M.

What career will the new generation choose? Suppose that, in the first period, the government chose to tax and redistribute through lump sum transfers to existing farmers. If the new generation become farmers, they don't get the transfer in the first period. Hence, if the new generation become farmers, the lifetime payoff of an individual from the new generation is

$$2F + T_F.$$

If the new generation become manufacturers there will be no taxes in the second period, so the lifetime payoff of an individual from the new generation is

$$M(1 - t) + M = M(2 - t).$$

Suppose, instead, that in the first period, the government chose to use taxes to fund price subsidies. Now a member of the new generation who becomes a farmer receives a transfer even in the first period, since she benefits from the price subsidies. That transfer will again be of value T_F. Hence, if the new generation become farmers, the lifetime payoff of an individual from the new generation is

$$2(F + T_F).$$

If the new generation become manufacturers, the lifetime payoff of an individual from the new generation is still

$$M(2 - t).$$

If, in the first period, the government chose to impose no taxes, then, if the new generation become farmers, the lifetime payoff of an individual from the new generation is

$$2F + T_F.$$

If the new generation become manufacturers, the lifetime payoff of an individual from the new generation is

$$2M.$$

Comparing, if the initial tax policy involves redistribution only to existing farmers, then the new generation become farmers if

$$2F + T_F \geq M(2 - t).$$

If the initial tax policy involves redistribution through price supports, then the new generation become farmers if

$$2(F + T_F) \geq M(2 - t).$$

If the initial tax policy involves no redistribution, then the new generation become farmers if

$$2F + T_F \geq 2M.$$

Importantly, the new generation are most willing to become farmers if the initial policy is redistribution through price supports.

Given all of this, what policy will the old generation of farmers choose? First, it is straightforward that the old farmers will implement some form of redistribution in the first period. Now let's focus on the interesting case where

$$2F + T_F < M(2 - t) < 2(F + T_F).$$

Here, the old generation of farmers faces a trade-off. On the one hand, if they choose a policy of redistribution through lump sum transfers, they get a larger initial transfer because they don't have to share it with the new generation. On the other hand, if they choose redistribution through price supports, they incentivize the new generation to become farmers, allowing their industry to retain power over government redistributive policy in the second period.

We can analyze their decision formally. If the old generation farmers choose redistribution through lump sum transfers, then the new generation become manufacturers. As a result, in the first period, each old farmer receives a transfer of

$$\frac{t\left((1-\delta)(1-\lambda)+\delta\right)M}{(1-\delta)\lambda}.$$

However, in the second period they are no longer in the majority and so receive no redistribution. Hence, the lifetime payoff to an old generation farmer, if they choose lump sum redistribution, is

$$2F + \frac{t\left((1-\delta)(1-\lambda)+\delta\right)M}{(1-\delta)\lambda}.$$

If, instead, the old generation farmers choose redistribution through price supports, then the new generation become farmers. As a result, the farmers retain their majority, receiving redistribution of value T_F in each period. Hence, the lifetime payoff to an old generation farmer, if they choose price supports, is

$$2(F + T_F).$$

Substituting for T_F and comparing, the old generation farmers will choose price supports if

$$\frac{\delta}{(1-\delta)^2} \leq \lambda(1-\lambda).$$

Recall that $\lambda > 1/2$. Hence, this condition says that two factors make the old generation farmers more likely to choose price supports rather than lump sum transfers. Price supports are more attractive when the new generation is small (δ small) and when the farmers hold a fairly small majority in the old generation (λ close to $1/2$). The intuition for the first of these conditions is straightforward. If the new generation is small, it costs relatively little to share the redistribution with the new generation, making price supports more palatable. The intuition for the second condition is similar. When the old generation has a large share of manufacturers, maintaining a political majority that allows for redistribution in the second period is very valuable, making the old generation farmers willing to adopt a policy that costs them in the first period in order to incentivize the new generation to become farmers.

The model illustrates a situation in which concerns about maintaining political power lead to inefficient policy, even when efficient policy instruments are available. The dominant industry in the old generation wants to maintain power, so they must convince the new generation to join their industry. To do so, they use policy instruments that reward people for joining their industry, even though that industry is less productive than other choices.

At heart, the inefficiency in this model is due to a commitment problem. If the new generation could commit to continuing redistribution to farmers in the future, even if farmers are a dwindling share of the population, then the old generation farmers would permit a non-distortionary policy that doesn't drive the new generation into a low-productivity field. But such a commitment is not credible. Once the new generation enters manufacturing, political power shifts, and there is no longer a coalition to support transfers to farmers. Anticipating this, farmers push for policies that maintain their political coalition.

This kind of story is, I think, broadly applicable to many areas of policymaking. Below are some examples of inefficient policies pursued by governments that can be understood as helping to maintain the power base of some political coalition.

Protectionist restrictions on imports are often justified by pointing to the declining fortunes of some domestic industry. It would be more efficient to make transfers to the current members of these declining industries than to restrict trade. But trade restrictions retain the size and power of the industry, while transfers will eventually lead the industry to decline and lose power. A savvy industry understands that once its political power declines, the transfers will disappear. Hence, it pushes for inefficient trade restrictions that prop up the industry for the long term.

Imagine a government controlled by a group of aristocrats, oligarchs, military officers, or other elites. Those elites have to decide whether to allow or block a new technology (e.g., industrialization, free trade, improved communication). This new technology will lead to increased economic growth. But it also makes it more likely that the elites will lose power because with growth comes the rise of the entrepreneurial, middle class. The members of the middle class cannot credibly commit not to use their economic power to seize political power in the future. Hence, the elites block the new technology for as long as they can. If the middle class could commit to not challenge the elites, then the elites would allow the technology, making the middle class richer. But because they can't so commit, the economy is kept stagnant.

Finally, consider immigration policy. Suppose the party in power believes that allowing immigration will improve economic growth or relieve a demographic problem in state-run pensions. If the incumbent politicians also believe that immigrants will eventually become citizens and support the other party, they might restrict immigration. If immigrants could commit to vote for the incumbent party, they would be allowed in and everyone would be better off. But they cannot credibly commit to do so, leading to inefficiently restrictive immigration policy.

8.3.1 The (Political) Second Best

The realization that policy changes can affect the distribution of political power renders the question of what constitutes good policy even more fraught than we've previously realized. Indeed, Acemoglu and Robinson (2013) argue that many textbook examples of policy advice derived from analyses like those in Part II don't stand up to a comprehensive analysis that takes seriously both the economic and political consequences of policy changes.

A simple version of this argument concerns the implications of effective policy reform on the longevity of leaders. Suppose an autocratic leader implements policies that, say, promote economic growth. If those policies improve the tax base and, so, provide the leader with more resources, they might contribute to that autocratic leader surviving in office longer than would otherwise be the case. Autocratic leaders do many things that are bad for their citizens. Hence, while efficient economic reform policies might seem obviously good, considered in isolation, when one factors in their impact on the distribution of political power, one's view might switch.

The same concern is expressed in contemporary debates over the merits of giving aid to bad leaders who invest in demonstrably good programs. For instance, the development economist Angus Deaton argues that[15]

> by providing health care for Rwandan mothers and children, [Rwandan President Paul Kagame] has become one of the darlings of the [aid] industry and a favorite recipient of aid. Essentially, he is "farming" Rwandan children, allowing more of them to live in exchange for support for his undemocratic and oppressive rule. Large aid flows to Africa sometimes help the intended beneficiaries, but they also help create dictators and provide them with the means to insulate themselves from the needs and wishes of their people.

We will return to the politics and political consequences of foreign aid in Chapter 11.3.

Our model tells a similar (though less tragic) story. In the model, efficient policy involves allowing the farming sector to decline in favor of the more efficient manufacturing sector. Suppose, however, that the society also faces an issue of pollution due to a failure to internalize externalities. Farmers might play an important role in a coalition against manufacturers pushing for welfare-enhancing environmental regulation. An unintended political consequence of allowing the agricultural sector to decline might be a diminution in the political power of the environmental coalition. If the welfare loss associated with decreased environmental regulation is larger than the welfare

---

[15]See http://bostonreview.net/forum/logic-effective-altruism/angus-deaton-response-effective-altruism.

gain associated with more efficient sorting into productive industries, then what looked like the optimal policy—letting agriculture decline—was actually suboptimal.

Acemoglu and Robinson's (2013) leading example is de-unionization. A textbook economic analysis suggests that unions (like monopolies) are inefficient because they exercise market power—giving union members rents through above-market wages, while creating distortions in the labor market that damage the overall economy. Hence, a standard piece of economic policy advice might be that Pareto efficiency requires reducing the power of unions.

However, Acemoglu and Robinson argue, unions do many things besides fight for higher wages for unionized workers. For instance, unions were central actors in democratization movements from the late nineteenth century in western Europe through the twentieth century in Latin America, Africa, and eastern Europe. The concern is that policies that reduce unions' market power also reduce their ability to attract members and, therefore, their political power. This diminution in political power may have serious consequences—for democratization, the distribution of income, and many other outcomes whose negative consequences more than offset any efficiency gains associated with eliminating wage distortions. Hence, Acemoglu and Robinson suggest, once one considers the (potentially unintended) political consequences of a policy that seems obviously beneficial from textbook policy analysis, its net benefits are less clear.

While this political caveat to standard policy advice is important, we should also note that it is, in a certain sense, nothing new to us. Acemoglu and Robinson's point is that sometimes taking actions that fix some problem—internalizing externalities, eliminating market distortions—create new problems as a result of political consequences. Hence, when evaluating policies, one must consider not only a policy's effect on the issue at hand, but its spillover effects on the political equilibrium. This is a specific, and particularly important, instance of the theory of the second best. As we discussed in Chapter 4, when choosing a tax or subsidy policy to make people internalize externalities, one doesn't aim for the first best because the taxes or subsidies create other sorts of problems that must be balanced against the benefits of internalizing the externality. Similarly, as we will discuss in Chapter 9, when designing incentives to extract information needed to set policy, one doesn't aim to extract all the information because doing so requires the inefficient expenditure of a huge amount of resources and opens up the risk of capture. We must also add political consequences to the list of the possible unintended consequences of policy changes that we have to think about when we do an analysis to identify the second best. This is a very important point—the second best isn't only about economic distortions due to taxation and the like, it is about any spillover from a policy change that affects welfare, including political spillovers—but it is also important to see that it is closely related to concepts we already understand.

8.4   Takeaways

- Dynamic considerations create a variety of constraints that prevent governments from implementing optimal policy solutions. These include commitment problems in the form of time inconsistency, incentives to sacrifice future interests for current interests, and the feedback between current policy and future political power.
- A time inconsistency problem occurs when the government announces a future policy and if the people believe the policy will be implemented as announced and make choices accordingly, then the government ends up wanting to implement a policy other than the announced policy.
- Fiscal manipulation—whereby current spending is funded by excessive borrowing from the future—can occur because of electoral threat, lack of concern for future generations, or because of rules that mandate discounting future payoffs. Balanced budget rules are often intended to prevent such manipulation, but in many circumstances governments can strategically adapt by finding new ways to borrow from the future.
- Changes to policy have the potential to change the distribution of political power. Such concerns can create incentives for leaders to adopt inefficient policies that preserve the power of some currently powerful group.
- Policy changes that alter the distribution of political power can have unintended consequences on other policy domains. Hence, the effect of policy changes on the distribution of political power creates another type of second-best constraint that must be taken into account when evaluating policies.
- Because of these various dynamic considerations, social welfare is sometimes higher when the government is constrained to follow preset rules, rather than given discretion over policy. This can be true even when the government is benevolent.

8.5   Further Readings

Kydland and Prescott (1977) is the initial articulation of the time inconsistency problem, though the model here is closer in spirit to Stokey (1989).

The model of deficits is in the spirit of Persson and Svensson (1989) and Alesina and Tabellini (1990).

The model of declining interests as a source of policy inefficiency is based on Acemoglu and Robinson (2001).

8.6 Exercises

1. Solve the model in Section 8.1 with a single consumer (i.e., so the consumer's savings decision has a one-for-one effect on the resources available to be taxed for public goods) and show that, in that case, there is no time inconsistency problem. That is, the government in fact achieves the first best.

2. Consider a government that controls the inflation rate through monetary policy. In particular, the government gets to choose a policy that determines the amount of inflation $\iota \in [0, 1]$. Wages are determined by bargaining inside an industry. In particular, the industry will choose an amount of wage increase $\omega \in [0, 1]$. The change in real wages (i.e., in the value of wages) is $\omega - \iota$.

    Economic productivity is increasing in inflation and decreasing in wages. In particular, it is $y = \iota - \omega$. The government's payoff is increasing in productivity, but decreasing in inflation. In particular, it is

    $$u_G(\omega, \iota) = y - \iota^2 = \iota - \omega - \iota^2.$$

    Since wages are determined as part of a bargain between labor and management, the goal of industry is to keep real wages constant. To capture this idea, suppose that industry's payoff is

    $$u_I(\omega, \iota) = -(\omega - \iota)^2,$$

    so it is maximized when $\omega = \iota$.

    (a) Suppose that industry first sets the wage increase and then the government sets inflation.

        i. What is equilibrium economic productivity?
        ii. What is the government's equilibrium payoff?
        iii. What is equilibrium wage growth?

    (b) Suppose, instead, that the government first sets inflation and then industry sets the wage increase.

        i. What is equilibrium economic productivity?
        ii. What is the government's equilibrium payoff?
        iii. What is equilibrium wage growth?

    (c) Explain how comparing these two scenarios suggests that in the first one the government faces a commitment problem that leads to worse policy outcomes.

(d) This kind of argument is often used to suggest that the government might be better off giving up its discretion over monetary policy and instead committing to a rule. Thinking a bit outside the model, what might be a downside to such a move?

3. In negotiations between rebels and a government, the government typically wants the rebel group to disarm as a condition of any peace agreement. Following such negotiations, there is typically a residual group of extremists who continue the rebellion. The government often depends on the former rebels' insider knowledge to fight this residual extremist group. Give an intuitive explanation, in terms of government commitment problems, for why, in light of this, the fact that there will be a residual extremist group might make it easier for the government and the main rebel group to reach a peace agreement.

4. It has been argued that one cause of the financial crisis of 2007 was banks taking excessive risk. Following the crisis, reform advocates argued for breaking up banks that were deemed "too big to fail." Provide an argument for the merits of this policy based on the analysis in this chapter.

9

The Need for Information

Providing social insurance is an essential governmental role. Government programs insure citizens against risk related to ill health, unemployment, disability, and so on. Social insurance programs can have significant utilitarian benefits. But they also have pitfalls. For instance, there is the problem of perverse incentives.

Suppose the government provides unemployment insurance, as many governments do. On the one hand, such a program provides support for people who cannot find work. On the other hand, such a program creates the possibility that an employable person could claim to be unable to find a job because that person prefers to collect unemployment insurance rather than work. It is difficult for the government to differentiate between such people. Moreover, were the government to simply ask, the employable types would have an incentive to lie. And so, if the government wants to minimize abuse, it must design the unemployment insurance program in a way that makes it attractive to people who genuinely can't find work, but unattractive to people who can.

A standard approach to this information and incentives problem is known as *workfare*. Under a workfare program, recipients must meet certain requirements—such as job training or unpaid labor—to qualify for benefits. The Earned Income Tax Credit in the United States is a version of workfare. So too are the welfare-to-work programs instituted in the 1996 welfare reform, which placed both a time limit and a minimum work requirement on recipients of public assistance. The Indian government's National Rural Employment Guarantee Act (NREGA) is the world's largest public employment program and is based on workfare principles. To qualify for benefits, the roughly 47 million annual NREGA beneficiaries work on local public works projects.

You can see how workfare has the potential to solve the government's information problem and mitigate the perverse incentives associated with social insurance. If a citizen must work in order to receive public assistance, then only citizens for whom such work is the best option will seek out the program. A citizen with the option to work in another sector will likely prefer to do so.

The workfare example highlights a general challenge for governments. Many of the policy recommendations that we have seen—subsidizing activities with positive externalities, taxing or regulating activities with negative externalities, pushing people toward efficient equilibria in coordination games—depend on the policymaker having a lot of information. For instance, in order to figure out the right tax, subsidy, or regulatory limit to impose in an externalities setting, the policymaker must be able to figure out the second best. This depends on knowing things about the participants' costs, benefits, and so on. Often such information is dispersed among the interested parties. This presents a problem because these interested parties might not be willing to release the relevant information. Indeed, as we will see, these sorts of informational asymmetries place a fundamental limit on how much good policymaking can do, even in the presence of social dilemmas that, in principle, present opportunities for Pareto improvements.

For instance, suppose the government is trying to diminish pollution. The optimal policy involves requiring firms to adopt some new, green technology if and only if the cost of doing so is below one million dollars. The policymaker doesn't know the true costs of adoption, while the firms do. If the policymaker asks the firms the cost of adopting the new technology, the firms have an incentive to say the cost is over a million dollars because doing so avoids new regulation.

The policymaker needs to design an incentive scheme to induce the firms to reveal their true information. The challenge is that the incentive scheme needs to do three things at once:

1. Induce truthful revelation of the relevant information.
2. Implement an efficient policy.
3. Be budget balanced.

The first point says the government needs to find a way to actually get the information.

The second point says that, once the government has the information, it must be free to implement the efficient policy. This is important because one way a policymaker might get the firms to reveal their information is to make a credible promise that the policy won't change, regardless of the information supplied. If the policymaker makes such a commitment, the firms have no reason to lie. So a commitment like this achieves point 1—firms will truthfully reveal their private information. But this is a Pyrrhic victory, since that information now can't actually be used to achieve a socially optimal outcome.

The third point says that there is no free lunch. You can't offer to pay the firms vast amounts of money, in excess of the benefits to be had from the information, in order to induce truth telling. We are trying to achieve Pareto improvements. At worst, we want society to break even on the deal.

The field dedicated to the study of this sort of incentive problem is called *mechanism design*. Since solving these sorts of problems is a basic challenge for governments, we will spend some time thinking about mechanism design. Doing so will give us a sense of the extent to which lack of information constrains government's ability to identify and implement Pareto improving policies. We will study three different, but related, problems. First, we will consider how a government might efficiently allocate an asset when it is uncertain about how various parties value the asset. Second, we will consider a government deciding whether to provide a public good and how to finance its provision, again while facing uncertainty about how various parties value the good. Finally, we will consider a government regulating an industry when it is doesn't know key facts about the production process.

Before commencing, I should say that the discussion in Sections 9.1–9.2 are heavily based on the wonderful lecture notes from Jeff Ely's microeconomics class at Northwestern.[1]

9.1 Auctions

Suppose the government has a valuable asset—say the right to transmit signals over some particular bands of the electromagnetic spectrum (for radio or cell phones), drill in a given oil field, take off and land on a particular airport runway, or occupy a location in geostationary orbit. There are lots of people who would like to have control of this asset. A player, i, places a monetary value of v_i on the asset. Players have quasi-linear utility. A player's valuation of the asset is her private information.

There is only one asset. So if Player i gets the asset, what is the utilitarian payoff? Each player who did not get the asset makes a payoff of zero. Player i makes a payoff of v_i. Thus, the utilitarian payoff is v_i. Given this, it is straightforward that the utilitarian optimal policy is to give the asset to the player with the highest valuation.

Even in this simple problem, we see a challenge for the government. In order to implement the utilitarian optimum, the government needs to figure out who has the highest valuation. One thing a government might do is simply ask the players their valuations and then give it to the player who says the highest number. But that won't work. All players have an incentive to say an arbitrarily large number, so the government will not be able to figure out who has the highest valuation.

Another thing the government might do is auction off the asset. Let's look at an auction that will work in this simple setting.

---

[1] http://cheaptalk.org/jeffs-intermediate-micro-course/

9.1.1 Second Price Auction

Suppose the government runs a *second price auction*. Each player submits a sealed bid. The government opens the bids and awards the asset to the highest bidder. The winner pays the amount bid by the second highest bidder.

I will show you that the government can implement the efficient policy by using a second price auction. That is, it is a Nash equilibrium for all players to bid their true valuation in a second price auction. Hence, the player with the highest valuation wins the asset. Indeed, I will show you something stronger. It is a *weakly dominant strategy* for each player to bid his or her true valuation in a second price auction. A strategy is weakly dominant if it is a best response to any profile of strategies by other players. Clearly, if each player is playing a weakly dominant strategy, then together they are playing a Nash equilibrium. (The opposite is not true: not all Nash equilibria are made up of weakly dominant strategies.) Throughout this chapter we will focus on looking for mechanisms that achieve the government's goals by making truthful play a weakly dominant strategy for each player.

I proceed in two steps. First, I show that, regardless of what the other players bid, Player i is always at least as well off if she bids her true valuation rather than something lower. Second, I show that, regardless of what the other players bid, Player i is always at least as well off if she bids her true valuation rather than something higher.

Consider a bid $b_i' < v_i$ by Player i. Suppose that the highest bid among the other players is B. Since she doesn't know B, from Player i's perspective, there are three possibilities:

1. $b_i' < v_i < B$: In this event, Player i loses whether she bids b_i' or v_i. Under either bid her payoff is 0. As such, in this case, she is indifferent between the two bids.
2. $b_i' < B < v_i$: In this event, if Player i bids v_i she wins and makes a payoff of $v_i - B > 0$. If she bids b_i' she loses and makes a payoff of 0. So she prefers to bid her true valuation, v_i, in this case.
3. $B < b_i' < v_i$: In this event, Player i wins whether she bids b_i' or v_i. Under either bid her payoff is $v_i - B > 0$. As such, in this case, she is indifferent between the two bids.

This analysis implies that bidding any $b_i' < v_i$ is weakly dominated by bidding v_i itself. The logic is straightforward. Changing her bid does not change how much she pays. It only changes the set of circumstances in which she wins. She wants to win whenever the price of the asset is less than her valuation of it, so she should bid her true valuation.

The logic for not bidding higher than her true valuation is the same. Consider a bid $b_i'' > v_i$. Again, suppose the highest bid among the other players is B. Since she doesn't know B, from Player i's perspective, there are three possibilities:

1. $v_i < b_i'' < B$: In this event, Player i loses whether she bids b_i'' or v_i. Under either bid her payoff is 0. As such, in this case, she is indifferent between the two bids.
2. $v_i < B < b_i''$: In this event, if Player i bids v_i she loses and makes a payoff of 0. If she bids $b_i'' > v_i$ she wins and makes a payoff of $v_i - B < 0$. So she prefers to bid her true valuation, v_i, in this case.
3. $B < v_i < b_i''$: In this event, Player i wins whether she bids b_i'' or v_i. Under either bid her payoff is $v_i - B > 0$. As such, in this case, she is indifferent between the two bids.

Again, bidding any $b_i'' > v_i$ is weakly dominated by bidding v_i itself. The logic is the same as above. Bidding more than v_i simply leaves her in a situation where she might win an asset for which she must pay more than her valuation of that asset.

The second price auction, thus, fulfills the government's goals. It gets each player to reveal her true valuation and awards the asset to the highest-valuation player.

Of course, auctions can get much more complicated. For instance, Milgrom (2004) describes spectrum auctions in which multiple assets are for sale and the value of asset 1 to Player i depends on who ends up owning asset 2 or 3. Clearly, this creates a variety of additional strategic complications.

Another example involves situations in which the value of the asset is unknown by the bidders. During the financial crisis of 2007–2008, the Troubled Asset Relief Program included provisions for auctioning so-called toxic assets—assets whose value was so uncertain that investment banks could find no buyers on their own. Often when the government auctions, say, offshore drilling rights for oil, bidders face uncertainty about the amount of extractable oil. In situations where there is uncertainty about valuations, but parties have some private information, it is particularly difficult to elicit truth telling. This is because of concerns over the "winner's curse" (see Thaler, 1988, for a discussion). A bidder only wins the auction if she bids higher than everyone else. This presumably only happens when her guess about the asset's value was higher than everyone else's guess, suggesting she probably paid too much.

9.2   Providing a Public Good

Now let's turn to a case in which the government is not allocating an excludable asset, but instead is considering providing a public good. The government's problem is that it doesn't know how much the interested parties value the

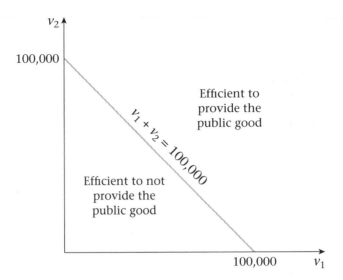

Figure 9.1. The efficient policy.

good. The parties know their individual valuations, but might have incentives to lie to the government. The government must devise incentives to extract the information, so it can figure out whether to provide the public good and who should pay for it.

To keep things as simple as we can, consider a society made up of two people. The society has to decide whether to provide a public good. We can think of this as a model of two neighborhoods deciding whether to build a shared park, two cities deciding whether to construct a bridge that connects them, or what have you. The public good costs $100,000. People have quasi-linear preferences. Each player, i, values the public good at $v_i \geq 0$. Players' valuations are their own private information.

What is the efficient policy here? If the public good is provided, then the social payoff is $v_1 + v_2 - 100,000$. If the public good is not provided, the social payoff is 0. Hence, the efficient policy (i.e., the utilitarian optimum) is to provide the public good if $v_1 + v_2 \geq 100,000$; that is, if the total value of the public good to the two players is at least as large as the cost of providing it. Figure 9.1 illustrates the efficient policy.

If the government knew the two players' valuations, it could simply implement the efficient policy. But it doesn't know those valuations, so it must try to get the players to reveal their private information. The willingness of players to tell their true valuations will depend on who has to pay for the public good, should it be provided.

Let's consider some possible approaches the government might take to try to learn what it wants to know.

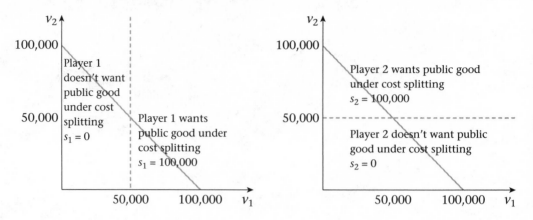

Figure 9.2. Best responses under split-the-costs.

9.2.1 Split-the-Costs

An intuitively appealing approach is to think that people should share the costs of the public good. Suppose that the government adopted a mechanism of the following sort:

- Each player states how much she values the public good. People can say any valuation greater than or equal to zero. Call player i's statement s_i.
- If the two statements sum to 100,000 or more, the public good will be provided and the costs will be split evenly—that is, each player will pay 50,000.

Under this set of rules, if the public good is provided, Player i will get a payoff of $v_i - 50,000$, since she pays half the cost. So Player i wants the public good to be provided whenever her personal valuation is greater than 50,000 and to not be provided whenever her personal valuation is less than 50,000.

If Player i's valuation is greater than 50,000, she can guarantee the public good will be provided by stating that her personal valuation is 100,000. Then, no matter what the other player says, the government will provide the public good. If player i's valuation is less than 50,000 she wants to minimize the chance that the public good will be provided. So she should say that her valuation is 0. These incentives are illustrated for each player in the two panels of Figure 9.2. The government has failed to elicit truthful revelation of people's valuations. People with valuations between 50,000 and 100,000 overstate their valuations and people with valuations less than 50,000 understate their valuations.

As a result, the government sometimes fails to implement the efficient policy. The public good ends up being provided whenever at least one party's valuation is greater than 50,000, even if the two valuations sum to less than 100,000.

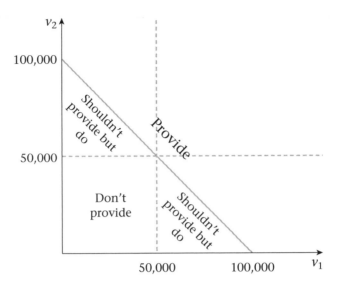

Figure 9.3. Inefficiency under split-the-costs with each player declaring valuation.

Intuitively, the split-the-costs rule creates externalities. If I bid 100,000, I get the full benefit of the public good, but I only bear half the cost, imposing the other half as a negative externality on you. Hence, there is too much public good provision relative to efficiency, as illustrated in Figure 9.3.

9.2.2 Veto and Split

Simply asking people their valuations and splitting the costs won't work because of negative externalities. What if, instead, we go the other way—split-the-costs, but rather than asking people their valuations (which allows them to impose the negative externalities), just let them say whether or not they want the public good, providing it if and only if both people say they want it. Now what happens? You shouldn't be surprised to learn that this too will not get us efficiency. Just as before, as illustrated in Figure 9.4, a player wants the public good provided if and only if her valuation is greater than 50,000. So a player with a valuation greater than 50,000 will support provision of the public good and a player with a valuation less than 50,000 will veto provision of the public good. Consequently, in any circumstance in which the sum of the valuations is greater than 100,000, but one of the individual valuations is less than 50,000, the public good will not be provided, even though it should be from a utilitarian perspective. This inefficiency is illustrated in Figure 9.5.

9.2.3 General Mechanisms

Since splitting the costs won't work, let's see if the government can do better with some more subtle mechanism.

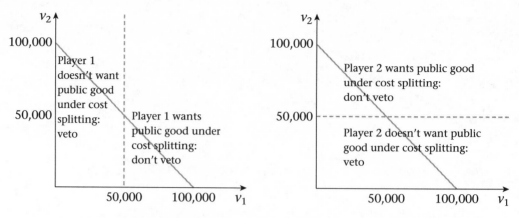

Figure 9.4. Best responses under split-the-costs with vetoes.

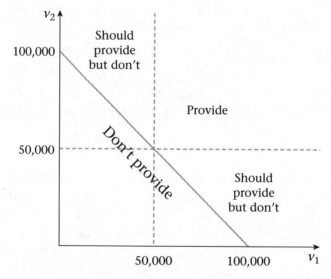

Figure 9.5. Inefficiency under split-the-costs with each player having a veto.

You could imagine all sorts of very complicated mechanisms in which the government asks lots of questions, makes people do all sorts of things, and then uses the output of this procedure to decide whether or not to provide the public good and how much to charge each player should the public good be provided. However, an important result, whose logic we will not explore here, says that this is unnecessary. The result is called the *revelation principle*. Roughly speaking, the revelation principle says this: if there is any complicated procedure that gets people to reveal their true valuation and then implements the utilitarian optimum, then there is also a very simple mechanism—called a *direct revelation mechanism*—that achieves the same thing. A direct revelation mechanism is a procedure in which the government does the following:

- Asks people to state their valuations.
- Before they make their statements, lays out whether or not the public good will be provided and who will pay what for each possible pair of stated valuations.

Our first split-the-costs mechanism is an example of a direct revelation mechanism. The government asks people their valuation. For any pair of statements that sums to at least 100,000, the government provides the public good and charges each player 50,000. For any pair of statements that sums to less than 100,000, the government doesn't provide the public good.

Another direct revelation mechanism would be to say that the public good is provided if and only if the statements sum to at least 100,000 and, if the public good is provided, charges each player according to his or her share of the sum. That is, if $v_1 + v_2 \geq 100{,}000$, then the public good is provided, player 1 is charged $\left(\frac{v_1}{v_1 + v_2}\right) \times 100{,}000$, and player 2 is charged $\left(\frac{v_2}{v_1 + v_2}\right) \times 100{,}000$.

To recap, the revelation principle says that *if* it is possible for the government to design some mechanism that gets people to tell the truth and then implements the utilitarian optimum, then the government can do so with a direct revelation mechanism. It doesn't say *any* direct revelation mechanism will do the job (we've already seen that split-the-costs won't). Nor does it say that there definitely exists a direct revelation mechanism that does the job. It says that if achieving efficiency is feasible at all, then it can be done with some direct revelation mechanism.

The revelation principle implies that if we can't find a direct revelation mechanism that achieves truthful revelation of information and efficient policy, then we also won't be able to find a more complicated procedure that achieves these goals. This is important because it means we don't have to look at all those complicated procedures. We can just look at direct revelation mechanisms. This makes our lives much easier.

So let's think about direct revelation mechanisms. The government asks each player to make a statement. Call player i's statement s_i. The government wants to come up with rules of the game (when to provide the public good and how much to charge each player) that induce players to choose $s_i = v_i$; that is, to tell the truth. If it can do so, then it will provide the public good when $s_1 + s_2 \geq 100{,}000$ and it will not provide the public good when $s_1 + s_2 < 100{,}000$.

The government's key lever is how much it charges each player as a function of the statements the players make. Can the government come up with amounts it will charge (as a function of the statements made) that make it weakly dominant for both players to tell the truth? That is, is there a mechanism under which, for any v_1, it is a best response for player 1 to tell the truth regardless of what player 2 says (and similarly for player 2)?

To answer this question, we will focus on player 1. (Player 2 is symmetric.) It turns out there is one and only one way to make truth telling a weakly dominant strategy. Whenever $s_1 + s_2 \geq 100{,}000$, so that the public good is provided, player 1 must be charged an amount $p^*(s_2) = 100{,}000 - s_2$. Notice, this says that the price player 1 is charged, should the public good be provided, is a function of the statement player 2 makes, not the statement person 1 makes. This is just as in the second price auction.

I will demonstrate that this is true in three steps. First, I will show you that if player 1 is charged $100{,}000 - s_2$ when the public good is provided, then truth telling is weakly dominant for any v_1. Second, I will show you that if player 1 will instead be charged some amount $p > 100{,}000 - s_2$, then truth telling is not weakly dominant for any v_1. Third, I will show that if player 1 will be charged some amount $p < 100{,}000 - s_2$, then, again, truth telling is not weakly dominant for any v_1.

First, suppose player 1 knows she will be charged $p^*(s_2) = 100{,}000 - s_2$ when the public good is provided. Of course, she doesn't know s_2. But let's see that, for any v_1, it is a best response for player 1 to state her true valuation, regardless of what s_2 turns out to be.

The government provides the public good if and only if $s_1 + s_2 \geq 100{,}000$. Rearranging, the government provides the public good if and only if $s_1 \geq 100{,}000 - s_2$. Now think about player 1's incentives. Player 1's payoff from the public good being provided is

$$v_1 - p^*(s_2) = v_1 - (100{,}000 - s_2).$$

Her payoff from the public good not being provided is 0. Hence, she wants the public good to be provided if and only if

$$v_1 \geq 100{,}000 - s_2.$$

Since the government provides the public good if $s_1 \geq 100{,}000 - s_2$, if player 1 chooses $s_1 = v_1$ (i.e., states her true valuation), the government provides the public good precisely when player 1 wants the government to do so (since this implies $v_1 \geq 100{,}000 - s_2$). Hence, choosing $s_1 = v_1$ is a best response by player 1 to any possible statement by player 2.

These incentives are illustrated in Figure 9.6. The upper panel shows that if the amount charged will be $p^*(s_2) = 100{,}000 - s_2$, then player 1 will state her true valuation when $v_1 > p^*(s_2)$. The lower panel shows that the same is true when $v_1 < p^*(s_2)$.

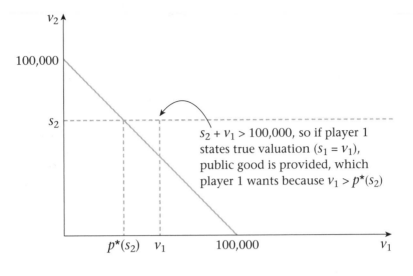

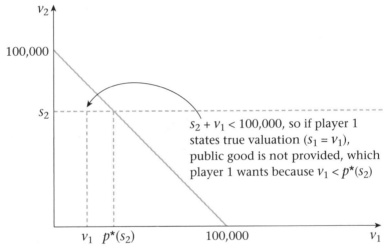

Figure 9.6. It is a weakly dominant strategy for player 1 to choose $s_1 = v_1$ when the cost of the public good to player 1 is $p^*(s_2) = 100{,}000 - s_2$.

Second, let's see that if player 1 will be charged some $p > 100{,}000 - s_2$ when the public good is provided, then for any v_1 there is some s_2 such that choosing $s_1 = v_1$ is not a best response. Player 1's payoff from the public good being provided is $v_1 - p$. Her payoff from the public good not being provided is 0. Hence, she wants the public good to be provided if and only if

$$v_1 \geq p.$$

Remember that $p > 100{,}000 - s_2$. Suppose player 2's statement, s_2, is such that player 1's valuation, v_1, is between $100{,}000 - s_2$ and p. Player 1 does not want the public good to be provided because her true valuation is less than her price. But if player 1 tells the truth, the public good will be provided because

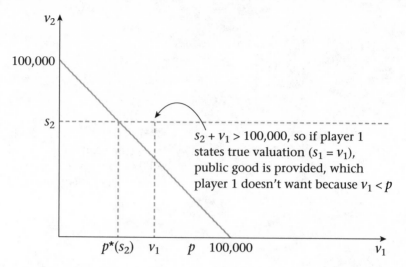

Figure 9.7. It is not a weakly dominant strategy to choose $s_1 = v_1$ when $p > p^*(s_2)$.

$v_1 + s_2 > 100,000$. Hence, player 1's best response is to lie—understating her valuation. This incentive is illustrated in Figure 9.7.

Finally, let's see that if player 1 will be charged $p' < 100,000 - s_2$ when the public good is provided, then for any v_1 there is an s_2 such that choosing $s_1 = v_1$ is not a best response. Player 1's payoff from the public good being provided is $v_1 - p'$. Her payoff from the public good not being provided is 0. Hence, she wants the public good to be provided if and only if

$$v_1 \geq p'.$$

Remember that $p' < 100,000 - s_2$. Suppose player 2's statement, s_2, is such that player 1's valuation, v_1, is between p' and $100,000 - s_2$. Player 1 wants the public good to be provided because her true valuation is greater than the price. But if player 1 tells the truth, the public good won't be provided because $v_1 + s_2 < 100,000$. Hence, player 1's best response is to lie—overstating her valuation. This incentive is illustrated in Figure 9.8.

Player 2's incentives are symmetric to player 1's. It is always a best response for player 2 to tell the truth, regardless of what statement player 1 makes, if and only if player 2 will be charged $100,000 - s_1$ whenever the public good is provided.

We have learned that any mechanism that makes revealing true valuations weakly dominant and uses that information to implement the efficient policy is equivalent to the following direct revelation mechanism:

- The public good is provided if and only if $s_1 + s_2 \geq 100,000$.
- Player 1 is charged $100,000 - s_2$ if the public good is provided.
- Player 2 is charged $100,000 - s_1$ if the public good is provided.

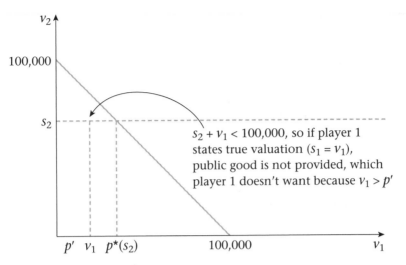

Figure 9.8. It is not a weakly dominant strategy to choose $s_1 = v_1$ when $p' < p^*(s_2)$.

This seems like good news. We have found a way for the government to learn the information it needs to pursue efficient policy. But there is a catch.

Suppose we are in a situation where the right policy is to provide the public good—that is, $v_1 + v_2 > 100,000$. Under our mechanism, $s_1 = v_1$ and $s_2 = v_2$, so the public good will be provided, at a cost of 100,000. How much revenue will be raised? Player 1 will be charged $100,000 - s_2$. Player 2 will be charged $100,000 - s_1$. So the total revenue generated is

$$100,000 - s_2 + 100,000 - s_1 = 200,000 - (s_1 + s_2)$$
$$= 200,000 - (v_1 + v_2).$$

But remember $v_1 + v_2 > 100,000$. So total revenue is *less* than the cost of providing the public good. Our mechanism doesn't have a balanced budget!

What does this mean? The presence of private information presents a real constraint on the ability of the government to pursue efficient public policy. *There is no budget balanced mechanism under which both players always tell the truth.* And since the government cannot create resources out of thin air, we must accept the fact that, at least some of the time, policymakers will be unable to elicit the information they need to implement optimal policies.

9.2.4 The Second Best

The fact that no mechanism exists that induces truth telling all the time does not mean the government must make policy with no information. There are mechanisms that induce truth telling some of the time. Such mechanisms

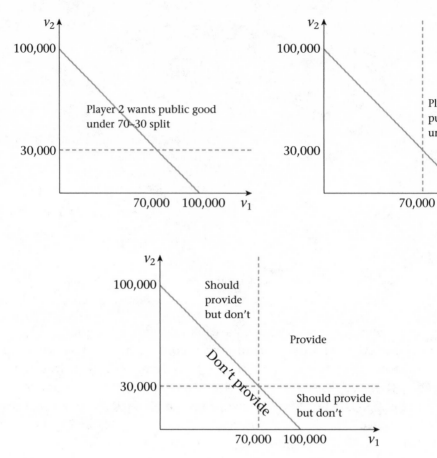

Figure 9.9. Incentives and inefficiency under a 70–30 split-the-costs arrangement with vetoes.

don't allow the government to always pursue Pareto efficient policies, but they certainly are better than making policy with no information.

We've actually already seen some examples of mechanisms like this in Figures 9.3 and 9.5. Each of these shows an example of a budget balanced mechanism that induces truth telling and allows the government to implement the Pareto efficient policy some of the time. You could imagine other such mechanisms. For instance, consider a mechanism that gives each player a veto and splits the costs 70-30 between player 1 and player 2. This mechanism is similar to the one described in Figure 9.5, but it shifts around when exactly policy fails to be efficient as well as how much of the cost each player pays, as illustrated in Figure 9.9.

We will refer to those mechanisms that do the best the government can as *second-best mechanisms*. This is in keeping with our notion of the second best from our earlier discussions. The second best is not the socially efficient outcome. But it is the best the government can do given the constraints under which it operates. In our earlier examples of the second best, the constraints came from the inefficiency inherent in imposing taxes, moral hazard, or other concerns. Here the constraints come from lack of information.

We will not fully characterize what the second best looks like in this public goods game. But, roughly speaking, the examples we've seen of mechanisms that choose a fixed division of the costs describe what the second-best mechanism looks like. The government must accept that, due to a lack of information, sometimes it will not provide the public good when it would be efficient to do so or will provide the public good when it is inefficient to do so. Comparing Figures 9.5 and 9.9, you can see that by changing how the costs are split, the government can change two things:

1. The valuations for which it fails to achieve efficiency.
2. The distribution of costs between the two players.

The first of these decisions may well be a question that the government can answer in terms of efficiency. If the government believes it is extremely unlikely that people have some particular set of valuations, then it should use a mechanism that leads to the government choosing the wrong policy in those instances, since those instances are relatively rare. The second question, however, is about the distribution of welfare. That is a decision not about how to make the pie larger, but rather, about how to divide it up. We will turn to questions about how players try to influence such decisions in Chapter 10.

9.3 Regulating a Monopolist

Markets characterized by monopoly power are a classic example of a situation in which government regulation can improve social welfare. Monopoly power exists when a single firm controls a market. As you know if you've taken microeconomics, monopolists have incentives to produce too little (relative to the utilitarian optimum) in order to inflate prices. Doing so gives them higher profits, but reduces consumer welfare.

There are a variety of reasons an industry might end up with a monopolist (or, more generally, with a small number of firms exercising oligopoly power). For instance, a firm might control a market because the dominant technology is its intellectual property. This is often the case, on a temporary basis, in markets for certain types of medicines. A firm might also control a market because there are high fixed costs to entering the market, making it too expensive for competitors to emerge. This is often thought to be the case in certain "natural monopolies," such as the provision of utilities like electricity, gas, and water. Regulating such monopolists is perhaps the paradigmatic example from economic theory of a Pareto improving policy intervention. And, indeed, governments do in fact regulate public utilities.

Governments can improve utilitarian social welfare by requiring monopolists to produce more than they otherwise would. Doing so increases consumer welfare by more than it reduces the monopolist's profits. The question is: how much more production should regulators require? In order to answer that question, the government needs to know the monopolist's marginal costs of production. Let's see why.

Imagine a simple economy with one firm that produces widgets. If the firm produces q widgets and sells them at price p, it makes revenues pq and bears costs of production cq. (I'm assuming constant marginal costs of production, c, which is to say perfectly elastic supply, because it makes the model simple. Nothing important in what I'm going to say depends on constant marginal costs.) Hence, the firm's profits are

$$\pi(p, q, c) = q(p - c).$$

Of course, prices are determined by the market. We will assume that the firm must charge the same price to all consumers. Moreover, at price p, demand for widgets is given by a simple, linear demand function:

$$D(p) = 100 - p.$$

That is, if the price per widget is \$5, then there is demand for 95 widgets. If the price per widget is \$20, then there is only demand for 80 widgets.

We can invert this demand function to find the price the market will bear, given the number of widgets produced. If the firm produces $q < 100$ widgets, all the widgets will be sold as long as the price is such that

$$D(p) = 100 - p \geq q.$$

Rearranging, when q widgets are produced, the highest price the monopolist can charge and still sell all the widgets is

$$p^*(q) = 100 - q.$$

Notice what this implies about the consumer's welfare (called *consumer surplus* in microeconomic parlance). If q widgets are produced, then the price per widget will be $100 - q$. For the qth widget, this is exactly the price that the marginal consumer is willing to pay. However, for all the other widgets produced, there were consumers willing to pay more than $100 - q$ per widget. Hence, for each of those widgets, a consumer is making positive surplus (i.e., her welfare is greater than 0). Indeed, for this reason, we can think of the demand curve as also representing the *marginal consumer surplus*.

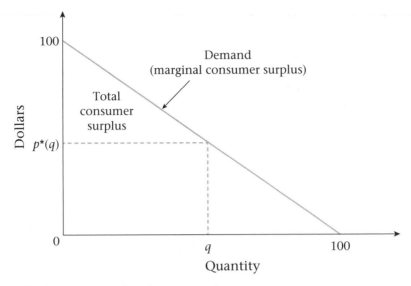

Figure 9.10. Consumer surplus given a quantity q.

Figure 9.10 shows how to calculate the *total consumer surplus*. The downward sloping line gives demand as a function of the quantity produced. We see that if the quantity produced is q, then the price will be $p^*(q)$—the price at which supply exactly equals demand. The total consumer surplus is represented by the area of the marked triangle. For the very first widget, someone was willing to pay 100, but got it for $p^*(q) = 100 - q$. That consumer made a surplus of $100 - p^*(q) = q$. For the next widget, the marginal consumer was willing to pay a little less, but still more than $100 - q$. Each subsequent consumer, then, values the widget slightly less and so makes slightly less surplus. This continues all the way to the consumer who values the widget at exactly $100 - q$ and, so, makes zero surplus. The area of the triangle gives the total surplus welfare that consumers enjoy by virtue of consuming widgets that they value at more than $100 - q$ but for which they pay only $100 - q$. This area is given by

$$\text{TCS}(q) = \frac{1}{2}\left(100 - p^*(q)\right)q.$$

Using the fact that $p^*(q) = 100 - q$, the total consumer surplus can be rewritten

$$\text{TCS}(q) = \frac{q^2}{2}.$$

9.3.1 Monopolistic Equilibrium

Now let's think about how much the monopolistic firm will produce if left to its own devices. The firm maximizes profits by solving

$$\max_q q(p^*(q) - c).$$

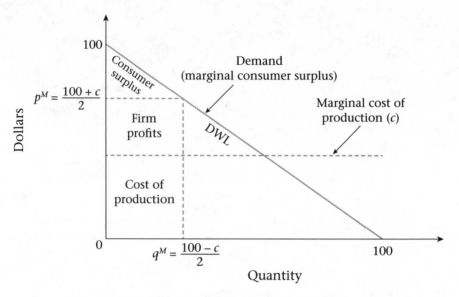

Figure 9.11. Outcome under a monopolist.

Since $p^*(q) = 100 - q$, this is equivalent to solving

$$\max_{q} q(100 - q - c).$$

Solving for the first-order condition, the monopolist's profit-maximizing level of production is

$$q^M = \frac{100 - c}{2}.$$

This implies that the price under a monopolist is

$$p^M = p^*(q^M) = 100 - \frac{100 - c}{2} = \frac{100 + c}{2}.$$

Social welfare is profits plus total consumer surplus:

$$\pi\left(p^M, q^M, c\right) + \text{TCS}\left(q^M\right) = \left(\frac{100 - c}{2}\right)\left(\frac{100 + c}{2} - c\right) + \frac{1}{2}\left(\frac{100 - c}{2}\right)^2$$

$$= \frac{3(100 - c)^2}{8}.$$

This sum of firm profits and consumer surplus can be seen graphically in Figure 9.11.

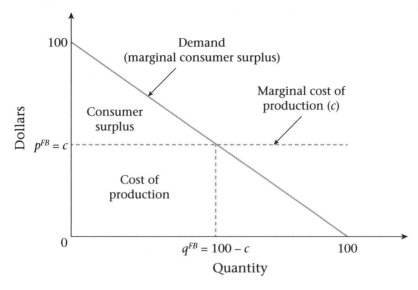

Figure 9.12. The first best.

9.3.2 Regulation with Full Information

Allowing the monopolist to choose the quantity produced does not maximize the utilitarian social welfare because the monopolist holds down production in order to keep prices and profits high. This behavior creates an inefficiency, known as *deadweight loss*, which is represented by the triangle labeled DWL in Figure 9.11. The deadweight loss exists because, at the monopolist's preferred level of production, there are still consumers whose value for widgets is higher than the firm's marginal cost of production. Hence, the deadweight loss represents social welfare that could be created if the firm produced more.

Suppose a utilitarian welfare maximizing government could regulate the monopolist, requiring a higher level of production. Such a government would increase production so that all of the deadweight loss was recovered. That is, it would make the firm keep producing until the marginal benefits of production (increased consumer surplus) exactly equaled the marginal costs of production. Graphically, this means setting the quantity to q^{FB}, represented in Figure 9.12. At this level of production, the price per widget exactly equals the firm's marginal cost of production. So the firm makes exactly zero profits (i.e., revenues equal production costs). But the consumers enjoy the largest feasible surplus. There is no deadweight loss.

Formally, the utilitarian government regulates the firm to produce the first-best quantity of widgets, q^{FB}, which solves

$$\max_{q} \overbrace{q(p^*(q) - c)}^{\text{Firm Profits}} + \overbrace{\frac{q^2}{2}}^{\text{Consumer Surplus}}.$$

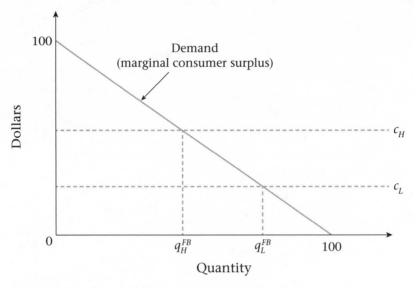

Figure 9.13. First best for two different marginal costs.

Substituting for $p^*(q) = 100 - q$ and maximizing, the first-best level of production is

$$q^{FB} = 100 - c.$$

The associated price is

$$p^{FB} = p^*(q^{FB}) = c.$$

At the first-best quantity, the price of widgets equals the marginal cost of production.

9.3.3 Regulation with Uncertainty

We are interested in what happens when the government doesn't have all the information it needs to optimally regulate the firm. So, suppose the government is uncertain of whether the firm has a high marginal cost of production (c_H) or a low marginal cost of production ($c_L < c_H$). The government believes the probability that the firm's marginal costs are low is $\lambda \in (0, 1)$. Let's also add one more constraint. While the government can regulate the firm, it cannot force the firm to operate at a loss, since the owners can always shut the firm down instead.

As above, if the government knew the firm's marginal cost, it would be easy to implement the first-best policy, illustrated in Figure 9.13. If the firm has low marginal costs, the government would like to require the firm to produce $q_L^{FB} = 100 - c_L$ and if the firm has high marginal costs, the government would like to require the firm to produce $q_H^{FB} = 100 - c_H$. In each case, the firm makes zero profits and utilitarian social welfare is maximized.

The challenge for the government is figuring out what to do without this critical piece of information.

CAN THE FIRST-BEST POLICY BE IMPLEMENTED?

One thing the government might do is simply ask the firm whether its marginal costs are high or low, and then implement the first-best policy assuming the answer is truthful. But this won't work. Let's see why.

Suppose the firm has high marginal costs. If it tells the government the truth, the government will set production at q_H^{FB} and the firm will make zero profits:

$$\pi(p = c_H, q = 100 - c_H, c_H) = (100 - c_H)(c_H - c_H) = 0.$$

If the firm lies and claims it has low marginal costs, then the government will set production at $q_L^{FB} = 100 - c_L$. The high-cost firm's profits from lying, then, are

$$\pi(p = c_L, q = 100 - c_L, c_H) = (100 - c_L)(c_L - c_H) < 0.$$

A high marginal cost firm makes zero profits from telling the truth and negative profits from lying, so a high marginal cost firm will tell the truth. This makes sense. Firms want to hold down production in order to increase prices and profits. The higher the government believes a firm's marginal costs to be, the lower it sets production. Hence, all the high marginal cost firm can achieve by claiming to have low marginal costs is to put itself in a position where production is even higher and prices even lower. It will not do so.

But what if the firm has low marginal costs? Now, by claiming to have high marginal costs, the firm can convince the government to reduce production, to the firm's benefit. Let's see this.

If the low marginal cost firm tells the truth, the government will set production at q_L^{FB} and the firm will make zero profits. If, instead, the firm claims to have high marginal costs, then the government will set production at $q_H^{FB} = 100 - c_H$ and the firm's profits will be

$$\pi(p = c_H, q = 100 - c_H, c_L) = (100 - c_H)(c_H - c_L) > 0.$$

This logic is illustrated in Figure 9.14, which shows that when a firm has low marginal costs, but production is set at q_H^{FB}, the firm makes positive profits. Hence, a low marginal cost firm will claim to have high marginal costs.

The analysis above shows that if the government attempts to implement the first-best policy, all firms will claim to have high marginal costs. When the firm actually has high marginal costs, the outcome will be socially optimal.

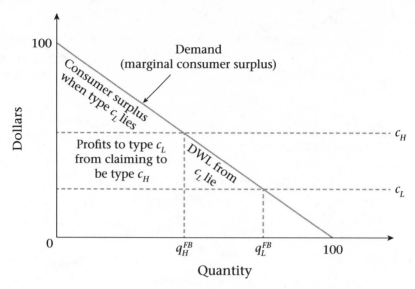

Figure 9.14. The first-best policy is manipulable by a low marginal cost firm when the government is uninformed.

However, when the firm actually has low marginal costs, the result will be underproduction and deadweight loss.

The expected decrease in social welfare (relative to the first best) associated with this policy is the deadweight loss suffered when the firm has low marginal costs multiplied by the probability that the firm has low marginal costs. The deadweight loss when the firm has low marginal costs is given by the area of the triangle in Figure 9.14:

$$\text{DWL} = \frac{1}{2}(q_L^{FB} - q_H^{FB})(c_H - c_L) = \frac{(c_H - c_L)^2}{2}.$$

Weighting this deadweight loss by the probability that the firm has low marginal costs (λ), the expected cost of government uncertainty, in terms of social welfare, under this policy, is

$$\frac{\lambda(c_H - c_L)^2}{2}.$$

THE SECOND BEST

The government can design a better mechanism than simply asking the firm to report its marginal costs and then attempting to implement the first best. How does it do so?

To induce a firm with low marginal costs to reveal that information, the government must compensate the firm for the profits it forgoes by not claiming

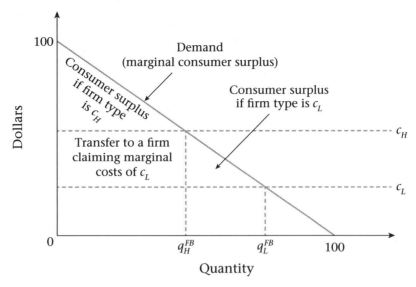

Figure 9.15. A mechanism that induces truth telling by making large transfers to firm claiming to have low marginal costs.

to have high marginal costs. Figure 9.15 illustrates a simple policy that achieves this goal as follows:

- If the firm claims to have high marginal costs, require production $q_H^{FB} = 100 - c_H$.
- If the firm claims to have low marginal costs, require production $q_L^{FB} = 100 - c_L$ and transfer an amount

$$t = \pi(p = c_H, q = 100 - c_H, c_L) = (100 - c_H)(c_H - c_L)$$

from the consumers to the firm.

This policy makes telling the truth a best response for both types of firms. Moreover, by eliminating the deadweight loss, this policy leaves the consumers better off than they otherwise would have been. Let's see how this works.

A high marginal cost firm that tells the truth makes zero profits. A high marginal cost firm that claims to have low marginal costs has to produce $q_L^{FB} = 100 - c_L$ at price c_L (so makes a loss on each sale) and gets a transfer $t = (100 - c_H)(c_H - c_L)$. So, by claiming to have low marginal costs, a high marginal cost firm's payoff is

$$(100 - c_L)(c_L - c_H) + (100 - c_H)(c_H - c_L) = (c_H - c_L)(c_L - c_H) < 0.$$

Even with the transfer, a high marginal cost firm prefers to truthfully reveal its costs.

A low marginal cost firm is willing to tell the truth since the transfer it receives when it reveals itself to have low marginal costs is exactly equal to the profit it makes by claiming to have high marginal costs.

If the government can make transfers from consumers to producers cost-lessly, then this policy gives the firm incentives to truthfully reveal its type and implements the first-best outcome. But now suppose, as we have in earlier chapters, that it is costly for the government to make transfers. In particular, as we have throughout, let's assume that if the government wants to transfer a dollar from consumers to the firm, it requires $\tau > 1$ dollars in revenue. By contrast, we'll assume that the government can transfer money from the firms to the consumers without any distortion. This is clearly a simplification, but there is an intuition for why transfers from firms to consumers should be less distortionary. The government can use revenue collected from firms as a substitute for revenue collected using distortionary tools such as income or sales taxes. Hence, moving money from firms to consumers is less distortionary because it is achieved by reducing distortionary taxes on consumers.

The policy just described, and illustrated in Figure 9.15, depends on large, distortionary transfers from consumers to low marginal cost firms. Since those transfers induce their own inefficiency, the government might want to look for a policy that reduces the size of the transfer it makes to the firm, while still inducing truthful revelation of marginal costs.

In order to hold down the level of distortionary transfers needed to induce truth telling by low marginal cost firms, the government must reduce how profitable it is for a low marginal cost firm to pretend to have high marginal costs. The government achieves this in two steps. First, it reduces the amount produced by a firm claiming to have high marginal costs. Second, it makes a (non-distortionary) transfer from a firm claiming to have high marginal costs to the consumers equal to the profits the high marginal cost firm would make under this lower level of production. Together, these two steps leave a high marginal cost firm with exactly zero profits (the government can't transfer more because it can't force a firm to operate at a loss) and reduce the attractiveness of lying for a low marginal cost firm. In so doing, they reduce the distortionary transfer required to induce truth telling by a low marginal cost firm.

Figure 9.16 illustrates this idea. If a firm claiming to have high marginal costs is made to produce q_H^{FB}, then a low marginal cost firm's profit from pretending to have high marginal costs is the sum of the rectangles $D + E$. Suppose, instead, that production by a firm claiming to have a high marginal cost is held down to $q_H' < q_H^{FB}$. Prior to transfers, this leaves a high marginal cost firm that tells the truth with profits equal to the rectangle B. Whenever a firm claims to have high marginal costs, the government transfers B from the firm to the consumers. So, after transfers, a high marginal cost firm makes zero profits. Prior to transfers, it leaves a low marginal cost firm that claims to have high marginal costs with

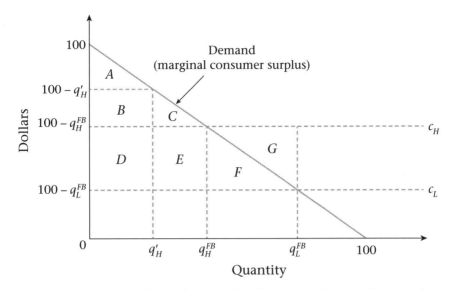

Figure 9.16. A mechanism that induces truth telling by making smaller transfers to a firm claiming to have low marginal costs, but also inducing some deadweight loss when the firm claims to have high marginal costs.

profits equal to the sum of the rectangles $B + D$. After the transfer of B from the firm to the consumers, a low marginal cost firm that claims to have high marginal costs is left with a profit of D. As such, to induce truth telling, the government need only transfer D to a firm claiming to have low marginal costs. By holding down production and making a transfer from firms to consumers when a firm claims to have high marginal costs, the government reduces the distortionary transfers it has to make from consumers to low marginal cost firms from $D + E$ down to just D.

Of course, reducing distortionary transfers in this way comes at a cost. When the firm actually has high marginal costs, there is deadweight loss from underproduction. That deadweight loss is represented by the triangle C in Figure 9.16. The second-best policy induces truth telling while balancing these benefits and costs.

Let's see how this works. Building on the argument above, suppose the government implements the following policy:

- If the firm claims to have high marginal costs, require production $q'_H < q_H^{FB}$ and transfer an amount $t'_H = q'_H(q_H^{FB} - q'_H)$ (i.e., the rectangle B) from the firm to consumers.
- If the firm claims to have low marginal costs, require production q_L^{FB} and transfer an amount $t'_L = q'_H(c_H - c_L)$ (i.e., the rectangle D) from the consumers to the firm.

We've already seen that such a policy will in fact induce truth telling by the firm.

Now we can solve for the second best. As we've already discussed, the trade-off is this: On the one hand, as q'_H gets smaller, the amount that must be transferred to low marginal cost firms (the rectangle D) decreases. This saves on distortionary transfers when the firm has low marginal costs. On the other hand, as q'_H gets smaller, the deadweight loss associated with underproduction when the firm has high marginal costs (the triangle C) gets larger. The second-best policy will balance these benefits and costs. Let's see how.

It will be useful to have notation for the first-best outcomes. Referring to Figure 9.16, when the firm has low marginal costs, utilitarian social welfare under the first best is

$$\Delta_L = A + B + C + D + E + F.$$

And when the firm has high marginal costs, utilitarian social welfare under the first best is

$$\Delta_H = A + B + C.$$

Suppose the firm has low marginal costs. Under the policy described above, the firm will reveal its true type and production will be q_L^{FB}. The government will then transfer D to the firm at cost τD to the consumers. Hence, for any given q'_H, if the firm has low marginal costs the total social surplus is

$$\Delta_L + D(1 - \tau).$$

Now suppose the firm has high marginal costs. Here, consumer surplus is $A + B$ and firm profits are 0. So total social surplus is equal to the first-best welfare when the firm has high marginal costs minus the deadweight loss associated with reduced production:

$$\Delta_H - C.$$

Recall that the probability that the firm has low marginal costs is λ. Hence, when the level of production for a firm that reports high marginal costs is q'_H, the expected social welfare from the policy described above is

$$U(q'_H) = \lambda(\Delta_L + D(1 - \tau)) + (1 - \lambda)(\Delta_H - C).$$

We can now substitute in for $D = q'_H(q_L^{FB} - q_H^{FB})$ and $C = \frac{(q_H^{FB} - q'_H)^2}{2}$ to get

$$U(q'_H) = \lambda\left[\Delta_L + q'_H\left(q_L^{FB} - q_H^{FB}\right)(1 - \tau)\right] + (1 - \lambda)\left[\Delta_H - \frac{(q_H^{FB} - q'_H)^2}{2}\right].$$

Neither Δ_L nor Δ_H are functions of q'_H. Maximizing with respect to q'_H, the first-order condition characterizing the second-best level of production for a high marginal cost firm (q_H^{SB}) yields

$$q_H^{SB} = q_H^{FB} + \frac{\lambda}{1 - \lambda}(1 - \tau)(q_L^{FB} - q_H^{FB}).$$

Recall that $\tau > 1$, so the second-best level of production by a high marginal cost firm is indeed lower than the first-best level of production. The larger is τ (i.e., the more distortionary are transfers from consumers to firms), the lower is the second-best level of production by a high marginal cost firm, since as τ gets large, avoiding large distortionary transfers becomes particularly important. The smaller is λ, the larger is the second-best level of production by a high marginal cost firm because, when λ is small, the firm is very likely to have high marginal costs, making it particularly important to avoid the deadweight loss associated with underproduction.

An important point to see, here, is that the government's lack of full information comes at a real cost—both in terms of deadweight loss due to underproduction and in terms of distortionary transfers by the government from consumers to producers. Moreover, these transfers from the government to the low marginal cost firm result in positive firm profits. This fact shows how the government's lack of information provides an account of behavior that may, at first blush, seem puzzling. The government has the legal authority to regulate monopolies. Yet we often observe the government negotiating with monopolistic firms over the terms of regulation. One might interpret this either as the government failing to exercise its authority or as evidence of malfeasance (e.g., the firm buying off the government). But our model offers a different view. When the firm possesses information that the government needs in order to exercise its regulatory authority effectively, the government cannot impose the optimal regulation. It must negotiate with the firm to extract the required information. And those negotiations will result in underproduction in some circumstances and government subsidization of the monopolist in other circumstances, not necessarily because of malfeasance or incompetence, but because of the power of information.

9.3.4 An Informed Regulator

A government might respond to limited information by employing expert regulators. For instance, a government might seek out regulators who previously worked in the regulated industry. This provides a rationalization for the commonly observed "revolving door"—whereby people move back and forth between employment in some regulated industry and employment in the agencies that regulate that industry. Of course, using such regulators, who have their own interests and agendas, comes with risks. To explore such issues, let's think about adding an expert to our model.

There is still a monopolistic firm, as above, with either low or high marginal costs. Now, however, the government appoints an expert regulator. The expert regulator investigates the firm's marginal costs. With probability μ the regulator indeed learns the firm's marginal costs and with probability $1 - \mu$ the regulator learns nothing. The regulator makes a report to the government. That report can be either a statement of the firm's marginal cost or a statement that the regulator did not learn anything in her investigation. The government, lacking expertise of its own, does not know whether or not the regulator really learned the firm's marginal costs.

Suppose the regulator makes an honest report. Then the government is in a better position with the informed regulator than without. If the regulator reveals the firm's marginal costs, the government can implement the first-best policy. If the regulator learns nothing, the government can still fall back on the second-best policy. Hence, at least some of the time, having an honest, informed regulator makes society strictly better off, and it never makes society worse off.

The question is, will the regulator tell the truth? To explore this, we want to think about the incentives of the regulated firm, which might want to try to corrupt or "capture" the regulator for its own purposes.

REGULATORY CAPTURE

Suppose that the regulator and the firm can collude by plotting for the regulator to issue a false report to the government. There is a fixed cost to collusion, $k > 0$, which might represent the risk of being caught. If the regulator and firm do collude, they split the costs and also split any resulting profits.

It is worth noting that our setup suggests a very stark interpretation—the firm is bribing the regulator. But matters need not be quite that clear cut. For instance, a variety of practices, short of bribery, might establish an implicit quid pro quo between regulators and a regulated industry. The revolving door is an obvious mechanism by which a quid pro quo might operate. Regulated firms could create incentives akin to those modeled here simply by structuring an environment in which regulators believe that their future job prospects depend on their behavior while in government.

If the government trusts the regulator, when will the firm and the regulator benefit from colluding?

Suppose the firm has high marginal costs. Under both the first- and second-best policies, a high marginal cost firm makes zero profits. So such a firm has no incentive to bear the costs of collusion.

What about a low marginal cost firm? If the regulator learns nothing (which happens with probability $1 - \mu$) and reports that honestly, the low marginal cost firm will make a profit equal to the rectangle D in Figure 9.17. If the regulator learns the firm's true marginal costs (which happens with probability μ)

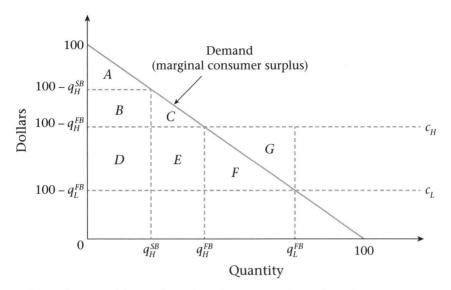

Figure 9.17. The second-best policy when there is no informed regulator.

and reports that honestly, the firm makes zero profits. Hence, absent collusion, the firm's expected profits are

$$(1 - \mu)D.$$

If, instead, the firm and the regulator collude, the regulator will simply always report that the firm has high marginal costs. The government will implement the first-best policy for a high marginal cost firm—requiring production q_H^{FB} and offering zero transfers. This will result in profits for the low marginal cost firm equal to the sum of the rectangles $D + E$ in Figure 9.17. Hence, collusion is worthwhile for the low marginal cost firm and the regulator if

$$D + E - k > (1 - \mu)D,$$

which is equivalent to

$$k < \mu D + E. \tag{9.1}$$

In this event, we say that the regulator will be *captured by industry*. When this happens, the government cannot trust the regulator's reports, undoing the benefit of using an informed regulator in the first place.

AVOIDING CAPTURE

If the government wants to gain the benefits of using an informed regulator, it needs to set policy such that the regulator will not be captured—that is, such that Condition 9.1 is not satisfied. In order to do so, it must ensure that

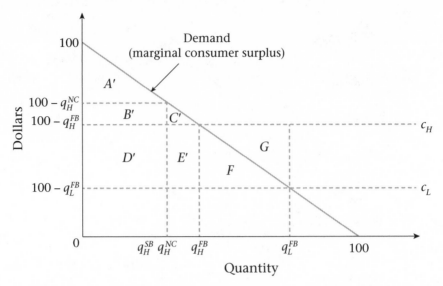

Figure 9.18. The optimal policy that avoids collusion between the firm and the regulator.

the profits a low marginal cost firm generates by lying are not sufficient to compensate for the costs associated with collusion.

To eliminate the incentive to collude, the government can adjust production when the regulator claims to be uninformed and the firm claims to have high marginal costs. This new production level (call it q_H^{NC} for "no collusion") must reduce $\mu D + E$ so that the firm and regulator do not want to collude. This involves choosing $q_H^{NC} > q_H^{SB}$, as illustrated in Figure 9.18.

Why does increasing production by the high marginal cost firm reduce incentives for collusion between the low marginal cost firm and the regulator? One benefit of collusion is that, by inducing the government to implement the first-best policy for a high marginal cost firm, collusion provides a profit equal to the rectangle E that would never be achieved without collusion. Second, by avoiding the possibility that the informed regulator will reveal that the firm has low marginal costs, collusion provides the firm with an extra profit of D in the event that the regulator is informed. By increasing the amount produced by a firm claiming to have high marginal costs when the regulator is uninformed, the government makes E smaller and D larger. That is, comparing Figures 9.17 and 9.18, $E' < E$ and $D' > D$. Since the E/E' rectangles represent a benefit of collusion that is realized with certainty, whereas the D/D' rectangles represent a benefit of collusion that is realized only probabilistically, the negative effect on the appeal of collusion associated with moving from E to E' is larger than the positive effect on the appeal of collusion associated with moving from D to D'. Hence, in order to reduce the appeal of collusion, the government wants $q_H^{NC} > q_H^{SB}$, so that $E' < E$ and $D' > D$.

THE IMPACT OF CAPTURE

There is an important point to note here. As we've just seen, the government can set policy so that the firm and regulator do not collude. Nonetheless, even if the government does so, the possibility of regulatory capture has an effect on policy and outcomes. In particular, when the government is uninformed, it will distort policy in a way that leads to more production by firms claiming to have high marginal costs, because the government knows that firms might try to capture the regulator. As a result of these government efforts to head off collusion, distortionary transfers to low marginal cost firms are larger than they otherwise would be. Thus, even if firms and regulators do not regularly collude with one another, the fact that they could in principle do so has a deleterious effect on policy.

To see this in the model, let's calculate the expected social welfare with and without the possibility of collusion.

Suppose collusion is simply impossible. With probability μ the government learns the true marginal cost and implements the first-best policy from our original model, generating social welfare of Δ_H if the firm has high marginal costs and Δ_L if the firm has low marginal costs. With probability $1 - \mu$ the government implements the second-best policy from our original model, generating social welfare of $\Delta_H - C$ if the firm has high marginal costs and $\Delta_L + (1 - \tau)D$ if the firm has low marginal costs. Hence, expected social welfare if collusion were impossible is

$$\Delta_H + \Delta_L + (1 - \mu)\left(-\lambda C + (1 - \lambda)(1 - \tau)D\right).$$

Now suppose collusion is possible. Again, if the regulator is informed, it will reveal the truth and the original first-best policy will be implemented. If the regulator is not informed, the government implements a policy that, if the firm has high marginal costs, generates a social welfare of $\Delta_H - C'$ and if the firm has low marginal costs generates a social welfare of $\Delta_L + (1 - \tau)D'$. Hence, the expected social welfare, given the possibility of collusion, is

$$\Delta_H + \Delta_L + (1 - \mu)\left(-(1 - \lambda)C' + \lambda(1 - \tau)D'\right).$$

Comparing these, the possibility of collusion makes social welfare worse if

$$-\lambda C' + (1 - \lambda)(1 - \tau)D' < -(1 - \lambda)C + \lambda(1 - \tau)D.$$

This inequality holds. (To see this, recall that q_H^{SB} was chosen to maximize $-(1 - \lambda)C + \lambda(1 - \tau)D$). Thus, even when we don't see direct evidence of collusive behavior, the possibility of collusion and regulatory capture may be affecting the way policy is set and harming social welfare.

9.4   Takeaways

- Identifying optimal policies often requires information that the policy-maker doesn't have.
- When relevant information resides with interested parties, the policy-maker must design incentives for those parties to reveal the information. The challenge is that revealing its information may sometimes lead to disadvantageous policy responses for a given party, giving that party an incentive to lie or fail to reveal information.
- Lack of information places an additional second-best constraint on how much good can be done through policy. As in our earlier examples of the second best, the government's limited access to information implies that policy cannot always get us all the way to Pareto efficiency.
- The possibility of collusion between regulated firms and expert regulators (through bribery, the revolving door, etc.) creates the threat of regulatory capture. Even if policy is set so that no collusion actually occurs, the threat of collusion due to informational asymmetries distorts policy.

9.5   Further Reading

Roger Myerson's "Perspectives on Mechanism Design in Economic Theory: Nobel Prize Lecture" is deep in content and context about the role of mechanism design in the theory of incentives.[2] Paul Milgrom's *Putting Auction Theory to Work* provides both an interesting informal discussion of the ways in which auction theory has been used in policy applications and a serious technical treatment of the important models.

Both the second price auction and the (not budget balanced) mechanism that induces truth telling in the public goods games are special cases of the Vickrey-Clarke-Groves mechanism (Vickrey, 1961; Clarke, 1971; Groves, 1973).

Stigler (1972) and Peltzman (1976) are the original treatments of regulatory capture. The model of regulating a monopolist is inspired by Dal Bó's (2006) overview and formal treatment of the relationship between asymmetric information and capture. It builds on the classic analyses of Baron and Myerson (1982) and Laffont and Tirole (1993).

Perhaps the most exciting work going on today on the interplay of policy and informational problems is in market design. This work addresses problems such as how to incentivize organ donation and allocate donated organs, how to match children with schools or doctors with residencies, and a host of other important topics. Al Roth's *Who Gets What—and Why* is a popular introduction. You should also read his market design blog.

---

[2]http://www.nobelprize.org/nobel prizes/economics/laureates/2007/myerson_lecture.pdf

9.6 Exercises

1. Consider an auction with two bidders. Bidder 1 values the object up for auction at v_1 and bidder 2 values it at v_2. If a bidder i wins the auction and has to pay price p, his payoff is $v_i - p$. If a bidder loses the auction, his payoff is 0.

    The auction is run as an "English Auction." That is, the auctioneer starts at a price of 1 and asks who will pay it. After the price is met, the auctioneer raises the price and asks who will pay that. The item is sold when no bidder is willing to match the new price. It is sold to the bidder who met the last stated price and it is sold at that price.

    Each bidder's strategy can be thought of as a number representing the last price to which she will say "yes." Call this the player's "price limit" and label player i's price limit as b_i (that is, player i's strategy says she'll pay any price up to and including b_i but not more).

    (a) Argue that there is at least one b_2 such that player 1 choosing $b_1 > v_1$ is not a best response.
    (b) Argue that there is at least one b_2 such that player 1 choosing $b_1 < v_1$ is not a best response.
    (c) Argue that player 1 choosing $b_1 = v_1$ is a best response to every b_2.
    (d) Player 2's problem is clearly symmetric. So for each player choosing a price limit equal to her true valuation is a weakly dominant strategy. If players follow this strategy, which player wins the auction? What price does the winner pay?
    (e) How do your answers to part (d) relate to the outcomes of the "second price auction" we studied in this text? Would the same or a different player win? Would that player pay the same or a different price?

2. Suppose there is a population of 20 people. Half of them are *healthy* and half of them are *sick*. Each individual knows whether she is healthy or sick.

    If a healthy person receives health care, her payoff is 10. If she does not receive health care, her payoff is 7. The price of providing health care to a healthy person is 3.

    If a sick person receives health care, her payoff is also 10. If she does not receive health care, her payoff is 0. The price of providing health care to a sick person is 5.

    Let's assume that health care can only be procured with health insurance. An individual cannot buy her own health care other than by buying insurance.

Suppose a not-for-profit insurance company is selling health care coverage. The first goal of the insurance company is to cover as many people as possible. Conditional on this, its goal is to charge as little as possible to sick people for their insurance. However, no matter what, it is not allowed to lose money.

(a) Suppose the insurance company knows if people are healthy or sick. What price will it charge sick people? What price will it charge healthy people?

(b) Now suppose the insurance company can't observe whether people are healthy or sick.

   i. Why won't it work for the insurance company to simply ask people whether they are sick or healthy and then charge them accordingly?
   ii. Suppose, then, that the insurance company charges everyone the same price. What price must it charge to break even, if everyone buys insurance?
   iii. At that price, who will buy insurance? Will the insurance company make or lose money?
   iv. Given this, what price will the insurance company in fact charge? Who will buy insurance?

(c) The phenomenon described in your previous answers is called the problem of *adverse selection*—because the pool of insurance buyers ends up being the sick, the price has to be so high that it erodes the insurance value. It was a major concern in the debates surrounding the Affordable Care Act because there was worry that young, healthy people would refuse to buy health insurance, despite the act's requirement that they do so. The solution in the Affordable Care Act is to fine people who don't buy health insurance.

   i. Suppose the insurance company charges a price $p \in (3, 5)$. What is the smallest possible fine, $f^*(p)$, the government can impose for not buying insurance, such that everyone buys insurance?
   ii. What is the lowest price, p, and associated fine, $f^*(p)$, such that everyone buys insurance and the insurance company at least breaks even?

3. Consider a public goods game with two players in which each player i chooses effort e_i and the total public goods produced are $e_1 + e_2$. Player 1 bears costs e_1^2. Player 2 bears costs $c \times e_2^2$. The parameter c is equal to either 1 or 2. Player 2 knows the true value of c, but the government is uncertain as to the true value of c.

Given knowledge of the true c, the first-best efforts are $e_1^{FB} = 1$ and $e_2^{FB} = \frac{1}{c}$. We are going to assume that the government can simply force people to choose whatever effort it wants them to take.

(a) Suppose the government asks Player 2 to report c and then implements the first best, naively assuming that Player 2 told the truth.

    i. Will a Player 2 with $c = 1$ tell the truth (i.e., report $c = 1$) or lie (i.e., report $c = 2$)?

    ii. Will a Player 2 with $c = 2$ tell the truth (i.e., report $c = 2$) or lie (i.e., report $c = 1$)?

(b) Suppose the government can now offer transfers from Player 1 to Player 2 conditional on Player 2's report of her c. Further assume that such transfers are inefficient—a transfer of t to Player 2 costs Player 1 an amount τt, with $\tau > 1$. Finally, suppose the probability that $c = 1$ is $\frac{1}{2}$.

    i. If the government wants to elicit truth telling as cheaply as possible, will it offer transfers to Player 2 following a report of $c = 1$, $c = 2$, or both?

    ii. What is the smallest such transfer it can offer that elicits truth telling?

(c) Continue to suppose the probability that $c = 1$ is $\frac{1}{2}$. What is the expected utilitarian payoff (as a function of τ) if the government pursues the smallest transfer policy that elicits truth telling. (Hint: Calculate the utilitarian payoff if it turns out that Player 2 has $c = 1$. Calculate the utilitarian payoff if it turns out that Player 2 has $c = 2$. Then multiply each of these by $\frac{1}{2}$ and sum to find the expected utilitarian payoff.)

(d) Continue to suppose the probability that $c = 1$ is $\frac{1}{2}$. Without any information, the best policy the government can pursue is $e_1 = 1$ and $e_2 = \frac{2}{3}$. Such a policy yields an expected utilitarian payoff of

$$2\left(1 + \frac{2}{3}\right) - 1^2 - \left(\frac{1}{2} \times 1 + \frac{1}{2} \times 2\right)\left(\frac{2}{3}\right)^2 = \frac{5}{3}.$$

For what values of τ is the expected utilitarian outcome better if the government offers the best transfer scheme that elicits truthful revelation of c instead of implementing this best uninformed policy?

(e) What do your answers to these questions tell us about the effect of lack of information on the government's ability to achieve good policy outcomes?

4.   A local government is trying to decide whether to build a school that will jointly serve two neighborhoods. The school will cost one million dollars to build. Neighborhood 1 values the school at value v_1 dollars and

neighborhood 2 values the school at v_2 dollars. The government does not know these valuations, though it knows that each is somewhere between 0 and one million. Assume all players have quasi-linear preferences.

(a) For which pairs of valuations is the utilitarian optimum to build the school and for which pairs of valuations is the utilitarian optimum not to build the school?

(b) Suppose the government proposes the following mechanism. Each neighborhood will say an amount it values the school. The neighborhoods can say any number they like between 0 and one million, they need not tell the truth. Call the statement from neighborhood one s_1 and the statement from neighborhood two s_2. If the sum of the two statements is greater than or equal to one million, the school will be built, with neighborhood 1 paying \$600,000 and neighborhood 2 paying \$400,000. If the two statements sum to less than one million, the school will not be built.

   i. Assume players play weakly dominant strategies. For which pairs (if any) of true valuations, v_1 and v_2, will the school be built?
   ii. Are there any pairs of true valuations, v_1 and v_2, where the policy that will be followed as a result of such behavior by the neighborhoods (build or don't build) is inefficient (i.e., not the utilitarian optimum)?

(c) Suppose the government proposes the following mechanism. Each neighborhood will say an amount it values the school. The neighborhoods can say any number they like between 0 and one million, they need not tell the truth. If the sum of the two statements is less than one million, then the school is not built. If the sum of the two statements is greater than or equal to one million, the school will be built, but in this mechanism, the price charged to each neighborhood can be a function of the stated valuations of the two neighborhoods.

   i. Identify a formula for the price (a function of the stated valuations of the two neighborhoods) the government can charge neighborhood 1 when the school gets built, such that, for any v_1, it is a best response for neighborhood 1 to state its true valuation regardless of what neighborhood 1 expects neighborhood 2 to say. Give a brief, informal explanation of why this works.
   ii. What, if anything, is wrong with a mechanism that uses this formula to determine the price?

(d) Briefly explain how your answers to (b) and (c) point to a fundamental tension between lack of information and efficient policy.

5.   Return to the game in Figure 6.6. Imagine that the government wants to achieve the utilitarian optimum and can force U to choose a level of investment, e, but can't force D to change the price it offers. Further, suppose the government doesn't know c, only U knows it.

(a) Suppose the government simply asks U what c is. U can choose, as an answer, any positive number. The government then naively assumes that this answer is the true c and imposes the utilitarian optimal level of investment given that c. Informally (i.e., no math necessary), will the c that U tells the government be larger than, smaller than, or equal to the true c? Why? Briefly explain how your answer points to a tension between lack of information and efficient policy choice.

(b) What c will U report to the government?

10

Influence over Elected Officials

Elections are the first line of defense against excessive rent seeking in democracies. They serve this function in at least two ways. First, elections allow voters to select politicians motivated and able to pursue the voters' interests. Second, they create incentives for politicians to do so. Madison put it eloquently in Federalist No. 57:

> The aim of every political constitution is, or ought to be, first to obtain for rulers men who possess most wisdom to discern, and most virtue to pursue, the common good of the society; and in the next place, to take the most effectual precautions for keeping them virtuous whilst they continue to hold their public trust.

Madison, of course, believed that achieving these goals requires more than just elections. He advocated for a whole suite of institutional checks and balances, most notably the separation of powers, to keep politicians "virtuous whilst they continue to hold their public trust." But there can be no question that electoral accountability plays a central role. As Madison wrote in Federalist No. 51:

> In framing a government which is to be administered by men over men, the great difficulty lies in this: you must first enable the government to control the governed; and in the next place oblige it to control itself. A dependence on the people is, no doubt, the primary control on the government.

This is a lofty vision, especially in light of our often cynical view of electoral politics. Leaving aside issues of fraud and violence that plague elections in much of the world, even in the best of circumstances, elections can struggle to establish "dependence on the people." Electoral concerns seem, at times, to drive politicians to pander to particularistic interests. Moreover, the realities of campaigning can give undo influence to organized or moneyed interests. Yet, at the same time, democratic elections do establish a relationship of accountability between the government and the governed. The question is, to what extent does that accountability relationship result in improved governance outcomes? In this chapter, we explore these issues through several models of electoral politics.

10.1 Particularistic Interests

We've discussed a variety of examples of inefficiency resulting from policies targeted to benefit some particular group of citizens at the expense of society at large. The home mortgage deduction benefits homeowners at the expense of economic efficiency. Professional licensing benefits incumbent members of a profession at the expense of new entrants and consumers. Political pork benefits the members of a particular legislative district at the expense of the rest of the taxpaying public. Low gasoline taxes benefit both transportation and agricultural interests at the expense of the environment. And so on. In Chapters 4.2.3 and 8.3 we saw various reasons that distributive politics might end up favoring certain groups over others. Here, we explore another possibility, rooted in electoral politics.

Politicians are motivated to win elections. If a politician's electoral prospects are more responsive to the welfare of one group of citizens, that politician has incentives to bestow benefits on that group at the expense of other, less responsive groups.

This kind of logic is not new, nor is it only for the cynical. In 1840, future President Lincoln coauthored a confidential memo giving the Whig Party's local electoral committees instructions for targeting responsive voters:[1]

> After due deliberation, the following is the plan of organization, and the duties required of each county committee.
>
> 1st. To divide their county into small districts, and to appoint in each a sub-committee, whose duty it shall be to make a perfect list of all the voters in their respective districts, and to ascertain with certainty for whom they will vote. If they meet with men who are doubtful as to the man they will support, such voters should be designated in separate lines, with the name of the man they will probably support.
>
> 2nd. It will be the duty of said sub-committee to keep a CONSTANT WATCH on the DOUBTFUL VOTERS, and from time to time have them TALKED TO by those IN WHOM THEY HAVE THE MOST CONFIDENCE, and also to place in their hands such documents as will enlighten and influence them.

There might be a variety of reasons that a particular group is more electorally responsive than another. Let's consider a few.

Many voters are concerned primarily with ideological issues that correspond to the platform of one party (or, in other settings, one ethnic group, religion, etc.). It would be essentially impossible for the other party to win the support of such voters. Hence, strongly partisan voters are typically thought to be relatively unresponsive to distributive issues. By contrast, other voters have little concern

---

[1]See *Collected Works of Abraham Lincoln*. Volume 1. University of Michigan Digital Library Production Services. http://quod.lib.umich.edu/l/lincoln/lincoln1/1:214?rgn=div1;view=fulltext

about broad ideological matters, but instead are focused on a single issue. For instance, in local elections, teachers may care primarily about school budgets and policy. Hence, a candidate for mayor might be able to win the support of a teachers' union by choosing an education policy of which the union approves, independent of any other policy position. Such single-issue voters are highly responsive.

Institutional factors can also affect responsiveness. For instance, in the United States, many functions of local government are carried out by so-called special purpose governmental units. Berry (2009, pp. 26–27) explains:

> Most special districts perform a single function.... Almost any service provided by a municipality can be provided by a special district government. The special district familiar to most Americans is the school district. Although school districts are the most numerous, they represent less than one-third of all special districts. Among the 35,000 nonschool special districts in existence as of 2002, some of the most common functions included providing fire protection, water, sanitation, parks, and libraries.

These special purpose governments are important. For instance, the combined revenues of all special district governments in the United States are roughly the same as the combined revenues of all city governments and are significantly larger than the combined revenues of all county governments. Most special purpose government officials are elected. And, interestingly, many special purpose governments do not hold their elections on election day in November. As a consequence, the voters who turn out for such elections are primarily those with a direct stake in whatever domain the special purpose government controls. If only these voters turn out, only they can be responsive.

Legislative districting creates yet another institutional source of non-responsiveness. From the perspective of the electoral fortunes of, say, a member of the United States House of Representatives, the voters in his or her district are responsive to pork-barrel projects brought to the district. But voters from other districts are not responsive. This means that each member of Congress has incentives to target only the voters in his or her district.

Finally, as we discussed in Chapter 4.2.3, concentrated interests are better able to organize themselves to take action than are diffuse interests. Thus, we might expect that concentrated interests are more responsive to issues about which they care than are diffuse interests.

Now that we've seen that voter responsiveness might vary for a host of reasons, let's consider how it affects policy in a simple model inspired by Dixit and Londregan (1996).

Two candidates, a and b, seek office. There are three groups of voters—the a-partisans (group A), the b-partisans (group B), and the independents (group I). The independents make up a share α of the electorate, while the

a- and b-partisans each make up a share $\frac{1-\alpha}{2}$. No group is a majority on its own (i.e., $\alpha < 1/2$). A candidate wins if she gets a majority of votes.

At the beginning of the election, each candidate proposes a platform, x, which represents the policies she will pursue if elected. Each candidate can propose one of three possible platforms:

1. Under the efficient platform, x_E, each group has a payoff equal to 1.
2. Under a partisan-biased platform (call this x_A for candidate a and x_B for candidate b), the relevant partisans get a benefit of π, while all other voters get 0.
3. Under the independent-biased platform, x_I, the independents get a benefit of π, while all other voters get 0.

Assume that $1 < \pi < \max\left\{\frac{1}{\alpha}, \frac{2}{1-\alpha}\right\}$, so that a biased platform is not a utilitarian optimum, but is preferred to the efficient platform by the privileged group.

After observing the platforms, the voters decide for which candidate to vote. The independent voters' payoffs come only from the platform payoffs just described. But the partisan voters also care about the identity of the politician in office—if a group's preferred candidate is elected, the members of that group get an extra benefit $\eta > 0$. If voters are indifferent, they flip a coin.

Suppose candidates care only about winning election. What do equilibrium policies look like?

The probability of winning, given platforms, depends on how biased the supporters are in favor of their preferred candidate (i.e., the size of η). Hence, there are two cases, represented separately in the following two tables (best responses are in bold):

		b's platform					b's platform		
		x_E	x_I	x_B			x_E	x_I	x_B
a's platform	x_E	$\frac{1}{2},\frac{1}{2}$	0, **1**	**1**, 0	a's platform	x_E	$\frac{1}{2},\frac{1}{2}$	**1**, 0	**1**, 0
	x_I	**1**, 0	$\frac{1}{2},\frac{1}{2}$	**1**, 0		x_I	0, **1**	$\frac{1}{2},\frac{1}{2}$	**1**, 0
	x_A	0, **1**	0, **1**	$\frac{1}{2},\frac{1}{2}$		x_A	0, **1**	0, **1**	$\frac{1}{2},\frac{1}{2}$

$$\eta > 1 \qquad\qquad\qquad\qquad \eta < 1$$

If partisans are highly attached to their preferred candidates ($\eta > 1$), in equilibrium both candidates propose a platform targeted at the independent voters. If partisans are more weakly attached to their preferred candidates ($\eta < 1$), in equilibrium policy is efficient. The logic is straightforward.

When attachments are weak, if (say) candidate a attempts to lure the independent voters by proposing x_I, candidate b can win the election by proposing the efficient policy and gaining the support of both groups A and B. Hence, in equilibrium, both candidates propose the efficient policy, preserving their electoral bases and competing for the independent voters.

By contrast, when attachments are strong, each candidate knows that no matter what, she will hold onto the support of her partisans and cannot gain the support of the other candidate's partisans. Only the independent voters are responsive. So each candidate has an incentive to target policy to benefit the independent voters.

The model, while simple, highlights an important point. Politicians, motivated by the desire to hold office, will pursue policies that benefit those citizens whose votes are responsive to policy choice. If a politician is certain that some group of voters will always support her or will never support her, she has little incentive to provide policy benefits to that group. Hence, in policy domains characterized by groups of highly responsive and unresponsive voters, policy will be biased away from efficiency and towards the interests of the responsive voters.

This simple insight provides leverage on many of our examples of inefficient policy choice. If homeowners are particularly responsive to the home mortgage deduction, sugar producers are particularly responsive to sugar subsidies, public sector workers are particularly responsive to public sector wages, and taxi drivers are particularly responsive to limits on ride sharing, then electoral considerations will drive politicians to target policies in those areas towards those particularistic interests.

The model is also consistent with empirical evidence. For instance, Berry and Gersen (2010, 2011) study a change to the California Electoral Code in the 1980s allowing school boards to shift from off-cycle (i.e., not in November) to on-cycle elections. As we've already discussed, off-cycle elections tend to attract only single-issue voters. If voters don't come to the polls, they certainly are not responsive to policy. Thus, the model would lead us to expect that, when a district moves to on-cycle elections, policy might become less targeted to single-issue education voters (e.g., teachers) because other voters become more responsive. And, indeed, this is what happened in California. When a school district moves from off-cycle to on-cycle elections, turnout roughly doubles on average. Moreover, policy becomes less favorable to teachers—for instance, teachers' salaries decreased by about $1,000 on average in on-cycle districts.

10.2 Special Interests and Campaign Donations

Of course, groups motivated to influence policy have tools at their disposal beyond the vote. Perhaps most importantly, they can use money to influence elected officials' policy choices.

The most disturbing possibility is that there might be a quid pro quo between politicians and organized interests—campaign donations in exchange for a politician taking policy actions that he or she otherwise would not have taken. But things need not be as nefarious as all that for money to matter for policy. Consider two other possibilities.

First, money might not buy policy concessions, but it might buy access—a politician may not be willing to change her behavior for a donor, but might be more open to giving a donor an opportunity to make a case. If there are circumstances in which new information or argument could persuade a politician to change his or her position, having such access could push policy outcomes in a donor's favor even without any quid pro quo.

Second, money might be useful for winning elections. For instance, imagine that politicians are precommitted (perhaps by their personal ideology or party affiliation) to a policy platform, so money can't possibly change their behavior. Money might still matter for policy outcomes if voters are responsive to campaigning (e.g., advertisements, speeches), so that having access to resources helps politicians win election. Organized interests might then donate to a politician whose ideology matches their own preferences in order to help her gain office. Nothing untoward is going on—campaign donations don't lead the politician to pursue any policy she wouldn't otherwise have pursued. Nonetheless, by helping candidates that are already sympathetic to its interests win election, an interest group does in fact use campaign contributions to secure policies from which it benefits.

If you believe either of these latter two stories, you might be inclined to think that the influence of money on politics is relatively unproblematic. In the first story, the politician is only changing her mind when convincing information or argument is presented. And, in the second story, campaign donations might be viewed as an expression of citizens' intensity of preference.

But let's remember the model of interest group organization from Chapter 4.2.3. There we saw that concentrated interests will have an easier time organizing to influence policy than will diffuse interests. Hence, even if campaign contributions only work through legitimate channels, they will nonetheless distort policy outcomes in favor of concentrated interests at the expense of diffuse interests. If money buys access, in those circumstances where information or argument could shift policy, organized interests will have the opportunity to make their case, while diffuse interests will not. Similarly, if money helps win campaigns, candidates who favor policies that benefit organized interests will have access to greater campaign resources and, thus, will win elections more often than candidates who favor diffuse interests. Indeed, as a result, we may simply not observe many candidates who advocate for policies that benefit diffuse interests.

There is considerable debate about the extent to which campaign money influences policy outcomes. On the one hand, by some measures, there is an awful lot of money in politics. For instance, Bombardini and Trebbi (2011) report that during the elections for the 106th Congress, the top 50 donor industries gave total campaign donations of almost $370 million. By the election of the 109th Congress, the amount had risen to almost $445 million. If money doesn't matter for policy, why are industries making these donations?

But, staggering as these numbers may seem, there is an argument that they are actually quite small. This argument derives from the so-called Tullock Paradox. Tullock (1972) points out a puzzle that emerges if we view campaign donations as an investment in policy outcomes. Ansolabehere, de Figueiredo, and Snyder (2003, p. 110) summarize Tullock's argument:

> In 1972, when Tullock raised this question, campaign spending was about $200 million. Assuming a reasonable rate of return, such an investment could have yielded at most $250–300 million over time, a sum dwarfed by the hundreds of billions of dollars worth of public expenditures and regulatory costs supposedly at stake.

And, they argue, the puzzle has only grown since the 1970s. I can do no better than to quote Ansolabehere, de Figueiredo, and Snyder (2003, pp. 110–111):

> [A]ll defense contracting firms and individuals associated with those firms gave approximately $10.6 million to candidates and parties in 1998 and $13.2 million in 2000. The U.S. government spent approximately $134 billion on defense procurement contracts in fiscal year 2000 (U.S. Census Bureau, 2000). Firms, individuals and industry associations of the oil and gas industry gave $21.6 million to candidates and party organizations in 1998 and $33.6 million in 2000. The Energy Information Administration (1999) of the U.S. Department of Energy values subsidies to the energy industry in 1999 at $1.7 billion. In agriculture, crop producers and processors contributed $3.3 million to candidates and parties in 2000; U.S. commodity loans and price supports equaled $22.1 billion that year (U.S. Department of Agriculture website). Dairy producers, who since 1996 have had to have subsidies renewed annually, gave $1.3 million in 2000 and received price supports worth almost $1 billion in the Farm Security and Rural Investment Act of 2002. In the case of sugar producers, Stratmann (1991, p. 615) estimates that a "$3,000 sugar PAC contribution maps into a yes vote with almost certainty." Without sugar industry contributions, he further estimates, the final vote on the sugar amendment to the 1985 agriculture bill would have been 203–210, effectively ending the sugar subsidy. With contributions, the subsidy survived: the final vote was 267–146. A U.S. General Accounting Office (1993) study values that the

annual transfer from consumers to sugar producers and processors at $1.1 billion a year from 1989 to 1991. In other words, $192,000 worth of contributions in 1985 bought more than $5 billion worth of value for the sugar industry over a five-year period.

The discrepancy between the value of policy and the amounts contributed strains basic economic intuitions. Given the value of policy at stake, firms and other interest groups should give more. The figures above imply astronomically high rates of return on investments.

Ansolabehere, de Figueiredo, and Snyder make sense of these findings by noting that campaign donations have a relatively small effect on electoral outcomes. As a result, they suggest, no matter which of the stories above you believe, donations will have relatively little impact on policy outcomes. If there is a quid pro quo (for policy concessions or access), donors have relatively little leverage over politicians because donations are not particularly valuable to politicians. And if money is simply a way of helping sympathetic candidates, it is relatively ineffective. In any case, the policy returns a donor can hope to garner are small. Indeed, on Ansolabehere, de Figueiredo, and Snyder's view, campaign donations are better understood as pure entertainment consumption by donors, rather than anything to do with shifting policy outcomes.

Bombardini and Trebbi (2011) take a different view of the evidence and its relationship to the Tullock Paradox. They point out that organized interests have at least two ways to influence politicians: money and votes. Whatever role you believe money plays in politics, the ability to directly deliver votes could serve as a substitute for campaign donations. They argue that perhaps the amount of campaign donations is small relative to the size of government, not because there isn't competition among interest groups to shape policy outcomes, but because that competition involves both money and votes. If this is correct, by ignoring the value of votes, Ansolabehere, de Figueiredo, and Snyder are overestimating the implicit rate of return from campaign contributions.

To illustrate this argument, Bombardini and Trebbi (2011, p. 588, footnote 2) offer the following quotation from Arizona Senator Dennis DeConcini:

> If I get a contribution from, say, Allied-Signal, a big defense contractor, and they've raised money for me. And then they come in and say, "Senator, we need legislation that would extend some rule of contracting that's good for us." They lay out the case. My staff goes over it. I'm trying to help them. Why am I trying to help them? The cynic can say: "Well, it's because they gave you 5,000 bucks. And if you ran again, they'll give you another 5,000 bucks." Or is it because they have 15,000 jobs in Arizona and this will help keep those jobs in Arizona? Now to me, the far greater motivation is those jobs, because those are the people that are going to vote for me. But I can't ignore the fact that they have given me money.

Bombardini and Trebbi go on to provide a variety of evidence to support the claim that both votes and money matter. Perhaps most compellingly, they show two facts. First, within a Congressional district, the largest donors tend to be medium-sized industries. Second, a given industry tends to give its largest donations in those districts where it is of medium size. They argue that the logic underlying both facts is the same. Industries don't give donations in districts where they are very small employers. In such districts, it would be too expensive to try to wield influence. Industries also don't give donations in districts where they are huge employers. In those districts, they can provide so many votes that they don't need to give large donations—for example, the auto industry may not need to make large donations to have influence in Michigan politics. Significant campaign donations make sense for industries that can provide some votes, but need to top those votes off with donations to have an impact on policy outcomes.

Using this approach, Bombardini and Trebbi estimate a rate of return for campaign donations, correcting for the ability to deliver votes. Doing so yields a much more reasonable estimate than the numbers presented by Ansolabehere, de Figueiredo, and Snyder might suggest. In particular, they report that the average rate of return to campaign donations is about thirteen cents on the dollar. With this more plausible number, it again becomes reasonable to think that interest groups may indeed be competing with one another for influence over policy outcomes, using both votes and money as tools to achieve their goals.

10.3 Electoral Accountability

The previous two sections discussed how electoral politics may create incentives for inefficient policy targeting or distortionary uses of money in politics. Problematic as such incentives may be, voters' ability to hold politicians accountable through elections also plays an indispensable role in creating the conditions for good governance.

If retaining office depends on achieving good outcomes for voters, then policymakers seeking reelection may be willing to take actions that they find personally costly but which benefit voters. Elections can, thus, create incentives for politicians to identify good policies, forgo corruption, choose policies preferred by voters even when they are not preferred by the politicians, and so on. In these ways, elections fulfill part of Madison's vision, by fostering a "dependence on the people" and, thereby "keeping [politicians] virtuous."

Elections also give voters an opportunity to identify and retain politicians with characteristics—for example, managerial skills, policy positions, honesty—that the voters value. Such *electoral selection* affects governance outcomes by allowing voters to screen for high quality or good leaders. In this way, elections fulfill Madison's goal "to obtain for rulers men who possess most wisdom to discern, and most virtue to pursue, the common good of the society."

In light of this, in this section we explore a basic model of electoral accountability and related empirical evidence. We do so with an eye toward answering several questions:

1. What are the mechanisms by which elections improve voter welfare?
2. What features of an electoral environment seem to increase incentives for politicians to act on behalf of voters?
3. Are stronger electoral incentives always beneficial to voters?

In our model of electoral accountability, there are three players: an incumbent, a challenger, and a voter. Each politician may be *high quality* or *low quality*. You can think of quality as reflecting the politician's management skills, knowledge of good public policy, or the ability of the politician's advisors and subordinates. Each politician is of high quality with probability $p \in (0, 1)$ and is of low quality with probability $1 - p$. A politician's quality is her private information.

In the first period, the incumbent chooses a level of effort to devote to policy, $e_1 \in [0, 1]$. The effort cannot be observed by the voter. Then a policy outcome is determined.

The policy outcome can be *good* or *bad*. The difference between high and low quality incumbents is that high quality incumbents always achieve a good outcome, while low quality incumbents only achieve a good outcome with probability e_1. You can think of this assumption in a couple of ways. High quality incumbents might always know what good policy is, while low quality politicians have to invest considerable effort and resources to try to identify good policies. Or high quality politicians might have good control over their staffs, so that their policy ideas are implemented faithfully, while low quality politicians might need to work hard to have any hope that their policy ideas are correctly implemented.

After the first-period policy outcome is determined, the voter forms beliefs about how likely the incumbent is to be high quality. Then the voter chooses to reelect the incumbent or replace the incumbent with the challenger (whom the voter believes is of high quality with probability p).

In the second period, the winner of the election chooses a new level of effort, $e_2 \in [0, 1]$, and a new policy outcome is determined. Once again, if the politician in office in the second period is of high quality, then the policy outcome is good for certain. If the politician in office in the second period is of low quality, then the policy outcome is good with probability e_2. The game ends after the second period.

Payoffs are as follows. A politician gains a benefit B, with $0 < B < 1$, for each period she is in office. In a period in which she is in office and chooses effort

e, she suffers a cost e^2. The voter cares only about policy outcomes, gaining a benefit of 1 in any period in which the policy succeeds and a benefit of 0 in any period in which the policy fails.

Let's solve this game from the end. In the second period, regardless of which politician is in office, she has no incentive to exert any effort, since there is not a future election. Thus, any equilibrium involves zero effort in the second period.

Now consider the voter's reelection decision. Given that the winner of the election will choose effort $e_2 = 0$, the probability of a good outcome in the second period is simply the probability that the winner is high quality. Thus, the only thing the voter cares about in the election is whether the first-period incumbent is more or less likely than the challenger to be high quality. If the first-period incumbent is more likely than the challenger to be high quality, the voter reelects the incumbent. Otherwise, the voter replaces the incumbent with the challenger.

Given the voter's reelection rule, the critical question is how the voter forms his beliefs about how likely the incumbent is to be high quality. Without going into the technical details, there is a simple intuition. If the incumbent is of high quality, then the outcome will be good for certain. If the incumbent is of low quality (and chooses effort $e_1 < 1$), then there is some chance of a bad outcome. Thus, if the voter observes a bad first-period outcome, he is certain the first-period incumbent is of low quality. If the voter observes a good first-period outcome, he is not sure whether the first-period incumbent is of low or high quality, but his assessment of the probability that the incumbent is of high quality goes up.[2] Thus, the voter will reelect the incumbent if the outcome is good and replace the incumbent with the challenger if the outcome is bad.

In light of this, how will the incumbent behave in the first period? Recall, a high quality incumbent succeeds for sure, so has no reason (or need) to exert effort. But if the incumbent is low quality, then hard work could help her achieve a good policy outcome and reelection. This is how the accountability re-

---

[2]Formally, we apply Bayes' rule: The probability of some event X given another event Y (written $\Pr(X|Y)$) is

$$\Pr(X|Y) = \frac{\Pr(Y|X)\Pr(X)}{\Pr(Y|X)\Pr(X) + \Pr(Y|\text{not } X)\Pr(\text{not } X)}.$$

So, if the voter believes a low quality incumbent will choose effort e_1, then the voter believes that the probability that the incumbent is high quality, given a good outcome, is

$\Pr(\text{High Ability}|\text{Good Outcome}) =$

$$\frac{\Pr(\text{Good Outcome}|\text{High Ability})\Pr(\text{High Ability})}{\Pr(\text{Good Outcome}|\text{High Ability})\Pr(\text{High Ability}) + \Pr(\text{Good Outcome}|\text{Low Ability})\Pr(\text{Low Ability})}$$

$$= \frac{1 \times p}{1 \times p + e_1 \times (1-p)}.$$

It is straightforward that this is greater than p, so following a good outcome, the voter prefers to reelect the incumbent.

lationship creates incentives for a politician to take costly effort that benefits the voter. Of course, the incumbent balances the benefits of increasing her chances of reelection against the costs of effort. She solves the following problem:

$$\max_{e_1} e_1 B - (e_1)^2.$$

Solving, the first-period effort by a low quality incumbent is

$$e_1^* = \frac{B}{2}.$$

The overall probability of a good outcome in the first period is

$$\Pr(\text{Good Outcome}) = p + (1-p)\frac{B}{2}.$$

10.3.1 Rewards of Office

One fact is immediate from this model. All else equal, the greater are the rewards to holding office (i.e., the higher is B), the more costly effort the voter is able to extract from the (low quality) incumbent and the better the expected policy outcome. This claim is consistent with some existing evidence. In Italy, mayors of larger towns (more than 5,000 residents) are paid significantly more than mayors of smaller towns. This kind of institutional variation in salaries provides a nice way to make an all-else-equal comparison of mayors with different benefits of holding office. Small towns and large cities are different in lots of ways, so one cannot simply compare the performance of their mayors and assume any difference is due to the fact that mayors of large cities are paid more. But, on average, towns just below and just above the 5,000 resident threshold are likely to be quite similar. So if we compare the performance of mayors in these two kinds of towns, we are coming close to isolating just the effect of salary differences. Gagliarducci and Nannicini (2011) do precisely this and find that, indeed, better paid mayors perform better. They decrease per-capita taxes and tariffs, while leaving the level of government expenditures unchanged.

10.3.2 Term Limits

A closely related implication of the model is that the behavior of politicians depends on whether or not they can stand for reelection. In the first period, reelection is possible and, so, electoral accountability creates incentives for effort by incumbent politicians. In the second period, the politician in office cannot stand for reelection and shirks no matter her quality.

de Janvry, Finan, and Sadoulet (2011) study this issue in the context of Brazil. In the early 2000s the Brazilian national government created a program to help keep children in school. Under the program, poor parents were offered a fairly large cash reward if their children did not drop out. Overall, the program was a success—decreasing drop out rates among those who had access to the program by about 8%. However, de Janvry, Finan, and Sadoulet find that different municipalities had very different results. The program performed 36% better in municipalities where the mayor was up for reelection compared to municipalities where the mayor could not seek reelection due to term limits, suggesting that reelection incentives played an important role incentivizing good implementation of the policy.

Finan and Ferraz (2011) also use Brazilian data to study the effects of term limits on corruption. The Brazilian central government randomly audited a collection of municipalities to assess the gap between grants to the municipality by the central government and actual spending by the municipality. The difference between these two numbers reflects resources wasted (or stolen) by the local government. Finan and Ferraz find that term-limited mayors are about 2 percentage points more corrupt than non-term-limited mayors.

10.3.3 Incentives and Screening

Elections, in this model, play two roles in improving government performance. The first, which we've already discussed, is to create incentives for politicians to exert costly effort for the benefit of the voters. These incentives come from the fact that the incumbent knows she can only gain reelection by achieving a good outcome. Elections also play a second role—they help voters screen politicians, retaining incumbents they believe are of high quality and replacing incumbents they believe are of low quality.

Alt, Bueno de Mesquita, and Rose (2011) separately estimate the magnitudes of these two effects of elections on the quality of governance. They do so for governors of American states, exploiting the fact that states vary in their term limit laws. Some states have two-term term limits, some have one-term term limits, some have no term limits, and individual states have changed their term limit laws over time.

This variation in term limit laws sets up two comparisons, each of which isolates one of the two effects. A first-term governor who is eligible to run again and a first-term governor who is term-limited have each won election only once, and so have each faced the same selection pressures. However, the governor who is eligible to run again has stronger incentives to work hard to impress voters and gain reelection. Comparing the performance of these two types of governors, thus, provides an estimate of the incentive effect.

A first-term, term-limited governor and a second-term, term-limited governor both face the same weak incentives. However, they differ in terms of the amount of electoral selection they have survived. Comparing the performance of these two types of governors, thus, provides an estimate of the electoral selection effect.

Alt, Bueno de Mesquita, and Rose estimate these two effects using data from the American states from 1950 to 2000. They use within-state variation (i.e., states that changed term-limit rules) to identify the different effects of incentives and selection. Their results suggest that, all else equal, economic growth is higher and taxes, spending, and borrowing costs are lower under reelection-eligible incumbents than under term-limited incumbents (incentives), and under second-term, term-limited incumbents than under first-term, term-limited incumbents (electoral selection). Moreover, according to their estimates, these two effects of elections on the quality of governance are of roughly equal magnitude.

10.3.4 Voter Information

Voter access to information about incumbent performance might also affect the power of electoral incentives and the quality of electoral selection. Voter information flows from a variety of sources—the news media, rival candidates, government transparency initiatives, and so on. Let's start by looking at a simple extension of our model that allows for variation in voter information. We will then discuss some evidence.

Keep the same model as above, with one change. When the policy fails, the voter definitely learns that it failed. However, when the policy succeeds, the voter only learns that fact probabilistically. In particular, following a good outcome, the voter observes what he perceives as a good outcome with probability $\pi \in (1/2, 1)$ and observes what he perceives as a bad outcome with probability $1 - \pi$. An increase in π is equivalent to an increase in voter information.

In this model, the behavior of politicians in the second period is just as above. The voter's behavior is also unchanged. It is still the case that the voter thinks the incumbent is more likely to be high quality following a perceived good outcome and more likely to be low quality following a perceived bad outcome.[3]

---

[3] Let H denote high quality, L denote low quality, G denote a good outcome, and B denote a bad outcome. If the voter believes a low quality incumbent will choose effort e_1, then the voter believes that the probability that the incumbent is high quality, given a good outcome, is

$$\Pr(H|G) = \frac{\Pr(G|H)\Pr(H)}{\Pr(G|H)\Pr(H) + \Pr(G|L)\Pr(L)} = \frac{\pi p}{\pi p + e_1 \pi (1 - p)}.$$

It is straightforward that this is greater than p, so the voter wants to reelect the incumbent following a good outcome. We also have

$$\Pr(H|B) = \frac{\Pr(B|H)\Pr(H)}{\Pr(B|H)\Pr(H) + \Pr(B|L)\Pr(L)} = \frac{(1 - \pi)p}{(1 - \pi)p + (1 - e_1 + e_1(1 - \pi))(1 - p)}.$$

It is straightforward that this is less than p, so the voter wants to replace the incumbent following a bad outcome.

Given this, the incumbent believes that she will be reelected if and only if the voter perceives a good outcome. So if a low quality incumbent chooses effort e_1, she believes that she will be reelected with probability πe_1.

As before, the low quality incumbent has incentives to exert effort to try to keep her job. But now the benefits of effort are somewhat reduced, since she is not certain that the voter will correctly perceive her successes. A low quality incumbent solves the following problem:

$$\max_{e_1} \pi e_1 B - (e_1)^2.$$

Maximizing, first-period effort by a low quality incumbent when voter information is imperfect (labeled e_1^π) is

$$e_1^\pi = \frac{\pi B}{2}.$$

The better the voter's information (the closer π is to 1), the stronger are the incumbent's incentives for effort. The intuition is straightforward. When the voter's information about policy success or failure is noisy, effort by the incumbent translates less directly into reelection than when policy success or failure is observed perfectly by the voter. As a result, the incumbent has weaker electoral incentives than in the baseline game where the voter always correctly perceived the outcome:

$$e_1^\pi = \frac{\pi B}{2} < \frac{B}{2} = e_1^*.$$

CHALLENGERS

One possible source of voter information is electoral challengers. A challenger has strong incentives to point out areas in which an incumbent politician's policies have not succeeded. Moreover, if voters know challengers have incentives to point out policy failures, they can infer from challenger silence on some issue that the incumbent probably had policy success. Hence, the presence of electoral challengers has the potential to improve voter information in a way very similar to that modeled above.

Gordon and Huber (2007) compare the behavior of judges in Kansas elected under two different systems. In some Kansas districts, judges run against challengers in competitive elections. In other Kansas districts, judges run in so-called retention elections—voters do not vote for the incumbent or a challenger, they just vote up or down on the incumbent. The previous paragraph suggests that voter information is stronger in competitive elections and, thus, that incumbents have stronger incentives in such systems.

This is indeed what Gordon and Huber find. Judges facing competitive elections behave differently than judges facing retention elections. Kansas has a guideline-based system for sentencing that depends on the severity of the crime and the criminal history of the defendant. Each criminal case is classified into a particular group based on these criteria. Using case-level data that controls for which sentencing group a case falls in (so comparing judicial behavior for very similar kinds of crimes), and a rich set of additional case-level controls, Gordon and Huber show that judges facing competitive rather than retention elections sentence defendants more harshly, incarcerating defendants about 16% more frequently. Assuming Kansas voters like strict law enforcement, this suggests that the presence of challengers increases the extent to which government officials take actions that represent the voters' interests. (We will consider an alternative interpretation in Section 10.3.5.)

MEDIA COVERAGE

Perhaps the most compelling evidence on the link between voter information and electoral accountability comes from Snyder and Strömberg (2010). They measure the amount of information voters have about their congressional representative using the congruence between congressional districts and media markets. Here's the idea. Imagine you live in a midsized city with a local daily newspaper. Suppose, further, that your city and your congressional district are basically the same. Then your local newspaper will cover your local congressperson closely—your congressional district is highly congruent with your media market. Suppose, now, that you live in a town 30 miles outside of that city. Your daily newspaper may still be the city's paper. But that newspaper is not terribly interested in reporting on your congressperson, since he or she represents relatively few of the newspaper's readers. Your congressional district is not very congruent with your media market. Snyder and Strömberg claim that changes in a localities congruence is a source of fairly random variation in the extent to which voters have information about their congressperson's performance. Their idea is, if arguments like those above are correct, congruence should correlate with performance.

Figure 10.1 documents the various relationships that Snyder and Strömberg find. Panel (a) shows that congruence does in fact predict news coverage of a congressperson. Each subsequent panel is then consistent with our model. First, panels (b) and (c) show that congruence leads to increased voter information— the more congruent a congressional district (the horizontal access) the more likely the voters are to have read news coverage of their congressperson (panel b) and to correctly answer survey questions about their congressperson (panel c). Panels (d) and (e) show that increased congruence leads congresspeople to behave in ways that are more representative of the interests of their constituents.

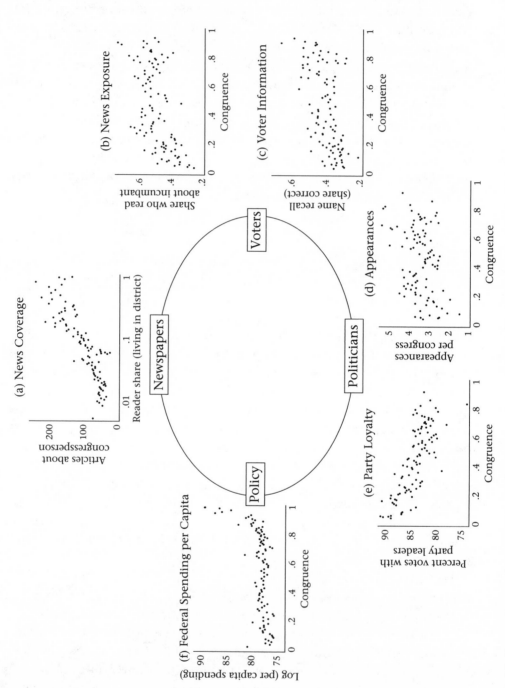

Figure 10.1. Media coverage and government performance in Congress. This figure uses Snyder and Strömberg's (2010) data to replicate analyses from their Figure 1.

Representatives from more highly congruent districts are more likely to stand as a witness before congressional committees on behalf of their districts (panel d) and less likely to vote in lockstep with the national party (panel e). Finally, panel (f) shows that this increased effort on the part of politicians in more congruent districts seems to translate into better outcomes for the district—the more congruent the congressional district with its media market, the more per capita federal spending flows to the district.

These pictures tell the basic story of how increased voter information can translate into better incentives and better outcomes. Snyder and Strömberg (2010) also do a lot of work to show that these relationships are not simply spurious correlations. For instance, they find these results even when controlling for characteristics of the district—indeed, they can show that when a locality gets redistricted such that it becomes more (or less) congruent with its media market, both the behavior of the congressperson and the level of federal spending directed to the locality change in the expected way. So the results are not, for instance, confounded by problems like big cities happening to both attract more federal spending and be more congruent.

VOTER RESPONSIVENESS

Berry and Howell (2007) present a different kind of evidence about the link between voter information and electoral accountability. They do not examine whether better voter information results in better governance outcomes. Rather, they investigate whether voter behavior becomes more responsive to governance outcomes when voters have better information. They find that the answer is yes.

Beginning in 2000, South Carolina instituted a school accountability system whereby the public was informed about school-level standardized test scores. During the 2000 school board elections, the raw test scores were reported to the public. However, for the 2002 school board elections and beyond, instead of raw test scores, the public was simply told whether each school was in one of four broad categories. Since schools fell into the same category, this change in the reporting system diminished the public's ability to distinguish good outcomes (improved test scores) from bad outcomes. In the 2000 election, the public could observe an improvement of any magnitude. In 2002, the public could only observe improvements that were large enough to move a school from one category to another. Thus, as in our model, in 2002, there might have been some policy successes (improvements in scores) that were observed as failures (no change in category).

Berry and Howell find that this decrease in voter information had an impact on voters' ability to use information about outcomes to make electoral decisions. In the 2000 election, improvements in test scores relate positively and significantly to electoral support for incumbent school board members. However, in elections following the 2002 changes in reporting systems, improvements in test scores no longer have any correlation with electoral support for incumbent school board members. Diminishing voter information made it impossible for voters to provide incumbent politicians with strong incentives for good performance.

10.3.5 The Risk of Electoral Pandering

We've seen important ways in which stronger electoral incentives can better align incumbent behavior with voter preferences. However, this need not always be the case. Sometimes increased electoral incentives actually distort the behavior of politicians away from voter interests. One interesting type of situation in which such distortions can occur is when politicians have an incentive to "pander." The technicalities of a pandering model are a bit too involved for our discussion here, but let me walk you through some intuitions and then discuss a bit of evidence.

To make things really stark, imagine a model with a voter and an incumbent who perfectly shares the voter's preferences. So, in the absence of electoral incentives, the incumbent would behave precisely as the voter wants her to.

The distortion comes from the fact that the voter faces two kinds of uncertainty. First, the voter is uncertain of the right policy choice. Suppose there are only two possible policies: A and B. The voter thinks that the right policy is probably A, but he isn't certain. (Since, all else equal, the voter would choose policy A, refer to A as the "popular" policy.) Second, the voter is uncertain of how competent the incumbent is. A competent incumbent always knows what the right policy is. An incompetent incumbent has more information than the voter—enough that she should choose B if her information says to do so—but is not perfectly informed.

The voter, for his part, will reelect the incumbent only if he thinks the incumbent is more likely to be competent than is the challenger. Given this, how should the incumbent behave?

If the incumbent's information indicates that policy A is the right policy, the incumbent's choice is clear—by choosing A she chooses the policy that both she and the voter believe is right. If the incumbent's information indicates that policy B is the right policy, things are more complicated. Choosing policy B, which the voter thinks is unlikely to be the right policy, carries some electoral risk for the incumbent. To see this, suppose the voter believes that the incumbent will follow her information. (This is what the voter would like the incumbent to do, even if she turns out to be the incompetent type, because even the incompetent type has pretty good information.) If the incumbent chooses policy B, the voter knows that one of two things is true. Either the correct policy is in fact B and the incumbent got the policy choice right. Or the correct policy is *A* and the incumbent got the policy choice wrong, which can only happen if the incumbent is incompetent. As such, upon observing the policy choice *B*, the voter starts to think it more likely that this was the right policy. But, since the voter started with the belief that *B* was unlikely to be the right policy, when he sees the incumbent choose *B*, he also starts to think the incumbent is more likely to be incompetent. This increased concern about incompetence can lead the voter to prefer the challenger. Thus, the incumbent has an incentive to pander—that is, even a competent incumbent who knows the right policy is *B* might choose the more "popular" policy, *A*, in order to avoid being perceived as incompetent.

These kinds of pandering incentives come directly from the desire for re-election. Thus, those features of the electoral environment that, in our earlier model, enhanced incentives, here can make voters worse off by increasing pandering. For instance, pandering can only exist with relatively informed voters. If all the voters observe is whether the government performs well or poorly, then the incumbent has incentives to choose policies that are likely to succeed. It is only the fact that voters can directly observe the substantive policy choice that creates incentives to pander. Similarly, the incentives to pander are strongest when the incumbent faces a competitive election. If the incumbent is term limited, or doesn't face a serious challenger, then convincing the voter that she is or is not competent doesn't matter for her future payoffs, so she has no incentive to pander. It is only when reelection is possible and contested that pandering becomes attractive.

Depending on how one thinks about the right sentencing behavior, one can view the evidence from Gordon and Huber (2007) discussed above as suggesting that judges pander to law-and-order voters only when they face serious electoral incentives. Similarly, Canes-Wrone and Shotts (2004) show that presidents propose budgets that are more in line with public opinion when two conditions hold: (*i*) the presidential election is close at hand, and (*ii*) presidential approval is such that the election is expected to be competitive. As with Gordon and Huber, one can interpret this finding as evidence of pandering to the public when electoral incentives are strong or as evidence of increased responsiveness to the legitimate demands of the voters when electoral competitiveness is high. Nonetheless, it is important to bear in mind that those forces that increase electoral incentives can increase or decrease the quality of governance, depending on whether you believe politicians achieve reelection by implementing good policy or by pandering to public opinion.

10.4 Takeaways

- Electoral concerns create incentives to target policy to benefit citizens whose political support is likely to be responsive to that policy. This can lead to policy distortions that favor concentrated interests, single-issue voters, non-partisan voters, and so on.

- There are a variety of ways in which interest groups might use money to affect electoral and policy outcomes—a quid pro quo between a policymaker and donor, using money to buy access to policymakers, or using money to help allied candidates win elections. There is some controversy over the extent to which money in fact influences policy outcomes.

- Electoral accountability plays at least two roles in affecting the quality of governance in a democracy: (*i*) the desire to gain reelection creates incentives for incumbents to take actions that they believe will please voters, and (*ii*) elections serve as a selection mechanism whereby voters replace incumbents whom the voters believe are of low quality on some dimension (e.g., competence, honesty, ideological fidelity with voters).

- Several factors affect the magnitude of incentives created by elections: benefits of office, term limits, voter information, the presence of challengers, and so on.

- Sometimes the incentive effect of elections can backfire by encouraging pandering. When incumbents believe that good policy outcomes are the path to reelection, factors that increase electoral incentives improve governance. However, when incumbents believe that pandering is the path to reelection, factors that increase electoral incentives reduce the quality of governance.

10.5 Further Reading

The model of electoral targeting is inspired by Dixit and Londregan (1996). There are many models similar to the model of electoral accountability (for a couple examples, see Ashworth and Bueno de Mesquita (2006) and Besley (2006)). Ashworth (2012) provides a stellar overview of the theoretical and empirical literatures. For models of pandering, have a look at Canes-Wrone, Herron, and Shotts (2001) and Maskin and Tirole (2004). Scott Gehlbach's terrific *Formal Models of Domestic Politics* provides a more advanced, textbook treatment of the various types of models discussed in this chapter.

10.6 Exercises

1. Based on the analysis in this chapter, offer two arguments in favor of term limits for elected politicians and two arguments against.

2.   The following is a common puzzle discussed by election observers. Often, some identifiable group of voters almost always votes for one political party over the other (e.g., African Americans vote overwhelmingly for Democrats and southern fundamentalist Christians vote overwhelmingly for Republicans). Yet, the argument goes, that political party often does little to help that loyal group of voters once in office. With reference to the analysis in Section 10.1, provide a potential explanation for this puzzle.

3.   Based on the analysis in Section 10.2, provide an assessment of the likely impact on the quality of public policy of significant restrictions on campaign donations and outside expenditures on campaigns.

4.   Consider the model from Section 10.3. But suppose the voter has an affinity for the incumbent, so that if the incumbent is reelected, the voter gets an additional payoff of α. (This could be because the incumbent is charismatic, because the voter and incumbent are from the same political party or ethnicity, etc.)

   From the analysis in footnote 2, if the voter believes that low ability incumbents choose effort e_1, then, conditional on seeing a good outcome, the voter believes the incumbent is of high ability with probability $\frac{p}{p+e_1(1-p)} > p$. If the voter observes the bad outcome, he is certain the incumbent is low ability.

   (a) What is the expected utility of electing the challenger?
   (b) If the voter believes low ability incumbents choose effort e_1, what is the expected utility of reelecting the incumbent after seeing a good outcome?
   (c) What is the expected utility of reelecting the incumbent after seeing a bad outcome?
   (d) If the voter believes low ability incumbents choose effort e_1, for what values of α does the voter reelect the incumbent no matter what? For what values of α does the voter reelect the incumbent only following a good outcome?
   (e) If α is such that the voter reelects the incumbent no matter what, what e_1 will the incumbent choose?
   (f) What does this imply about the effect of voter affinities for one candidate over the other on electoral accountability?
   (g) We can think of higher levels of voter affinity as corresponding to less competitive elections. Does this model suggest that competitive elections are good or bad for accountability?

5. (This problem is due to Scott Ashworth.) An elected official must decide whether to behave or to be corrupt. If he is corrupt, then he gets a private benefit worth B, while he gets no private benefit from behaving. After the official makes his choice, he stands for reelection. Winning the election is worth $R > B$ to the official. The voter strictly prefers for the politician to behave rather than act corruptly.

    (a) Suppose the voter does not have any information about the official's corruption choice prior to voting. Is there any reelection rule that (if anticipated by the politician) induces good behavior by the official? If yes, what is it? If no, why not?

    (b) Now assume that there are n newspapers, each of which can report on corruption if and only if it happens. (Corruption is perfectly observed by the reporters.) A newspaper that reports on corruption gets a boost in sales, giving it a benefit of M. The voter observes the newspaper reports before voting. Is there a reelection rule that (if anticipated by the politician) induces good behavior by the official? If yes, what is it? If no, why not?

    (c) Now assume that the official can offer bribes to the newspapers after he chooses to be corrupt. Both B and M are measured in dollars, with $B > M$. Newspapers care only about profits. How much does the official have to offer in bribes to get away with corruption? How many newspapers are needed to deter corruption?

    (d) What does this imply about the market structure of the media and democracy?

11

Institutions, Incentives, and Power

Bueno de Mesquita et al. (2003) tell the following story of Leopold II. Leopold was the king of Belgium from 1865 through 1909. Beginning in 1885, he was also the private owner of the Congo Free State—an area of land in Africa more than seventy-five times the size of Belgium.

Leopold faced very different political constraints in the two polities of which he was the leader. His governance of Belgium, a constitutional monarchy, was constrained by elected parliaments and cabinets. Moreover, the government of Belgium was chosen by majority rule from a voting population that, at the beginning of his reign, had over 100,000 members and, by the end of his reign, was made up of all of Belgium's adult male citizens.

Leopold held the Congo Free State as his personal property. He controlled the Congo with a mercenary army—the Force Publique. The members of the Force Publique were the only constituency to which Leopold was accountable in Africa. The easiest way to stay in power was by extracting and distributing private goods to his cronies.

This case is interesting because we observe one person, simultaneously facing two different sets of institutions. So how did Leopold behave as leader of each place?

As the constitutional monarch of Belgium, Leopold was generally viewed as one of the great reformers of his day. He advocated for universal male suffrage, gave workers the right to unionize and strike, instituted child labor laws, funded large public works projects (including road and railroad construction), and took measures to diminish unemployment. Under his leadership, Belgium experienced prosperity and rapid economic growth. All told, Leopold was regarded as a progressive and highly successful leader in Belgium.

Leopold's story is quite different in the Congo. He ran the Congo as an extractive slave state, first focusing on ivory and later on rubber. Leopold restricted foreign access to the Congo and allowed the Force Publique to enslave the native population. Work and compliance were enforced through torture, mutilation, and murder. The Force Publique was given enormous financial incentives to maintain Leopold's leadership, in the form of commissions based on the amount of rubber its slaves produced. Estimates vary as to how many people were murdered during Leopold's genocidal rule over the Congo. The low end of estimates are on the order of two million, with some scholars putting the number as high as fifteen million.

Under one set of institutions, Leopold was a noted progressive. Under another set of institutions, the self-same Leopold was one of the great genocidal murderers of modern history—on par with Stalin, Hitler, Pol Pot, and Mao. Certainly other factors, like racism, play a role in explaining Leopold's horrendous crimes in Africa. But, it seems likely that the unconstrained political environment in Congo was an important factor in Leopold's decision to implement horrific policies that benefited himself and his cronies while decimating millions of lives.

In this final chapter, we will think at a general level about how such differences in political institutions affect the incentives of political leaders who wish to stay in office. Following the analysis in Bueno de Mesquita et al. (2003), we will describe institutions according to two features:

1. The size of the *selectorate*: The proportion of the population that has some chance of playing a role in the selection of the leader.
2. The size of the *winning coalition*: The portion of the selectorate needed to keep a leader in power.

Our standard notions of regime type can be located within this selectorate/winning coalition typology. In a democracy, the selectorate is citizens with voting rights and a winning coalition is some majority or plurality of those citizens (depending on the exact electoral rules). In a Soviet-style autocracy, the selectorate is the members of the party and a winning coalition is made up of some central committee of those party members. In a junta or monarchy, the selectorate is a group of elite military officers or nobles and clergy, while a winning coalition is some small critical group of those elites.

We will study a model of a leader choosing between two kinds of policies: providing public goods (i.e., good public policy) and providing private goods to the members of the leader's winning coalition. Think of public goods as things like economic growth, peace, or solving social dilemmas. Think of private goods as corruption, direct transfers of wealth, patronage, and so on.

We will assume that leaders are primarily motivated by the desire to remain in office. Then we will examine how different institutions (i.e., different sizes of the selectorate and winning coalition) affect incentives to provide public and private goods.

The motivating idea is this: in order to stay in office, a leader must prevent challengers from recruiting away winning coalition members. So, in small winning coalition systems, a leader needs to keep relatively few people happy to retain power. It is relatively inexpensive to do so by providing private goods for the members of the winning coalition. Indeed, within such a system, money spent on providing public goods for the population (beyond those that the members of the winning coalition themselves demand) is, speaking politically, a waste of resources that could potentially be exploited by challengers. That is, in small winning coalition systems, *bad policy is good politics.*

The incentives are different in large winning coalition systems. In those systems, it is very expensive to provide private goods to all the members of the winning coalition, because there are so many of them. Hence, in a large winning coalition system, the most effective way to stay in power is to provide public goods for everyone. That is, within a large winning coalition system, *good policy is good politics.*

This logic predicts some interesting things. First, we should expect better policy outcomes in large winning coalition systems. Second, and more surprisingly, we should expect the survival of leaders to be negatively related to the quality of public policy in small winning coalition systems. That is, autocratic leaders who provide bad policy outcomes are expected to survive in office longer because bad policy is good politics. The opposite is expected in large winning coalition systems. Bueno de Mesquita et al. show patterns in data that are broadly consistent with this second prediction.

Let's now turn to a model that captures these intuitions.

11.1 A Selectorate Model

There are two politicians: an incumbent leader, L, and a challenger, C. There is also a selectorate, made up of S individuals. The incumbent leader starts the game with a preexisting winning coalition of size $W < S$.

The government has resources, R. (For technical convenience, assume $R > S$.) Each politician proposes a policy, which is an amount of public goods (g) to be provided and an amount of private goods (x) to be provided to each member of the politician's winning coalition. (For simplicity, I assume each member of the winning coalition gets the same private goods.) Each member of the selectorate then chooses which politician to support. The incumbent leader loses power if and only if two things happen:

1. The challenger gets the support of a group of at least size W.
2. The leader loses the support of at least one member of her winning coalition.

The price of a unit of public goods is p, so g units of public goods costs $p \times g$ dollars. Private goods are measured directly in dollars. Policy proposals must have a balanced budget. So any proposal, (g, x), must satisfy

$$pg + Wx \leq R.$$

Payoffs are quasi-linear. Suppose a member of the selectorate, i, receives private goods x_i and public goods g. Her payoffs are linear in x_i and are increasing, but with decreasing marginal returns, in g. In particular, let's assume the utility from some amount of public goods, g, is the natural log of g (denoted $\ln g$). This is a simple functional form that captures the idea that payoffs are increasing in public goods, but with decreasing marginal returns. Thus, her payoffs are

$$U_i(x_i, g) = x_i + \ln g.$$

The payoff to a politician who is not in office is 0. The payoff to a politician who is in office includes a benefit from holding office, $B > 0$, and a benefit from any resources not spent on policy, $u(R - pg - Wx)$, where u is an increasing function. Thus, the politician who wins leadership has payoffs

$$B + u(R - pg - Wx).$$

I make one further assumption. The incumbent leader is committed to the members of her winning coalition. If she retains office, any member of her winning coalition who supported her remains in the winning coalition. The challenger cannot make a similar commitment. It is not until the challenger takes office that the members of the selectorate learn who will be in the challenger's inner circle—that is, the winning coalition. From the perspective of a selectorate member, each member of the selectorate is equally likely to end up in the challenger's winning coalition, should the challenger take power.

11.1.1 Equilibrium

I focus on a Nash equilibrium in which both politicians attempt to secure the support of exactly W people and in which each member of the selectorate supports the politician whose platform he or she prefers.[1]

Suppose the incumbent proposes (g^L, x^L) and the challenger proposes (g^C, x^C). Who will the members of the selectorate support?

If the incumbent retains office, a member of the winning coalition makes a payoff of $x^L + \ln g^L$, while a member of the selectorate not in the winning coalition makes a payoff of $\ln g^L$. If the challenger wins, each member of the selectorate ends up in the new winning coalition with probability $\frac{W}{S}$. So the expected payoff to a member of the selectorate from the challenger winning is $\frac{W}{S} \times x^C + \ln g^C$. Given this, a member of the incumbent's winning coalition

---

[1]This last restriction is the common assumption that players don't play weakly dominated strategies. It rules out equilibria in which I support a politician I dislike because I know my support has no effect on the outcome. That is, it rules out certain kinds of coordination traps.

continues to support the incumbent if

$$x^L + \ln g^L \geq \frac{W}{S} \times x^C + \ln g^C, \tag{11.1}$$

while a member of the selectorate not in the incumbent's winning coalition supports the incumbent if

$$\ln g^L \geq \frac{W}{S} \times x^C + \ln g^C. \tag{11.2}$$

The incumbent leader has an advantage over the challenger in holding on to the support of the members of her winning coalition—she can guarantee them continued access to private goods, while the challenger cannot because he cannot commit to the makeup of his winning coalition. Given this, we want to see whether there is any offer a challenger can make that will allow him to unseat the incumbent.

The most attractive proposal a challenger can make to the members of the selectorate is to spend the entire budget, R, and to divide it between public and private goods in a way that maximizes a selectorate member's expected utility (remembering that the selectorate members do not know if they will end up in the winning coalition should the challenger win). This proposal solves the following:

$$\max_{(g,x)} \frac{W}{S} x + \ln g \quad \text{subject to } pg + Wx = R. \tag{11.3}$$

Notice, from the budget constraint, we have the following condition:

$$pg + Wx = R \Rightarrow x = \frac{R - pg}{W}.$$

This says that, given that the challenger is going to spend the whole budget, the choice of how much to spend on public goods (g) tells you, through simple accounting, how much she will spend on private goods (x). Hence, she really just has to make one choice: how much to spend on public goods. In our model, we can see this by substituting $x = \frac{R-pg}{W}$ into Equation 11.3. This transforms the two-dimensional maximization problem subject to a budget constraint into a simple one-dimensional problem of how much to spend on public goods:

$$\max_{g} \frac{W}{S} \times \frac{R - pg}{W} + \ln g.$$

Using the fact that the derivative of $\ln g$ with respect to g is $\frac{1}{g}$, the following first-order condition gives the challenger's optimal spending on public goods (labeled g^C):

$$\frac{1}{g^C} = \frac{p}{S} \Rightarrow g^C = \frac{S}{p}.$$

Substituting back into the budget constraint tells us how much the challenger will propose to spend on private goods for her winning coalition. Putting this all together, the challenger's best policy proposal is

$$g^C = \frac{S}{p} \qquad x^C = \frac{R-S}{W}. \tag{11.4}$$

This implies that, for any member of the selectorate, the expected payoff from the challenger winning is

$$\frac{W}{S} \times \frac{R-S}{W} + \ln\frac{S}{p} = \frac{R-S}{S} + \ln\frac{S}{p}.$$

Let's label this payoff, which is the best expected payoff that the challenger can offer to members of the selectorate in exchange for their support, as $\overline{U}^C$.

To stay in office, the incumbent leader has to provide the members of her winning coalition with a better payoff than the challenger can offer. Assume, for the moment, that everyone not in the winning coalition will support the challenger. Then each member of the winning coalition is pivotal—if any member leaves the winning coalition, the incumbent leader falls. As such, the leader must offer a package (g^L, x^L) that convinces each member of the winning coalition that having her in office is better than having the challenger in office. That is, (g^L, x^L) must satisfy

$$x^L + \ln g^L \geq \overline{U}^C \qquad \text{and} \qquad pg^L + Wx^L \leq R.$$

The leader can in fact make a proposal that will keep her in office. Why is this? The members of the leader's winning coalition understand that if they stick with her, they get to stay in the winning coalition, so they get the private goods she offers for certain. If they defect to the challenger, they may or may not end up in the new winning coalition, so they may or may not get the private goods. Thus, it is clear from Condition 11.1, if the incumbent leader offered the same proposal as the challenger, the incumbent's existing winning coalition members would support her.

Of course, the incumbent leader will not make the same proposal as the challenger. She wants to remain in power as cheaply as possible, since she gets to keep any resources she doesn't allocate to public or private goods. As we just said, all else equal, the leader's existing winning coalition members strictly prefer her to the challenger because they are certain to remain in her winning coalition if she wins. Hence, the leader can retain her winning coalition members' loyalty even if she offers them somewhat less than the challenger is offering to his winning coalition (whose membership is uncertain). Let's see exactly what the incumbent leader offers.

Suppose the leader were going to propose spending a total amount Δ on providing public and private goods. She wants to use those resources to make the members of her winning coalition as happy as possible. Doing so will allow her to keep Δ as small as possible while still staying in office. To do so, she maximizes the winning coalition members' utility, given a total expenditure Δ. That is, the leader solves

$$\max_{x,g} x + \ln g \quad \text{subject to } \Delta = Wx + pg.$$

Just as we did for the challenger, we can use the budget constraint to reduce this to a one-dimensional problem, since whatever share of Δ the incumbent doesn't spend on public goods, she spends on private goods for her winning coalition members. (She then keeps $R - \Delta$ for herself.) The budget constraint implies that $x = \frac{\Delta - pg}{W}$. Hence, the incumbent's maximization problem can be rewritten

$$\max_{g} \frac{\Delta - pg}{W} + \ln g.$$

The first-order condition for this problem is

$$\frac{p}{W} = \frac{1}{g^L} \Rightarrow g^L = \frac{W}{p}.$$

For any amount $\Delta \geq W$ that the leader spends, she will divide it as follows:

$$g^L(\Delta) = \frac{W}{p} \quad x^L(\Delta) = \frac{\Delta - W}{W}. \tag{11.5}$$

Notice, if $\Delta < W$, our formula in Equation 11.5 calls for an $x < 0$. Since this is not allowed, the leader is stuck at what is called a "corner solution." That means that if she spends $\Delta < W$, she will allocate it all to public goods, providing no private goods to her winning coalition.

The analysis above already reveals two important pieces of intuition. First, when the winning coalition is small, private goods are shared among a small group of people. Hence, the incumbent has particularly strong incentives to allocate a lot of her spending to private goods (i.e., x^L is decreasing in W). As the winning coalition gets larger, the leader spends more and more resources on public goods. Indeed, if the winning coalition gets large enough relative to the budget allocated ($W > \Delta$), the leader provides only public goods, spending nothing on private goods for the winning coalition.

Second, compare the incumbent leader's division of resources in Equation 11.5 to the challenger's division of resources in Equation 11.4. The incumbent allocates a bigger portion of the resources she spends to private goods than does the challenger. (You can see this clearly if you consider the case of $\Delta = R$.) This is because the incumbent's winning coalition members know for certain that they will be in her winning coalition in the future. Hence, they place greater value on private goods. But the challenger's supporters don't know if they will end up in her winning coalition or not. So they put less value on private goods and more value on public goods.

Now the incumbent must decide how much to spend in total. She will spend just the amount needed to keep her in office. Call this amount Δ^*. Let's assume that $\overline{U}^C > \ln \frac{W}{p}$, so that the incumbent leader must spend more than W to keep the winning coalition happy. This implies that $\Delta^* > W$, so the leader's optimal allocation between public and private goods is given by Equation 11.5. Using this fact, the minimal Δ^* that keeps the members of the incumbent leader's winning coalition loyal satisfies

$$\frac{\Delta^* - W}{W} + \ln \frac{W}{p} = \overline{U}^C.$$

Rearranging, the incumbent's total spending is

$$\Delta^* = W \left(\overline{U}^C + 1 - \ln \frac{W}{p} \right). \tag{11.6}$$

11.1.2 Outcomes and Institutions

What do we learn from this analysis? Let's start by studying the amount that is spent by the government. If we substitute the definition of $\overline{U}^C$ into Δ^* (recall $\overline{U}^C = \frac{R-S}{S} + \ln \frac{S}{p}$), we find that the incumbent leader spends

$$\Delta^* = W \left(\frac{R}{S} + \ln \frac{S}{W} \right).$$

Differentiating with respect to W shows that total government spending is increasing in the size of the winning coalition.[2] The larger the size of the winning coalition, the more of the budget the leader spends and the less she misappropriates. Hence, for leaders, small winning coalition systems are better than large winning coalition systems in that they offer the leader more opportunities for personal corruption.

---

[2] $\frac{d\Delta^*}{dW} = \frac{R}{S} + \ln \frac{S}{W} - 1$. Since we have $R > S > W$, the first term is greater than 1 and the second term is positive. Together, then, the first two terms are greater than 1, so the whole derivative is positive.

To see what drives this fact, it helps to study the policy choices. Recall, from above, that the per-person level of private goods is

$$x^L(\Delta^*) = \frac{\Delta^* - pg^L}{W}.$$

Substituting for Δ^* and for $g^L(\Delta^*) = \frac{W}{p}$, we get

$$x^L = \frac{R}{S} + \ln \frac{S}{W} - 1.$$

Thus, the per-person public and private goods provided by the incumbent leader are

$$g^L = \frac{W}{p} \quad x^L = \frac{R}{S} + \ln \frac{S}{W} - 1.$$

The level of public goods provided is increasing in the size of the winning coalition and the level of private goods provided to members of the winning coalition is decreasing in the size of the winning coalition.

As the size of the winning coalition increases, it becomes more expensive to provide private goods. So, increasingly, as the winning coalition gets large, the cheapest way for the leader to make the members of the winning coalition happy is to provide public goods.[3] When the winning coalition is small, it is quite cheap to provide private goods. Hence, in small winning coalition systems, the leader provides lots of private goods and relatively few public goods.

These results highlight another important point—public goods are all that matter to a member of society who is not in the winning coalition. Large winning coalitions create incentives for leaders to provide public goods rather than private goods. Hence, for a person not in the winning coalition, large winning coalitions are better.

Taken together, all of these results suggest the following point. In large winning coalition systems, good policy is good politics. In small winning coalition systems, bad policy is good politics. Governments are not benevolent social welfare maximizers. Leaders are not inherently motivated to achieve Pareto improvements. Rather, political leaders have their own preferences and incentives. The desire to stay in office is a powerful source of such incentives. So leaders pursue policies that benefit those people who are in a position to keep them in office. If that group of people has preferences that are broadly similar to most of society (i.e., if most of society is in the selectorate and the winning coalition is large), then leaders have incentives to pursue policies that are pretty benevolent. If that group of people has preferences that are quite different from

---

[3]Indeed, as we discussed earlier, if the winning coalition is really big, the leader provides no private goods at all to the members of the winning coalition.

most of society, then leaders have incentives to pursue policies that may well be quite bad for society.

There could be many reasons why the winning coalition ends up being small—autocratic institutions, widespread inattention by voters, special interests capturing control of the political process, and so on. In this sense, the lesson of the selectorate model is similar to the lesson of our model, from Chapter 10.1, of elected incumbents who target policy to the interests of responsive voters.

All of this is to say that politics act as a real and important constraint on whether or not the social dilemmas we discussed in Part II get solved. If the institutions of government create incentives such that the government is, broadly speaking, working for the people, then policy is likely to be good. If the institutions of government create incentives such that the government is not, broadly speaking, working for the people, then rational politicians are likely to choose policies that are not good for society, but rather are good for their political coalition.

If this argument is right and the social dilemmas discussed throughout this book are important, then we should expect the quality of political institutions to have a big impact on the type of policy pursued and the welfare outcomes for society. In the remainder of this chapter, we explore whether this is the case in a couple of settings.

11.2 Institutions and Development

The selectorate model provides a formalization of the idea that political institutions play an important role in determining whether governments pursue good or bad public policy. Given the arguments of the rest of this book—that good public policy plays an important role in determining citizen welfare—you might wonder whether there is any systematic evidence of a link between the quality of political institutions and welfare. In this section, we will look briefly at some evidence on this question, focusing especially on whether good governance institutions lead to economic growth.

Answering this question is tricky. Consider the simplest comparison you might make to assess the answer—comparing economic outcomes in countries with good institutions to economic outcomes in countries with bad institutions. Unfortunately, even if you controlled for lots of other things in that comparison, you would not convincingly answer the question. Suppose you found a correlation between good institutions and good economic outcomes. You would not know whether the good institutions caused the economic outcomes or whether a good economy causes good institutions. Perhaps, for example, as the economy grows, people become more educated, and more educated people demand better government institutions. To make things even more complicated, there could be no causal relationship between the two at all. Perhaps there is some third factor—say climate or ethnic fractionalization—that creates the correlation by affecting both institutions and the economy.

Given these deep causal inference problems, if one wants to figure out the relationship between good institutions and economic outcomes, one has to be a bit more clever.

One way to start to see that governance institutions really might matter for growth is to think anecdotally about some more convincing comparisons. As Acemoglu, Johnson, and Robinson (2005) discuss, prior to the late 1940s, North and South Korea shared a common history and culture. They were also quite similar economically, with the north the more industrially developed of the two. But after World War II, the two parts of Korea ended up with very different political systems—North Korea came under Communist control, while South Korea's nationalist government aligned with the West. Starting in the late 1960s, South Korea had one of the highest growth rates in modern history, while the North Korean economy basically failed to grow at all. By the year 2000, South Korea's per capita GDP was more than sixteen times North Korea's. Government institutions seem to matter. Although even here the inference is questionable. After all, the two Koreas differ in many ways (beyond political institutions) in the postwar period. For instance, their different political alignments resulted in different military alliances, trading partners, diplomatic relationships, and so on.

11.2.1 Settler Mortality, Institutions, and the Economy

If you want to assess the impact of institutions on economic outcomes, you have to find a way to set up a comparison that is something like an experiment. That is, you need some countries to get good institutions and other countries to get bad institutions for reasons not having to do with their current or expected future economic outcomes. This is a tough challenge. Perhaps the most famous research attempting to do so is Acemoglu, Johnson, and Robinson (2001).

Here is their idea. European colonialists established different kinds of institutions in different places. One source of variation was simply the home country of the colonist—the French set up different institutions from the British or the Dutch. Another source of variation was whether the colonists planned to live in the colony. In places where the colonists themselves planned to live, they set up European-like governance institutions. In places where the colonists planned to establish, say, extractive colonies, but did not plan to live, they established much less enlightened institutions. (Remember the story of King Leopold.) So, Acemoglu, Johnson, and Robinson reason, where colonists planned to live was an important source of variation in the quality of governance institutions at the time of colonization.

Institutions are sticky. A country that gets good institutions at the time of colonization tends to have good institutions later, and likewise with bad institutions. This suggests that settlement patterns at the time of colonization exert an influence on the quality of institutions, even today.

If colonial settlement patterns were unrelated to factors that affect contemporary economic outcomes, then we have something like the experiment we want. But is this true? Surely the settlers chose to stay in locations with lots of natural resources and good economic prospects, factors that might carry through to economic growth today.

Acemoglu, Johnson, and Robinson argue that a major determinant of settlement patterns at the time of colonization was the disease environment. Colonists did not want to settle in locations rife with malaria and yellow fever, as they would not survive. Further, they argue, the diseases that constituted the major risks to colonists at the time of settlement are unlikely to have a serious impact on economies today because those diseases have either been eradicated or effectively controlled. As such, they argue, the bit of variation in settlement patterns that is due to the disease environment at the time of colonization might have affected institutions, while having no other relationship to current economic outcomes. That variation is like an experiment—countries that have good institutions because of their deep historical disease environments and countries that have bad institutions because of their deep historical disease environments can be compared to learn about the effect of institutions because deep historical disease environment is "as if random" (i.e., assigned almost as if for an experiment) relative to modern economic outcomes. We'll come back to how airtight this argument is later. For now, though, let's look at a little data.

At a very simple level, if Acemoglu, Johnson, and Robinson's argument is right, we should see a relationship between historic disease environments and modern economic outcomes. Figure 11.1 shows that relationship. The horizontal axis is a measure of settler mortality. The vertical axis is a measure of per-capita income in 1995. Each point is a country. (They are labeled with three-letter country codes.) There is clearly a negative relationship—the less pleasant a location was to settle, the worse its economy today.

This simple picture doesn't tell the whole story. In particular, it leaps directly from settler mortality to modern economic outcomes. What we really want to see is a two-step relationship. First, settler mortality at the time of colonization should predict worse institutions today. Second, we want to isolate the bit of variation in institutions today that is due to settler mortality and see that it is associated with worse economic outcomes today.

Figure 11.2 shows the first step. On the horizontal axis, again, is a measure of settler mortality. On the vertical axis is a measure of the quality of modern institutions—in particular, a measure of whether the government respects property rights (higher numbers mean better institutions). Again, the relationship is clearly negative.

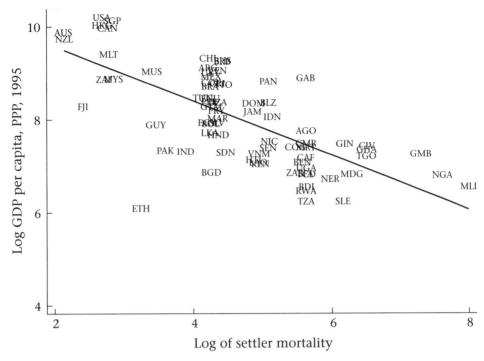

Figure 11.1. Log settler mortality at time of colonization against log 1995 GDP per capita. This figure uses Acemoglu, Johnson, and Robinson's (2001) data to replicate their Figure 1.

Showing the second of these relationships is a bit more involved, since you must isolate the bit of variation in the quality of institutions that is due to settler mortality and then relate just that bit of variation to GDP. The details of how one does this are not important for us.[4] What is important is that, having done so, Acemoglu, Johnson, and Robinson find the expected relationship—good institutions seem to lead to better economic outcomes. In particular, their estimates suggest that moving from the twenty-fifth percentile (roughly Nigeria) to the seventy-fifth percentile (roughly Chile) in quality of institutions yields a sevenfold increase in GDP.

Of course, there are reasons you might be skeptical of this interpretation. First, since the evidence is historical and across many countries, there are inevitably some measurement concerns (Albouy, 2012). Second, it seems possible that settler mortality has ways to affect economic outcomes today besides just institutions. For instance, Glaeser et al. (2004) point out that, along with good institutions, colonists who actually settled in the colonies brought along their human capital. If human capital leads to investment in infrastructure, health, more human capital, or what have you, it could have a persistent effect

---

[4]If you are interested in this kind of empirical research, you should read Angrist and Pischke (2008).

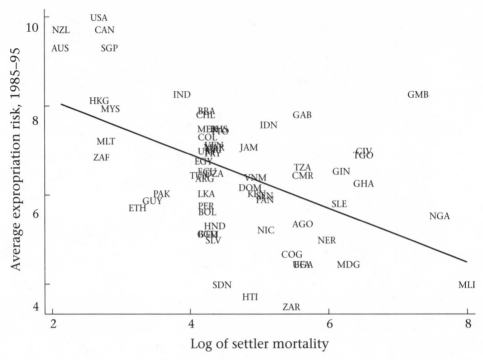

Figure 11.2. Log settler mortality at time of colonization against modern expropriation risk (higher expropriation risk means more respect for property rights). This figure uses Acemoglu, Johnson, and Robinson's (2001) data to replicate their Figure 3.

on the economy. Hence, Glaeser et al. argue, one cannot be certain that the relationship between settler mortality and modern economic outcomes is due to institutions. Nonetheless, Acemoglu, Johnson, and Robinson provide some really interesting, if inevitably limited, evidence. In the next section, we will look at some more evidence of a link between institutions, policy choices, and welfare.

11.3 Foreign Aid

We have looked at both a model and some evidence related to two key claims. First, that government policy actually matters for outcomes we care about. Second, that the type of incentives created for policymakers by political institutions affect the kind of policies made and, thus, the welfare outcomes for citizens. In this section we will look at both of these questions again, within the context of a particular policy domain, foreign aid.

In our discussion of foreign aid, let's start with the traditional account of how aid works. This is the account typically given by development specialists and others who advocate foreign aid as a (at least partial) solution to global poverty. We will then turn to some critiques from within the tradition of development economics. Finally, we will think about a political economy account of the politics of foreign aid policy, using the selectorate model to motivate our discussion.

11.3.1 Poverty Traps and Foreign Aid

In Chapter 5.2 we discussed the standard account of the role of foreign aid, based on the theory of poverty traps (Sachs, 2006; Collier, 2007). Poor countries lack human capital, infrastructure, health, and a variety of the other features of a congenial investment environment. As such, they cannot attract foreign investment. This inability to attract capital leads poor countries to become ever poorer, making it even harder to invest in human capital, infrastructure, and so on. Poverty creates a vicious cycle. And so, poor countries are caught in a *poverty trap*, unable to develop and grow precisely because they are poor. This problem, the argument goes, is only exacerbated by globalization. As capital becomes increasingly mobile, the disadvantages of those countries that cannot attract foreign investment are magnified.

Foreign aid is thought to be a solution to poverty traps. Aid can be used by poor countries to invest in the infrastructure and human capital needed to make poor countries more attractive destinations for foreign capital. Once foreign investment begins to flow to the country, wealth will increase. This allows for further investment in infrastructure and human capital, which then attracts even more investment. Aid is intended to break the vicious cycle of poverty, replacing it with a virtuous cycle of investment and growth.

On this account, a country is not expected to depend on aid for the long term. Rather, like in the case of the Tennessee Valley Authority creating an agglomeration economy in manufacturing, aid is meant to be a short- to medium-term measure that allows a big push in infrastructure and human capital investment. This big push is meant to shift the country into the virtuous cycle of economic growth, eventually eliminating the need for foreign aid.

11.3.2 Does Foreign Aid Work through Poverty Traps?

Perhaps the most prominent critic of the poverty traps view of foreign aid is the development economist William Easterly.[5] Easterly rejects the poverty trap view, primarily on empirical grounds, and suggests a different model for how foreign aid could be effective.

He starts by pointing out that it is very difficult to find any evidence of even a correlation between foreign aid and future economic growth. Any relationship that has been found, Easterly notes, is highly fragile to both specification of the statistical model (e.g., whether or not to control for domestic economic policy)

---

[5] See, for example, Easterly (2003, 2006) and Easterly and Pfutze (2008).

and to the inclusion of new data (e.g., as more years become available). The first-order fact one notices from the data is essentially no relationship between aid and growth.

Easterly further questions whether poverty traps exist at all. There is no doubt that there are some very poor countries. But that is not evidence of a poverty trap. A poverty trap requires two things to be true: (*i*) the poor get poorer over time because the rich can attract investment while the poor can't, and (*ii*) poverty is a persistent trait of a country (i.e., certain countries are caught in poverty). Easterly questions whether either of these features of the poverty trap model actually describes the world. He points to the following evidence. From 1950 to 2001, the growth rates of the richest 8% of countries and poorest 20% of countries were indistinguishable (both around 2.5%). If one looks only from 1985 to 2001, then the poorest 20% of countries grew more slowly. However, if one accounts for both their poverty prior to 1985 and the quality of their government institutions prior to 1985, the quality of government was a better predictor of low growth than was initial poverty. And of the 28 countries that constitute the poorest 20% in 1950, eleven were no longer among the poorest 20% in 1985.

Taken together, Easterly argues, this kind of evidence calls into question whether poverty traps exist. Poor countries seem not to be stuck in a cycle of negative growth relative to rich countries. And, to the extent that there is any evidence that they are (e.g., by looking only from 1985 on), the reason seems to be because of bad governance, not poverty traps. Moreover, poverty does not seem to be persistent. There are always poor countries. But the identity of the poor countries changes over time.

Given that Easterly does not believe poverty traps exist, it is not surprising that he is unpersuaded by the argument for big push foreign aid as a solution to poverty. After all, the argument for big push foreign aid hinges on the existence of poverty traps. And, indeed, Easterly presents some evidence to suggest that foreign aid programs designed to address poverty traps do not work. From 1950 to 2001, among the poorest 20% of countries, those that received aid failed to grow at a faster rate than those that did not. There was a huge aid push in Africa during this period. For instance, in the 1990s the average African country received aid equal to 15% of GDP. Yet during this same time, economic growth in Africa plummeted. And of the 88 countries that received aid between 1965 and 1995, only 6 had economic growth of more than a dollar per dollar of foreign aid. Notice, even if aid sparks no growth, mechanically there is economic growth of a dollar per dollar of aid (since a dollar of aid itself increases GDP by a dollar). The 6 countries that had growth in excess of a dollar per dollar of aid were Hong Kong, China, Morocco, Tunisia, Sri Lanka, and Malta—not the countries evoked by the poverty traps story.

None of this evidence, on its own, settles the matter. For instance, perhaps aid recipients failed to grow faster than non-aid recipients because they were in worse economic shape to begin with. More generally, a critical question that such facts don't address is whether those countries that received aid would have faired even worse absent aid. But taken together, Easterly's evidence certainly raises some questions about how common poverty traps are and how much good aid is in fact doing.

11.3.3 Effective Aid?

Empirical scholarship is divided on the question of the efficacy of aid.[6] The most heralded study purporting to show aid's positive effects on economic growth is Burnside and Dollar (2000), which finds that multilateral aid is correlated with economic growth in countries that have good economic policies (e.g., trade openness) in place. However, Easterly (2003) claims that these findings are highly sensitive to empirical specification and disappear with the addition of more years of data. Indeed, such non-robustness characterizes much of the literature (Roodman, 2007). Moreover, none of these studies has a source of variation in aid that is sufficiently close to random to justify a causal interpretation one way or the other.

Among studies with more convincing causal interpretations, the evidence remains equivocal. On the positive side, Galiani et al. (2014) show that countries that just qualify for aid have higher growth rates than similar countries that just fail to qualify for aid. Werker, Ahmed, and Cohen (2009) show mixed effects of aid flows from wealthy OPEC countries to poor Muslim countries resulting from shocks to world oil prices—they find no effect on growth, a positive effect on consumption, and a negative effect on savings. Other studies find that aid has a variety of deleterious effects. Djankov, Montalvo, and Reynal-Querol (2008) report that receiving aid is associated with a decrease in democratic governance. Svensson (2000) shows a positive relationship between aid and corruption. Rajan and Subramanian (2011) find that aid reduces the growth of export industries. And Nunn and Qian (2014), Crost, Felter, and Johnston (2014), and Dube and Naidu (2015) use a variety of clever sources of variation to show that aid appears to have increased conflict in several countries.

Easterly reads this evidence, on balance, as suggesting that aid does more harm than good. His explanation is that the foreign aid system is broken. Aid agencies have bad incentives—they do things that get noticed, whether or not they make a difference. International institutions and governments rely on incorrect theories of poverty traps and state building to motivate unrealistic, utopian visions of the effects of aid. As a result, aid ends up doing little to relieve suffering and much to prop up dictators and kleptocrats in poor countries.

---

[6] See Qian (2015) for an overview on which the summary below is based.

So what are we to do? On Easterly's view, there are a few simple steps. The first step is to accept that aid cannot change societies, economies, or governments. Economic growth, in Easterly's view, must come from homegrown development of markets and entrepreneurship. This cannot be done for people; it must arise organically.

A second step is to stop giving aid to corrupt leaders. Aid directed in this way does not help the poor. It simply allows bad leaders to steal money, use it to stay in power, and continue to implement bad policies.

Third, aid should be given to relieve the suffering associated with great poverty. Rather than attempting to transform societies or economies, we should use aid for the more modest purpose of making people's lives less miserable. Inherent in this goal is giving money to local, direct service organizations doing measurable and accountable good on the ground, rather than to dictators.

Easterly's recommendations strike me as sensible. (I'm not a development specialist, so there's no reason you should care about my opinion.) But I also believe his analysis misses a critical piece of the puzzle. In particular, he seems both outraged and puzzled as to why rich governments have persisted in pursuing failed aid policies—policies that prop up dictators, hurt the poor, and fail to achieve their stated goals—for so long. I think his puzzlement derives from the fact that this may not be a question for a development economist, but rather for a political economist. So at the risk of appearing just a little too cynical for my own good, I want to think for a moment about the political economy of foreign aid.

11.3.4 A Political Economy of Foreign Aid

Let's apply the intuitions about leader incentives from the selectorate model to the politics of foreign aid (Bueno de Mesquita and Smith, 2007, 2009). Perhaps governments are following what, from Easterly's perspective, are failed foreign aid policies, not because they do not understand the development economics, but because those policies, while not economically optimal, are politically optimal. Here's what I mean.

Imagine two countries, A and B. The leader of country A offers the leader of country B some resources (which we can call foreign aid) in exchange for country B making a policy concession of some sort. Think of the United States offering Egypt aid in exchange for maintaining peace with Israel or offering Colombia aid in exchange for crackdowns on drug cartels. The leader of country B can accept the aid and make the policy concession, or she can reject the aid and not make the policy concession. Each leader faces domestic political competition as in the selectorate model.

Without solving a whole new model, let's think about the incentives at work here, given what we know about selectorate politics.

When will country A's leader be willing to trade aid for policy? The cost to country A's leader is that resources spent on foreign aid could have been used to provide public and private goods to her winning coalition. Hence, foreign aid potentially opens up an opportunity for her challenger. The benefit to country A's leader is that the foreign aid expenditures induce country B to enact a pro-A policy. This policy, presumably, is a public good for the citizens of country A. The larger the winning coalition of country A, the more valuable it is for country A's leader to provide public goods to her citizens. This suggests the following. First, aid-for-policy deals are more attractive to the leader of country A when the amount of aid needed to buy the policy concession from country B is small. Second, aid-for-policy deals are more attractive to the leader of country A the larger A's winning coalition is.

Now think about country B. Country B's leader will accept an aid-for-policy deal as long as the aid more than compensates for the costs of the policy concessions. How costly the policy concessions are depends on at least two factors. First, how bad the policy change is for country B. Second, how much the leader of country B cares about implementing suboptimal policies. The larger country B's winning coalition is, the more costly the leader of country B finds it to make a policy concession. Hence, the amount of aid A will have to provide to get an aid-for-policy deal from B is increasing in the size of B's winning coalition.

Taken together, this story about aid-for-policy deals has some interesting implications. Let me start with some empirical implications and then talk about the implications for social welfare. Three empirical predictions follow from the argument above:

1. Aid will primarily be provided by countries with large winning coalitions, since policy concessions are particularly valuable to them.
2. Most aid will go to countries with small winning coalitions, since they are the cheapest to buy off.
3. While aid will go to small winning coalition countries more often than to large winning coalition countries, when it does go to a large winning coalition country, the aid package will be unusually large, since such countries are expensive to buy off.

The data, sadly, turn out to be supportive of all three of these predictions. Bueno de Mesquita and Smith (2009) find the following in data on aid from countries within the OECD. The larger the winning coalition of an OECD country, the more likely it is to give aid (point 1). Controlling for poverty and need, the larger the winning coalition of a country (i.e., the more democratic it is), the *less* likely it is to receive aid (point 2). Conditional on receiving an aid package, large winning coalition countries receive a larger number of dollars (point 3).

The empirical findings in Bueno de Mesquita and Smith (2007, 2009) are certainly not slam-dunk convincing. In particular, they do little to isolate causal relationships in the data and one could certainly tell other stories for some of the findings. That said, the theory yields some subtle and counterintuitive implications that seem to be borne out in the data. Further, there is other evidence, less directly tied to this particular theory, but more convincing causally, that also suggests politics play an important role in determining foreign aid policy. In perhaps the most important such study, Kuziemko and Werker (2006) uncover political motivations in foreign aid by exploiting a natural experiment in the value of the concessions a recipient country can offer a donor. The variation comes from the interaction of two sources—rotating membership of the non-permanent members of the United Nations Security Council and variation in the importance of the issues facing the security council in any given year. The idea is that a vote on the security council (which might be bought with a foreign aid package) is of greater value when there are high-stakes issues before the council. And, indeed, Kuziemko and Werker find that countries receive more foreign aid when they have a vote on the security council in high-stakes years, suggesting that foreign aid is being used, at least in part, to buy votes in the United Nations.

Having looked at a bit of evidence, let's now turn to the implications of this theory for social welfare.

Start by asking who benefits from aid-for-policy deals, on this political economy account. Clearly, the leaders of both country A and country B benefit. If they didn't, they wouldn't agree to the deal in the first place. The donor country's leader benefits because she gets a policy concession that is worth more to her than are the resources spent on foreign aid. The recipient country's leader benefits because she gets resources that are more valuable to her (presumably for providing private goods for herself and her coalition partners) than the lost public goods associated with the policy concessions. Finally, the citizens of the donor country also benefit from the aid-for-policy deal. The citizens of that country (which typically has a large winning coalition) have a leader who is concerned with providing public goods. That leader was willing to make the deal precisely because the public goods associated with the recipient country's policy concessions were more valuable than whatever public goods could have been purchased with the aid money.

Only one group, on this account, is hurt by the aid-for-policy deal—the citizens of the recipient country! Remember, a key prediction of the political economy model of aid is that aid flows primarily to dictators, since they are relatively inexpensive to buy off. The citizens of recipient countries, thus, typically have leaders who are not motivated to pursue good policy, but rather to provide private goods to a small group of critical supporters (precisely as Deaton and Easterly both note). Hence, aid-for-policy deals result both in costly policy concessions and resources flowing to dictatorial leaders who use those resources to stay in office. Both of these make the citizens of aid recipient countries worse off.

You may have thought Easterly's take on foreign aid was discouraging. But the political economy view is even more so. It suggests that rich governments may be giving aid to dictatorial governments, not because they don't understand how to use aid properly, but because they are using aid as a political tool. The leaders of democratic countries have incentives to improve the welfare of *their* citizens, since it is their citizens who keep them in office. They do not have clear incentives to improve the welfare of citizens of other countries. Hence, they use foreign aid as a tool to buy policy concessions. And because dictatorial leaders are cheaper to buy off than are democratic leaders, foreign aid resources flow to dictators, actually hurting the citizens of the country receiving aid.

I tell you this story not to induce despair, but because it lets us end on an absolutely critical point for thinking about politics and policymaking. If you want to understand and lead policy debates, politics matter. It will not do to come in with some first-best (or even second-best) theory of policy interventions and assume that, once you explain it to them, politicians will do the optimal thing. Politicians and other policymakers are embedded within strategic environments and are driven by their own interests and incentives. If you want to move policy in some direction, you must take those political constraints seriously in selecting your goals, in deciding for what policies to advocate, and in formulating a strategy for getting your ideas implemented.

11.4 Takeaways

- Different political institutions create different incentives for political leaders. Leaders have incentives to pursue policies that benefit the people on whom they depend to remain in power.
- Institutions that make leaders' hold on power contingent on the support of a small group make bad policy good politics. Institutions that make leaders' hold on power contingent on the support of large groups of citizens make good policy good politics.
- The fact that a leader has incentives to provide good policy for her own citizens does not mean that she has incentives to provide good policy around the globe. So, for instance, democratic leaders are willing to pursue foreign aid policies that secure policy concessions that benefit their own citizens at the expense of the citizens of the recipient country. This phenomenon is exacerbated by the fact that autocratic leaders don't depend on providing good policy to stay in power and, so, are cheaper to buy policy concessions from than are democratic leaders.

- When thinking about how to achieve policy change, or the likely effects of a policy change, it is critical to think about how the institutions of government affect the incentives of the leaders who must adopt and enforce the policies.

11.5 Further Reading

Bruce Bueno de Mesquita, Alastair Smith, Randolph M. Siverson, and James D. Morrow's *The Logic of Political Survival* is the fullest articulation of the selectorate model. Bueno de Mesquita et al. (2001) is a non-technical introduction. Daron Acemoglu and James A. Robinson's *Why Nations Fail* is an exhaustive treatment of the roll of political institutions in economic development. For a different tradition of thinking about institutions and development, see Douglass C. North and Robert P. Thomas's classic *The Rise of the Western World* and Douglass C. North, John J. Wallis, and Barry R. Weingast's *Violence and Social Orders*.

For accessible treatments of the foreign aid debate, compare Jeffrey Sachs's *The End of Poverty*, Paul Collier's *The Bottom Billion*, William Easterly's *The White Man's Burden*, and Bruce Bueno de Mesquita and Alastair Smith's *The Dictator's Handbook*. As I mentioned in the text, Qian (2015) provides an overview of empirical studies of the effects of foreign aid, focusing on the economics literature.

11.6 Exercises

1. The United States' government gives over \$1 billion per year in aid to Egypt's government. Moreover, U.S. law forbids the continued flow of aid from the United States to a country whose government has been formally found to have been overthrown by a coup. Yet, following the 2013 coup in Egypt that overthrew a democratically elected government, the White House stated:

   > The law does not require us to make a formal determination as to whether a coup took place, and it is not in our national interest to make such a determination.

   Give an account of this policy decision based on the selectorate model.

2. Historically, when a democracy defeats another country in war and has the opportunity to set up a new government in that country, the victorious democracy rarely sets up a democratic government in the defeated country. (The Marshall Plan is a famous exception.) It is much more common for the victorious democracy to set up some form of autocracy in the defeated country.

(a) From the perspective of the selectorate model, why might this be?

(b) Suggest some way that a citizen of a democracy who was interested in spreading democracy to other countries might work to encourage his/her government to behave differently after war.

3.   Recall from the analysis of the selectorate model that total spending by the leader is

$$\Delta^* = W \left(\frac{R}{S} + \ln \frac{S}{W} \right).$$

If we differentiate this with respect to the size of the selectorate, we get

$$\frac{d\Delta^*}{dS} = \frac{W(S-R)}{S^2},$$

which is negative since $R > S$. This implies that, holding fixed the size of the winning coalition, the leader is better off with a larger selectorate.

(a) Give an intuition for why this is the case.

(b) What does this imply about how we should expect to see non-democratic leaders shape their political institutions?

4.   Even though only the members of the leader's winning coalition are relevant to her decision making, the leader in the selectorate model nonetheless provides some public goods.

(a) Why is this the case?

(b) This suggests that better policy outcomes could be achieved by increasing the importance of public goods to members of the winning coalition (even without changing their importance to citizens in general). Identify two policies that outside forces could pursue that might have this effect.

(c) The amount of public goods the leader provides is decreasing in p, the price of public goods. Identify two policies outside forces might pursue that would decrease p.

Summing Up Constraints on Good Governance

In Part III we've seen that we should not expect the government to function as a Pareto improving machine. Indeed, this is precisely why we need to study the political economy of public policy. If the government were simply in the business of identifying and implementing second-best policy interventions, politics wouldn't much matter for policy.

We examined two types of governance constraints. First, we considered technological constraints—limits on the ability of even a benevolent government to implement optimal policy. These include the ability of the governed to adapt their behavior to avoid policy interventions, commitment problems and other dynamic constraints inside government, and lack of information. We can think of the government's limited ability to overcome each of these challenges as another set of second-best constraints that affect the extent to which policy can improve social welfare.

Next we considered incentive constraints—facts about the institutions of government that shape the kinds of policies that are in policymakers' interests to pursue. We focused on incentives that come from policymakers' desire to maintain power. These include incentives derived from the electoral process—such as the incentive to target responsive voters, the need to raise money, and the accountability relationship. Our analysis highlighted features of the electoral environment that improve both incentives and selection, but also showed that there are sometimes trade-offs and risks of perverse effects (e.g., strengthening incentives can lead to pandering). Finally, we considered a more general model of incentives in democratic and autocratic regimes. Broadly speaking, in institutions where leaders require the support of a large number of citizens to retain power, good policy is good politics. But in institutions where leaders' hold on power depends on a small number of supporters, good policy is bad politics. By taking this model into the realm of foreign aid we saw how the interaction of leaders who themselves face different types of domestic constituencies make these politics, and their welfare implications, even more complex.

I purposefully did not provide an in-depth treatment of particular governance institutions—the legislature, courts, bureaucracy, executive, central bank, and so on. Such institutions also shape incentives and impose important constraints. Understanding these institutions is essential. But, as I stated at the outset, I have tried to focus on high level technological and incentive problems. The particulars of institutional incentives is a big topic, best left to a book dedicated to that topic.

Concluding Reflections on Politics and Policy

In the event that you haven't been paying attention, this book has, broadly speaking, attempted to convey three messages. In Part I we explored the normative foundations of policy, discovering how difficult it is to say anything conclusive about what good public policy is. In Part II we developed models to learn about some fundamental dilemmas of social life. We found that if we are willing to embrace a weak form of consequentialism—defining a good policy change as one that makes some people better off and no one worse off—then externalities, coordination problems, and commitment problems all create opportunities for a variety of policies to do a lot of good. Finally, in Part III we started to take seriously the politics of policymaking. Governments are not Pareto improving machines. Policies are made by individuals with their own beliefs, interests, and goals operating in highly constrained and strategic political environments. For reasons having to do with fundamental technological constraints and the incentives created by the institutions of government and the desire for power, sometimes policymakers take actions that benefit society and sometimes they take actions that do not benefit society. Often, whether a policy is a good idea—in the sense of addressing a social dilemma—is neither here nor there with respect to whether that policy will be pursued or implemented.

The realization that policymaking is so fundamentally political can sit uncomfortably with the traditions of policy analysis and policy education, which tend to focus on technocratic concerns such as cost-benefit analysis, program evaluation, and public administration. Once we accept that the merits of a policy are, at best, but one input into the highly political policymaking process we are left wondering, what role is there for traditional policy analysis? And are traditional approaches likely to lead to good outcomes?

These questions can be unsettling. After all, if policymaking is all about politics, and politics follows its own strategic logic revolving around the pursuit of power, what is the point of spending all this effort trying to understand and articulate good policies? Why did we bother with Part II? We could have jumped right from Chapter 1 (there is no such thing as good policy) straight to Chapter 11 (policymakers don't really care about doing good anyway) and been done with it. As the economist Dani Rodrik put it in an influential and thoughtful essay, "If politicians' behavior is determined by the vested interests to which they are beholden, economists' advocacy of policy reforms is bound to fall on deaf ears. The more complete our social science, the more irrelevant our policy analysis."[1] I want to conclude with just a few thoughts on these issues.

There are, of course, important roles for traditional policy analysis. Let me suggest two.

First, in plenty of settings, politicians want to pursue something at least approximating an optimal policy. In such happy circumstances, when leaders' incentives and the principles of good policymaking coincide, policymakers are in need of technocratic advice of the sort traditional policy analysis provides.

Second, ideas themselves are powerful. It is important for informed people to shout good policy ideas from the mountain tops, even if they often fall on the deaf ears of political leaders. At least some of the time, good ideas change minds. If enough people come to believe in a particular idea, political incentives can shift. Who knows, in another couple of generations, we might yet see politicians embrace fighting global warming through a carbon tax or paying for a sustained effort to avoid asteroid-induced mass extinction.

All of that said, my own view is that, if you want to lead policy change (whether from within government or from without), depressing though it may be, it is almost always a mistake to embrace traditional policy analysis while ignoring the politics of the policymaking process. There is a dangerous tendency to think of the second-best policy as the optimal policy given all the constraints except those that come from the policymaking process itself. But politics are a fundamental constraint on what policy outcomes are possible. The real second best is the optimal policy, *given all the constraints*—technological, informational, economic, and political.

We need some idealists fighting for good, if perhaps infeasible, ideas. But we also need practical policymakers and policy entrepreneurs, willing to rigorously think through what can actually be achieved and how to achieve it. This kind of thoroughgoing policy analysis requires not only understanding what problems need addressing and what policies might work to address them. It requires taking seriously political constraints that can fundamentally change our notion of good policy.

Often what seems the second-best policy is not politically feasible. As we discussed at the very outset of this book, absent political considerations, a carbon tax coupled with an offsetting reduction in some other distortionary tax seems an obvious, Pareto improving response to global warming. But once we consider the need for a policy reform to have a coalition of political support, both in the short and long run, a cap-and-trade system without a revenue generating auction may be preferable. The fact that the benefits of increased efficiency are left with the regulated firms (a concentrated interest), rather than

---

[1]Dani Rodrik. "The Tyranny of Political Economy," *Project Syndicate*, February 8, 2013. http://www.project-syndicate.org/commentary/how-economists-killed-policy-analysis-by-dani-rodrik

transferred to the diffuse citizenry, may make cap-and-trade more politically feasible than a carbon tax in the short run, since the regulated firms have a reason to support reform. Moreover, a cap-and-trade system creates a natural constituency for the long-run sustainability of reform in at least two ways. First, firms that reduce emissions below the amount allowed by their permits can bank the surplus for future use or sale. Firms with a significant amount of carbon permits banked would strongly oppose any attempt to undo reform, since such regulatory rollback would reduce the value of their banked assets. Second, the presence of a market gives a new set of previously irrelevant actors an interest in the sustainability of the reform—financial services companies and others involved with the actual operation of the market. For both of these reasons, cap-and-trade creates a natural coalition to ensure long-run viability (recall our discussion of dynamic consistency). A carbon tax, by contrast, has no natural constituency beyond environmentalists, making it vulnerable to repeal by policymakers looking to score political points through tax cutting.

Policies, even once put into law, are implemented and enforced by political actors whose incentives can distort the policy in myriad ways. These incentives must also be taken into consideration when evaluating the likely effects of a policy. Failure to do so can lead one to support policies that end up having little, or even deleterious, effects. We saw an example of this in our discussion of foreign aid. That analysis suggested that advocates for increased foreign aid may be doing more harm than good for the world's poor. Foreign aid, if implemented properly, might well address poverty traps or, at least, relieve intense misery. But political leaders, following their political incentives, may use foreign aid in a way that systematically harms aid recipients—propping up autocratic leaders who pursue policies that hurt their own people but help the donor nations.

Finally, the study of political economy opens up the possibility of a whole new set of policy concerns. Political incentives and political institutions are themselves key determinants of whether leaders make and enforce good policies. Hence, the design and adoption of political institutions that give leaders good incentives is a fundamental policy issue in its own right, one with which anyone concerned with good governance and good policy must grapple.

Understanding politics, then, is essential to understanding policy. Politics is a central determinant of the types of policies that can and do get implemented. Frustrating and limiting as it may seem at times to talk about politics when you want to talk about policy solutions, no thoroughgoing analysis of public policy can ignore something so fundamental. It is my hope that the tools in this book will help you bring the insights of political economy to bear on your own policy concerns. It is my belief that doing so will lead to a more rigorous and realistic analysis and, ultimately, more effective policy responses to society's woes.

PART IV

Appendices on Game Theory

A

Utility, Strategic-Form Games, and Nash Equilibrium

A rational person in a supermarket deciding what kind of bread to buy has a pretty easy problem. She has preferences over the different breads, over money spent, and so on. All she has to do is think about some simple trade-offs (perhaps one type of bread is more delicious than another, but also costs more) and buy the bread that she most prefers, given the prices. This is a classic, non-strategic, rational choice problem. It is not strategic because the outcome for the decision maker (what bread she gets, how much she spends) does not depend on the behavior of anyone but herself. It is a rational choice problem because she has rational preferences and acts based on them.

Much of what is interesting about the social world is not like buying a loaf of bread. Most interesting situations are situations of *strategic interdependence*. That is, situations in which the outcome for one person depends not only on her own behavior, but also on the behavior of others.

Understanding such strategic interdependence is critical for identifying opportunities for public policy to do good in the world. It is also essential for understanding some of the challenges that limit the extent to which policy-makers do so. Unfortunately, analyzing situations of strategic interdependence can be complicated because a person's actions may depend on what she believes others will do. Game theory is the mathematical tool that we use to structure our thinking about such situations. It is used extensively throughout this book.

Game theory is a powerful and flexible tool that can be used to study quite complicated strategic environments—environments with many players, asymmetric access to information, a variety of kinds of uncertainty, and so on. Our goal, however, is not to learn game theory for game theory's sake. Rather, our purpose is to learn just enough game theory to grasp the social dilemmas and governance challenges that are the core substantive concerns of this book. So these appendices are limited to two relatively simple classes of games, which will be sufficient for our purposes.

Before we get to game theory, however, we need to say a little bit more about our model of rational decision makers.

A.1 Utility

In Chapter 2 I describe a rational person as someone whose preferences are complete and transitive. For now, let's stick with that.

Preferences are a bit unwieldy to work with, if only because you have to constantly write this symbol, $\succ$. Happily, it turns out that the preferences of a rational individual can be represented in a much more user-friendly way, with numbers.

Suppose a person has rational preferences over a set of alternatives, A. That means the person can take all the alternatives in A and line them up in order of preference (there might be some stacks, representing indifference). Suppose we line them up from least preferred to most preferred. If we then assign each alternative a number in ascending order (giving the same number to all alternatives in an indifference stack), we have constructed a *utility function*.

Person i's utility function is any function that assigns a number to each alternative and satisfies the following condition: person i's utility from alternative x is greater than her utility from alternative y if and only if $x \succ_i y$ and her utility from alternative x is equal to her utility from alternative y if and only if $x \sim_i y$. Utility functions are useful because it is easier to work with numbers than it is to work with preference relations. Typically, we will write person i's utility from alternative x as $u_i(x)$, which, again, is just a number.

One point is worth noting. There are many utility functions that represent a given preference. If i prefers x to y, then this utility function represents that preference:

$$u_i(x) = 10 \quad u_i(y) = 1$$

and so does this utility function:

$$u_i(x) = 1{,}000{,}000 \quad u_i(y) = -132.42323.$$

This is because, as we've defined them thus far, all the information a utility function communicates is ordinal (about the order of preference) not cardinal (about the magnitude of preference). Importantly, this means that the notion of utility that we've used to define rationality is fundamentally different from the notion of utility that underlies utilitarianism—for utilitarianism to make sense, utilities need to be comparable across individuals (i.e., need to be on a common scale), whereas even within an individual's preferences, let alone across individuals, the scale is meaningless for our ordinal notion of utility.

A.1.1 Expected Utility

Sometimes we want to be able to think about the preferences of rational people who face some uncertainty. (We talk about this in our discussion of preferences behind the veil of ignorance in Chapter 1.) Consider, for example, a rational person deciding whether or not to carry an umbrella without knowing for certain whether it is going to rain. Such a person faces four possible outcomes:

1. No Umbrella, No Rain (*NN*)
2. Umbrella, No Rain (*UN*)
3. No Umbrella, Rain (*NR*)
4. Umbrella, Rain (*UR*)

Presumably it is unpleasant to get wet and also a little annoying to carry an umbrella around. So, if such a person knew it wasn't going to rain, she would not carry an umbrella. And if she knew it was going to rain, she would carry an umbrella (assuming getting wet is more annoying than carrying an umbrella). But she doesn't know whether or not it will rain. All she knows is the probability it is going to rain according to the weather report. We need a way to model how she uses her information about the probability of rain and her preferences over these four possible outcomes to make a decision.

Our standard utility functions, unfortunately, are not up to the task of addressing this issue. That is because, in order to answer questions like "how high does the probability of rain need to be for me to be willing to carry an umbrella?" we need some information about the cardinality of my preferences—how intensely do I dislike being wet relative to my annoyance at carrying an umbrella?

To think about such choices, we model a decision maker choosing between alternatives that are themselves *lotteries*. A lottery is a probability distribution over various possible outcomes. For instance, suppose the probability of rain is p. Then a decision maker choosing whether or not to carry an umbrella is choosing between the following two lotteries:

Lottery 1 (don't carry an umbrella): "No Umbrella and Rain" with probability p and "No Umbrella and No Rain" with probability $1 - p$.

Lottery 2 (carry an umbrella): "Umbrella and Rain" with probability p and "Umbrella and No Rain" with probability $1 - p$.

In order to deal with preferences over lotteries, we need people's preferences to have a little more structure than just being complete and transitive. In particular, suppose their preferences satisfy two additional requirements:

1. **Continuity:** Suppose there are three lotteries $\mathcal{L}_1, \mathcal{L}_2,$ and $\mathcal{L}_3$ such that person i has preferences

$$\mathcal{L}_1 \succ_i \mathcal{L}_2 \succ_i \mathcal{L}_3.$$

Then there exists a probability p such that person i is indifferent between lottery $\mathcal{L}_2$ and a new lottery that gives lottery $\mathcal{L}_1$ with probability p and lottery $\mathcal{L}_3$ with probability $1 - p$.

2. **Independence:** Suppose there are three lotteries $\mathcal{L}_1, \mathcal{L}_2$, and $\mathcal{L}_3$ and person i has preference

$$\mathcal{L}_1 \succ_i \mathcal{L}_2.$$

Then for any probability p, person i prefers a new lottery that gives lottery $\mathcal{L}_1$ with probability p and lottery $\mathcal{L}_3$ with probability $1 - p$ to a new lottery that gives lottery $\mathcal{L}_2$ with probability p and lottery $\mathcal{L}_3$ with probability $1 - p$.

I'm not going to go into technicalities, but it turns out that if preferences over lotteries are complete, transitive, continuous, and independent, then preferences can be described by a *von Neumann-Morgenstern (vnm) utility function*, which has the following property. For each possible outcome, the vnm utility function assigns a number, just like a normal utility function. If you want to know whether a person prefers one lottery to another, you compare their *expected utilities*. You find a person's expected utility for a lottery by multiplying the utility associated with each outcome by the probability of that outcome occurring, and then summing.

Let's go back to our rain example and assume some person, i, has preferences described by the following vnm utility function:

$$u_i(NN) = 9 \quad u_i(UN) = 6 \quad u_i(NR) = 0 \quad u_i(UR) = 3.$$

Suppose the probability of rain is $\frac{1}{3}$. If person i carries an umbrella she faces the following lottery: the outcome is UN with probability $\frac{2}{3}$ and the outcome is UR with probability $\frac{1}{3}$. So her expected utility from carrying an umbrella, given that the probability of rain is $\frac{1}{3}$, is

$$EU_i\left(\text{Umbrella}|\frac{1}{3}\right) = \frac{2}{3} \times 6 + \frac{1}{3} \times 3 = 5.$$

If she chooses not to carry an umbrella, she faces the following lottery: the outcome is NN with probability $\frac{2}{3}$ and the outcome is NR with probability $\frac{1}{3}$. So her expected utility from not carrying an umbrella, given that the probability of rain is $\frac{1}{3}$, is

$$EU_i\left(\text{No Umbrella}|\frac{1}{3}\right) = \frac{2}{3} \times 9 + \frac{1}{3} \times 0 = 6.$$

Given that the probability of rain is $\frac{1}{3}$, person i prefers not to carry an umbrella, since an expected utility of 6 is greater than an expected utility of 5.

Notice, we can also now ask the more general question, "how high must the probability of rain be in order for person i to carry an umbrella?" To answer this question, we solve for the probability of rain that makes the expected utility of carrying an umbrella higher than the expected utility of not carrying an umbrella. Suppose the probability of rain is some number p between 0 and 1. This implies the probability of no rain is $1 - p$. Given this, person i's expected utility of carrying an umbrella is

$$EU_i\left(\text{Umbrella}|p\right) = (1 - p) \times 6 + p \times 3 = 6 - 3p.$$

(Notice, for $p = \frac{1}{3}$, this equals 5, as we found above.) Her expected utility from not carrying an umbrella is

$$EU_i\left(\text{No Umbrella}|p\right) = (1 - p) \times 9 + p \times 0 = 9 - 9p.$$

(Again, for $p = \frac{1}{3}$ this equals 6, as we found above.)

Person i prefers to carry an umbrella if and only if the expected utility of carrying an umbrella is greater than the expected utility of not carrying an umbrella, given that it rains with probability p:

$$6 - 3p > 9 - 9p.$$

Rearranging, this holds if $p > \frac{1}{2}$. So, in this particular case, person i prefers to carry an umbrella if the probability of rain is greater than one-half.

There is nothing special about a probability of rain equal to one-half. That just happened to be the threshold for carrying an umbrella in this example. Suppose, for instance, that another person, j, has a vnm utility function given by

$$u_j(NN) = 12 \quad u_j(UN) = 6 \quad u_j(NR) = 0 \quad u_j(UR) = 3.$$

Person j's expected utility from carrying an umbrella, given a probability of rain p, is

$$EU_j\left(\text{Umbrella}|p\right) = (1 - p) \times 6 + p \times 3 = 6 - 3p.$$

Person j's expected utility from not carrying an umbrella is

$$EU_j\left(\text{No Umbrella}|p\right) = (1 - p) \times 12 + p \times 0 = 12 - 12p.$$

So person j prefers to carry an umbrella if

$$6 - 3p > 12 - 12p.$$

Rearranging, this holds if $p > \frac{2}{3}$. Person j, who really values not carrying an umbrella on sunny days, only carries an umbrella if he believes the probability of rain is at least two-thirds.

It is worth noting that a vnm utility function does let us compare the relative value of alternatives within an individual's preferences. That is, it lets us make statements like, "I care more about avoiding getting wet than about the annoyance of carrying an umbrella." But even this isn't strong enough to provide a foundation for utilitarianism. For that, we need to be able to compare strength of preference across people. That is why we rely on quasi-linearity for much of the book.

A.2   Games in Strategic Form

Now that we have a technology for modeling payoffs let's turn to game theory. We will start by focusing on games in *strategic form*. Such games are described by three components:

1. **Players:** The collection of people playing the game.
2. **Strategies:** For each player, a list of things that player can do in the game.
   - We will call a collection (or, more correctly, a profile) of strategies—one for each player—an *outcome* of the game. The idea is, if you know how everyone will play, you know what will happen in the game.
3. **Payoffs:** A description of each player's preferences over the set of possible outcomes.

It will help to look at some examples.

A.2.1 Where to Eat?

Suppose a married couple, Ethan and Rebecca, are deciding where to eat. They have two options: a delicious pork restaurant or a not-so-delicious vegetarian restaurant. Sadly, they are both coming straight from work and their cell phones are dead, so they can't talk. Each must simply go to a restaurant and hope the other has chosen the same place.

A strategy for each player is simply a choice of restaurant. Thus, the strategies available to each player are *pork* (P) or *vegetarian* (V). An outcome of the game is a strategy profile (one strategy for each player). Let's write a strategy profile as a pair, with Ethan's strategy first. There are four possible outcomes of this game: (P, P), (P, V), (V, P), and (V, V).

		Rebecca	
		P	*V*
Ethan	*P*	4, 3	1, 1
	V	0, 0	3, 4

Figure A.1. Where to eat?

		Kid 2	
		H	*T*
Kid 1	*H*	1, –1	–1, 1
	T	–1, 1	1, –1

Figure A.2. Matching pennies.

The last thing we need to describe our game is payoffs. As it turns out, Ethan loves pork. Rebecca, being a rabbi, prefers to eat vegetarian. However, they love each other, so the most important thing to each of them is to eat together. Their payoffs are given by the following vnm utility functions:

$$u_E(P,P) = 4 \quad u_E(P,V) = 1 \quad u_E(V,P) = 0 \quad u_E(V,V) = 3$$

$$u_R(P,P) = 3 \quad u_R(P,V) = 1 \quad u_R(V,P) = 0 \quad u_R(V,V) = 4$$

These payoffs reflect two things. Each player prefers to go to his or her less-preferred restaurant with the other than to go to his or her more-preferred restaurant alone. That said, conditional on both being together, Ethan would prefer they were eating pork and Rebecca would prefer they were eating vegetarian. And, conditional on eating separately, they agree that Ethan should eat pork and Rebecca should eat vegetarian.

It is sometimes useful to represent a simple game like this as a matrix. In Figure A.1, Ethan's strategies are the rows and Rebecca's strategies are the columns. The payoffs in each cell represent Ethan's and Rebecca's payoffs (with the row player's always written first) from the outcome associated with that cell's strategy profile.

A.2.2 Matching Pennies

There are two kids, 1 and 2. Each has a penny. Simultaneously, each kid shows heads (H) or tails (T). If the pennies match, kid 1 wins and gets to keep both pennies. If the pennies don't match, kid 2 wins and gets to keep both pennies. Each kid cares only about money. This game is represented in the matrix in Figure A.2.

A.2.3 Cleaning an Apartment

There are two roommates, 1 and 2. They must each decide how hard to work on cleaning up their apartment. Each will choose a level of work. Call Player i's level of work s_i and assume that s_i is chosen from the set of real numbers greater than or equal to zero. The total cleanliness of the apartment is

$$\pi(s_1, s_2) = s_1 + s_2 + \frac{s_1 \times s_2}{2}.$$

This says that the harder each works, the cleaner the apartment will be. Moreover, the third term $(s_1 \times s_2/2)$ indicates that the harder Player 1 works, the more effective Player 2's effort and vice versa.

To see this last point, suppose $s_1 = 1$. If Player 2 increases her effort from 1 to 2, total cleanliness goes from

$$\pi(1, 1) = 1 + 1 + \frac{1 \times 1}{2} = 2.5$$

to

$$\pi(1, 2) = 1 + 2 + \frac{1 \times 2}{2} = 4.$$

So, when $s_1 = 1$, an increase in effort by Player 2 from 1 to 2 increases cleanliness by $4 - 2.5 = 1.5$.

Now suppose $s_1 = 2$. If Player 2 increases her effort from 1 to 2, total cleanliness goes from

$$\pi(2, 1) = 2 + 1 + \frac{2 \times 1}{2} = 4$$

to

$$\pi(2, 2) = 2 + 2 + \frac{2 \times 2}{2} = 6.$$

Here an increase in effort by Player 2 from 1 to 2 increases cleanliness by $6 - 4 = 2$. Player 2's increase in effort makes more of a difference for total cleanliness when Player 1 is working harder. We refer to situations like this as Player 1's effort and Player 2's effort being *complements*.

Players enjoy a clean apartment. However, the players also suffer costs for their individual effort. To capture these costs in a simple model, let's assume that if Player i works s_i, she suffers costs s_i^2.

Given all this, Player 1's payoff from an outcome (s_1, s_2) is

$$u_1(s_1, s_2) = \pi(s_1, s_2) - (s_1)^2 = s_1 + s_2 + \frac{s_1 \times s_2}{2} - (s_1)^2$$

and Player 2's payoff is

$$u_2(s_1, s_2) = \pi(s_1, s_2) - (s_2)^2 = s_1 + s_2 + \frac{s_1 \times s_2}{2} - (s_2)^2.$$

There are an infinite number of outcomes in this game, so we can't represent it in a matrix. Nonetheless, it is a perfectly well-specified game that we might want to analyze.

A.2.4 Choosing a Number

There are two players who have \$10 to split. Each bids a number between 0 and 10, inclusive. Call Player 1's bid s_1 and Player 2's bid s_2. If the two bids sum to 10 or less (i.e., $s_1 + s_2 \leq 10$), then each player receives his or her bid. If the two bids sum to more than 10, then each player receives nothing. Each player cares only about his or her individual, monetary payoffs.

Player 1's payoff from any outcome (s_1, s_2) is

$$u_1(s_1, s_2) = \begin{cases} s_1 & \text{if } s_1 + s_2 \leq 10 \\ 0 & \text{if } s_1 + s_2 > 10. \end{cases}$$

Player 2's payoff from any outcome (s_1, s_2) is

$$u_2(s_1, s_2) = \begin{cases} s_2 & \text{if } s_1 + s_2 \leq 10 \\ 0 & \text{if } s_1 + s_2 > 10. \end{cases}$$

Again, this game has an infinity of possible outcomes, so we cannot represent it in a matrix.

A.3 Nash Equilibrium

Situations of strategic interdependence are complicated—for both the players and the analyst. In this section, we develop the main tool we use for figuring out what might happen in such situations: *Nash equilibrium.*

Recall that a strategy profile is a collection of strategies, one for each player in the game. A Nash equilibrium is a strategy profile that meets a particular condition. I'm going to start by telling you the condition and what it means. Later we'll turn to the question of why you should care about or believe in Nash equilibrium as a prediction of what will happen in a game. But first things first, let's define a Nash equilibrium.

Intuitively, a strategy profile is a Nash equilibrium if no individual has a *unilateral* incentive to change her behavior. What does that mean? A strategy profile lists what each player will do in the game. The profile is a Nash equilibrium if each individual is taking an action that leads to an outcome that is as good for her as possible, holding all other players' behavior fixed. Now let's be a little more formal.

- Suppose our game has N players.
- The set of all possible strategies for a Player i is S_i.
- A particular strategy for Player i is $s_i \in S_i$.
- A strategy profile, $(s_1, s_2, \ldots, s_N)$, is a list of strategies, one for each player. We will sometimes notate this strategy profile as $\mathbf{s}$, where $\mathbf{s} = (s_1, s_2, \ldots, s_N)$.
- We will sometimes want to be able to talk about the list of strategies for everyone but some Player i. We will notate this reduced profile as $\mathbf{s}_{-i} = (s_1, \ldots, s_{i-1}, s_{i+1}, \ldots, s_N)$.
- We will often, then, reconstruct the full profile by combining the reduced profile and the missing player's strategy, writing $\mathbf{s} = (s_i, \mathbf{s}_{-i})$.
- Player i's utility (or payoff) from the strategy profile $\mathbf{s} = (s_1, s_2, \ldots, s_N)$ is $u_i(\mathbf{s})$.

To make this notation clearer, let's do an example.

EXAMPLE A.3.1 (BIDDING FOR $10 WITH 3 PLAYERS)

Consider a game with three players. Each gets to name a real number from 0 to 10. Call the number a player chooses her *bid*. If the three bids sum to 10 or less, each player gets a dollar amount equal to her bid. If the three bids sum to more than 10, each player gets nothing. Each player has utility equal to the money she receives.

We can apply the notation above to this game.

- There are three players, so $N = 3$.
- For any player, i, the set of strategies is $S_i = [0, 10]$; that is, the real numbers from 0 to 10.
- A particular strategy for a Player i is just one of these real numbers.
- A strategy profile takes the form of three numbers, a bid by Player 1, a bid by Player 2, and a bid by Player 3. For instance, $\mathbf{s} = (1, 4, 7)$ is a strategy profile.
- We could also consider that strategy profile without Player 2's strategy. Then we would have $\mathbf{s}_{-2} = (1, 7)$. Similarly, that strategy profile without Player 1's strategy is $\mathbf{s}_{-1} = (4, 7)$ and without Player 3's strategy is $\mathbf{s}_{-3} = (1, 4)$.
- We can reconstruct the full profile by saying $\mathbf{s} = (s_2, \mathbf{s}_{-2}) = (4, (1, 7))$.

(Continued on next page)

- Player i's utility from an outcome $\mathbf{s} = (s_1, s_2, s_3)$ is

$$u_i(\mathbf{s}) = \begin{cases} s_i & \text{if } s_1 + s_2 + s_3 \leq 10 \\ 0 & \text{if } s_1 + s_2 + s_3 > 10. \end{cases}$$

Having established this notation, we can now formally define Nash equilibrium.

Definition A.3.1. Consider a game with N players. A strategy profile $\mathbf{s}^* = (s_1^*, s_2^*, \ldots, s_N^*)$ is a **Nash equilibrium** of the game if, for every player i,

$$u_i(s_i^*, \mathbf{s}_{-i}^*) \geq u_i(s_i', \mathbf{s}_{-i}^*)$$

for all $s_i' \in S_i$.

This formalizes the intuitive definition I gave above. A strategy profile gives a strategy for each player: $(s_1^*, s_2^*, \ldots, s_N^*)$. This profile is a Nash equilibrium if every player, i, wants to play s_i^*, assuming everyone else plays according to the strategy in $\mathbf{s}^*$. That is, no player has a unilateral incentive to change her behavior.

As a quick aside, it is worth noting that we have actually defined what is called a "pure strategy Nash equilibrium." The phrase "pure strategy" refers to the idea that players take some action for certain—they don't randomize among various strategies. For instance, in the bidding game, each player chooses one real number. We don't consider the possibility that a player might use a strategy like "flip a coin and bid 2 if it comes up heads and bid 7 if it comes up tails." (Such a strategy, constructed by playing some pure strategy with some probability and another pure strategy with some probability, is called a "mixed strategy.") Since we only study pure strategy Nash equilibria in this book, I don't qualify the term Nash equilibrium with the phrase "pure strategy," though if you go on to study more game theory, you will see that terminology.

A.4   Why Nash Equilibrium?

There are several reasons that Nash equilibrium is an appealing prediction for how people will behave in strategic situations. Let me suggest a few.

A.4.1 No Regrets and Social Learning

Perhaps the most appealing feature of Nash equilibrium is that it satisfies a sort of "no regrets" criterion. Suppose players use strategies that are part of a Nash equilibrium. Then no player looks at the outcome of the game and believes she made a mistake or wishes she had done something different.

This is an important and appealing stability property. Imagine a group of players playing a game in the same society over time. Suppose the players start at some random strategy profile and then adjust their behavior according to a simple social learning procedure. For instance, suppose at some iteration, t, each player chooses the behavior that would have made her best off in the previous iteration, $t - 1$, given what all the other players did in iteration $t - 1$. That is, she naively chooses her action today to make her payoff as high as possible, assuming no other players change their behavior from yesterday. If players find themselves, at some point, at a Nash equilibrium, no individual has an incentive to change her behavior in the next iteration or any iteration thereafter. By the definition of a Nash equilibrium, every individual is maximizing her payoff, given what everyone else did. Hence, under this kind of social learning story, once the people in a society find themselves playing a Nash equilibrium in a particular game, they will keep playing it forever. It is a stable, or self-reinforcing, pattern of behavior.

Relatedly, if some strategy profile is not a Nash equilibrium, then at least one player is making a mistake, given what everyone else is doing. Such a person will therefore change her behavior in the next iteration—that is, the non-Nash profile is not stable. Now, nothing guarantees that a process of adjustment like this will lead to a Nash equilibrium. This kind of social learning process may remain unstable forever—with people adjusting their behavior in every iteration. But if behavior ever does settle down to something stable, that stable behavior will be a Nash equilibrium.

A.4.2 Self-Enforcing Agreements

Another appealing feature is that you can think of a Nash equilibrium as a self-enforcing agreement. Suppose you and I are in some interaction with one another. We want to reach a deal about how we will behave, but we cannot write a binding contract that will be enforced by a court. For instance, suppose you are my research assistant. I am deciding whether to write you a good letter of recommendation, and you are deciding whether to work hard on my research project. In such a situation, all you and I can do is make an agreement and hope that the other person honors it. If you agree to work hard in exchange for a good letter and then I write you a bad letter, there is nothing you can do. Similarly, if I write you a good letter in exchange for hard work, and then you shirk, there is nothing I can do.

We can describe the interaction over which we are trying to make an agreement as a game. It might look something like the situation modeled in Figure A.3 (though I hope not).

		RA	
		Work hard	Shirk
Professor	Good letter	4, 3	0, 4
	Bad letter	3, 1	1, 2

Figure A.3. Professor and research assistant game.

In such a situation, any agreement that you and I will find credible must be *self-enforcing*—that is, each of us must individually want to honor the agreement. What is a self-enforcing agreement that we would all actually honor upon playing this game? It is a Nash equilibrium. If we agree to play a Nash equilibrium profile, then we will actually be willing to do so, since the definition of a Nash equilibrium is that, given what you are doing, the thing I'm supposed to do is, in fact, in my interest and vice versa. If, however, we try to agree to play a profile that is not a Nash equilibrium, it is not self-enforcing. At a profile that is not a Nash equilibrium, at least one of us has an incentive to change behavior.

A.4.3 Analyst's Humility

Finally, for an analyst, there is one more reason to like Nash equilibrium as a prediction. Suppose you predicted the outcome of a game would be some profile that is not a Nash equilibrium. Implicitly, you would be asserting that you know things about the environment that the players themselves do not know.

Why is this? You apparently have information that supports the conclusion that a non-Nash profile will be played. The players must not have this same information. A non-Nash profile is a profile where at least one player would be better off changing behavior. Thus, if the players had your information, at least one of them would alter her behavior and your prediction would be wrong.

While it is not impossible to imagine situations where the analyst believes she knows things about the game that the players in the game don't know, as a general matter this seems a strange assumption. After all, you are just sitting around solving the game. The players are living it. Who do you think you are?

A.5 Solving for Nash Equilibrium

Okay, we've defined a Nash equilibrium and talked about why it may be the right prediction for what will happen in games. Now let's talk about how to actually find a Nash equilibrium.

The basic tool for solving for a Nash equilibrium is called a player's *best response* to the other players' strategies. A best response by Player i to a profile of strategies for all the other players is a strategy for Player i that maximizes her payoff, given what all the other players are doing.

Definition A.5.1. A strategy, s_i, is a *best response* by Player i to a profile of strategies for all the other players, $\mathbf{s}_{-i}$, if

$$u_i(s_i, \mathbf{s}_{-i}) \geq u_i(s_i', \mathbf{s}_{-i})$$

for all $s_i' \in S_i$.

Notice, there need not be a unique best response to a given profile of strategies by others. Given what everyone else is doing, Player i may have multiple strategies that are optimal. An example will help to fix ideas.

EXAMPLE A.5.1 (BIDDING OVER $10 WITH 3 PLAYERS)

Recall the game from Example A.3.1.

Consider Player 1's best response to the profile of strategies for Players 2 and 3, $(9, 9)$. In this scenario, regardless of what Player 1 bids she will get a payoff of 0. Hence, any bid is a best response for Player 1.

Now consider Player 1's best response to a profile of strategies for Players 2 and 3, $(3, 3)$. If Player 1 bids an amount of money less than or equal to 4, she gets that amount of money. If she bids an amount of money greater than 4, she gets nothing. Hence, her unique best response to $(3, 3)$ is to bid exactly 4.

We would like to be able to think about Player i's best response to any possible profile of strategies for the other players. To do this, we will think about Player i's *best response correspondence*. Player i's best response correspondence is a mapping that tells you Player i's best responses to any given profile of strategies for the other players.

Definition A.5.2. Player i's *best response correspondence*, BR_i, is a mapping from profiles of strategies for all players other than i into subsets of S_i (Player i's set of possible strategies) satisfying the following condition: For each $\mathbf{s}_{-i}$, the mapping yields a set of strategies for Player i, $\mathrm{BR}_i(\mathbf{s}_{-i})$, such that $s_i \in \mathrm{BR}_i(\mathbf{s}_{-i})$ if and only if s_i is a best response to $\mathbf{s}_{-i}$.

We've worked through these pretty unpleasant definitions because they provide us with a straightforward way to solve for Nash equilibria. A Nash equilibrium is a strategy profile, $\mathbf{s}^*$, where each Player i's strategy, s_i^*, is a best response to what the other players are doing, $\mathbf{s}_{-i}^*$. Thus, if we can figure out each player's best response correspondence, it will be easy to find Nash equilibria.

Let's do this in a bunch of examples so you can see what I'm talking about.

A.6 Nash Equilibrium Examples

In this section, we will work our way through the examples of strategic-form games from Section A.2, solving for Nash equilibria in each of them.

Rebecca

		P	V
Ethan	P	4, 3	1, 1
	V	0, 0	3, 4

Figure A.4. Where to eat?

A.6.1 Where to Eat?

Recall the game about where a married couple should eat represented in Figure A.4. Let's solve for each player's best responses. Suppose Ethan believes Rebecca will play P. Then his payoff from playing P is 4 and his payoff from playing V is 0. So he wants to play P. Now suppose Ethan believes Rebecca will play V. Then his payoff from playing P is 1 and his payoff from playing V is 3. So he wants to play V. Given this, Ethan's best response correspondence is

$$\text{BR}_E(P) = P \quad \text{BR}_E(V) = V.$$

The logic for Rebecca is the same:

$$\text{BR}_R(P) = P \quad \text{BR}_R(V) = V.$$

A Nash equilibrium in this game is a strategy profile (s_E^*, s_R^*), such that s_E^* is a best response for Ethan to s_R^* and s_R^* is a best response for Rebecca to s_E^*. There are four possible strategy profiles—(P, P), (P, V), (V, P), (V, V). Which of these is a Nash equilibrium?

First consider (P, P). If Rebecca plays P, then Ethan's best response is $\text{BR}_E(P) = P$. So Ethan is playing a best response to Rebecca's strategy. Similarly, if Ethan plays P, then Rebecca's best response is $\text{BR}_R(P) = P$. So Rebecca is playing a best response to Ethan's strategy. Thus, this profile is a Nash equilibrium.

Next consider (P, V). If Rebecca plays V, then Ethan's best response is $\text{BR}_E(V) = V$. So Ethan is not best responding to Rebecca's strategy. Thus, this profile is not a Nash equilibrium. Ethan would be better off by unilaterally changing his behavior to V. (It turns out, Rebecca would also be better off unilaterally changing her behavior.)

Next consider (V, P). This also is not a Nash equilibrium. If Rebecca is playing P, then Ethan's best response is $\text{BR}_E(P) = P$, so Ethan could make himself better off by unilaterally changing his behavior to P. (Rebecca could also unilaterally make herself better off.)

Finally, consider (V, V). If Rebecca plays V, then Ethan's best response is $\text{BR}_E(V) = V$. So Ethan is best responding to Rebecca's strategy. Similarly, if Ethan plays V, then Rebecca's best response is $\text{BR}_R(V) = V$, so Rebecca is also best responding to Ethan's strategy. Hence, this strategy profile is a Nash equilibrium.

Kid 2

		H	T
Kid 1	H	1, −1	−1, 1
	T	−1, 1	1, −1

Figure A.5. Matching pennies.

This list is exhaustive. The game has two (pure strategy) Nash equilibria. In one (delicious) equilibrium, both players eat pork. In the other (regrettable) equilibrium, both players eat vegetarian.

A.6.2 Matching Pennies

Recall the matching pennies game represented in Figure A.5:
Once again, it is not hard to calculate best responses.

$$\text{BR}_1(H) = H \quad \text{BR}_1(T) = T$$

and

$$\text{BR}_2(H) = T \quad \text{BR}_2(T) = H.$$

These best responses say that kid 1 always wants to try to match kid 2, while kid 2 always wants to do the opposite of what kid 1 did. From these best responses it should be clear that there are no (pure strategy) Nash equilibria of this game. In any profile in which both players are doing the same thing—(H, H) or (T, T)—kid 2 is not playing a best response. In any profile in which the two players are doing different things—(H, T) or (T, H)—kid 1 is not best responding.

This implies that our Nash equilibrium concept fails to make a prediction for what will happen in this game. An expanded notion of Nash equilibrium that allowed for mixed strategies (i.e., kids randomize between heads and tails) does make a prediction for this game. You might not be surprised to learn that, in such an equilibrium, each kid will flip her coin.

A.6.3 Cleaning an Apartment

In our cleaning an apartment game, two roommates (1 and 2) each chose how hard to work at cleaning the apartment. The choices are labeled s_1 and s_2. The total cleanliness of the apartment is $\pi(s_1, s_2) = s_1 + s_2 + \frac{s_1 \times s_2}{2}$. Player i's cost of work is s_i^2. Player 1's payoff from a profile (s_1, s_2) is

$$u_1(s_1, s_2) = \pi(s_1, s_2) - (s_1)^2 = s_1 + s_2 + \frac{s_1 s_2}{2} - (s_1)^2$$

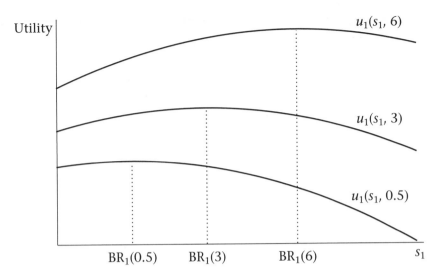

Figure A.6. Player 1's best responses to three of Player 2's possible strategies.

and Player 2's payoff is

$$u_2(s_1, s_2) = \pi(s_1, s_2) - (s_2)^2 = s_1 + s_2 + \frac{s_1 s_2}{2} - (s_2)^2.$$

Before we solve for the players' best response correspondences, let's draw a player's payoffs. The three curves in Figure A.6 each represent Player 1's utility as a function of her effort choice, s_1 (which increases as we move from left to right on the horizontal axis). There are three curves because I've drawn Player 1's utility as a function of s_1 for three different values of s_2 ($s_2 = 0.5$, $s_2 = 3$, and $s_2 = 6$).

Finding a player's best response correspondence, here, is mathematically a bit different from in our previous two games. In this game, there are literally an infinite number of things the other player can do. A player's best response correspondence must tell her what her best strategy is for any possible strategy by the other player.

Graphically, it is clear what Player 1's best response correspondence looks like. For each s_2, we find the s_1 that maximizes Player 1's utility. These best responses are shown in Figure A.6 for three values of s_2.

More generally, we can find Player 1's best response to a choice s_2 by maximizing Player 1's utility function, treating s_2 as fixed. We do so by taking the first derivative, with respect to s_1, and setting it equal to zero. The first derivative is

$$\frac{\partial u_1(s_1, s_2)}{\partial s_1} = 1 + \frac{s_2}{2} - 2s_1.$$

The term $1 + \frac{s_2}{2}$ represents Player 1's *marginal benefit* from increased effort—that is, how much an incremental increase in her work increases cleanliness. The term $-2s_1$ represents Player 1's *marginal cost* from increased effort—that is, how much an incremental increase in her work increases her personal costs.

Player 1's best response to s_2 can be found by setting this derivative equal to zero—that is, setting the marginal benefits equal to the marginal costs. So if some s_1' is a best response to s_2 it must satisfy the following first-order condition:

$$1 + \frac{s_2}{2} = 2s_1'.$$

Rewriting this in terms of best responses, we have that for any s_2

$$1 + \frac{s_2}{2} = 2 \times \mathrm{BR}_1(s_2).$$

This can be rewritten

$$\mathrm{BR}_1(s_2) = \frac{1}{2} + \frac{s_2}{4}.$$

A similar argument shows that

$$\mathrm{BR}_2(s_1) = \frac{1}{2} + \frac{s_1}{4}.$$

What, then, is a Nash equilibrium of this game? At a Nash equilibrium, Player 1 is playing a best response to Player 2 and vice versa. That is, if (s_1^*, s_2^*) is a Nash equilibrium, we need the following to hold:

$$s_1^* = \mathrm{BR}_1(s_2^*) = \frac{1}{2} + \frac{s_2^*}{4}$$

and

$$s_2^* = \mathrm{BR}_2(s_1^*) = \frac{1}{2} + \frac{s_1^*}{4}.$$

Hence, we have a system of two equations and two unknowns. If we solve for the unknowns, we will have a Nash equilibrium.

To find a pair that satisfies these two requirements, we can substitute. In the first expression, we can replace s_2^* with $\frac{1}{2} + \frac{s_1^*}{4}$, since we know that in an equilibrium, this is what s_2^* must equal. Doing so, we can rewrite the first condition as

$$s_1^* = \frac{1}{2} + \frac{\frac{1}{2} + \frac{s_1^*}{4}}{4}.$$

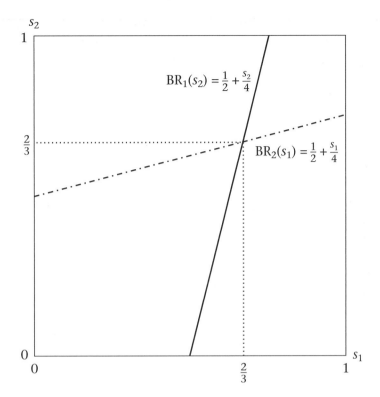

Figure A.7. Best responses in the apartment cleanup game.

Solving for s_1^*, we get

$$s_1^* = \frac{2}{3}.$$

Given this, it is not difficult to find Player 2's equilibrium strategy:

$$BR_2(s_1^*) = \frac{1}{2} + \frac{\frac{2}{3}}{4} = \frac{1}{2} + \frac{1}{6} = \frac{2}{3}.$$

Thus, the unique Nash equilibrium of this game is both players choosing effort equal to $\frac{2}{3}$.

Above, we solved for the Nash equilibrium algebraically. But we can also see it graphically, by plotting each player's best response correspondence. In Figure A.7, the horizontal axis is Player 1's effort and the vertical axis is Player 2's effort. You read the figure as follows. To find Player 1's best response to some s_2, move horizontally rightward from s_2 (on the y-axis) to the line labeled $BR_1(s_2)$, then drop down vertically to the x-axis to find the s_1 that is a best response for Player 1 to that s_2. To find a best response for Player 2 to some s_1, move vertically upward from that s_1 (on the x-axis) to the line labeled $BR_2(s_1)$, then move horizontally leftward to the y-axis to find the s_2 that is a best response for

Player 2 to that s_1. A Nash equilibrium is a point where each player is playing a best response to the other—that is, where the best response correspondences intersect. Hence, the only Nash equilibrium is $\left(\frac{2}{3}, \frac{2}{3}\right)$.

A.6.4 Choosing a Number with Two Players

Let's turn to the easier "choosing a number" game—the one with two players. Each player bids a number between 0 and 10, inclusive. Call Player 1's bid s_1 and Player 2's bid s_2. If the two bids sum to 10 or less, then each player receives the dollar value of his or her bid. If the two bids sum to more than 10, then each player receives nothing. Each player cares only about his or her individual, monetary payoffs.

Player i's payoff from any profile (s_1, s_2) is

$$u_i(s_1, s_2) = \begin{cases} s_i & \text{if } s_1 + s_2 \leq 10 \\ 0 & \text{if } s_1 + s_2 > 10. \end{cases}$$

Let's think about Player 1's best response correspondence. First, suppose Player 2 makes a bid $s_2 < 10$. If Player 1 bids $s_1 > 10 - s_2$, she makes zero. If Player 1 bids $s_1 \leq 10 - s_2$, she makes s_1. Hence, Player 1 maximizes her payoff by choosing $s_1 = 10 - s_2$. Next, suppose Player 2 bids $s_2 = 10$. Then, for any bid, Player 1 makes a payoff of 0. Hence, any bid is a best response to $s_2 = 10$. So Player 1's best response correspondence is

$$BR_1(s_2) = \begin{cases} 10 - s_2 & \text{if } s_2 < 10 \\ \text{Any } s_1 \in [0, 10] & \text{if } s_2 = 10. \end{cases}$$

Player 2's best response correspondence follows the same logic:

$$BR_2(s_1) = \begin{cases} 10 - s_1 & \text{if } s_1 < 10 \\ \text{Any } s_2 \in [0, 10] & \text{if } s_1 = 10. \end{cases}$$

To find the Nash equilibria of this game, we look for pairs (s_1^*, s_2^*), such that $s_1^* \in BR_1(s_2^*)$ and $s_2^* \in BR_2(s_1^*)$. Let's start by ruling out some profiles.

Consider a profile, (s_1, s_2), such that $s_1 + s_2 < 10$. No such profile is a Nash equilibrium because if the two bids do not sum to at least 10, then one player could unilaterally increase her bid a little bit and improve her payoff.

Next, consider a profile such that $10 < s_1 + s_2 < 20$. Such a profile also cannot be a Nash equilibrium. Since $s_1 + s_2 < 20$, at least one of s_1 or s_2 is less than 10. For the sake of argument, suppose $s_2 < 10$. Then Player 1's unique best response is $BR_1(s_2) = 10 - s_2$. But, since $s_1 + s_2 > 10$ we know that Player 1 is

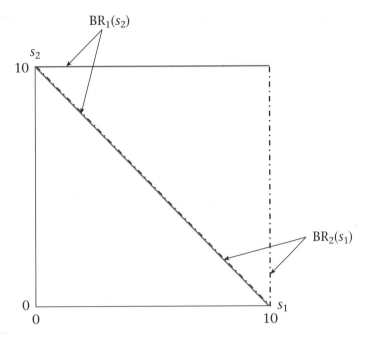

Figure A.8. The best responses in the two-player number bidding game. Intersections of the best response correspondences are Nash equilibria.

actually choosing $s_1 > 10 - s_2$, which is not a best response. So this profile is not a Nash equilibrium. Substantively, if the sum of the bids is greater than 10 and at least one player is bidding less than 10, then the other player could make herself better off by decreasing her bid so that the bids sum to 10. Doing so, she moves from a payoff of 0 to a positive payoff.

Now consider a profile such that $s_1 + s_2 = 10$. Any such profile is a Nash equilibrium. If $s_2 < 10$, then Player 1 is best responding by playing $10 - s_2$. If $s_2 = 10$, then any bid by Player 1 is a best response, including 0. Similarly, if $s_1 < 10$, then Player 2 is best responding by playing $10 - s_1$ and if $s_1 = 10$, then any bid by Player 2 is a best response, including 0.

The only profile left to consider is $(10, 10)$. If Player 2 bids 10, then Player 1 is indifferent over all her possible bids, so 10 is a best response. Similarly, if Player 1 bids 10, then Player 2 is indifferent over all his possible bids, so 10 is a best response. Hence, at $(10, 10)$, both players are best responding.

This analysis implies that the full set of Nash equilibria of this game is

- Any pair (s_1^*, s_2^*) satisfying $s_1^* + s_2^* = 10$
- $(10, 10)$.

We can see these equilibria graphically by drawing the two best response correspondences, as in Figure A.8. The horizontal axis is Player 1's bid and the vertical axis is Player 2's bid. The solid line is Player 1's best response correspondence. Hence, for any s_2, moving over to the solid line and dropping down to the horizontal axis tells you the s_1 (or set of s_1's) that is a best response by Player 1 to that s_2. For any s_2 less than 10, this identifies a unique best response: $10 - s_2$. For $s_2 = 10$ this shows that any s_1 is a best response. Similarly, the dash-dot line is Player 2's best response correspondence. For any s_1, moving up to the dash-dot line and then moving to the left to the vertical axis tells you the s_2 (or set of s_2's) that is a best response by Player 2 to that s_1. For any $s_1 < 10$, this identifies a unique best response: $10 - s_1$. For $s_1 = 10$ this shows that any s_2 is a best response.

Nash equilibria are points where these two best response correspondences intersect—along the diagonal line that identifies pairs $s_1 + s_2 = 10$ and at the point $(10, 10)$.

A.7 Takeaways

- A *best response* by Player i to the strategies of all other players is a strategy for Player i that gives her at least as good a payoff as any of her other strategies, given the strategies being played by all other players.
- Player i's *best response correspondence* tells you Player i's best responses to all possible profiles of strategies by other players.
- A *Nash equilibrium* is a profile of strategies (i.e., one strategy for each player) with the property that each player's strategy is a best response to what all the other players are doing.
- Nash equilibrium is the primary tool we use to generate predictions from games. It can be justified on a variety of grounds including no regrets, self-enforcing agreements, social learning, and analyst humility.

A.8 Exercises

1. Consider a person deciding whether to go back to graduate school next year. The person is making this decision facing uncertainty about what next year's job market is likely to look like. Her most preferred outcome is not to go to school and have a good job market. Her next most preferred outcome is to go to school and have a good job market. Her next most preferred outcome is to go to school and have a bad job market. And, from her perspective, the worst possible outcome is to not go to school and have a bad job market. Suppose she has a vnm expected utility function over the four

possible outcomes given by

$$u(\text{No School, Good Job Market}) = 10$$

$$u(\text{School, Good Job Market}) = 8$$

$$u(\text{School, Bad Job Market}) = 7$$

$$u(\text{No School, Bad Job Market}) = 1.$$

Suppose, finally, that she believes the probability of a good job market is a number p between 0 and 1.

(a) Calculate her expected utility from going to school.

(b) Calculate her expected utility from not going to school.

(c) For what values of p is going back to school a best response?

2. Consider the game in Figure A.9, in which each player can either act *collaboratively* or *selfishly*. If the players both collaborate, then they get a very good outcome. But if one player acts selfishly, the other wants to act selfishly.

(a) Write down each player's best response correspondence.

(b) Identify all the (pure strategy) Nash equilibria of the game.

Player 2

		C	S
Player 1	C	3, 3	0, 2
	S	2, 0	1, 1

Figure A.9. Collaboration game.

3. Consider the game of chicken in Figure A.10. A player can *continue* or *swerve*. The goal is to continue and have your opponent swerve. But if you both continue, you crash, which is bad.

(a) Write down each player's best response correspondence.

(b) Identify all the (pure strategy) Nash equilibria of the game.

Player 2

		C	S
Player 1	C	0, 0	3, 1
	S	1, 3	2, 2

Figure A.10. Chicken.

4. Consider the military escalation game in Figure A.11:

(a) Write down each player's best response correspondence.

(b) Identify all the (pure strategy) Nash equilibria of the game.

| | Country 2 | |
	Don't arm	Arm
Country 1 Don't arm	4, 4	0, 3
Arm	3, 0	1, 1

Figure A.11. Military escalation.

5. Consider a game in which there are 3 people. Each player can either *participate* or *not participate* in a revolution. If at least 2 people participate, the revolution succeeds.

    If the revolution succeeds, each player gets a benefit of B. If the revolution fails, each player gets a benefit of 0. Each player who participates bears a cost $c < B$, whether or not the revolution succeeds.

    (a) Write down each player's best response correspondence.
    (b) Is it a Nash equilibrium for no players to participate? Why or why not?
    (c) Is there a Nash equilibrium in which only one player participates? Why or why not?
    (d) Is there a Nash equilibrium in which only two players participate? Why or why not?
    (e) Is it a Nash equilibrium for all three players to participate? Why or why not?

6. Two firms each decide how many widgets to produce. Firm 1 produces s_1 widgets and Firm 2 produces s_2 widgets. The price per widget is $100 - s_1 - s_2$. The cost of producing s widgets is s^2. Hence, Firm 1's profits are

    $$(100 - s_1 - s_2) \times s_1 - s_1^2$$

    and Firm 2's profits are

    $$(100 - s_1 - s_2) \times s_2 - s_2^2.$$

    Firms' utilities are equal to their profits.

    (a) What is Firm 1's best response if Firm 2 produces 100 or more widgets?
    (b) Use calculus to derive each firm's best response correspondence, assuming the other firm produces fewer than 100 widgets.
    (c) Draw the best response correspondences and identify the Nash equilibrium graphically.
    (d) Now solve for the Nash equilibrium. Do this in three steps:
        • Substitute Firm 2's best response correspondence (assuming Firm 1 produces fewer than 100 widgets) into Firm 1's best

response correspondence to find out Firm 1's equilibrium number of widgets.

- Substitute this back into Firm 2's best response correspondence to find Firm 2's equilibrium number of widgets.
- Confirm that these are in fact less than 100.

(e) Argue that there is not an equilibrium where either firm produces 100 or more widgets.

7.   Four students—let's call them 1, 2, 3, and 4—are in a study group together. Each must simultaneously and independently decide whether or not to study before their study session. Studying will help them pass their midterm. The value to a student of passing the midterm is 8. The value of failing is 0.

A student who does not study passes with probability 1/8. A student who studies passes with probability $n/4$, where n is the number of students (including himself) who studied. By way of example, if only students 1, 2, and 3 studied, they would each pass with probability 3/4 and student 4 would pass with probability 1/8.

Different students face different costs from studying. In particular, the cost to student 1 is 1, the cost to student 2 is 2, the cost to student 3 is 6, and the cost to student 4 is 8.

Suppose each student aims to maximize her expected payoff. Expected payoffs are found as follows. Suppose only students 1, 2, and 3 study. Then student 1's expected payoff is $\frac{3}{4} \times 8 - 1 = 5$, student 2's expected payoff is $\frac{3}{4} \times 8 - 2 = 4$, student 3's expected payoff is $\frac{3}{4} \times 8 - 6 = 0$, and student 4's expected payoff is $\frac{1}{8} \times 8 = 1$.

(a) Is it a Nash equilibrium for all students to study?
(b) Is it a Nash equilibrium for students 1, 2, and 3 to study, but not student 4?
(c) Is it a Nash equilibrium for students 1 and 2 to study, but not students 3 and 4?
(d) Is it a Nash equilibrium for just student 1 to study?
(e) Is it a Nash equilibrium for no one to study?

B

Extensive-Form Games

Thus far, we have studied games in strategic form, which can be fully represented in terms of players, strategies, and payoffs. The strategic form can be understood to represent complex games with multiple moves over time. The way to do so is to think about a player's strategy in such a game as a *complete contingent plan* which states what a player would do in every possible contingency that could arise. If all players submitted such a complete contingent plan to a computer, the computer could play the game for the players and tell them the outcome. Hence, all that we need to describe such a game is the players, all their possible strategies (this could get very complicated, since a complete contingent plan in a long game is a very big object), and payoffs for the outcome associated with every possible profile of strategies.

To see what I'm talking about, think about the game tic-tac-toe. This game is played dynamically—first the X player moves, then the O player moves, then the X player moves again, and so on. We can think of a tic-tac-toe strategy as a complete contingent plan for the game and then represent the game in strategic form.

What would a strategy look like for the X player? It would say what X does as a first move. Then it would say what X does for a second move for *every possible* combination of first moves by X and second moves by O. Then it would say what X does as a third move for every possible combination of first moves by X and O and second moves by X and O. And so on.

You can imagine, even in a simple game like tic-tac-toe, a complete contingent plan for a player will get *very* complicated. Nonetheless, in theory, we could write such a strategy down. Indeed, we could write down all the possible complete contingent plans for each player, so that we knew the full set of strategies, S_i, for each Player i. And once we'd done so, we could analyze the game for its Nash equilibria.

All that said, sometimes it is useful to explicitly model the dynamic nature of a game. In this appendix, we will learn how to do so.

B.1 Games in Extensive Form

We model the dynamics of a game using the *extensive form*. A game in extensive form is described by four things:

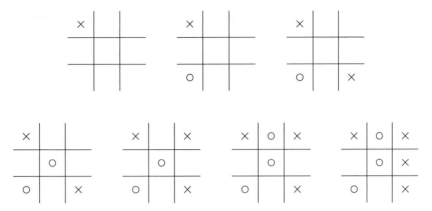

Figure B.1. A terminal history of tic-tac-toe in which X wins.

1. A list of players.
2. A *player function* which tells us whose turn it is to move at every possible point in the game.
3. A list of possible paths through the game, called *terminal histories*.
4. Player *preferences* over terminal histories (i.e., over things that can happen in the game).

These four pieces of information fully describe the game.

Figures B.1 and B.2 show two terminal histories of tic-tac-toe. In Figure B.1, the X player wins. In Figure B.2, there is a tie. Of course, there are many other terminal histories of this game.

You can also see from this example why preferences are defined over terminal histories in games like this. In the case of tic-tac-toe, players care about winning—which is determined by a terminal history. For instance, presumably the X player likes the terminal history in Figure B.1 better than the terminal history in Figure B.2.

Fascinating as tic-tac-toe is, let's move on to an example with a little more substantive motivation.

B.1.1 A Model of International Crisis

Consider two countries—call them A and B—engaged in a dispute over a piece of land which B currently controls. At the beginning of the game, Country A decides whether or not to demand the land from Country B. If A makes no demand, the game ends peacefully. If A makes a demand, Country B must decide whether to acquiesce to A's demand or start a war. If B acquiesces, then A gets the land and the game ends. If B starts a war, then the game ends with the two countries fighting.

A's most preferred outcome is to get the land. A's least preferred outcome is to fight a war. B's most preferred outcome is to keep the land peacefully. B's least

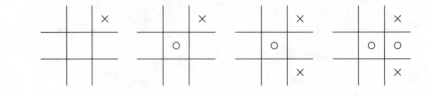

Figure B.2. A terminal history of tic-tac-toe in which there is a tie.

preferred outcome is to fight a war. This story constitutes a complete description of an extensive-form game.

- **Players:** A and B

- **Player Function:**
    - At the beginning of the game A moves.
    - If A makes a demand, B moves.

- **Terminal Histories:**
    - No Demand
    - (Demand, Acquiesce)
    - (Demand, War)

- **Preferences:**
    - $u_A(\text{Demand, Acquiesce}) = 3$, $u_A(\text{No Demand}) = 2$, $u_A(\text{Demand, War}) = 1$
    - $u_B(\text{No Demand}) = 3$, $u_B(\text{Demand, Acquiesce}) = 2$, $u_B(\text{Demand, War}) = 1$

Before we learn to analyze such games, let's find an easier way to represent them.

B.2   Game Trees

It is often convenient to represent an extensive-form game with a game tree. A game tree is a full description of the game. It shows the players, player function, preferences, and terminal histories.

B.2.1 International Crisis Game

Figure B.3 represents the international crisis game on a tree. The *A* at the top of the figure indicates that Country *A* moves at the beginning of the game. The two branches are labeled with each of *A*'s possible actions—*D* for demand and *ND* for no demand. If *A* makes no demand, the game ends (i.e., *ND* is a terminal history). At the end of that branch, the two numbers indicate the players' payoffs (2 for *A* and 3 for *B*). If *A* makes a demand, then it is *B*'s turn to move (as indicated on the tree). *B* can do one of two things: declare war (the left branch) or acquiesce (the right branch). Either move by *B* takes us to the end of a terminal history and payoffs are indicated, with Country *A*'s payoffs first because Country *A* moved first in the game.

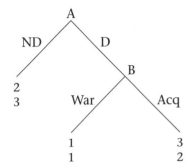

Figure B.3. International crisis game on a tree.

B.2.2 A Budget Game

Figure B.4 represents a game between the Congress and the president. Congress starts the game by passing a large budget or a small budget. The president then decides whether to sign or veto the budget. Let's assume Congress wants a small budget and the president wants a large budget. Moreover, the president dislikes the small budget enough that she is willing to veto it. Payoffs are represented after each terminal history, with Congress's listed first.

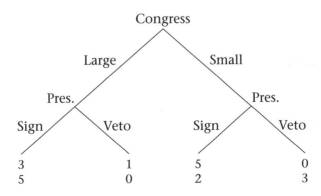

Figure B.4. The budget game in extensive form.

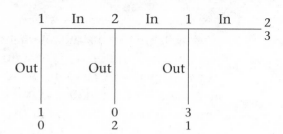

Figure B.5. The centipede game.

B.2.3 The Centipede Game

Figure B.5 represents another classic game—the centipede game (named for the shape of the tree that represents it). In this game, there are two players. The game starts with Player 1 choosing *In* or *Out*. If he goes *Out*, the game ends. If he goes *In* the game continues and Player 2 chooses *In* or *Out*. If she goes *Out*, the game ends. If she goes *In* the game continues and Player 1 again chooses *In* or *Out*, at which point the game ends regardless of what Player 1 did.

At each terminal history, payoffs are shown. Player 1's payoffs are always listed first. The key feature of the centipede game is that, if a player goes *In*, he or she raises the future payoffs for the other player. So this is a game that captures some interesting dynamics about players trying to establish trust with one another. We will discuss it in greater detail later.

B.3 Strategies as Complete Contingent Plans

Now that we've seen what a game in extensive form is, we need to be a little more precise about strategies. As I said at the outset, a strategy for a player is a *complete contingent plan*. That is, it is a statement of what that player would do at every point in the game where it is that player's turn to play. The definition of a strategy in an extensive-form game is often a major source of confusion, so we are going to go through each of our examples in detail.

B.3.1 International Crisis Game

Strategies are easy in the international crisis game in Figure B.3. Each player moves only once. Country *A* has two strategies: Demand or No Demand. Similarly, Country *B* has two strategies: War or Acquiesce. Notice, given the dynamic structure of this game, Country *B* only gets to move if Country *A* chooses Demand. Thus, one should understand Country *B*'s strategy "War" as being a contingent plan of the form: "If Country *A* makes a demand, I will go to war," and similarly with the strategy Acquiesce.

B.3.2 Budget Game

Strategies are only a little more complicated in the budget game represented in Figure B.4. Congress moves in only one place and has only two actions available. So, Congress has two strategies: Small and Large.

The president, however, has the potential to move in two different places: following a large budget proposal and following a small budget proposal. A strategy for the president must specify what she would do in either circumstance.

I will write a strategy for the president as a pair, where the first element of the pair represents what she would do following Large and the second element of the pair represents what she would do following Small. The president has four possible strategies:

- (Sign, Sign)
- (Sign, Veto)
- (Veto, Sign)
- (Veto, Veto)

Remember, a strategy for the president is a complete contingent plan. So, for instance, the strategy (Sign, Veto) should be understood to mean: "If Congress passes a large budget, I will sign. If Congress passes a small budget, I will veto."

B.3.3 The Centipede Game

Things are even a little more complicated in the centipede game represented in Figure B.5. Here, Player 1 has two potential opportunities to move—at the beginning of the game and after both players play In. Hence, a strategy for Player 1 must say what Player 1 will do at each of the points where he might be called on to play. I will write a strategy for Player 1 as a pair, where the first element in the pair says what Player 1 does at the beginning of the game and the second element in the pair says what Player 1 would do if called on to play at the end of the game. Player 1 has four strategies:

- (In, In)
- (In, Out)
- (Out, In)
- (Out, Out)

It is at this point that things tend to get confusing for people. I suspect you are wondering to yourself what the strategies (Out, In) and (Out, Out) could possibly mean. If Player 1 knows he is going to play Out at the beginning of the game, there is no way he could possibly be called on to act later in the game. So it is weird that his strategy has a plan for later in the game. To see what I mean, notice that the strategy (Out, In) means "Play Out at my first move. If I played In at my first move and Player 2 played In, then play In at my second move." Why must Player 1's strategy say what he will do in his second move following In by both himself and Player 2, when he knows he will actually play Out at his first move?

Country B

		War	Acquiesce
Country A	Demand	1, 1	3, 2
	No demand	2, 3	2, 3

Figure B.6. International crisis game.

The answer is this. Player 1's strategy must be a complete contingent plan. It says what he would do were he to reach any point in the game where he might be called on to play—even if he knows he will not reach that point. That may seem strange. It will become clear why we define strategies this way. For now, I simply ask that you accept that strategies are so defined and play along.

A strategy for Player 2 in this game is more straightforward. Player 2 only has one spot where she can move. Hence, she has only 2 possible strategies: In or Out.

B.4 Representing an Extensive-Form Game as a Strategic-Form Game

Now that we understand that a strategy is a complete contingent plan, it is straightforward to move back and forth between extensive-form and strategic-form representations of games. Let's do so for each of our examples.

B.4.1 The International Crisis Game

In the international crisis game represented in Figure B.3, each player has two strategies. Country A can make a demand or no demand. Country B can start a war or acquiesce. Thus, there are four possible strategy profiles: (Demand, War), (Demand, Acquiesce), (No Demand, War), and (No Demand, Acquiesce).

While the game has four strategy profiles, it only has three terminal histories (and, so, three sets of payoffs). The reason for the discrepancy is that the strategy profiles (No Demand, War) and (No Demand, Acquiesce) lead to the same terminal history: No Demand. When we move from representing this game on a tree, to representing it in a matrix, this will mean that the cells representing these two strategy profiles will have the same payoffs in them. Figure B.6 is a matrix representation of the international crisis game.

B.4.2 The Budget Game

In the budget game from Figure B.4, Congress has only two strategies: Large or Small. The president, however, has four strategies: (Sign, Sign), (Sign, Veto), (Veto, Sign), and (Veto, Veto). As a result, when we put this game in a matrix, as in Figure B.7, there are four columns (one for each strategy of the president) and two rows (one for each strategy of the Congress).

President

Congress	(Sign, Sign)	(Sign, Veto)	(Veto, Sign)	(Veto, Veto)
Large	3, 5	3, 5	1, 0	1, 0
Small	5, 2	0, 3	5, 2	0, 3

Figure B.7. Budget game.

Player 2

Player 1	In	Out
(In, In)	2, 3	0, 2
(In, Out)	3, 1	0, 2
(Out, In)	1, 0	1, 0
(Out, Out)	1, 0	1, 0

Figure B.8. Centipede game.

Although the matrix has eight cells, there are only four terminal histories of the game. For instance, the strategy profile (Large, (Sign, Sign)) and the strategy profile (Large, (Sign, Veto)) lead to the same terminal history (and, so, the same payoffs): the Congress proposes a large budget and the president signs it. The reason the two profiles lead to the same payoffs is that, once the Congress has proposed a large budget, it is irrelevant for the outcome of the game what the president would have done had the Congress proposed a small budget. Nonetheless, since the president's strategy is a complete contingent plan, her strategy has to say what she would have done in that eventuality.

B.4.3 The Centipede Game

Finally, in the centipede game, Player 1 has four strategies while Player 2 has only two. Again there are eight strategy profiles and four terminal histories. Figure B.8 shows the game in a matrix.

B.5   Nash Equilibria of Extensive-Form Games

A Nash equilibrium in an extensive-form game is no different than a Nash equilibrium in a strategic-form game. It is a strategy profile—that is, one complete contingent plan for each player—in which each player is playing a best response to what the other players are doing.

Let's solve for the Nash equilibria in each of our examples.

B.5.1 International Crisis Game

It is straightforward to calculate best responses for the international crisis game represented in Figures B.3 and B.6. Country A's best response correspondence is

$$BR_A(\text{War}) = \text{No Demand}$$

$$BR_A(\text{Acquiesce}) = \text{Demand}.$$

This says that if Country A believes that Country B will go to war if challenged, then Country A should back down, making no demand. However, if Country A believes Country B will acquiesce, then Country A should make a demand.

Now consider Country B's best response correspondence:

$$BR_B(\text{Demand}) = \text{Acquiesce}$$

$$BR_B(\text{No Demand}) = \{\text{War}, \text{Acquiesce}\}.$$

B's best response correspondence is slightly more subtle. If Country B believes Country A will make a demand, then she is best off playing the strategy Acquiesce, since

$$u_2(\text{Demand}, \text{Acquiesce}) = 2 > 1 = u_2(\text{Demand}, \text{War}).$$

However, if Country B believes Country A will make no demand, then she is indifferent between her two strategies. This is because, in the event that Country A makes no demand, what Country B would have done had Country A made a demand is irrelevant in terms of payoffs.

Given these best response correspondences, the international crisis game has exactly two Nash equilibria:

1. (Demand, Acquiesce)
2. (No Demand, War)

To see that the first is a Nash equilibrium, note that Demand is a best response to Acquiesce and that Acquiesce is a best response to Demand. To see that the second is a Nash equilibrium, note that No Demand is a best response to War and that War is a best response to No Demand. I leave it to you to convince yourself that the other two possible strategy profiles are not Nash equilibria.

This analysis may seem a bit fishy to you. In particular, you may be worried that the (No Demand, War) equilibrium doesn't make any sense. In this equilibrium, Country B plays the strategy "go to war if Country A makes a demand." Country A makes no demand. The reason it is a best response for Country A to make no demand in this equilibrium is as follows: if Country A made a demand, then according to Country B's strategy, Country B would go to war, which Country A wants to avoid. Thus, Country A is deterred. But it is deterred in a weird way. After all, going to war is bad for Country B. She would prefer to acquiesce. The strategy War is *only* a best response for Country B because Country A makes no demand, which implies that Country B's planned action ends up having no effect on her payoffs, since she is not called on to act. But we've already seen that if Country A were to make a demand, surely Country B would want to acquiesce, making a payoff of 2 instead of 1. Why, then, should Country A believe and be deterred by Country B's strategy of playing war?

I agree, the strategy profile (No Demand, War) doesn't make any sense as a predicted outcome of this game. For now, however, it is important to see that (No Demand, War) *is* a Nash equilibrium. It is just that Nash equilibrium, as a prediction for what happens in the game, is failing to capture some of our strategic intuitions. We will come back to this shortly and propose a refinement of the Nash equilibrium solution concept that will do a better job. Be patient.

B.5.2 The Budget Game

Now consider Nash equilibria of the budget game represented in Figures B.4 and B.7. If the president believes Congress will propose a large budget, she wants to sign it and is indifferent as to what she would have done had Congress passed a small budget. If the president believes Congress will propose a small budget, she wants to veto it and is indifferent as to what she would have done had Congress passed a large budget. Hence, the president's best response correspondence is

$$BR_P(\text{Large}) = \{(\text{Sign, Sign}), (\text{Sign, Veto})\}$$

$$BR_P(\text{Small}) = \{(\text{Sign, Veto}), (\text{Veto, Veto})\}.$$

Congress's most preferred outcome is a small, signed budget. But it prefers a large signed budget to a veto. If its proposal must be vetoed, then it prefers to have a large budget vetoed. Here, then, is Congress's best response correspondence:

$$BR_C(\text{Sign, Sign}) = \text{Small}$$

$$BR_C(\text{Sign, Veto}) = \text{Large}$$

$$BR_C(\text{Veto, Sign}) = \text{Small}$$

$$BR_C(\text{Veto, Veto}) = \text{Large}.$$

Given these best responses, this game has a unique Nash equilibrium: (Large, (Sign, Veto)). To see that this strategy profile is a Nash equilibrium, it suffices to see that no player would be better off by unilaterally changing behavior. If Congress were to switch to proposing a small budget, the president's strategy calls on her to veto, leaving Congress worse off. If the president were to change her strategy, either nothing would change (if she were to switch to (Sign, Sign)) or she would end up vetoing a large budget, making herself worse off.

Let's now look at one non-Nash profile to see why it isn't an equilibrium. Consider the profile (Large, (Sign, Sign)), which might seem like it should be an equilibrium, since it leads to the same terminal history as (Large, (Sign, Veto)). But, notice, if the president is using the strategy (Sign, Sign), then it is not a best response by Congress to choose Large. Instead, if Congress anticipates that the president will sign any budget (i.e., play (Sign, Sign)), then Congress's best response is to propose a small budget. Hence, (Large, (Sign, Sign)) is not a Nash equilibrium.

I leave it to you to check that no other profile is a Nash equilibrium.

B.5.3 The Centipede Game

Consider Nash equilibria of the centipede game represented in Figures B.5 and B.8. First let's find Player 1's best responses. If Player 1 believes Player 2 will play In, then Player 1's best response is (In, Out). If Player 1 believes Player 2 will play Out, then Player 1 has two best responses—(Out, In) and (Out, Out)—both of which lead to the same terminal history: Out. So Player 1's best response correspondence is

$$BR_1(In) = (In, Out)$$

$$BR_1(Out) = \{(Out, In), (Out, Out)\}.$$

Player 2's best response correspondence is found similarly and given by

$$BR_2(In, In) = In$$

$$BR_2(In, Out) = Out$$

$$BR_2(Out, In) = \{In, Out\}$$

$$BR_2(Out, Out) = \{In, Out\}.$$

Clearly, from these best responses, there is no Nash equilibrium where Player 2 plays In. To see this, note that if Player 2 plays In, then Player 1's best response is (In, Out). But if Player 1 plays (In, Out), then Player 2's best response is Out.

So the only possibility for a Nash equilibrium is a profile in which Player 2 plays Out. If Player 2 plays Out, both (Out, In) and (Out, Out) are best responses by Player 1. And, since both of those strategies involve Player 1 playing Out immediately, any strategy by Player 2 is a best response for her. Hence, there are two Nash equilibria: ((Out, In), Out) and ((Out, Out), Out). Both equilibria lead to the same terminal history—Player 1 goes Out immediately.

B.6   Subgame Perfect Nash Equilibrium

As we've already noted, sometimes the Nash equilibria of extensive-form games don't make a lot of sense as predictions. For instance, in the international crisis game, there was an equilibrium in which Country A did not make a demand because it believed Country B would start a war following a demand. That equilibrium is strange because, once a demand is actually made, Country B clearly prefers to acquiesce. So why should Country A believe that Country B would really start a war following a demand? It seems as though Country A was being deterred by a non-credible threat.

If the threat was non-credible, why was Country B able to make it? The answer comes from the logic of Nash equilibrium. In a world in which Country B actually succeeds at deterring Country A, Country B is never called on to carry through on the threat. The fact that Country B would have gone to war (against its interests) in a part of the game that never actually got played has no effect on Country B's payoffs. As such, when considering a unilateral change in strategy by Country B, we found that Country B's planned action did not affect Country B's payoffs (because Country B was never actually forced to act). Thus, we had a Nash equilibrium.

This equilibrium strains credulity for a couple of reasons. First, it seems hard to believe that Country A couldn't "look down the tree" and anticipate that Country B would in fact choose to acquiesce if called on to act. If Country A can do so, it should not believe that Country B will go to war. Instead, Country A should say to itself, "Country B is rational. At the point where it is called on to make a decision, after I make a demand, surely it will acquiesce, since doing so will be in its best interest." And if Country A believes its own thinking, it will make a demand, counting on Country B's rationality to lead to acquiescence.

Second, think of Country B. When playing the strategy War as part of a Nash equilibrium, Country B is leaning quite strongly on its complete certainty that A will not make a demand. If Country B thinks there is even a tiny chance that Country A will make a demand, then Country B should play the strategy Acquiesce. The strategy War is only a best response because, when there is absolutely no chance Country A will make a demand, Country B is exactly indifferent between its two strategies. If Country B assigns any positive probability, however small, to actually having to act, then Country B strictly prefers to acquiesce.

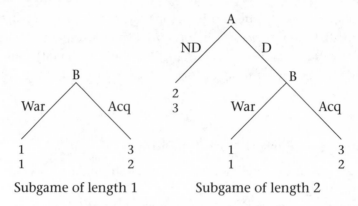

Figure B.9. International crisis game subgames.

For both of these reasons, we want to think about a prediction for games like this that refines Nash equilibrium to rule out non-credible threats of this sort. The concept we use is called *subgame perfection*.

B.6.1 Subgame Perfection

The basic idea of subgame perfection is that players play best responses not just in the full game, but at every possible point in the game where they might be called upon to move. Defining subgame perfection formally requires a bit more notation than I'd like to present, so I will be a little informal. But we do need some terminology.

A *subgame* of an extensive-form game is another extensive-form game made up of part of the original extensive-form game. You can find a subgame of an extensive-form game by cutting the tree at any decision point. Then, everything from that decision down constitutes a subgame of the original game. Games are also always considered subgames of themselves.

We also talk about the *length* of a subgame, which is the largest number of actions that could be taken in a terminal history of a subgame. Looking at our examples will help to fix ideas. Figures B.9–B.11 show the subgames of the international crisis game, the budget game, and the centipede game, respectively.

Now we can develop the refinement of Nash equilibrium that rules out non-credible threats. A strategy profile is a *subgame perfect Nash equilibrium* if every player is playing a best response to what the other players are doing, not only in the game as a whole, but in every subgame.

To see how subgame perfection rules out non-credible threats, let's revisit the international crisis game. There we had two Nash equilibria: (Demand, Acquiesce) and (No Demand, War). Earlier, we argued that the Nash equilibrium (No Demand, War) depended on a non-credible threat. Consider the subgame of length one shown in Figure B.9. Subgame perfection requires that, if we treat

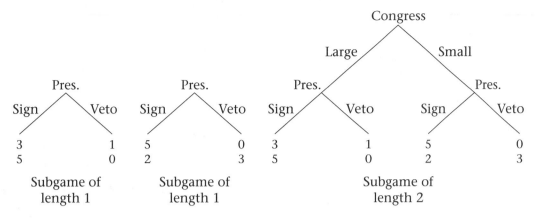

Figure B.10. Budget game subgames.

this subgame as a game unto itself, the actions that are specified by the strategy profile must be best responses. The strategy profile calls on Country B to play War. But, clearly, in the simple one-player game created by considering just this subgame, Country B's best response (i.e., optimal action, since there are no other players) is to choose Acquiesce. Hence, the profile (No Demand, War) is not a subgame perfect Nash equilibrium, since it involves a player taking an action that is not a best response in one of the subgames.

Now consider the other Nash equilibrium, (Demand, Acquiesce). In the subgame of length one, shown in Figure B.9, Country B, by choosing Acquiesce, is playing a best response. And, given this, Country A is playing a best response by choosing Demand. Thus, this profile satisfies the requirements of subgame perfection. Subgame perfection rules out the unreasonable Nash equilibrium that depended on a non-credible threat, leaving only the reasonable Nash equilibrium as a prediction for what will happen.

B.6.2 Backward Induction

Solving for a subgame perfect Nash equilibrium is quite easy. It can be done by following a simple algorithm called *backward induction*. Here is the idea.

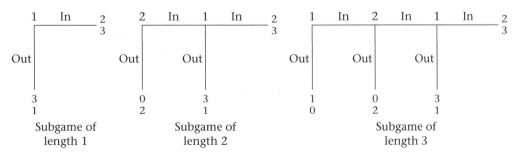

Figure B.11. Centipede game subgames.

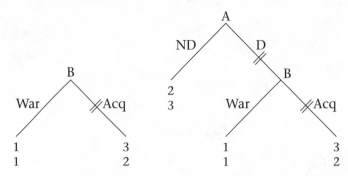

Figure B.12. Finding the subgame perfect Nash equilibrium of the international crisis game through backward induction.

Start by finding all of the subgames of length 1. Figure out the best responses of the relevant player in each of those subgames. Now find all the subgames of length 2. Find the best responses of all the relevant players in those games, taking as fixed the actions in the subgames of length 1 that you already identified. Now take the actions you've found in subgames of length 1 and 2 as given and do the same thing for subgames of length 3. Continue this procedure until you get to the beginning of the game.

Any strategy profile you identify following this backward induction algorithm is a subgame perfect Nash equilibrium. The reason should be clear—by doing backward induction, you are making sure players are playing best responses at every subgame. Any subgame perfect Nash equilibrium will be found using backward induction.

Let's go through our three examples. In the international crisis game, there is one subgame of length 1. It is Country B's choice. In that subgame, as we've already discussed, Country B's best response is Acquiesce. Now we take this action as fixed and look at the one subgame of length 2. Taking B's action as fixed means that we assume Country A knows that if it makes a demand, Country B will acquiesce. Hence, Country A's best response, given Country B's behavior, is to make a demand. Thus, there is a unique subgame perfect Nash equilibrium: (Demand, Acquiesce).

Figure B.12 shows the logic of the backward induction. The hash-marked line in the first panel shows Country B's best response in the subgame. The hash-marked line in the second panel shows, given Country B's behavior in the subgame, that Country A's best response is Demand.

In the budget game, there are two subgames of length 1. In each of them, the president decides whether or not to veto. In the subgame following a large budget proposal, the president's best response is to sign the budget. In the subgame following a small budget proposal, the president's best response is to veto the budget.

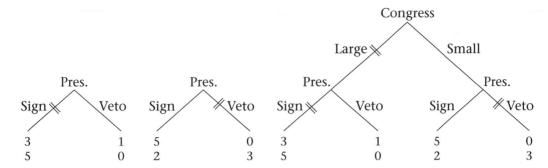

Figure B.13. Finding the subgame perfect Nash equilibrium of the budget game through backward induction.

Taking these actions as fixed, now consider the single subgame of length 2—in which Congress makes a choice of what type of budget to pass. Congress anticipates that if it proposes a large budget, the budget will be signed and Congress will make a payoff of 3. Congress also anticipates that if it passes a small budget, the budget will be vetoed and Congress will make a payoff of 0. Hence, Congress's best response is to propose a large budget and the unique subgame perfect Nash equilibrium is (Large, (Sign, Veto)). Figure B.13 illustrates the backward induction for this game.

There are two things to point out here. First, notice how I've written the equilibrium. I did not write (Large, Sign). That is what happens—that is, the terminal history in this equilibrium—but it is not the equilibrium itself. An equilibrium is a strategy profile. A strategy profile is made up of one strategy for each player. And a strategy for a player is a complete contingent plan. Hence, when describing the equilibrium, you must report a full strategy for each player—that is, what the player does in the places he is actually called on to play and what he would have done everywhere else.

The budget game actually makes it clear why it is so important to write a strategy as a complete contingent plan. Proposing a large budget is only a best response for Congress because the president would veto a small budget. If the president would sign a small budget, Congress would propose a small budget. Hence, Congress's incentives depend on what action the President would take in the subgame that is never actually reached as part of equilibrium play.

It is worth noting that the subgame perfect Nash equilibrium of this game is the same as the unique Nash equilibrium of the game. This is because subgame perfection is a refinement of Nash. All subgame perfect Nash equilibria are Nash equilibria. But not all Nash equilibria are subgame perfect (as we saw in the International Crisis example).

In the centipede game, there is one subgame of length 1, one subgame of length 2, and one subgame of length 3. In the subgame of length 1, Player 1 will choose Out. Anticipating this behavior, in the subgame of length 2, Player 2 will

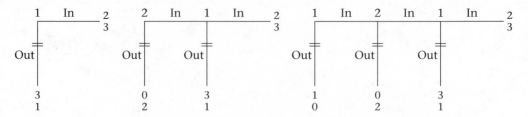

Figure B.14. Finding the subgame perfect Nash equilibrium of the centipede game through backward induction.

choose Out. And, anticipating both of these decisions, Player 1 will choose Out in the subgame of length 3. Hence, the game has a unique subgame perfect Nash equilibrium: ((Out, Out), Out). This analysis is illustrated in Figure B.14.

B.6.3 Indifference and Multiple Equilibria

Subgame perfect Nash equilibria need not be unique. Sometimes a player has more than one best response in a subgame. Which action the player is expected to choose from amongst her best responses can affect what happens earlier in the game. In such circumstances, to find all of the subgame perfect Nash equilibria, you must go case-by-case, considering each possible best response and its implications for behavior up the tree.

To see how this works, consider the example in Figure B.15. The key point comes from studying the subgame that follows an action of A by Player 1 and an action of C by Player 2. In this subgame of length 1, Player 1 is indifferent between the actions G and H. Hence, when we do the backward induction, we have to allow for the possibility of either action.

Let's first do the backward induction in the case where Player 1 chooses G in that subgame, as illustrated in the left-hand cell of Figure B.15. In the other subgame of length 1, Player 1 has a clear best response, I. Now there are two subgames of length 2. In the subgame on the left, Player 2 anticipates that Player 1 will choose G down the tree. Hence, she plays D, making a payoff of 5 rather than 2. In the subgame of length 2 on the right, Player 2 anticipates that Player 1 will choose I down the tree, so Player 2 chooses E, making a payoff of 4 rather than 3. Finally, hold all of this behavior fixed and consider the subgame of length 3. Player 1 anticipates that if he chooses A, Player 2 will choose D and he'll make a payoff of 5. If, instead, he chooses B, Player 2 will choose E and then Player 1 will choose I, yielding a payoff of 4. Hence, Player 1 chooses A. The subgame perfect Nash equilibrium we've identified is $((A, G, I), (D, E))$.

Now we must go back and redo our backward induction for the case where Player 1 chooses H instead of G. As illustrated in the right-hand cell of Figure B.15, doing so identifies a second subgame perfect Nash equilibrium: $((B, H, I), (C, E))$.

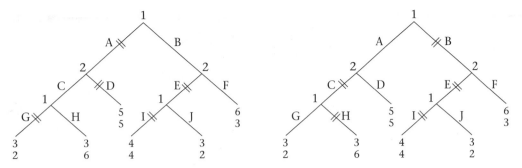

Figure B.15. The backward induction when Player 1 chooses *G*.

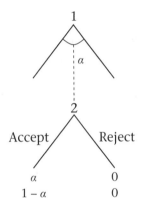

Figure B.16. The ultimatum game.

B.6.4 Continuous Choices

Another issue that arises involves extensive-form games in which at least one of the players makes a choice from a continuum. For instance, consider the ultimatum game in Figure B.16. In the ultimatum game, Player 1 proposes a division of a dollar, keeping a share $\alpha \in [0, 1]$ for herself. Player 2 then either accepts or declines the offer. If Player 2 accepts, Player 1 gets a payoff of α and Player 2 gets a payoff of $1 - \alpha$. If Player 2 declines, both players get nothing. In Figure B.16, the fact that Player 1 has a continuous choice (any α between 0 and 1) is represented by the curve at her decision node. The dashed line coming from this choice indicates that there are actually a continuum of subgames after Player 1's decision. Player 2's strategy must specify an accept or reject decision at each of these infinity of subgames.

Let's analyze this game using backward induction. For any proposal $\alpha \neq 1$, Player 2 strictly prefers to accept Player 1's offer. But if $\alpha = 1$, Player 2 is indifferent between accepting and rejecting. So, as we saw in the previous section, we must do the backward induction twice.

First, assume that Player 2 accepts any offer $\alpha < 1$ and rejects if $\alpha = 1$. Player 1's best response is to propose the largest α that Player 2 will accept. So

Player 1 wants to propose the largest $\alpha \in [0, 1)$. Now we run into a technical problem. There is no largest $\alpha \in [0, 1)$. For any $\alpha < 1$, we can find an α' such that $\alpha < \alpha' < 1$. Hence, there is no equilibrium because, for technical reasons, Player 1 has no best response. That said, the basic incentives are clear. Player 1 wants to make a proposal that leaves Player 2 all but indifferent.

Second, suppose Player 2 will accept any α, including $\alpha = 1$. Then Player 1 wants to propose the largest $\alpha \in [0, 1]$. This is straightforward to do; Player 1 keeps the whole dollar for herself. Thus, the unique subgame perfect Nash equilibrium of this game is that Player 1 proposes $\alpha = 1$ and Player 2 accepts any $\alpha \in [0, 1]$.

B.7 Discounted Payoffs

Another important type of extensive-form game is the infinitely repeated game. We define an infinitely repeated game by first specifying a strategic-form game. We then create an extensive-form game in which players play that strategic-form game over and over.

In an infinitely repeated game, we think of players getting the payoff from the strategic-form game in each period. However, we can't simply have them sum those payoffs. We need a way to model how players think about the value of future payoffs relative to current payoffs.

A given payoff today is worth more than the same payoff tomorrow. (Think about whether you'd rather have a thousand dollars right now or in five years.) We model this by assuming that players discount future payoffs by a *discount factor*, $\delta \in (0, 1)$. The idea is that a unit of utility to be delivered a period from now is worth δ units of utility now. That further implies that a unit of utility to be delivered two periods from now is worth δ^2 units of utility now. Hence, future payoffs are getting less and less valuable as they get further and further away from being realized. In an infinitely repeated game, a player's payoff from some terminal history is the discounted sum of the payoffs she made throughout the game.

The following mathematical fact will prove useful:

Fact B.7.1. *If $\delta \in (0, 1)$, then the infinite series $1 + \delta + \delta^2 + \delta^3 + \ldots$ is equal to $\frac{1}{1-\delta}$. You can see this as follows. Assuming the series converges (i.e., the sum approaches some finite number), which it does, we can let that number be called Z:*

$$Z = 1 + \delta + \delta^2 + \delta^3 + \ldots$$

Then we have

$$\delta Z = \delta + \delta^2 + \delta^3 + \ldots.$$

Subtracting the two left-hand sides from each other and the two right-hand sides from each other, we have

$$Z - \delta Z = \left[1 + \delta + \delta^2 + \delta^3 + \ldots\right] - \left[\delta + \delta^2 + \delta^3 + \ldots\right].$$

Distributing the Z on the left-hand side and canceling things on the right-hand side, we have

$$Z(1 - \delta) = 1 \Rightarrow Z = \frac{1}{1 - \delta}.$$

Using the definition of Z, we get

$$Z = 1 + \delta + \delta^2 + \delta^3 + \ldots = \frac{1}{1 - \delta}.$$

B.8 Takeaways

- In some extensive-form games, some of the Nash equilibria involve players committing to non-credible threats "off the path of play" (i.e., in parts of the game tree that are never actually reached).
- Subgame perfection refines the Nash equilibrium concept to rule out strategy profiles in which players make such non-credible threats. It does so by requiring that players play best responses in every subgame, whether or not that subgame is actually reached on the path of play.
- You solve for a subgame perfect Nash equilibrium by backward induction.
- A strategy in an extensive-form game is a complete contingent plan— that is, a statement of the action a player would take at every point in the game where she can be called on to play.

B.9 Exercises

1. Consider the game in Figure B.17.

   (a) How many strategies does player 1 have? How many strategies does player 2 have? What are they?
   (b) Solve the game for all of its Nash equilibria.
   (c) Solve the game for all of its subgame perfect Nash equilibria.
   (d) Give an intuition for why the answers to (b) and (c) are different.

2. Consider a game between an administrative agency and a court. At the beginning of the game, the administrative agency can choose to regulate or

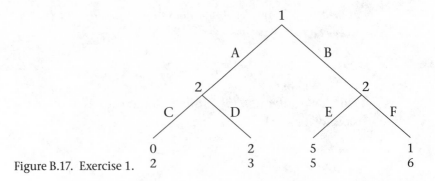

Figure B.17. Exercise 1.

Figure B.18. A repeated game.

	Player 2	
	A	*B*
A	10, 10	5, 15
B	15, 5	4, 4

Player 1

not. If the agency chooses not to regulate the game ends. If the agency chooses to regulate, the court can uphold the regulation or strike it down. The agency's most preferred outcome is to successfully regulate and its least favorite outcome is to have its regulation struck down. The court's most preferred outcome is no regulation and its least preferred outcome is to have to strike down regulation by the agency.

(a) Represent this game in a matrix and on a tree.

(b) What are all the Nash equilibria of this game?

(c) What is the subgame perfect Nash equilibrium? Explain the intuition for why this equilibrium is the "right" prediction for the outcome of the game.

(d) Explain how, intuitively, if the court could develop a reputation as enjoying conflict with the agency, it could make itself better off.

3.   Suppose the game in Figure B.18 is repeated infinitely and that each player discounts the future according to discount factor δ (with δ between 0 and 1).

(a) Consider the strategy: "Start playing *A* and continue to play *A* if all players have always played *A*. If any player (be it me or you) has ever played *B*, play *B* forever." Give conditions on δ such that this strategy is a Nash equilibrium. (Hint: all you have to do is check whether, given that the other player follows this strategy, you want to play *A* rather than *B*.)

(b) Consider the strategy: "In *Cooperate Mode* play *A*. In *Punishment Mode* play *B*. Switch from Cooperate Mode to Punishment Mode if either player plays B while in Cooperate Mode. Switch from Punishment Mode to Cooperate Mode after one period of Punishment Mode, regardless of what happened." Give conditions on δ such that this strategy is a Nash equilibrium. (Hint: all you have to do is check whether, in Cooperate Mode, a player wants to play A rather than B assuming that, if she plays B, they will both play B for one period and then revert to both playing A.)

(c) Give an intuition for why the conditions in your answers to (a) and (b) are different.

Bibliography

Acemoglu, Daron and James A. Robinson. 2001. "Inefficient Redistribution." *American Political Science Review* 95(3):649–661.

Acemoglu, Daron and James A. Robinson. 2006. *Economic Origins of Dictatorship and Democracy.* Cambridge, UK: Cambridge University Press.

Acemoglu, Daron and James A. Robinson. 2012. *Why Nations Fail: The Origins of Power, Prosperity, and Poverty.* New York, NY: Crown Business.

Acemoglu, Daron and James A. Robinson. 2013. "Economics versus Politics: Pitfalls of Policy Advice." *Journal of Economic Perspectives* 27(2):173–192.

Acemoglu, Daron, Simon Johnson and James A. Robinson. 2001. "The Colonial Origins of Comparative Development: An Empirical Investigation." *American Economic Review* 91(5):1369–1401.

Acemoglu, Daron, Simon Johnson and James A. Robinson. 2005. "Institutions as a Fundamental Cause of Long-Run Growth." *Handbook of Economic Growth* 1:385–472.

Albouy, David Y. 2012. "The Colonial Origins of Comparative Development: An Empirical Investigation: Comment." *American Economic Review* 102(6):3059–3076.

Alesina, Alberto and Guido Tabellini. 1990. "A Positive Theory of Fiscal Deficits and Government Debt." *Review of Economic Studies* 57(3):403–414.

Alt, James E., Ethan Bueno de Mesquita and Shanna Rose. 2011. "Disentangling Accountability and Competence in Elections: Evidence from U.S. Term Limits." *Journal of Politics* 73(1):171–186.

Angrist, Joshua D. and Jörn-Steffen Pischke. 2008. *Mostly Harmless Econometrics: An Empiricist's Companion.* Princeton, NJ: Princeton University Press.

Angrist, Joshua D., Parag A. Pathak and Christopher R. Walters. 2013. "Explaining Charter School Effectiveness." *American Economic Journal: Applied Economics* 5(4):1–27.

Angrist, Joshua D., Susan M. Dynarski, Thomas J. Kane, Parag A. Pathak and Christopher R. Walters. 2012. "Who Benefits from KIPP?" *Journal of Policy Analysis and Management* 31(4):837–860.

Ansolabehere, Stephen, John M. de Figueiredo and James M. Snyder, Jr. 2003. "Why is There so Little Money in U.S. Politics?" *Journal of Economic Perspectives* 17(1):105–130.

Appiah, Kwame Anthony. 2011. *The Honor Code: How Moral Revolutions Happen.* New York, NY: Norton.

Arrow, Kenneth J. 1950. "A Difficulty in the Concept of Social Welfare." *Journal of Political Economy* 58(4):328–346.

Arrow, Kenneth J. 1999. Discounting, Morality, and Gaming. In *Discounting and Intergenerational Equity*, ed. Paul R. Portney and John P. Weyant. Washington, DC: Resources for the Future, pp. 13–21.

Ashworth, Scott. 2012. "Electoral Accountability: Recent Theoretical and Empirical Work." *Annual Review of Political Science* 15:183–201.

Ashworth, Scott and Ethan Bueno de Mesquita. 2006. "Delivering the Goods: Legislative Particularism in Different Electoral and Institutional Settings." *Journal of Politics* 68(1):169–179.

Austen-Smith, David and Jeffrey Banks. 1999. *Positive Political Theory I: Collective Preference.* Ann Arbor, MI: University of Michigan Press.

Azariadis, Costas. 1996. "The Economics of Poverty Traps Part One: Complete Markets." *Journal of Economic Growth* 1(4):449–486.

Baker, George. 2002. "Distortion and Risk in Optimal Incentive Contracts." *Journal of Human Resources* 37(4): 728–751.

Barnett, Michael L. and Jeffrey A. Linder. 2014. "Antibiotic Prescribing to Adults with Sore Throat in the United States, 1997–2010." *JAMA Internal Medicine* 174(1):138–140.

Baron, David P. and Roger B. Myerson. 1982. "Regulating a Monopolist With Unknown Costs." *Econometrica* 50(4):911–930.

Bartels, Daniel M. and David A. Pizarro. 2011. "The Mismeasure of Morals: Antisocial Personality Traits Predict Utilitarian Responses to Moral Dilemmas." *Cognition* 121(1):154–161.

Beghin, John C., Barbara El Osta, Jay R. Cherlow and Samarendu Mohanty. 2003. "The Cost of the U.S. Sugar Program Revisited." *Contemporary Economic Policy* 21(1):106–116.

Berry, Christopher R. 2009. *Imperfect Union: Representation and Taxation in Multilevel Governments.* New York, NY: Cambridge University Press.

Berry, Christopher R. and Jacob E. Gersen. 2010. "The Timing of Elections." *University of Chicago Law Review* 77(1): 37–64.

Berry, Christopher R. and Jacob E. Gersen. 2011. "Election Timing and Public Policy." *Quarterly Journal of Political Science* 6(2):103–135.

Berry, Christopher R. and William G. Howell. 2007. "Accountability and Local Elections: Rethinking Retrospective Voting." *Journal of Politics* 69(3):844–858.

Besley, Timothy. 2006. *Principled Agents: Motivation and Incentives in Politics.* Oxford, UK: Oxford University Press.

Black, Duncan. 1958. *The Theory of Committees and Elections.* London, UK: Cambridge University Press.

Bombardini, Matilde and Francesco Trebbi. 2011. "Votes or Money? Theory and Evidence from the US Congress." *Journal of Public Economics* 95(7):587–611.

Broome, John. 2012. *Climate Matters: Ethics in a Warming World.* New York, NY: W.W. Norton and Company.

Bueno de Mesquita, Bruce and Alastair Smith. 2007. "Foreign Aid and Policy Concessions." *Journal of Conflict Resolution* 51(2):251–284.

Bueno de Mesquita, Bruce and Alastair Smith. 2009. "A Political Economy of Aid." *International Organization* 63(2):309–340.

Bueno De Mesquita, Bruce and Alastair Smith. 2011. *The Dictator's Handbook: Why Bad Behavior is Almost Always Good Politics.* New York, NY: PublicAffairs.

Bueno de Mesquita, Bruce, Alastair Smith, Randolph M. Siverson and James D. Morrow. 2003. *The Logic of Political Survival.* Cambridge, MA: MIT Press.

Bueno de Mesquita, Bruce, James D. Morrow, Randolph M. Siverson and Alastair Smith. 2001. "Political Competition and Economic Growth." *Journal of Democracy* 12(1):58–72.

Bueno de Mesquita, Ethan. 2007. "Politics and the Suboptimal Provision of Counterterror." *International Organization* 61(1):9.

Burnside, Craig and David Dollar. 2000. "Aid, Policies, and Growth." *American Economic Review* 90(4):847–868.

Butler, Christopher C., Stephen Rollnick, Roisin Pill, Frances Maggs-Rapport and Nigel Stott. 1998. "Understanding the Culture of Prescribing: Qualitative Study of General Practitioners' and Patients' Perceptions of Antibiotics for Sore Throats." *BMJ* 317(7159):637–642.

Caliendo, Lorenzo and Fernando Parro. 2015. "Estimates of the Trade and Welfare Effects of NAFTA." *Review of Economic Studies* 82(1):1–44.

Canes-Wrone, Brandice and Kenneth W. Shotts. 2004. "The Conditional Nature of Presidential Responsiveness to Public Opinion." *American Journal of Political Science* 48(4):690–706.

Canes-Wrone, Brandice, Michael C. Herron and Kenneth W. Shotts. 2001. "Leadership and Pandering: A Theory of Executive Policymaking." *American Journal of Political Science* 45(3):532–550.

Clarke, Edward H. 1971. "Multipart Pricing of Public Goods." *Public Choice* 11(1):17–33.

Coase, Ronald Harry. 1960. "The Problem of Social Cost." *Journal of Law and Economics* 3:1–44.

Cohen, Gerald Allan. 2009. *Why Not Socialism?* Princeton, NJ: Princeton University Press.

Collier, Paul. 2007. *The Bottom Billion: Why the Poorest Countries are Failing and What Can Be Done About It.* New York, NY: Oxford University Press.

Cooper, Richelle J., Jerome R. Hoffman, John G. Bartlett, Richard E. Besser, Ralph Gonzales, John M. Hickner and Merle A. Sande. 2001. "Principles of Appropriate Antibiotic Use for Acute Pharyngitis in Adults: Background." *Annals of Internal Medicine* 134(6):509–517.

Cooper, Russell and Thomas W. Ross. 2002. "Bank Runs: Deposit Insurance and Capital Requirements." *International Economic Review* 43(1):55–72.

Crost, Benjamin, Joseph Felter and Patrick Johnston. 2014. "Aid Under Fire: Development Projects and Civil Conflict." *American Economic Review* 104(6):1833–1856.

Dal Bó, Ernesto. 2006. "Regulatory Capture: A Review." *Oxford Review of Economic Policy* 22(2):203–225.

de Janvry, Alain, Frederico Finan and Elisabeth Sadoulet. 2011. "Local Electoral Incentives and Decentralized Program Performance." *Review of Economics and Statistics* 94(3):672–685.

Diamond, Douglas W. and Philip H. Dybvig. 1983. "Bank Runs, Deposit Insurance, and Liquidity." *Journal of Political Economy* 91(3):401–419.

Dixit, Avinash and John Londregan. 1996. "The Determinants of Success of Special Interests in Redistributive Politics." *Journal of Politics* 58(4):1132–1155.

Dixit, Avinash and Victor Norman. 1986. "Gains from Trade without Lump-Sum Compensation." *Journal of International Economics* 21(1):111–122.

Djankov, Simeon, Jose G. Montalvo and Marta Reynal-Querol. 2008. "The Curse of Aid." *Journal of Economic Growth* 13(3):169–194.

Downs, Anthony. 1957. *An Economic Theory of Democracy.* New York, NY: Harper.

Dube, Oeindrila and Suresh Naidu. 2015. "Bases, Bullets, and Ballots: The Effect of U.S. Military Aid on Political Conflict in Colombia." *Journal of Politics* 77(1):249–267.

Dworkin, Ronald. 1981*a*. "What is Equality? Part 1: Equality of Welfare." *Philosophy and Public Affairs* 10(3):185–246.

Dworkin, Ronald. 1981*b*. "What is Equality? Part 2: Equality of Resources." *Philosophy and Public Affairs* 10(4):283–345.

Easterly, William. 2003. "Can Foreign Aid Buy Growth?" *Journal of Economic Perspectives* 17(3):23–48.

Easterly, William. 2006. *The White Man's Burden: Why the West's Efforts to Aid the Rest Have Done So Much Ill and So Little Good.* New York, NY: Penguin.

Easterly, William and Tobias Pfutze. 2008. "Where Does the Money Go? Best and Worst Practices in Foreign Aid." *Journal of Economic Perspectives* 22(2):29–52.

Enders, Walter and Todd Sandler. 1993. "The Effectiveness of Antiterrorism Policies: A Vector-Autoregression-Intervention Analysis." *American Political Science Review* 87(4):829–844.

English, Richard. 2003. *Armed Struggle: The History of the IRA.* Oxford, UK: Oxford University Press.

Fearon, James D. 1995. "Rationalist Explanations for War." *International Organization* 49(3):379–379.

Fearon, James D. 1998. Commitment Problems and the Spread of Ethnic Conflict. In *The International Spread of Ethnic Conflict: Fear, Diffusion, and Escalation*, ed. David Lake and Donald Rothchild. Princeton, NJ: Princeton University Press.

Fearon, James D. 2011. "Self-Enforcing Democracy." *Quarterly Journal of Economics* 126(4):1661–1708.

Fearon, James D. and David D. Laitin. 1996. "Explaining Interethnic Cooperation." *American Political Science Review* 90(4):715–735.

Feltham, Gerald A. and Jim Xie. 1994. "Performance Measure Congruity and Diversity in Multi-Task Principal/Agent Relations." *Accounting Review* 69(3):429–453.

Fey, Mark and Kristopher W. Ramsay. 2007. "Mutual Optimism and War." *American Journal of Political Science* 51(4):738–754.

Finan, Frederico and Claudio Ferraz. 2011. "Electoral Accountability and Corruption in Local Governments: Evidence from Audit Reports." *American Economic Review* 101:1274–1311.

Foot, Philippa. 1967. "The Problem of Abortion and the Doctrine of Double Effect." *Oxford Review* 5:5–15.

Foucault, Michel. 2008. *The Birth of Biopolitics: Lectures at the Collège de France, 1978–1979*. New York, NY: Palgrave Macmillan.

Friedman, Milton and Anna J. Schwartz. 1963. *A Monetary History of the United States, 1867–1960*. Princeton, NJ: Princeton University Press.

Gagliarducci, Stefano and Tommaso Nannicini. 2011. "Do Better Paid Politicians Perform Better? Disentangling Incentives from Selection." *Journal of the European Economic Association* 11(2):369–698.

Galiani, Sebastian, Stephen Knack, Lixin Colin Xu and Ben Zou. 2014. "The Effect of Aid on Growth: Evidence from a Quasi-Experiment." World Bank Policy Research Working Paper No. 6865.

Gans, Joshua S. and Michael Smart. 1996. "Majority Voting with Single-Crossing Preferences." *Journal of Public Economics* 59(2):219–237.

Geanakoplos, John. 2005. "Three Brief Proofs of Arrow's Impossibility Theorem." *Economic Theory* 26(1):211–215.

Gehlbach, Scott. 2013. *Formal Models of Domestic Politics*. New York, NY: Cambridge University Press.

Gibbons, Robert. 2010. "Inside Organizations: Pricing, Politics, and Path Dependence." *Annual Review of Economics* 2:337–365.

Giere, Ronald N. 2006. *Scientific Perspectivism*. Chicago, IL: University of Chicago Press.

Glaeser, Edward L. 2010. *Agglomeration Economics*. Chicago, IL: University of Chicago Press.

Glaeser, Edward L. 2011. *Triumph of the City: How Our Greatest Invention Makes Us Richer, Smarter, Greener, Healthier, and Happier*. New York, NY: Penguin.

Glaeser, Edward L., Rafael La Porta, Florencio Lopez de Silanes and Andrei Shleifer. 2004. "Do Institutions Cause Growth?" *Journal of Economic Growth* 9(3):271–303.

Gordon, Sanford C. and Gregory A. Huber. 2007. "The Effect of Electoral Competitiveness on Incumbent Behavior." *Quarterly Journal of Political Science* 2(2):107–138.

Greenstone, Michael, Richard Hornbeck and Enrico Moretti. 2010. "Identifying Agglomeration Spillovers: Evidence from Winners and Losers of Large Plant Openings." *Journal of Political Economy* 118(3):536–598.

Groves, Theodore. 1973. "Incentives in Teams." *Econometrica* 41(4):617–631.

Hacking, Ian. 1983. *Representing and Intervening: Introductory Topics in the Philosophy of Natural Science*. Cambridge, UK: Cambridge University Press.

Hardin, Garrett. 1968. "The Tragedy of the Commons." *Science* 162(3859):1243–1248.

Harrod, Roy F. 1948. *Towards a Dynamic Economics*. London, UK: Macmillan.

Harsanyi, John C. 1953. "Cardinal Utility in Welfare Economics and in the Theory of Risk-Taking." *Journal of Political Economy* 61(5):434–435.

Harsanyi, John C. 1977. *Rational Behavior and Bargaining Equilibrium in Games and Social Situations*. Cambridge, UK: Cambridge University Press.

Hart, Oliver D. 1988. "Incomplete Contracts and the Theory of the Firm." *Journal of Law, Economics, and Organization* 4(1):119–139.

Holmström, Bengt and Paul Milgrom. 1991. "Multitask Principal-Agent Analyses: Incentive Contracts, Asset Ownership, and Job Design." *Journal of Law, Economics, and Organization* 7:24–52.

Hornbeck, Richard and Suresh Naidu. 2014. "When the Levee Breaks: Black Migration and Economic Development in the American South." *American Economic Review* 104(3):963–990.

Hutchings, Jeffrey A. 1996. "Spatial and Temporal Variation in the Density of Northern Cod and a Review of Hypotheses for the Stock's Collapse." *Canadian Journal of Fisheries and Aquatic Sciences* 53(5):943–962.

Jacob, Brian A. 2005. "Accountability, Incentives and Behavior: the Impact of High-Stakes Testing in the Chicago Public Schools." *Journal of Public Economics* 89(56):761–796.

Kant, Immanuel. 1997. *Groundwork of the Metaphyscis of Morals*. Cambridge, UK: Cambridge University Press.

Kleiman, Mark. 2011. "Surgical Strikes in the Drug Wars: Smarter Policies for Both Sides of the Border." *Foreign Affairs* 90(5):89–101.

Klein, Benjamin, Robert G. Crawford and Armen A. Alchian. 1978. "Vertical Integration, Appropriable Rents, and the Competitive Contracting Process." *Journal of Law and Economics* 21(2):297–326.

Kleiner, Morris M. 2006. *Licensing Occupations: Ensuring Quality or Restricting Competition?* Kalamazoo, MI: W. E. Upjohn Institute for Employment Research.

Kleppner, Daniel and Norman Ramsey. 1985. *Quick Calculus: A Self-Teaching Guide, 2nd Edition*. New York, NY: Wiley.

Kline, Patrick and Enrico Moretti. 2014. "Local Economic Development, Agglomeration Economies and the Big Push: 100 Years of Evidence from the Tennessee Valley Authority." *Quarterly Journal of Economics* 129(1):275–331.

Kraay, Aart and David McKenzie. 2014. "Do Poverty Traps Exist? Assessing the Evidence." *Journal of Economic Perspectives* 28(3):127–148.

Krehbiel, Keith. 2010. *Pivotal Politics: A Theory of U.S. Lawmaking*. Chicago, IL: University of Chicago Press.

Krugman, Paul R. 1991. *Geography and Trade*. Cambridge, MA: MIT Press.

Krugman, Paul R. 1995. *Development, Geography, and Economic Theory*. Cambridge, MA: MIT Press.

Kuziemko, Ilyana and Eric Werker. 2006. "How Much Is a Seat on the Security Council Worth? Foreign Aid and Bribery at the United Nations." *Journal of Political Economy* 114(5):905–930.

Kydland, Finn E. and Edward C. Prescott. 1977. "Rules Rather than Discretion: The Inconsistency of Optimal Plans." *Journal of Political Economy* 85(3):473–491.

Laffont, Jean-Jacques and Jean Tirole. 1993. *A Theory of Incentives in Procurement and Regulation*. Cambridge, MA: MIT Press.

Lafontaine, Francine and Fiona Scott Morton. 2010. "Markets: State Franchise Laws, Dealer Terminations, and the Auto Crisis." *Journal of Economic Perspectives* 24(3):233–250.

Lane, Philip R. 2012. "The European Sovereign Debt Crisis." *Journal of Economic Perspectives* 26(3):49–67.

Lapan, Harvey E. and Todd Sandler. 1988. "To Bargain or Not to Bargain: That Is the Question." *American Economic Review (Papers and Proceedings)* 78(2):16–21.

Lipsey, Richard G. and Kelvin Lancaster. 1956. "The General Theory of Second Best." *Review of Economic Studies* 24(1):11–32.

Locke, John. 1980. *Second Treatise of Government*. Indianapolis, IN: Hackett.

Mackie, Gerry. 1996. "Ending Footbinding and Infibulation: A Convention Account." *American Sociological Review* 61(6):999–1017.

Mankiw, N. Gregory. 2009. "Smart Taxes: An Open Invitation to Join the Pigou Club." *Eastern Economic Journal* 35(1):14–23.

Mas-Colell, Andreu and Hugo Sonnenschein. 1972. "General Possibility Theorems for Group Decisions." *Review of Economic Studies* 39(2):185–192.

Maskin, Eric and Jean Tirole. 2004. "The Politician and the Judge: Accountability in Government." *American Economic Review* 94(4):1034–1054.

May, Kenneth O. 1952. "A Set of Independent Necessary and Sufficient Conditions for Simple Majority Decision." *Econometrica* 20(4):680–684.

McLaren, John and Shushanik Hakobyan. 2010. "Looking for Local Labor Market Effects of NAFTA." NBER Working Paper #16535.

Mickolus, Edward F. 1982. *International Terrorism: Attributes of Terrorist Events, 1968–1977 (ITERATE 2)*. Ann Arbor, MI: Inter-University Consortium for Political and Social Research.

Milgrom, Paul R. 2004. *Putting Auction Theory to Work*. New York, NY: Cambridge University Press.

Milgrom, Paul R., Douglass C. North and Barry R. Weingast. 1990. "The Role of Institutions in the Revival of Trade: The Law Merchant, Private Judges, and the Champagne Fairs." *Economics and Politics* 2(1):1–23.

Morgan, Mary S. 2012. *The World in the Model: How Economists Work and Think*. New York, NY: Cambridge University Press.

Morris, Stephen and Hyun Song Shin. 2003. Global Games: Theory and Applications. In *Advances in Economics and Econometrics: Theory and Applications, 8th World Congress of the Econometric Society*, ed. Mathias Dewatripont, Lars Peter Hansen and Stephen J. Turnovsky. Cambridge, UK: Cambridge University Press.

Myerson, Roger B. 2013. "Fundamentals of Social Choice Theory." *Quarterly Journal of Political Science* 8(3):305–337.

Myerson, Roger B. and Mark A. Satterthwaite. 1983. "Efficient Mechanisms for Bilateral Trading." *Journal of Economic Theory* 29(2):265–281.

Neal, Derek and Diane Whitmore Schanzenbach. 2010. "Left Behind by Design: Proficiency Counts and Test-Based Accountability." *Review of Economics and Statistics* 92(2):263–283.

North, Douglass C. and Robert Paul Thomas. 1973. *The Rise of the Western World: A New Economic History*. New York, NY: Cambridge University Press.

North, Douglass C., John Joseph Wallis and Barry R. Weingast. 2009. *Violence and Social Orders: A Conceptual Framework for Interpreting Recorded Human History*. New York, NY: Cambridge University Press.

Nozick, Robert. 1974. *Anarchy, State, and Utopia*. New York, NY: Basic Books.

Nunn, Nathan and Nancy Qian. 2014. "U.S. Food Aid and Civil Conflict." *American Economic Review* 104(6):1630–1666.

O'Hare, Michael. 2015. "Museums Can Change—Will They?" *Democracy: A Journal of Ideas* 36(Spring):66–78.

Olson, Mancur. 1965. *The Logic of Collective Action: Public Goods and the Theory of Groups*. Cambridge, MA: Harvard University Press.

Osborne, Martin J. 2003. *An Introduction to Game Theory*. New York, NY: Oxford University Press.

Ostrom, Elinor. 1990. *Governing the Commons: The Evolution of Institutions for Collective Action.* Cambridge, UK: Cambridge University Press.

Patashnik, Eric M. 2008. *Reforms at Risk: What Happens After Major Policy Changes Are Enacted.* Princeton, NJ: Princeton University Press.

Peltzman, Sam. 1976. "Toward a More General Theory of Regulation." *Journal of Law and Economics* 19(2):211–240.

Persson, Torsten and Lars E. O. Svensson. 1989. "Why a Stubborn Conservative Would Run a Deficit: Policy with Time-Inconsistent Preferences." *Quarterly Journal of Economics* 104(2):325–345.

Powell, Robert. 2004. "The Inefficient Use of Power: Costly Conflict with Complete Information." *American Political Science Review* 98(2):231–241.

Powell, Robert. 2007. "Defending Against Terrorist Attacks with Limited Resources." *American Political Science Review* 101(3):527–541.

Qian, Nancy. 2015. "Making Progress on Foreign Aid." *Annual Review of Economics* 7:277–308.

Rajan, Raghuram G. and Arvind Subramanian. 2011. "Aid, Dutch Disease, and Manufacturing Growth." *Journal of Development Economics* 94(1):106–118.

Ramsey, Frank. 1928. "A Mathematical Theory of Saving." *Economic Journal* 38(152):543–549.

Rawls, John. 1971. *A Theory of Justice.* Cambridge, MA: Harvard University Press.

Robinson, Joan. 1962. *Essays in the Theory of Economic Growth.* London, UK: Macmillan.

Roemer, John E. 1998. *Theories of Distributive Justice.* Cambridge, MA: Harvard University Press.

Roodman, David. 2007. "The Anarchy of Numbers: Aid, Development, and Cross-Country Empirics." *World Bank Economic Review* 21(2):255–277.

Rose, Mark H. and Raymond A. Mohl. 2012. *Interstate: Highway Politics and Policy since 1939, Third Edition.* Knoxville, TN: University of Tennessee Press.

Roth, Alvin E. 2015. *Who Gets What—and Why: The New Economics of Matchmaking and Market Design.* New York, NY: Houghton Mifflin Harcourt.

Rousseau, Jean-Jacques. 1968. *The Social Contract.* London, UK: Penguin.

Sachs, Jeffrey. 2006. *The End of Poverty: Economic Possibilities for Our Time.* New York, NY: Penguin.

Schelling, Thomas C. 1960. *The Strategy of Conflict.* Cambridge, MA: Harvard University Press.

Sen, Amartya. 1970*a*. *Collective Choice and Social Welfare.* Amsterdam: North Holland.

Sen, Amartya. 1970*b*. "The Impossibility of a Paretian Liberal." *Journal of Political Economy* 78(1):152–157.

Sen, Amartya. 1980. Equality of What? In *The Tanner Lectures on Human Values, Volume 1*, ed. Sterling McMurrin. Salt Lake City, UT: University of Utah Press.

Shepsle, Kenneth A. 2010. *Analyzing Politics: Rationality, Behavior, and Institutions, 2nd edition.* New York, NY: Norton.

Simmons, Beth A. 2001. "The International Politics of Harmonization: The Case of Capital Market Regulation." *International Organization* 55(3):589–620.

Singer, Peter. 2011. *Practical Ethics, 3rd Edition.* New York, NY: Cambridge University Press.

Smith, Adam. 1979. *An Inquiry into the Nature and Cases of the Wealth of Nations, Volume 1.* Oxford, UK: Oxford University Press.

Snyder, James M. and David Strömberg. 2010. "Press Coverage and Political Accountability." *Journal of Political Economy* 118(2):355–408.

Solow, Robert M. 1974. "The Economics of Resources or the Resources of Economics." *American Economic Review (Papers and Proceedings)* 64(2):1–14.

Stigler, George J. 1972. "Economic Competition and Political Competition." *Public Choice* 13(1):91–106.

Stokey, Edith and Richard Zeckhauser. 1978. *A Primer for Policy Analysis.* New York, NY: Norton.

Stokey, Nancy L. 1989. "Reputation and Time Consistency." *American Economic Review* 79(2):134–39.

Sunstein, Cass R. 2005. "Cost-Benefit Analysis and the Environment." *Ethics* 115(2):351–385.

Sunstein, Cass R. 2014. "The Real World of Cost-Benefit Analysis: Thirty-Six Questions (and Almost as Many Answers)." *Columbia Law Review* 114(1):167–211.

Sunstein, Cass R. and Richard H. Thaler. 2003. "Libertarian Paternalism is Not an Oxymoron." *University of Chicago Law Review* 70(4):1159–1202.

Svensson, Jakob. 2000. "Foreign Aid and Rent-Seeking." *Journal of International Economics* 51(2):437–461.

Swift, Adam. 2006. *Political Philosophy: A Beginners' Guide for Students and Politicians, 2nd edition.* Cambridge, UK: Polity.

Thaler, Richard H. 1988. "Anomalies: The Winner's Curse." *Journal of Economic Perspectives* 2(1):191–202.

Thaler, Richard H. and Cass R. Sunstein. 2003. "Libertarian Paternalism." *American Economic Review* 93(2):175–179.

Thomson, Judith Jarvis. 1985. "The Trolley Problem." *Yale Law Journal* 94(6):1395–1415.

Tullock, Gordon. 1972. "The Purchase of Politicians." *Western Economic Journal* 10(3):354–55.

Turner, Leslie J. 2014. "The Road to Pell is Paved with Good Intentions: The Economic Incidence of Federal Student Grant Aid." University of Maryland typescript.

Vickrey, William. 1961. "Counterspeculation, Auctions, and Competitive Sealed Tenders." *Journal of Finance* 16(1):8–37.

Walters, Christopher R. 2014. "The Demand for Effective Charter Schools." NBER Working Paper #20640.

Weingast, Barry R. 1997. "Political Foundations of Democracy and the Rule of Law." *American Political Science Review* 91(2):245–263.

Werker, Eric, Faisal Z. Ahmed and Charles Cohen. 2009. "How Is Foreign Aid Spent? Evidence from a Natural Experiment." *American Economic Journal: Macroeconomics* 1(2):225–244.

Williamson, Oliver E. 1975. *Markets and Hierarchies: Analysis and Antitrust Implications*. New York, NY: Free Press.

Williamson, Oliver E. 1985. *The Economic Institutions of Capitalism*. New York, NY: Free Press.

Zame, William R. 2007. "Can Intergenerational Equity Be Operationalized?" *Theoretical Economics* 2(2):187–202.

Index of Referenced Authors

General Index